P9-DEV-931

Also by Strobe Talbott

Endgame: The Inside Story of SALT II (1979)
The Russians and Reagan (1984)

Translator and editor:
Khrushchev Remembers (1970)
Khrushchev Remembers: The Last Testament (1974)

Deadly
Gambits

Strobe Talbott

Deadly Gambits

The Reagan Administration and the Stalemate in Nuclear Arms Control

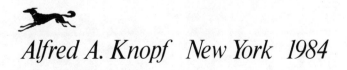

Alfred A. Knopf   New York   1984

This Is a Borzoi Book
Published by Alfred A. Knopf, Inc.
Copyright © 1984 by Strobe Talbott
All rights reserved under International and Pan-American
Copyright Conventions. Published in the United States by
Alfred A. Knopf, Inc., New York, and simultaneously in
Canada by Random House of Canada Limited, Toronto.
Distributed by Random House, Inc., New York.

Library of Congress
Cataloging in Publication Data
Talbott, Strobe.
Deadly gambits.

Includes index.
1. Strategic Arms Reduction Talks.
2. Atomic weapons and disarmament.
3. United States—Foreign relations—1981–   . I. Title.
JX1974.76.T34   1984   327.1′74   84-47781
ISBN 0-394-53637-1

Manufactured in the United States of America
Published October 15, 1984
Second Printing, November 1984

To my wife,
Brooke Lloyd Shearer,
with love and thanks

Contents

Foreword

For a generation, the United States and the Soviet Union have negotiated with each other to control nuclear weapons. From the first probes on the possibility of a test ban under Dwight Eisenhower and Nikita Khrushchev in 1958 until the conclusion of the second round of the Strategic Arms Limitation Talks (SALT II) by Jimmy Carter and Leonid Brezhnev in 1979, nuclear arms control was an ongoing, albeit fitful, enterprise. It survived repercussions from the intrinsic antagonism of the Soviet-American relationship, from the brutality of Soviet foreign policy, and from the upheavals of American domestic politics.

Sometimes the negotiations have been intense and productive, culminating in agreements to regulate various aspects of the Soviet-American military rivalry. But there have also been setbacks and periods of stagnation. The breakdowns have been as much a part of the history of arms control as the breakthroughs. The pages that follow are a chronicle of the most serious and protracted breakdown to date.

I started this book at the end of 1980 and finished it at the beginning of 1984. I conceived it as a sequel to *Endgame* (Harper & Row, 1979), my account of SALT II. That story had ended with President Carter's decision, in the wake of the Soviet invasion of Afghanistan, to withdraw the SALT II treaty from consideration by the Senate.

But the broader saga was far from over. Both the objective need and the political demand for arms control were greater than ever. At the same time, however, the obstacles were higher than ever. By the end of the Carter Administration, Soviet-American relations had been deteriorating for some years. Scientists were inventing arms faster than negotiators could contrive ways of controlling them. Distinctions in weaponry had led to a new division in the diplomatic proceedings, and the division complicated the diplomats' work (not to mention the chronicler's). *Endgame* dealt with one set of Soviet-American negotiations under the banner of one set of initials, SALT; its sequel is about two: INF, the Intermediate-range Nuclear Forces talks, and START, the Strategic Arms Reduction Talks.

But there was another, far more portentous development: when Ronald Reagan became President, the arms-control enterprise came into the hands of a group of people who were extremely critical of the results of that enterprise as it had been conducted by the previous three administrations. These people differed in many important ways from their predecessors—in their world outlook, their view of America's adversaries in Moscow, their conception of their own opportunities and obligations. A number of key officials in the new Administration believed that arms control had been, in their phrase, "bad medicine"; SALT and other agreements of the détente era, they felt, had not only failed to mitigate the Soviet threat but had actually worsened it; arms control was partly—perhaps even largely—to blame for what they saw as the weakening of America's defenses.

The new U.S. leadership was determined to change not just the name of the game in nuclear arms control (from SALT to INF and START) but the rules and objectives as well. For three years, the Reagan Administration attempted to redefine both what was possible and what was desirable in arms control. Some officials questioned the desirability of any agreement that entailed accommodation with America's principal adversary and limitation of America's military options. If forced to keep up the appearance of playing the old arms-control game, they believed, the U.S. would do best with gambits at the negotiating table that would lead to diplomatic stalemate; that way the U.S. might more freely acquire and deploy new pieces on its side of the board and position itself, if necessary, to make winning military moves against the Soviet Union.

The Administration's conduct of the INF talks and START brought about an unprecedented crisis in the already strained quarter-century-old arms-control process. And the crisis in arms control contributed to three others: in the alliance between the U.S. and Western Europe; in the partnership between the executive and legislative branches of the U.S. government; and in the Soviet-American relationship. Even if it proved temporary, the deadlock in the negotiations lasted long enough to become one of the factors making Ronald Reagan's stewardship of foreign policy and national security a contentious issue in the 1984 presidential election.

I have, in the pages that follow, concentrated on the first three years of the Administration, from the formulation of its proposals in the INF negotiations and START through the suspension of both sets of talks at the end of 1983. They remained suspended well into 1984. By then, the Administration had begun to consider new initiatives and concessions that it hoped would induce the Soviets to resume negotiations. The Republicans did not want to go into the fall elections vulnerable to the charge that they had presided over the collapse of arms control.

When the Soviet leader, Yuri Andropov, died in February 1984, the

White House and the State Department believed that his successor, Konstantin Chernenko, might be willing to start afresh—not with some bold new approach, but with a return to an old one. By May, however, it was clear that the Soviets were in no hurry to resume the negotiations that they had broken off six months before, and that had been so fruitless and acrimonious for two years before that.

As in 1980, the saga was still not over. But the prospects for the immediate future were bound to be deeply influenced by the record of the recent past. The Administration's proposals of 1981–83 had left a lasting mark on the arms-control process, as indeed their designers intended them to do. Even though these proposals might yet be fundamentally modified if not abandoned, the Administration's original approach was certain to have consequences with which President Reagan and his successors would have to cope for a long time. Therefore it is important to understand what happened, and why.

I conducted the reporting and much of the writing while the various negotiations—not only the Soviet-American ones but the transatlantic ones within the Western alliance and the intramural ones within the American government—were in progress. Official records of many events described here will remain classified, and participants constrained from freely discussing their roles, for years to come. Therefore I cannot, here or in the pages that follow, acknowledge the sources that allowed me to keep a running account of events as they unfolded.

I can, however, thank a number of people who helped me to turn that record into this narrative: James Moore, my literary agent; Lissa August, who assisted me with the research; and Sidney Drell, Alton Frye, William Hyland, Jan Lodal, Thomas Longstreth, Bruce Nelan, Walter Slocombe, and Ted Warner, who read all or part of the manuscript at various stages, offered useful suggestions, and shared with me their considerable knowledge of the field. Laurence Barrett, Douglas Brew, William Bundy, Rick Jones, Stanley Resor, Barrett Seaman, and William E. Smith also assisted me along the way.

I am particularly indebted to Michael Mandelbaum, who helped me not only with the substance of the material but with its organization and presentation, and whose own thinking and writing on the problems of national security, international relations, and nuclear weapons have been an inspiration to me.

This project stemmed directly from my reporting for *Time,* and distillations of what I learned have appeared in its pages. The managing editor, Ray Cave, and the chief of correspondents, Richard Duncan, have been extraordinarily supportive.

Throughout my career, I have had outstanding editors, and that same good fortune has now carried over to my association with the publishers of this book. Ashbel Green and Charles Elliott were patient, painstaking, and skillful.

Finally, thanks to my sons, Devin and Adrian, for putting up with my habit of disappearing in order to write about "rocket ships" for long hours that I would rather have spent with them; and to my wife, Brooke Shearer. She, too, helped me in many ways to tell this story, and she kept up my spirits when both the story and the telling of it threatened discouragement. That is one of the many reasons that this book is dedicated to her.

S.T.
Washington,
May 1984

Deadly
Gambits

Prologue

For the Administration of Ronald Reagan, 1983 was to be, in a slogan coined by the State Department, "the Year of the Missile." It was to be the moment of truth in the long-standing American effort to introduce new offensive weapons into both Western Europe and the U.S.'s own arsenal of last resort. Until the buildup in Western defenses was well underway, nuclear arms control would be a matter of keeping up appearances, of limiting damage, of buying time, and of laying the groundwork for agreement later.

Perhaps an agreement might be possible in 1984. By then, it was hoped, the United States would be able to negotiate from strength. The Soviets would be impressed by the resolve of the U.S. leadership and by the solidarity of the Western alliance. An American presidential campaign would have begun, and Reagan—who was expected to seek a second term—would be able to make good use of his reputation as a strong leader on the foreign scene. The rulers in the Kremlin, calculating that the U.S.S.R. could get a better deal before the 1984 election than after, would agree to a summit meeting early in that year. The Administration would get an agreement and vindicate the tough line it had been following throughout its term, and, by the time Americans went to the polls, the Republicans would have outflanked the Democrats on the war-and-peace issue.

That was the Administration's hope, and its timetable. In mid-November 1983 new American missiles began arriving in Britain and West Germany, right on schedule. But then things began to go wrong. On November 23, after a meeting that had lasted less than half an hour, a Soviet diplomat named Yuli Kvitsinsky stood in front of an office building on the Avenue de la Paix in Geneva, the headquarters of the U.S. arms-control delegations, and delivered a brief statement. The Soviet government, he said, had "discontinued the present round of negotiations without setting a date for their resumption." Demonstrators who had set up a "peace camp" nearby on the edge of the city's botanical gardens broke off their chants of "Keep talking! Keep talking!" Some lay down in front of Kvitsinsky's car and were dragged away by police.

Soon afterward, reporters were summoned to the U.S. headquarters for a press conference with Kvitsinsky's American counterpart, Paul Nitze. Nitze's face was drawn with exhaustion, his voice hoarse from a lingering cold, but he put the most positive interpretation possible on what had happened. The Soviets had not said they were withdrawing from the talks forever; he hoped they would be back. In Washington, President Reagan went further: he not only hoped but predicted that the Soviets would, after a brief sulk in Moscow, return to the negotiating table in Geneva.

The next day, Thanksgiving, Reagan's counterpart, Yuri Andropov, had his say from Moscow: the American leaders were kidding themselves; either that, or they were deliberately deceiving their allies and peace-loving people everywhere. The talks, he said, were not just in recess; they were over; the U.S. had made their continuation impossible.

In response to the arrival of new American missiles in Europe, Andropov announced an array of Soviet military "countermeasures." Even if they were little more than a repackaging of existing Soviet programs, these measures seemed certain to complicate diplomacy for years to come. Nor was that all. A parallel set of U.S.-Soviet negotiations in Geneva, on strategic or intercontinental weaponry, also ended abruptly—not with a walk-out but a breakoff. The Soviet Union refused to agree to a date for resumption in the new year. Those talks, too, had been deadlocked from the beginning, and the Soviets vowed ominously to "reassess" their negotiating position in light of the new American weapons in Europe. Such reassessment could only further dim the chance of eventual progress. A similar suspension occurred in negotiations taking place in Vienna between the North Atlantic Treaty Organization (NATO) and the Warsaw Pact on conventional (that is, non-nuclear) forces.

The Year of the Missile had, in short, lived up to its billing, but not the way the State Department intended. For the first time in nearly fifteen years, the Americans and the Soviets were no longer negotiating in any forum. Instead of exchanging proposals or putting the finishing touches on agreements, they were now almost totally consumed with exchanging recriminations and maneuvering for advantage amidst the wreckage of their failed policies. On January 25, 1984, fifteen days before his death, *Pravda* quoted Andropov as saying: "It is an open secret now that for almost two years the representatives of the United States in Geneva have been, so to say, beating the air." Actually, it was a good description of what both sides had been doing—not only in Geneva, but in Moscow and Washington as well.

Of all the ways in which the U.S. and the Soviet Union compete, none is of greater importance and danger than their rivalry in the acquisition and deployment of nuclear weaponry. Should the superpowers ever come to blows, it would almost certainly be with these arms that they would strike each other, if not at the outset of hostilities, then as soon as one side felt it was losing. Yet those weapons are so powerful and numerous that they have, in a curious, paradoxical, and somewhat reassuring way, negated their own military utility. For if either side ever resorted to the use of nuclear weapons, the result would probably be that side's own destruction as well as mass destruction inflicted on its enemy.

What utility nuclear weapons have, therefore, is not so much military as political. Nuclear missiles and bombs are symbols of power. The way in which their custodians, the leaderships of the U.S. and the Soviet Union, manipulate these symbols is a key factor in how successful their other policies will be. In that respect, nuclear weapons exist to be talked about, not to be used. Largely for that reason, it is another central and, again, paradoxical part of their nature that they exist to be controlled. At least implicitly, the terms for the non-use of these weapons are always on the agenda of the superpower relationship, no matter how tense and antagonistic that relationship may be.

Nuclear arms control has been one of the most critical enterprises in American foreign policy since the early 1960s. Like the Soviet-American relationship itself, arms control involves both cooperation and competition. Because the weapons under negotiation symbolize power of the most awesome kind, each side can use them as part of its ongoing effort to gain political advantages over the other, even as it seeks to avoid direct military conflict. An American administration's handling, or mishandling, of nuclear arms control has a major bearing on how that administration is judged by its constituents in the polls, by its legislative partners in government, by its allies in the councils of NATO, and also, of course, by its rivals in the Kremlin.

Since the beginning of the Cold War—but particularly since the Watergate scandal undermined Richard Nixon's presidency and, as a by-product, aborted the policy of détente—the U.S. has searched for the right combination of inducements and deterrents for dealing with the Soviet Union. Managing the Soviet-American rivalry, particularly in its military dimension, is difficult in itself, given the propensity of the U.S.S.R. to bully first and negotiate later, its instinctive stubbornness and secretiveness, its acquisition of the instruments of war on a scale out of all proportion to what its neighbors perceive as legitimate defensive interests, and its habit of defining its own security in a way that makes other states feel insecure. But the task has been all the harder since any U.S. administration must sustain support for its policies from a democratic society as well as from its independent, unpredictable, and sometimes recalcitrant allies.

Moreover, arms control always has been inherently controversial. On the one hand, it almost defies common sense for a nation to compromise with adversaries over the composition of its defenses. On the other hand, it is senseless not to attempt to keep a contest that could destroy the world from getting out of hand. In the 1970s, liberals and conservatives alike exaggerated what arms control could accomplish, loading it down with burdens of hope it could not bear or blame it did not deserve, and expecting it to work wonders by itself.

In fact, arms control cannot work wonders at all, least of all by itself. It can be useful only as a component of a larger strategy for Soviet-American relations. Arms control is not a substitute for defense. It is defense conducted by other means. Those means are diplomatic: the mutually agreeable rules of the road in the arms race—rules that will make the competition somewhat more predictable, that will set limits on the most dangerous kinds of weapons and help avert the sudden appearance of new weapons systems that might upset the balance. Arms control for the U.S. is a way of setting bounds to the twin threats of Soviet aggression and nuclear war—but not of ending them. Arms control does not involve trusting or relying on the good will of the other side. It is a matter of reaching accords that both sides deem to be in their mutual interest and of assuring each side's ability independently to verify the compliance of the other.

The Reagan Administration presided over a particularly tumultuous episode in the history of arms control. A number of problems came home to roost. Some were inherent in the process of arms control itself and in the adversary nature of the Soviet-American relationship. Some were inherited from previous leaderships, or they were a function of trying to make policy in a democracy and in an alliance of democracies, or they were aggravated by Soviet actions and attitudes. But other problems were a function of the Reagan Administration's own assumptions.

Principal among these was the belief that the U.S. was now No. 2 in its military competition with the U.S.S.R. and must therefore try harder. This alarm had been sounded before. John F. Kennedy had campaigned for the presidency warning about a gap in the relative nuclear strength of the U.S. and the Soviet Union, but once in office, he acknowledged that the U.S. was on the winning side of that gap. In every administration since Kennedy's, American military planners and political leaders have worried about the loss of superiority by the U.S., the achievement of equality, or parity, by the Soviet Union, and the danger that unless the U.S. improved its defenses the Soviets would pull ahead in the future. There were analysts in the Pentagon and National Security Council staff during the Carter Administration who feared that the future had already arrived.

Never before Reagan, however, had a President made pessimism about the existing state of the military balance a basic and continuing tenet of his world view and program. At a news conference in March 1982, he said, "The truth of the matter is that on balance the Soviet Union does have a definite margin of superiority." Reagan also believed that arms control as practiced in the past, particularly in the Strategic Arms Limitation Talks

(SALT) of 1969–1979, had contributed to American military inferiority and, if continued, would lock the U.S. permanently into second place. Because the U.S. was behind, and because arms control was partly to blame, this logic said that the best course would be to suspend bilateral bargaining and concentrate on American rearmament. Once the U.S. had reestablished equality or, better yet, a "margin of safety," it could resume talks and negotiate from strength. The 1980 Republican party platform explicitly called for the reestablishment of overall military and technological superiority over the U.S.S.R., and a number of people who helped draft that platform became members of, or advisers to, the Administration.

Thus, Reagan and his Administration came into office not really wanting to pursue arms control at all. But two key constituencies wanted them to pursue it anyway: the Western Europeans and, speaking for the American public, Congress. Both constituencies had leverage. The Europeans could block the deployment of new missiles in Europe; the Congress could thwart the Administration's ambitious plans to build up the nation's strategic defenses. In the longer run, of course, the American electorate could even deny Reagan reelection in 1984.

Realizing that he was forced for reasons of political expediency to engage in arms control before the rearmament was well underway, Reagan believed that the U.S. must find a way of pursuing an American arms buildup simultaneously with cutbacks in Soviet forces. In SALT, the U.S. had sought and achieved measures that mainly served to cap the competition, to slow down the proliferation of the most dangerous weapons on both sides. But Reagan wanted to distinguish his brand of arms control from his predecessors' by giving dramatic prominence to the quest for reductions. Because of his basic belief that the U.S.S.R. was ahead, reductions meant first and foremost reductions on the Soviet side. The U.S. must insist on drastic cutbacks in the most modern and potent Soviet weapons already deployed; no comparable reductions should be considered in existing American forces. Arms control should be used to effect nothing less than a top-to-bottom overhaul of the Soviet Strategic Rocket Forces, and to accomplish changes in the nuclear balance that the U.S. had not been able to bring about by means of its own defense programs.

The logic of these objectives was that if the U.S. was not going to build up to a position of strength from which it could negotiate in the future, then the Soviet Union must build down. For many years, American analysts had worried about the composition of the Soviet arsenal, particularly the reliance on intercontinental ballistic missiles, or ICBMs, armed with multiple independently targetable reentry vehicles, or MIRVs, which are potential first-strike weapons. There had been attempts in SALT to include in various proposals inducements for the Soviets to "move out to sea"—that is, develop more submarine-launched ballistic missiles (SLBMs) and fewer large

ICBMs.* Not until the Reagan Administration, however, did it become the predominant and unabashed purpose of arms control virtually to dictate to the U.S.S.R. an entirely new sort of arsenal, one more to America's liking and one that required the wholesale scrapping of the Soviets' very latest, most cost-effective, most powerful, and most highly valued weapons.

Reagan also came into office with a new attitude toward bargaining with the U.S.S.R. There is a time-honored tradition in negotiations—whether over labor contracts, corporate mergers, divorce settlements, or the sale of used cars—that both sides come in with their maximum demands, then eventually settle for something approximately halfway between. Reagan felt that this dynamic should not necessarily apply when, as he saw it, the object of negotiation is the very basis of U.S. defenses, the negotiating partner enjoys unfair and threatening advantages, and that partner (as he asserted in his first press conference) reserves "the right to commit any crime, to lie, to cheat." He believed his Administration should dispense with what had traditionally been a criterion in American arms-control policy: "negotiability," an accommodation to what the other side might reasonably be expected to accept in an agreement.

Earlier administrations had sought to put their own stamp on arms control, but sooner rather than later they came around to picking up where their predecessors had left off. Ronald Reagan was the first President who set about to break with the past and who, in one of his own favorite phrases, stayed the course, right up until the Soviet walkout in Geneva at the end of 1983. One reason he did so was an underlying concern in his Administration that even if a "good" arms-control agreement could be reached—one that lived up to the various desiderata of rolling back Soviet forces and allowing the U.S. to surge forward with its rearmament—there would still be reason for wariness about signing such a thing: Americans tend to take arms control as an excuse for not spending enough on defense.

Versions of this viewpoint were heard even before the advent of the Reagan Administration. Henry Kissinger, the dominant figure in SALT, feared that détente, if oversold, might undercut support for defense. Jimmy Carter's National Security Adviser, Zbigniew Brzezinski, noted in his journal in 1978 that he and Secretary of Defense Harold Brown "both worried that SALT will be used to generate such euphoria about American-Soviet relations that it will be difficult to face realistically either the Soviet military or the Soviet regional challenge." The implication was that the Soviets were capable of ruthlessly self-interested arms control in a way that the West was not. The U.S. was on the losing side of a tough-mindedness gap. In the

---

*Abbreviations like SALT, ICBM, SLBM, and MIRV are unavoidable in this book and, by now, are relatively familiar. "Reentry vehicle," the RV in MIRV, is not a precise synonym for warhead, but it is close enough so that warhead is usually used instead in the pages that follow.

Reagan Administration, an awareness of the possible lulling effects of negotiations and agreements came to reinforce a persistent, deep-seated distrust of the very enterprise of arms control.

Not surprisingly, the Administration had great difficulty converting this cluster of attitudes into a policy and even greater difficulty converting that policy into progress in negotiations. The President and his Cabinet knew they wanted to pursue a more ambitious program than their predecessors, with more stringent consequences for the Soviet Union. But, as they sought to practice the art of the possible, they were less certain of what they would settle for; their instincts differed and their lack of experience showed. They relied to an unprecedented extent on lower levels of the government. That is why this book is largely the story of bureaucratic battles at the second, third, and even fourth echelons of the government. That is where policy was made, unmade, and remade.

The top ranks of the Executive Branch had been assembled by a small group of men who had served in Reagan's earlier campaigns and in his gubernatorial administration in California. The principals were Edwin Meese, Michael Deaver, Lyn Nofziger, Caspar Weinberger, and William Clark. They were conservatives from the West Coast with little background or interest in foreign affairs. They represented a geographical as well as ideological break with the East Coast establishment's traditional concerns. The new President's views and those of his closest advisers on foreign policy tended to be simple, with more than a touch of nostalgia for the good old days of global American predominance and the Cold War. They were less impressed than the leaders of previous administrations had been by the differences between Chinese and Soviet Communists; if they saw the Third World at all, it was as an arena of Manichean struggle between the superpowers; they had little understanding of, and even less patience with, Western Europe.

Nonetheless, Reagan's two key appointments in the area of national-security policy were at first reassuring to moderates. Instead of choosing as Pentagon chief one of the many fire-breathing right-wing defense specialists available to him, Reagan picked Weinberger. He was known as "Cap the Knife," and it was governmental fat, not Communist flesh, that had felt his blade. It was hoped by some, feared by others, that he would approach the Defense Department as the ultimate manifestation of federal overspending. A number of conservatives initially worried that Weinberger would be as tough on weapons programs as he had been on social programs during his earlier cabinet assignments as director of the Office of Management and Budget and Secretary of Health, Education, and Welfare in the Nixon Administration.

To compensate for their own lack of experience in foreign affairs, the members of the Reagan inner circle knew they needed a Secretary of State with an established reputation. Alexander Haig looked like a good choice. He was a useful combination of tough guy and good guy—a soldier, a former Supreme Allied Commander in Europe, much respected by the Europeans, and a unique sort of patriotic hero. During Watergate, he had been a White House official whose reputation had actually been enhanced by the scandal. The depiction of him as the man who kept the government from falling apart was not universally credited, but it was widely enough believed to serve Haig well when Ronald Reagan was looking for a Secretary of State.

Despite his credentials, the White House was wary of Haig. For one thing, he had made soundings for a run of his own at the Republican nomination in 1980, deciding against it because of lack of support and poor health (he had undergone open-heart surgery). In his confirmation hearings, he denied categorically that he still harbored any lingering ambitions, but Reagan's men were not so sure. Moreover, Haig had served earlier administrations, and particularly those heavily involved in SALT and détente. The same quality that made him reassuring to the West Europeans and other foreigners made him suspect in Reagan's inner circle.

There was also a historical tension between the White House and the State Department. When a new occupant comes into the White House, he cleans the place out, bringing with him a new staff, made up largely of loyalists known to him or to his closest aides. A new boss at the State Department, by contrast, changes the names on the doors of a cluster of offices on the seventh floor and a handful on the sixth. The rest of that huge building is populated with career foreign-service officers who have served under earlier administrations and will serve under later ones. The 16,000 or so "working-level" professionals in Foggy Bottom and in diplomatic posts scattered around the world constitute an entrenched bureaucracy that can pose an obstacle to the implementation of bold new policy initiatives.

From John Kennedy to Jimmy Carter, presidents had quickly come to rely on the National Security Council staff, headquartered in the White House basement and next door in the Old Executive Office Building, as a mechanism for managing and often circumventing the State Department. The result was that Assistants to the President for National Security Affairs, who sat near to the Oval Office, ended up as powerful rivals to the Secretary of State.

Reagan was determined to avoid repeating that pattern, partly because any NSC director suffered from a kind of historical guilt by association: Henry Kissinger had achieved the apotheosis of power in that job, and Kissinger was anathema to the new Administration. Reagan deliberately downgraded the NSC staff. The Assistant for National Security Affairs, who also functioned as director of the NSC staff, was Richard Allen, who had served as Reagan's foreign-policy adviser during his campaign for the presidency. Twelve years before, Allen had held the same job in Richard Nixon's entourage, only to end up being elbowed aside by Kissinger. Unlike his predecessors, who had direct access to the President, Allen was to report through Edwin Meese. Meese had cabinet rank and the title of Counselor to the President, but his background was limited to the Governor's office in Sacramento and the Alameda County District Attorney's office. Under Meese and Allen, the NSC staff was weak; it failed to coordinate and synthesize the work of other agencies effectively. It failed particularly to act as a buffer between State and Defense, and thus contributed by default to the tensions that arose between those two departments.

Allen and Meese were bedrock Reaganauts in their view of the world, and accordingly mistrustful of Haig. They were always looking for ways of checking Haig's influence on the President. One opportunity was in filling the job of director of the Arms Control and Disarmament Agency (ACDA). The original candidate for the directorship of ACDA was Edward Rowny. A retired Army general, Rowny had been the military representative on the delegation that negotiated the SALT II treaty; he resigned in protest at the time of its signing by Jimmy Carter and Leonid Brezhnev in 1979, and he campaigned against its ratification. That was enough to earn him a place in the new Administration. But Allen and Meese worried that Rowny would not stand up to Haig. So Allen came forward with a new candidate to head ACDA: Eugene Rostow, an elder statesman, law professor, and leading light of the Committee on the Present Danger, a private group that had fought against SALT II and in favor of new weapons programs.

Thus both the initial and the eventual choices for the leadership of the agency in charge of arms control were men whose principal attraction in the eyes of the White House was their vigorous opposition to arms control as it had been practiced by the preceding three administrations. And of the two, Rostow got the job because he was seen as more likely to counterbalance Haig's suspected softness on the issue. Moreover, because of the shift in the lineup, Rostow was one of the last senior officials designated in 1981. This initial uncertainty over its directorship made the Arms Control Agency even less important than it would have been otherwise at the outset of the Administration. Once confirmed, Rostow did indeed stand up to Haig—and to everyone else, including Reagan, which proved to be his undoing. The bureaucratic combat between Rostow and Haig made for constant friction between their agencies, which further hampered the Administration's ability to make coherent policy.

Another part of the White House effort to keep tabs on the State Department was its pressing for the appointment of Reagan's close friend William Clark as Deputy Secretary of State. Haig agreed to the choice, but Clark then had to pass before the Senate Foreign Relations Committee. His tenure as Governor Reagan's executive secretary in Sacramento and a stint on the

California State Supreme Court had not prepared "Judge" Clark, as he would continue to be called, for the oral examination on current events that the senators administered. But they were forgiving; they wished him luck and approved him for the No. 2 job in the State Department. From there, slightly better prepared, he would eventually move to succeed Allen at the NSC.

Haig picked as his own right-hand man a professional foreign-service officer, Lawrence Eagleburger. First Haig made Eagleburger Assistant Secretary of State for European Affairs, then promoted him to be Under Secretary for Political Affairs. Here was yet another reason for the White House to keep a close eye and a short leash on the department. Eagleburger personified what Reagan's men rejected. He was a veteran diplomat who had served every president since Dwight Eisenhower, but had risen to the top working for Henry Kissinger. That was how Haig had come to know and admire him. It was also how Allen had come to resent him: Eagleburger was the man whom Kissinger had assigned the task of easing Allen out of the Nixon Administration.

Haig and Eagleburger had both served on Kissinger's NSC (and, in Eagleburger's case, at the State Department as well) when SALT and détente were in their heyday. But their responsibilities had been more managerial than substantive, so neither was tarred with the brush of policies which the new Administration was sworn to repudiate. However, it also meant that neither had a strong background for the task of guiding policy-making in the esoteric and controversial field of arms control. Haig was all for arms control, he said, particularly in Europe. That enterprise, he promised in his own distinctive idiom, would be "in the vortex of cruciality." SALT II, however, had failed "because of its substantive inadequacies." Yet, on a number of occasions, Haig revealed an understanding of the treaty's substance that was superficial and on some points downright inaccurate.

Like Haig, Eagleburger had spent years in intimate professional contact with the high priesthood of nuclear-weapons and arms-control theology, but he had never shared their fascination with the subject. The issues were too abstract for his taste, too much a matter of hardware and theories and mercifully implausible scenarios. He preferred the hurly-burly of international and intragovernmental relations, with an accent on the making of deals, the forming of alliances, and the defeating of enemies. Therefore, he brought with him as his own right-hand man another professional, David Gompert, who had worked on SALT and related issues not only in the Kissinger days but in the Carter State Department. But what made him valuable to Eagleburger made him vulnerable to attack from hard-liners inside the Administration and on Capitol Hill. Gompert had to be constantly defended against the charge that he would be better suited to a liberal Democratic administration. Haig and Eagleburger had to keep Gompert in a middle-level job and find someone less contaminated by previous government service to put in control of arms control for the department—and, they hoped, for the government bureaucracy as a whole.

Haig's choice for that job was Richard Burt, a defense intellectual who was then covering national-security affairs for *The New York Times.* Burt had met with Haig on a number of occasions, but the two men did not know each other well. Burt was urged upon Haig by the team that was assembling lists of candidates for subcabinet jobs during the transition between the election and the inauguration. Both the transition team and Haig were attracted to Burt's record of writing and speaking critically about SALT. He had stressed the pitfalls of letting arms control become an end in itself, divorced from the military imperatives of national security.

Burt was put in charge of the Bureau of Politico-Military Affairs, or PM, the State Department's own inhouse mini-Pentagon. It was an office charged with coordinating diplomacy with defense—a task that went to the heart of Burt's criticism of SALT. At one of his first meetings with his staff, he declared that his mission was to wage a "one-man crusade" to reintegrate arms-control policymaking with military planning, to turn his bureau into a "bridge" between the State and Defense departments, and to preside over a process that would yield compromises between the two.

He moved quickly to push through a plan that would put him in charge of the Interagency Groups, or IGs, that were to guide the National Security Council on arms control; that would give him bureaucratic supremacy over the Pentagon and the Arms Control Agency. He also wanted to participate in Defense Department decisionmaking and to merge into a single committee, with himself as chairman, the two NATO groups that represented the defense and foreign ministries on arms-control and defense planning. Burt's plans also included the hope that he would help Haig establish, and then negotiate arms-control agreements through, a "back channel" to the Kremlin via the Soviet ambassador to Washington, Anatoly Dobrynin. That is the way Henry Kissinger had done it. That is the way Haig wanted to do it. But Kissinger had the advantage of being a nuclear-weapons scholastic in his own right; Haig did not. Burt saw himself as being Haig's alter ego on the substance of arms control. In that capacity, he was hoping to emerge as the preeminent "working-level" policymaker in the government.

One way or another, in varying degrees, he was frustrated in many of these ambitions. Burt logged many hours of intensive, substantive discussion with Soviet diplomats, but he never became, in their eyes, the indispensable American. His difficulties were partly a function of his boss's. As it became apparent, almost from Inauguration Day, that Haig's tenure would be a rocky one, Burt's effectiveness suffered accordingly.

Burt was a man of exceptional intelligence. He could talk lucidly, fluently, and persuasively about the most arcane aspects of nuclear arms doctrine, accurately calibrating his presentation to the level of interest and knowledge of his audience. He was also one of the few people in a high position in the new order who respected the need not to tear down the old order. He was genuinely devoted to achieving progress in arms control, and not just for the sake of advancing his own career.

But, like Haig, Burt combined great skill, natural ability, and dedication with a volatile, hard-driving, often moody personality that sometimes made him his own worst enemy. He came into office at the age of thirty-three. He had never served in a comparable job, inside of government or out. He had spent most of his adult years in universities and at the International Institute for Strategic Studies in London. In the Washington bureau of *The New York Times* he had a reputation for brilliance marred by arrogance and abrasiveness. He was quick to dismiss non-experts, and even fellow experts, as fools whom he suffered ungladly. He tended to take credit liberally and dispense it sparingly for new ideas, particularly ones that worked out. He was better at the theory of diplomacy and politics than at the practice.

West Europeans with whom Burt dealt sometimes complained about his being insensitive and glib. Yet they still regarded him as one of their few friends in court in Washington. With members of his own staff, Burt was often secretive to an extent that was sometimes demoralizing. He would often fail to brief them on his meetings with Dobrynin's deputy, Alexander Bessmertnykh, and sometimes even on his breakfasts with Haig. As director of Politico-Military Affairs, he made a number of lasting enemies in the European Bureau, who resented him for poaching on their turf. That would complicate his life, not to mention theirs, when he took charge of the European Bureau in 1982. Eagleburger, too, found Burt on occasion difficult, even immature. But he also regarded him as talented, tenacious, and fundamentally a moderate, a pragmatist, and an Atlanticist. That orientation, along with his grasp of arms-control issues and his rough-and-tumble instinct for bureaucratic machinations, made him the State Department's best weapon against the more extreme elements in the Administration.

As Eagleburger observed early in 1981, the Reagan Administration had the look of a coalition government. Haig, Eagleburger, and Burt were the leaders of one faction, those who believed that it was critically important to maintain close ties with America's allies and that it was still possible for the U.S. to make agreements with the Soviets that were in the interests of America and the West.

At the other end of the spectrum, and on the other side of the Potomac, were the Pentagon civilians. They put more faith in Fortress America than in the Western alliance, and they tended to the view that the U.S. could not ultimately count on its allies and should not really do business with the Soviet Union. They saw it as self-deluding to think that the West could compromise in the military rivalry. While committed to avoiding, if possible, a nuclear war, they prided themselves on being hard-headed enough to accept the possibility that the planet might not, in the end, be big enough for both superpowers. The principal figure in this camp was Richard Perle.

Just as the State Department had its mini-Pentagon in the Politico-Military Bureau, the Pentagon had its mini-State Department under the Assistant Secretary of Defense for International Security Affairs (ISA). This office was charged with making sure that military procurements and programs fit into the context of U.S. foreign policy—and that the Defense Department had its say in formulating that policy. In the Reagan Administration, ISA was expanded, reorganized, and renamed, and the predominant official was Perle, the Assistant Secretary of Defense for International Security Policy (ISP). He was Richard Burt's Pentagon counterpart. At the beginning of the Administration, both men hoped they would be partners. Perle had been a member of the State Department transition team that helped pick Burt for his job as director of PM. Within a few months, however, the two Richards, as they were soon dubbed, were at loggerheads and would remain so. Much of the story of the Reagan Administration's arms-control policy is the story of the struggle between them.

Perle's many enemies called him the Prince of Darkness, but he was usually the picture of mildness. He had a youthful, almost cherubic face, an easy smile, and a calm, quiet, earnest but soothing manner almost no matter what he was saying. Even when criticizing colleagues, to their faces or behind their backs, he usually managed to suggest that he was doing so more in sorrow than in anger. In a city and a profession filled with workaholics, Perle tried harder than most to keep his job from putting undue strain on his personal and family life. He made a point of getting home for supper with his wife and infant son, of spending weekends and taking vacations with them, and bringing his wife along on business trips whenever possible. Partly as a result, he was often able to enter the fray of bureaucratic warfare refreshed in a way that his opponents were not. By most accounts, he was a considerate boss, inspiring hard work and loyalty from clerical assistants, military aides, and arms-control professionals on his staff, some of whom had feared him by reputation but came to respect him.

Perle had a dark side to his personality, too, but it was only occasionally apparent. He was capable of savage, bullying outbursts and bouts of deep depression. He sometimes saw himself as a lonely, beleaguered warrior in a righteous but losing cause. He contemplated and threatened resigning many times. He made no secret of his impatience to get government service behind him, to make some "real money on the outside." After a knock-down drag-out battle over one of the countless issues that divided the Defense and State departments, he went home and told his wife: "I don't know how much longer I'm going to stay around there if I have to keep fighting the same issues over and over again. It's a little like the Israelis: they have to win every war they fight, because the first one they lose, it's curtains."

Perle had spent years working for Senator Henry Jackson, the Democrat from Washington State. With Perle's help, Jackson had become the leading critic of arms control as practiced by Republican and Democratic presidents alike. Jackson's anti-Sovietism and his commitment to unilateralism in defense transcended partisan politics. That made Perle just the sort of Democrat that the Reagan Administration was eager to recruit. It was an ideological administration more than a partisan one: Kissinger Republicans were unwelcome; Jackson Democrats were much in demand. This was the bipartisanship of the right wing on national-security issues, and Perle was a veteran of the cause. He was only six years older than Burt (thirty-nine on taking office), but he had had thirteen years' experience in government—and that was thirteen years more than Burt.

Perle had been a *bête noire* of Henry Kissinger's. In 1974, shortly after Jackson and Perle had struck a crippling blow against détente with a legislative restriction on Soviet-American economic ties, Kissinger, quivering with frustration and anger, remarked, "You just wait and see! If that son of a bitch Richard Perle ever gets into an administration, after six months he'll be pursuing exactly the same policies I've been attempting and that he's been sabotaging."

But Kissinger was wrong.

Other critics confidently predicted that Perle would not be able to make the transition from the opposition to the policymaking branch of the government. Having been a guerrilla fighter who laid ambushes for the Executive Branch from his stronghold on Capitol Hill, Perle, it was expected, would be his own worst enemy in the more genteel world of interagency politics. It turned out to be true that in the Pentagon, just as in the Congress, Perle's principal mission was to stop things from happening; even as an insider, he was still very much an oppositionist. But he was an extremely successful one. To the dismay of his critics, he turned out to be a masterful bureaucrat. As a rule, naysayers have an advantage in a struggle over policy. It is relatively easy to block progress by raising objections and diverting debate. Also, the government as a whole is usually looking for a consensus, and that often means accommodating the more recalcitrant if not obstructionist elements of the bureaucracy. But in addition to these natural advantages, Perle had the benefit of intelligence, ingenuity, determination, and an unswerving, passionate conviction that he was right.

On the department's organization chart, he was subordinate to Fred Iklé, the Under Secretary for Policy. Iklé was a bona-fide expert on nuclear strategy and arms control. But he was no match for Perle in deftness and assertiveness. After the SALT I agreements were approved by the Senate in 1972, Senator Jackson demanded that Nixon purge the SALT delegation and the Arms Control and Disarmament Agency. Perle played an important part in picking Iklé, who was then at the Rand Corporation, the Air Force–

sponsored think tank in California, as the new director of ACDA.

In that position, Iklé was instrumental in preventing Kissinger from reaching a SALT II breakthrough with the Soviets early in 1976. Iklé's deputy at ACDA had been John Lehman, who later went briefly into the defense consulting business with Perle. Now, with the onset of the Reagan Administration, Lehman was Secretary of the Navy. From that post, he too would obstruct efforts to work out compromises in strategic arms control. Iklé and Lehman were members of what was sometimes called "the Perle mafia," the wide circle of Perle's former associates, protégés, and mentors scattered throughout the new Administration and, of course, still in place on Capitol Hill.

Perle ended up having more impact on policy in arms control than any other official in the U.S. government, an achievement that was all the more remarkable in that he held a third-echelon job. Part of his success was that he was as personally charming, intellectually brilliant, and politically well connected as he was ideologically self-assured and therefore unyielding. Perle's near-dominance of the arms-control process during the critical first year and a half of the Administration had another explanation as well: he was able to fill the partial vacuum of experience, expertise, and interest in arms control that existed at the highest levels of the government, including on the part of his ultimate superior, Reagan, and his immediate superior, Defense Secretary Weinberger.

To the consternation of many who had admired him, Weinberger left his budget-cutting knife behind and adopted an attitude of more is better, most is best. He virtually turned over the Pentagon's arms-control portfolio to Perle. In that sense, Weinberger, too, became a member of the Perle mafia. And since Weinberger, unlike Haig, was also a member of President Reagan's inner circle, that gave Perle special advantages over Burt.

While Burt made it his goal to reestablish the close linkage between arms control and defense, Perle was determined to separate arms control from the vicissitudes of American domestic politics and to postpone further agreements with the U.S.S.R. until the U.S. had greatly improved its leverage by dint of a unilateral buildup. He and like-minded officials, he once remarked, were going to "teach the nation a lesson in the virtues of supply-side arms control." He remarked at an interagency meeting early in 1981 that the Administration might have only a few years to shatter the mold of the past. Perle was fond of saying that, in the otherwise dismal annals of Soviet-American diplomacy, the only agreement truly in the interests of the West was the Austrian State Treaty of 1955, which ended the partial Soviet occupation and guaranteed the neutrality of Austria. Then he would add pointedly that it had taken ten years to negotiate that pact: "That's the precedent we should have in mind, not SALT." In early 1983, Perle remarked to Richard Staar, the departing chief American negotiator in the deadlocked Mutual Balanced Force Reduction Talks between NATO and the Warsaw Pact, "Congratulations! You obviously did a good job because nothing happened."

Perle's more charitable critics suspected that in pursuing the best in arms control he was making it the enemy of the good. Others accused him of opposing any and all arms control; of propounding principles that were a smokescreen for obstructionism; and of cynically promoting, then defending, proposals that he knew perfectly well were non-negotiable. Perle steadfastly denied that charge many times, including in testimony in July 1983 before a special panel on arms control of the House Armed Services Committee.

> I believe that the principal difference between this Administration and its critics on the subject of arms control lies in the standard we each set for the reaching of agreement. I confess that I believe we set a higher standard than our detractors. . . . In all the confusion that surrounds the subject of arms control there is none so serious as the issue of seriousness. It has become commonplace for the Administration's critics to accuse it of a lack of seriousness about arms control. In support of this accusation there are learned journalistic excursions into the bureaucratic world of the heroic but ineffective "good guys" (who are serious about arms control) and the dominant "bad guys" (who are secretly opposed to arms control and block it at every turn but go through the motions in a false show of seriousness). And by some obscure litmus test we are—all of us—herded into one camp or the other in an ever upward spiral of cant and calumny. . . . The burden of advice we are receiving from many of our critics amounts to little more than that we should modify our proposals so as to permit the Soviets to retain a vastly larger strategic arsenal than the levels the Administration has proposed. According to this view, seriousness is to be found on the side of the big guns—or, in this case, the big missiles. Demand too much restraint on the part of the Soviets, and you are not serious. Hold out for an agreement worthy of our children's respect (and with some chance of protecting their safety and liberty) and you are not serious. Seriousness resides with those who don't worry too much about the terms of an agreement as long as something gets signed.

Perle's statement was a rebuttal not only to the many commentaries that had already appeared labeling him as the chief saboteur of arms control; it was also an anticipatory defense against the harsh judgments that would come later, especially after it became apparent in late 1983 that the Soviets were simply not willing to conduct arms control according to the standards espoused by Perle and the Administration he served.

Part One
The Intermediate-Range
Nuclear Forces Talks

1 Decision and Indecision

The most numerous, far-reaching, and powerful of American nuclear weapons are in the U.S., in the bomb bays of aircraft ready to take off from bases or on top of ICBMs in underground silos, or they are aboard submarines in international waters. These are so-called strategic weapons. "Strategic" in this usage refers primarily to mission; it means they can strike the Soviet enemy's homeland, at the source of his military, economic, and political power. The strategic arsenal is intended to pose a believable threat of devastating retaliation should the Soviet Union ever contemplate a nuclear attack against the U.S.

But strategic weapons have had another purpose: to threaten retaliation in case the Soviet Union should ever consider an attack—conventional or nuclear—on Western Europe, Japan, or South Korea. American intercontinental and submarine-launched ballistic missiles (ICBMs and SLBMs) are instruments of "extended deterrence." They represent the extension of the U.S. military umbrella to cover its allies. The U.S. is the only member of the Western alliance with sufficient nuclear capability to give the Soviets serious pause; therefore, Western Europe depends on American nuclear weapons to deter the Soviet Union. By promulgating the doctrine of extended deterrence, the U.S. was warning the Soviet Union that an attack on America's allies would incur the same retaliatory response as an attack on the American homeland.

Originally, extended deterrence was the primary purpose of American nuclear weapons. After World War II, it was apparent that Western Europe was economically, politically, and culturally aligned with the U.S., yet geographically closer to the Soviet Union and therefore militarily almost defenseless. American bombs, and bombers, were the great equalizers. If the Communist takeover of Czechoslovakia or the Berlin blockade of 1948 had led to Soviet aggression against Western Europe, American long-range aircraft could have done to Soviet cities what they had done to Hiroshima and Nagasaki in 1945.

During the 1950s, the U.S. had little fear of a Soviet nuclear attack against North America. The U.S.S.R. had a relatively small number of bombers that could reach the U.S. on one-way suicide missions from Soviet bases, while the far more numerous and powerful aircraft of the U.S. Strategic Air Command could drop atomic and hydrogen bombs on the U.S.S.R. from bases both in North America and overseas. The purpose of the American arsenal of nuclear weapons during those years was to deter, and if necessary to defeat, a Soviet attack on Western Europe.

During the sixties, the Soviet Union developed ICBMs, so the U.S. itself became vulnerable to attack. This posed a problem not just for American self-defense, but for the defense of Europe as well: the threat of American nuclear retaliation against the Soviet Union in response to a Soviet attack on Western Europe became less credible, for now the Soviets could respond in turn with a nuclear attack on the continental U.S. Virtually all of the planning, expenditures, and distribution of nuclear weaponry within NATO were devoted, directly or indirectly, to addressing this problem by making sure that nuclear deterrence of Soviet aggression as exercised by the U.S. on its own behalf would also protect Western Europe.

The difficulty has always been making this threat one that both allies and adversaries would believe, and would therefore take account of in their political as well as their military calculations. The U.S. has not relied exclusively on its "central," or strategic, arsenal to provide nuclear deterrence for Europe. It has kept nuclear weapons in and around the territories of its allies as well: bombs and missiles on fighter-bombers in Britain and on warplanes aboard aircraft carriers in the Mediterranean and Atlantic; 108 Pershing I ballistic-missile launchers in West Germany (plus 72 more in the hands of the West German Army); and a variety of shorter-range missiles and nuclear artillery shells. These weapons have had ranges sufficient to deliver nuclear bombs or warheads against Warsaw Pact targets in Eastern Europe or against any attacking Soviet army that might advance upon Western Europe.

NATO's nuclear forces in Europe have been considered a kind of forward auxiliary to the U.S.'s strategic arsenal. It has never been deemed wise to make them carry the full burden of deterring Soviet aggression. Planners could too easily imagine the Soviets reaching the point where they might calculate that they could overwhelm the portion of NATO's retaliatory capability that is confined to Europe itself. If the Soviets could find some way of excluding American ICBMs, missile-firing submarines, and the B-52 bombers of the Strategic Air Command from their calculations, they might be more likely to decide that the conquest of Western Europe, or the take-over of West Germany, was feasible. They might also conclude that the costs were acceptable, since the battle could not be brought to the Soviet home-land. Furthermore, if the West Europeans had reason to doubt that the nuclear defenses on their own territory were backed up by more numerous and powerful weapons in the U.S., they would be more susceptible to out-right intimidation or more subtle pressures from the Soviets.

Therefore, it has been a cardinal principle of American and allied planning that the Soviets must be forced to contend with the very real possibility that an attack on Europe would trigger a punitive response from American weapons based in the U.S. itself, or from its strategic submarines. Extended deterrence has been a way of making it more difficult for the Soviets to pursue a divide-and-conquer strategy toward NATO; it has been a way of "coupling" American and West European defenses.

From time to time, Europeans have worried about the danger of "decoupling." They could imagine circumstances in which the U.S., faced with the necessity of retaliating against the Soviet Union on Western Europe's behalf, might utilize (and sacrifice) the nuclear forces it had deployed in Europe but hold back its central forces against the possibility of a Soviet attack on the continental U.S. In the background, and sometimes in the foreground, of these dark imaginings has been the West European fear that the superpowers might end up in a nuclear war against each other—but fought out on a European battlefield. American weapons might be stationed in Europe to deter Soviet aggression, but in a crisis they might have the thoroughly undesirable effect of attracting a Soviet preemptive attack, with devastating results for any country that hosted the American weapons. A missile launcher or an airfield is by definition a prime target for the other side. Depending on what sort of worries a West European has about how the war will go, he may well regard an American missile-launching facility on the outskirts of his city not as something that makes him sleep more soundly at night but as the cause of nightmares.

Thus, NATO planners have always had to keep in mind two thresholds. If they fall below a certain point in strength, American nuclear forces in Europe would be *inadequate* both as a symbol of American power and as an immediately available reservoir of firepower. This would be a form of decoupling. If they rise above a certain point, American nuclear forces in Europe would be *excessive*, insofar as they might constitute an excuse for the U.S. to hold back on the use of its ultimate weapons, ICBMs and SLBMs. This would be another form of decoupling. Those two thresholds have always been difficult to define. They have moved up and down in response not just to the hard, cold numbers of Soviet weaponry arrayed against NATO but to much softer and more mercurial indicators, such as the confidence that West European constituencies have in their leaders and the confidence that those leaders have in the U.S. In that respect, decisions about how many of what kind of American weapons to put in and around Europe have always been as much political as military. So, in fact, have all decisions about these weapons, since they are not intended for use in military conflict so much as they are intended to serve as symbols and safeguards of political arrangements.

In the late 1950s and early '60s, NATO decided to put some American ballistic missiles, Thors and Jupiters, in Britain, Italy, and Turkey. In West Germany, a young Social Democratic member of Parliament who was already making a name for himself as an outspoken defense intellectual, Helmut Schmidt, argued that long-range American missiles on West German territory would be too vulnerable to Soviet preemptive attack; better to rely on American ICBMs and SLBMs. For much the same reason, the Thors and Jupiters were soon removed from Britain, Italy, and Turkey as well. Minuteman ICBMs in the U.S. and Polaris SLBMs at sea made them seem redundant. The Minutemen in their underground silos back in the Great Plains, it was true, were far away from the Europeans whom they were supposed to protect, but their very remoteness was, in those days, seen as an advantage: it meant that they were harder for the Soviet Union to get at, yet the American missiles could still reach the Soviet Union in about half an hour.

In the early sixties another, more senior European politician, President Charles de Gaulle of France, made public a more profound concern about the very idea of extended deterrence: In the event of Soviet aggression against Western Europe, he asked, could the Americans be trusted to make good on their promise to retaliate as though the U.S. itself had been attacked, knowing that by doing so American cities would be exposed to what might be called extended aggression, or counterretaliation, by the U.S.S.R.? The answer, de Gaulle felt, was no. France, for this reason and others, needed its own independent deterrent. Britain, too, had long since decided that its security and its self-esteem as a world power, albeit a fading one, required that it possess a similar ability.

Over time, the French and British nuclear forces came to consist of a lopsided, miniature version of the U.S.'s own strategic triad—a deterrent made up of three "legs," on land, in the air, and at sea. On land there were ballistic missiles in southern France. For the air leg of the triad, both Britain and France had rather antiquated bombers: the Vulcan, which was to see action and gain worldwide attention during the Falkland Islands war between Britain and Argentina in 1982; and the Mirage IV, which had been the centerpiece of de Gaulle's original *force de frappe* in 1963. The most potent and numerous weapons in the two arsenals were SLBMs aboard British and French submarines.

The French called their weapons, both land- and sea-based, *stratégique,* since they could reach Soviet territory. The Soviets, of course, considered them strategic in the same sense; they sought to include them in SALT and would try even harder to include them in new negotiations on European nuclear forces. But by American reckoning they should not figure in the only strategic equation that mattered, the one between the U.S. and the U.S.S.R. For while British nuclear forces remained formally committed to NATO, France's did not, and while both arsenals were sizable and powerful enough to qualify as genuine independent national deterrents, they were too puny compared to the Soviet arsenal to contribute more than marginally to deterrence on behalf of the alliance as a whole.

By indulging in nuclear nationalism, France and Britain could each legitimately claim to have enhanced its own safety, but neither could claim very persuasively to have enhanced the collective security of the West. That responsibility lay with the U.S. Helmut Schmidt and his countrymen—who were generally seen as the most likely victims of Soviet aggression or intimidation—did not count on British and French forces to dissuade the Soviet Army from pouring into West Germany. Their insurance policy was American strength, and in the seventies, there was reason to worry that the value of that insurance policy might be diminishing.*

There has been, in the minds of those who have designed nuclear weapons and developed doctrines to justify them, an elaborate interconnection among the various categories of weaponry, all the way from intercontinental-range nuclear missiles down to conventional forces. For winning a battle, the U.S. has tanks, rifles, grenades, mortars, and, for that matter, bayonets. It also has "tactical" nuclear weapons in short-range projectiles such as artillery shells. For prevailing in a regional conflict confined to a theater of operations adjacent to the U.S.S.R. (such as Western Europe or the Persian Gulf), it has intermediate-range, or "theater," nuclear forces. Some theater weapons have strategic missions; some theater weapons are capable of tactical missions. But to win the war, to defeat the Soviet Union itself and destroy Soviet targets on Soviet territory, the U.S. has central forces (ICBMs, SLBMs, and intercontinental bombers), backed up by theater nuclear forces.

Each level and category of weaponry is supposed to reinforce the credibility of the other as a deterrent, or, in the event that deterrence fails, to reinforce the effectiveness of the other as an instrument of war. Conventional, tactical nuclear, theater, and strategic weapons are all part of what is conceived as a single system. The U.S.S.R. has numerical and geographical advantages over the U.S. in Europe in its conventional forces. But it is less likely to use those forces—to take advantage of its advantage, as it were —as long as there is a plausible danger that doing so will trigger nuclear retaliation, and as long as the U.S. can pose the threat of retaliation at various levels.

The theory of deterrence borrows much of its terminology from bridge, chess, and poker; it is critical that the U.S. not be trumped, checked, or have its bluff called at any point. If one level of deterrence is weak, the U.S.S.R. might be tempted to exploit that weakness, win the conflict at that level, and

---

*For a thorough but highly readable explanation of the historical background, and a sensible critique of the assumptions underlying Western policies, see *NATO's Nuclear Dilemmas*, by David N. Schwartz, published by the Brookings Institution in 1983.

count on the other side to throw in its cards—or concede the game—at the next higher level rather than permit the conflict to escalate. That, at least, is the prevailing view of those who have worked through the gamesmanship of nuclear war and nuclear peace.

In gauging the balance between them, each side has insisted on taking account of its own special circumstances. The U.S.S.R. has demanded "compensation" for two facts: first, that, unlike the U.S., it has potential enemies on both its eastern and western borders; and second, that the U.S. has weapons in countries adjacent to the U.S.S.R., while there are no such Soviet "forward bases" in, say, Canada or Mexico. Thus, in the Soviet view, the proximity of Western Europe, which is made up largely of American allies, is a disadvantage and a threat to the Soviet Union.

In the American and West European view, however, it is just the other way around: Western Europe is close to the U.S.S.R. and therefore all the more vulnerable to Soviet attack, while the U.S., in its capacity as guarantor of its allies' security, is an ocean away. American nuclear weapons were traditionally supposed to be the great equalizers, the trump card, the ace in the hole; they were supposed to make up for the U.S.S.R.'s menacing proximity to Western Europe. They were also supposed to counterbalance the underlying assumption of all Western strategy, that the U.S. and NATO would never commit aggression against the U.S.S.R. and the Warsaw Pact, while aggression in the other direction is a clear, present, and permanent danger.

Many experts believe that even Soviet-American equality can be destabilizing (that is, likely to lead to conflict in a crisis), or decoupling. Outright Soviet superiority is, obviously, much worse, and that means superiority at any level. NATO planners in the seventies had long since agreed that a gap favoring the U.S.S.R. already existed at the level of conventional forces, and they feared that another had developed higher up, at the level of theater nuclear forces, or TNF. They were concerned that because the U.S.S.R. had the upper hand on the TNF "rung" in the so-called "ladder of escalation dominance," there was a greater possibility that the Soviets might use their military power to bully or blackmail Western Europe.

The men and women who thought professionally about these matters were not so much preoccupied with the actual possibility of a nuclear war occurring as they were concerned about what political benefits the U.S.S.R. might realize if its generals and political leaders were to go through the same tortuous logic and conclude that they did indeed have NATO "beaten" on paper, on the chessboard, or in the cards they were holding: thus perceiving their military advantage, the Soviets might try to use it for political purposes.

The concern over a TNF gap arose because of adverse developments both in the military balance between East and West and in the political climate within the Western alliance. It arose because of some new weapons in the Soviet

Union and some old anxieties in Western Europe, exacerbated in the late 1970s by the policies of the leader of the alliance's senior partner, Jimmy Carter.

Parity and the Pioneer

De Gaulle's doubts about the credibility of U.S. nuclear protection spread to Germany. During the Carter Administration, the European who voiced these doubts most forcefully was Helmut Schmidt, who had by then risen, by way of the post of Defense Minister, to be Chancellor of West Germany. In October 1977, he delivered a speech before the International Institute for Strategic Studies in London. It was widely interpreted as a warning that extended deterrence was in serious trouble for a combination of reasons having to do with Soviet military deployments, the military wisdom and political resolve of the alliance, and American arms-control policies.

As long as the U.S. enjoyed a clear margin of superiority over the Soviet Union as measured in strategic nuclear power (ICBMs, SLBMs, and long-range bombers), the U.S. possessed a surplus of firepower which it could invest in the defense of its allies. But as a result of their buildup in the late sixties and seventies, the Soviets drastically reduced and may have eliminated the American margin. They attained what was described as parity or rough equivalence. In the view of many, the credibility of extended deterrence eroded accordingly. As long as the U.S. had seemed, on paper, to have the Soviet Union beaten in a hypothetical World War III, the American threat to respond to aggression in Europe as though it were aggression against the U.S. stood up. It seemed now, however, that the Soviet Union might soon be in a position to rely on its own central, strategic forces to hold the U.S. in check while it used its conventional and shorter-range nuclear forces to subdue Western Europe.

This was a problem that policymakers and theoreticians had seen coming for decades and had tried, at various times and various ways, to head off; but now Schmidt was heard to be proclaiming that the day of reckoning had arrived. The threat that the U.S. would use its central nuclear forces against the Soviet Union now carried with it a danger to the American people and therefore a profound dilemma for American leaders. Once the U.S. fired its ICBMs against targets deep in the Soviet Union, the American homeland would become fair game for Soviet counterretaliation.

As time went on, Schmidt's concern was fueled by doubts about the consistency and competence of the Carter Administration. Jimmy Carter grossly mishandled the question of whether NATO needed a specially refined version of the hydrogen bomb intended for use against a Soviet tank attack. The enhanced radiation weapon, or neutron bomb, would minimize blast and radioactive fallout while it maximized the emission of lethal neutron radiation in a concentrated area. It was an attempt to make more credible the threat that NATO would detonate nuclear weapons against Soviet targets, such as attacking tanks, on West European territory. The reasoning was that the Soviets would take more seriously the possible use of "clean" neutron bombs against their armies than of older, "dirtier" nuclear weapons, which would do more "collateral" damage to a larger area and release more poisonous radioactivity. For much the same reason that military planners liked the neutron bomb, however, many politicians and advocates of disarmament detested it: it made nuclear war seem more "fightable," therefore more feasible, therefore more likely to occur. Since the neutron bomb was a weapon designed with a war in Europe in mind, and more particularly a war in West Germany, it was a very hot potato for Schmidt.

Nonetheless, it was one he was willing to handle. He stood up to a wave of widespread, emotional public protests and to opposition from within his own Social Democratic party. But that was not good enough for Carter. He wanted Schmidt, in effect, to accept the full onus of the decision to deploy the new weapon by *asking* the U.S. to put it in West Germany. This tactic of Carter's made an awkward situation nearly untenable for Schmidt; it also deepened the Chancellor's doubts about Carter's judgment and reliability.

Schmidt was already uneasy with what he was hearing about the Carter Administration's conduct of SALT II. The Administration was now pursuing a treaty that would constrain, and perhaps modestly reduce, the strategic weaponry of the two superpowers at levels not far below those that already existed. Schmidt believed that in an era of strategic equality, *in*equalities at lower, substrategic levels of the East-West military rivalry took on new importance, and that here the West was at a disadvantage. This was one of the principal themes in his London speech:

> SALT neutralizes [the superpowers'] strategic nuclear capabilities. In Europe, this magnifies the significance of the disparities between East and West in nuclear tactical and conventional weapons. . . . [S]trategic arms limitation confined to the United States and the Soviet Union will inevitably impair the security of the West European members of the Alliance *vis-à-vis* Soviet military superiority in Europe if we do not succeed in removing the disparities of military power in Europe parallel to the SALT negotiations.

If, in addition to their strategic missiles aimed against targets in the U.S., the Soviets were allowed to come forward with a new class of very potent missiles aimed at American military targets in Europe as well—if SALT did nothing to constrain these weapons, and if NATO did nothing to offset the regional advantage they created for the Soviets—then the old fear of decoupling would seem finally to have been realized.

Schmidt's attention was focused on a particular new Soviet weapon: the SS-20 missile, which had come into deployment within the previous few months. There were indications that the secret Soviet code name for it was Pioneer, which is even more innocent-sounding in Russian than in English. Pioneers are not intrepid adventurers but the Soviet equivalent of Cub Scouts, Boy Scouts, and Campfire Girls—kids who have wholesome fun in the great outdoors. The Soviets took the view that the SS-20 was part of their own program to "modernize" aging defenses. (Both sides used the euphemism "modernization" for the introduction of whole new generations of weaponry.) The SS-20, said Soviet officials, was nothing more than a somewhat updated, upgraded replacement for SS-4 and SS-5 ballistic missiles that had been around since the late fifties and into the sixties. These were old missiles that had achieved considerable notoriety when Nikita Khrushchev tried to station some in Cuba in 1962, precipitating the most serious showdown of the nuclear age.

The SS-4 was well on its way to being a candidate for an air-and-space museum. The rocket drew heavily from the technology of the V-2 that the Germans developed near the end of World War II; twelve tractors with special trailers, manned by a crew of about twenty, were required to transport, erect, and fire one weapon. Once in flight, the SS-4 corrected its course by the primitive and highly fallible device of external fins. It was typical of the Soviet reluctance to retire even the most outmoded hardware that the SS-4 stayed in service. The SS-5 was a bit more sophisticated. Its trajectory was controlled by vanes acting on the motor exhaust, and it had a range nearly twice that of the SS-4.

In the sixties, most of the SS-4s and -5s had been aimed at Europe. Others were directed against the Middle East, South Asia, and East Asia. China at first had not been a target even of the SS-4s and -5s. In the late sixties, the U.S.S.R. began to retire the SS-4s and -5s, replacing them at first with ICBMs like the single-warhead SS-11, and adding China to their assigned targets.

Along came SALT I, with its limits on strategic weapons. The SS-20 was apparently designed to circumvent those limits. It was two generations ahead of the SS-4s and SS-5s in every respect. It was fueled by solid propellant, which is more reliable and manageable than liquid fuel; it had two stages rather than one; it was armed with three MIRVs rather than a single warhead. The SS-20 had a greater range, one approaching 5,000 kilometers*, and it could be moved about on trucklike vehicles. SALT II banned, at least for the time being, mobile ICBMs, but because the SS-20 was just shy of the highly arbitrary 5,500-kilometer range that defined an ICBM for purposes of SALT, it was deemed an intermediate-range ballistic missile (IRBM) and thus exempt.

---

*A debate continued for years over the exact range of the SS-20s. The CIA for a long time put the figure at 4,400 kilometers.

In addition to being tipped with three MIRVs, there was reason to fear that the SS-20s might be designed to be deployed in pairs. In that case, each launcher could readily be reloaded and refired, delivering six warheads rather than three. And it could do so with considerable accuracy. If it was set up at a presurveyed site, its warheads were believed capable of coming within 1,200 feet of a target nearly 3,000 miles away.

The SS-20 was a classic example of the Soviet penchant for playing as close as possible to the edge of what is permissible under existing or prospective arms-control agreements, stopping just short of violating the letter of those agreements but nonetheless upsetting the stability and predictability that arms control is meant to help achieve.

Also of concern to Schmidt was the Soviet Union's Backfire bomber. It was bigger, faster, farther-reaching, more heavily armed, and altogether a much more impressive airplane than the old Blinder which it was meant to replace. Backfire was first spotted in 1970, shortly after SALT I had begun. It seemed designed to operate at ranges just short of those that the SALT negotiators were using to define intercontinental bombers. By 1977, when Schmidt delivered his speech, it was clear that the Soviets would probably succeed in exempting Backfire from the main limitations of SALT II. But the Backfire, at least, had its American counterparts—F-111s based in Britain and FB-111s on the East Coast of the U.S., available for quick dispatch to Europe in a crisis. The SS-20 was different. It had no American counterpart.

By giving the Soviets a monopoly in a whole category of weapons— modern land-based, intermediate-range ballistic missiles—the SS-20 created the perceived gap at the level of theater nuclear forces, or TNF, in the "continuum," or "spectrum," of deterrence. It thus undercut the credibility of American doctrine for the defense of Europe.

One way to solve the problem would be for SALT—preferably SALT II, but failing that, SALT III—to impose limits leading to reductions on the Backfire and SS-20. Another way would be for the West to come forward with new weapons of its own in order to deprive the Soviets of their monopoly. Later, officials in the Reagan Administration, particularly Secretary of Defense Caspar Weinberger, would talk about the need for the U.S. to "match" the SS-20s. That was not, strictly speaking, the original idea, at least as conceived by Schmidt or the American officials who listened carefully to his message. What the Europeans needed, Schmidt was saying, was a more tangible guarantee that the U.S. would not sit out a European conflict.

America did have its shorter-range nuclear missiles in Europe, and it had aircraft, such as the F-111s and others, that could deliver nuclear bombs. But the former could not reach Soviet territory, and the latter were considered too vulnerable to Soviet air defense. What was needed in the face of the SS-20s was longer-range missiles, invulnerable to air defenses, that could reach into the U.S.S.R. In that sense, they would be "Euro-strategic" —American-made, American-operated, but European-based and capable of striking against the Soviet homeland. Faced with a Soviet attack on the countries where these weapons were to be based, the U.S. would have to "use them or lose them." Using them, the U.S. would be engaging the U.S.S.R. directly, thereby coupling its own military response to Soviet attack with the defense of Europe. Once again, the rationale for such new American weapons had to do not with a strategy for winning, or even playing out, a game, but with anticipating and checking possible moves that the other side might make, so as to assure that the game was not played at all. In short, deterrence: planning not for the event, but to make the event less likely to occur.

As it happened, the U.S. had a weapon in the works, the cruise missile, that seemed well suited to this task, or so it appeared to Europeans like Schmidt. Therein lay another source of transatlantic tension, for the cruise missile had a different appeal in Washington. Rather than deploying cruise missiles in NATO as a way of offsetting the intermediate-range SS-20s, the Carter Administration was inclined to trade cruise missiles away in SALT for concessions in Soviet intercontinental-range systems.

The cruise missile is a small, relatively inexpensive, jet-powered, slow, low-flying drone. While ballistic missiles avoid air defenses by hurtling too high and too fast overhead to be shot down en route to their targets, cruise missiles sneak in under air defenses. They can also deliver a thermonuclear warhead with almost pinpoint accuracy. In prospect, these weapons represented a considerable American advantage over the Soviet Union. Their guidance systems, which work by matching a computerized map against the terrain over which they are flying, rely on microelectronics and other high technology in which the U.S. has been considerably ahead of the U.S.S.R.

Cruise missiles can be launched from air, land, or sea. Of the three versions, the Soviets have been least concerned about air-launched cruise missiles, since the bombers that carry them can be detected a long way off and therefore may be vulnerable to interception even if the cruise missiles themselves are not. Sea-launched and ground-launched cruise missiles, however, can be scattered on and around the continent of Europe. Ground launchers, since they are small and mobile, can be dispersed to evade enemy targets. Sea-launched cruise missiles can be fired from submarines, which are hard for the other side to track. At a minimum, the Soviets were determined in SALT to prevent the deployment of sea- and ground-launched cruise missiles with ranges sufficient to cross the buffer zone of Eastern Europe and penetrate the Soviet Union itself.

The Soviets had faced that threat once before, in an earlier period of the nuclear age, and they were determined not to face it again. In the fifties and sixties, the U.S. nuclear forces in Europe included, in addition to the Thor and Jupiter ballistic missiles in Britain, Italy, and Turkey, two types of cruise missiles, called the Matador and the Mace B. They were based in concrete-hardened sites in West Germany. They were armed with nuclear warheads and were capable of reaching into the western U.S.S.R. But Matador and Mace B were primitive compared to the Tomahawk ground-launched cruise missile that the U.S. Air Force was developing for deployment in 1983. The Tomahawk would be far more accurate and reliable, and it would be mobile. Four Tomahawks would be carried in a canister, called an armored box launcher, on a semi-trailer towed by a truck or tractor. The whole machine could rumble camouflaged around the countryside and forests, or it could be loaded aboard a military transport plane and moved rapidly to some other part of the country or continent. In a crisis, large numbers of Tomahawk launchers could be rushed to Europe on fairly short notice from bases back in the U.S.

So the Soviets did not want to see cruise missiles deployed, and at the time of Schmidt's October 1977 speech in London, there was talk coming out of Washington and Geneva indicating that the weapons might indeed be subject to a variety of constraints in SALT II—if not in the treaty proper, then in the shorter-term protocol, or accompanying agreement. As it turned out, SALT II limited the number of air-launched cruise missiles that could be deployed on bombers, while the protocol banned altogether the deployment of long-range sea- and ground-launched cruise missiles, thus establishing a precedent that some Europeans (and some Americans, too) found disturbing.

The same month that Schmidt spoke, the alliance's defense ministers set up a permanent subcommittee of experts from their staffs to address the problem of enhancing extended deterrence. It was called the High Level Group, or HLG, and was chaired by an American Assistant Secretary of Defense. (It would be primarily in the capacity of chairman of the HLG that Richard Perle would deal with the allies.) In the early deliberations of the High Level Group during the Carter Administration, the West European members were much more inclined than their American colleagues to press for the introduction of some new American weapons in Europe to shore up NATO against the SS-20s, and cruise missiles were the obvious candidate. The Americans insisted that existing strategic weapons were adequate, since they could cover all the relevant targets. The Europeans disagreed.

The issue was not really a matter of whether available American weapons could hit Soviet targets and counter Soviet weapons; it was a matter of confidence, of atmosphere, of psychology. In early 1978, Carter deepened doubts about his leadership and reawakened the controversy over the neutron bomb in a way that suggested he had learned all the wrong lessons the previous year. The Pentagon had lobbied the West German defense ministry hard, finally getting the Bonn government to agree that it would ask for the weapon if other European countries followed suit. Then suddenly, without consultation and with little explanation, Carter reversed himself and postponed production of the weapon. That left Schmidt out on a limb.

The Carter Administration quickly realized that military pros and cons about whether to put new weapons in Europe were now secondary to political considerations, and the overriding political imperative was to undo the damage done by the neutron-bomb fiasco. The U.S. had to demonstrate to its allies that it was capable of coming up with a plan to enhance the defense of Europe, and then of sticking with it. Carter's advisers suppressed their doubts about the military necessity of new land-based American weapons in Europe; they climbed, wearily and apprehensively, aboard the bandwagon for such deployments that European leaders themselves had started.

Looking back on the whole matter in an article published in 1982, Carter's National Security Adviser, Zbigniew Brzezinski, offered an extraordinarily candid reconstruction of the rationale that drove his own thinking, and that of the Administration in which he served:

> I was personally never persuaded that we needed [the new weapons] for military reasons. I was persuaded reluctantly that we needed [them] to obtain European support for SALT. This was largely because Chancellor Schmidt made such a big deal out of the so-called Eurostrategic imbalance that was being generated by the Soviet deployment of the SS-20. To keep him in line we felt that some response in Europe on the intermediate level would be necessary.

But, even as it was admitting the political need for new weapons in Europe in order to keep the alliance content, Washington's heart was still in the pursuit of an agreement with Moscow.

The Right Missiles for Europe

Once it had been decided that new weapons were necessary for NATO, the U.S. and its allies had to agree upon what sort of weapons, and in what quantity. There were five principal choices: (1) the Tomahawk ground-launched cruise missile; (2) a sea-launched cruise missile that would be put on submarines or surface ships assigned to NATO; (3) the Army's Pershing II XR (extended range) intermediate-range ballistic missile, a successor to the Pershing I missile already in West Germany; (4) a new medium-range ballistic missile called Longbow, which the Air Force was thinking about building; and (5) the FB-111H bomber, which would have a somewhat longer range and larger payload than the FB-111A already assigned to the Strategic Air Command.

Sea-launched cruise missiles, because they would be submerged somewhere off shore, would not have the desired visibility and political impact of land-based systems. If they were put on surface ships belonging to the West European navies, moreover, there would have to be American officers on board to approve their handling and possible use. That prospect was too reminiscent of the ill-fated scheme of the early 1960s for a "multilateral force."*

The Longbow, since it was a newly conceived rocket, would take too long to perfect for deployment by the mid-1980s. (By contrast, the Pershing II was supposed to make use of available, proven technology from the Pershing I.) Also, the Longbow would be perceived, and criticized, as representing an escalation of the arms race.

The only remaining choices for missiles were the ground-launched Tomahawk and the Pershing II. Each had what at the time seemed like advantages in its limitations as well as its capabilities. The Tomahawk was highly mobile. Its launchers could be picked up and moved around by air, within Europe or from the U.S. to Europe in a crisis. Its low "flight profile," several hundred feet or less, combined with a zigzag path, would give it the ability to dodge and duck below Soviet air defenses. But it flew subsonically, much more slowly than manned warplanes—about six hundred miles per hour. That meant it did not constitute a first-strike threat, and it enjoyed the reputation among most Western theoreticians of being purely retaliatory, a "stabilizing" factor in the military balance.

The Pershing II was to be a considerable improvement on the Pershing I. In addition to more than twice the range, it would have a "terminally guided" reentry vehicle, or warhead, that would home in on its target, correcting its course as it plunged toward earth. As the warhead reentered the atmosphere, it would take a radar reading of the area below, especially the target and landmarks in the surrounding terrain. Then it would compare that live image with a reference map assembled from satellite photos and stored in the warhead's computerized brain. Depending on the match between where the warhead was headed and where it was supposed to land, signals would be relayed to four small fins, which would maneuver the warhead and adjust its descent accordingly as it plunged toward earth. If everything worked properly, the warhead would come within twenty to forty meters of its target, about ten times closer than the Pershing I.

All these technological wonders of the Pershing II had yet to be perfected in laboratories and on test ranges back in the U.S. They were part of the sales pitch for the rocket, but they were still the object of an intense development

---

*The multilateral nuclear force, or MLF, was an American plan that envisaged the deployment of a mixed-nationality NATO fleet of twenty-five surface vessels, manned by crews and commanded by officers from a number of member states. The ships would be equipped with Polaris missiles. The U.S. would have a veto over the firing of the missiles. France rejected the idea because it violated the cherished principle of an independent French deterrent; Britain rejected it, too. The Soviet Union had a field day with propaganda about how the MLF would put German fingers on the nuclear trigger. The plan died a slow, painful, but in the end unmourned death.

and testing program that was to be marred by highly publicized fizzles for some years thereafter, right up until the deadline for deployment.

Because of the increased accuracy it was supposed to have when it was finally operational, some advocates of the Pershing II said that its warhead could afford a somewhat lower yield, or destructive capability, than the Pershing I. Lower yield meant less "collateral damage." That was the same supposed asset that made the neutron bomb so controversial. A more usable weapon was justified as a more credible deterrent. The Pershing II was to require less support equipment and personnel than the Pershing I and could be readied for firing more quickly, which improved its "survivability" in a crisis and therefore, once again, its utility as a weapon and its credibility as a deterrent.

Also, its designers and proponents claimed at the time that, despite its increased range, the Pershing II could not reach Moscow from those parts of West Germany where it was to be stationed. Targets in the western regions of the U.S.S.R. were fair game, but not the Soviet capital or the command-and-control centers east of Moscow, from which that nation's leaders would direct a full-scale war with the U.S. This limitation in range was seen as making the Pershing II less provocative.

However, earth-penetrating warheads were being prepared for the Pershing II that would make it devastating to underground bunkers that had been "superhardened," or protected by layers of reinforced concrete, in the western parts of the U.S.S.R., from which the Soviets might otherwise be tempted to wage an attack against West Germany. The Pershing II was billed as the ultimate "theater" weapon, greatly bolstering regional deterrence but not posing a "strategic" threat to the U.S.S.R. It also had the cosmetic advantage of being distinguished in designation from the Pershing I only by a Roman numeral. That made it easier to advertise as an upgrading of an existing system.

Once NATO had settled on the Tomahawk and Pershing II as the best means of bolstering the credibility of American extended deterrence, the next question was how many of each would be deployed and where. It was decided, in a rather arbitrary and obscure series of guesses and compromises, that the total number of new American missiles in Europe should be between 200 and 600. Less than 200 would be a flimsy token, lacking the desired political impact. Military experts figured they would need about 600 new warheads to cover key targets in the western parts of the Soviet Union from which a Soviet attack would emanate and be controlled. But political experts worried that more than 600 long-range American missiles in Europe would be decoupling: they would make it look as though the U.S. was trying to buy its way out of its commitment to use its central, strategic nuclear weapons in defense of Europe. So it was decided to keep the number under 600.

The range of the Pershing IIs was shorter than that of the Tomahawks, so they had to be placed as far to the east as possible within NATO. That meant West Germany. There were already 108 Pershing I launchers to be replaced, so that meant 108 Pershing II launchers.

Tomahawks came in "flights" of 16 (four launchers with four missiles each), so the number of cruise missiles in the package would have to be a multiple of 16. Twenty-nine flights of Tomahawks meant 464 cruise missiles in all. Along with the Pershings, that brought the total up to 572—just under 600.

The West Germans made clear that even though their Chancellor had argued for the new missiles in the first place, the Federal Republic, slated to get the 108 Pershing IIs, was not willing to accept the full burden of the 464 cruise missiles as well. Schmidt and his Social Democratic colleagues still had their own version of détente, *Ostpolitik,* to protect, and they also had a vociferous left-wing opposition within their own party to worry about. The U.S. and the rest of NATO were sympathetic. It made no sense for West Germany to take the lonely lead in NATO's nuclear modernization, especially given the Soviets' fear of renascent German militarism. Soviet propagandists had quickly taken the line that GLCM, the initials for ground-launched cruise missile, might as well stand for German-launched cruise missile. The High Level Group decided by April 1979 that the cruise missiles should be spread out among as many NATO member states as possible. The Pentagon's "deployment package" called for stationing Tomahawks in West Germany, Great Britain, Italy, Belgium, and Holland.

However, it bears remembering that, if military experts had been left strictly to their own calculations and devices, they would probably not have assembled such a package at all. Instead, to protect Europe they would have continued to rely on central, strategic systems as instruments of extended deterrence, despite the heavy-breathing arrival on the scene of SS-20. From the standpoint of hardware alone, the U.S. still had plenty of warheads to cover Soviet targets. It was the software of intra-alliance self-confidence that was showing wear and tear.

Two Tracks: Collision and Derailment

Already in 1978 there was a powerful imperative within NATO to have it both ways—to prepare to deploy new weapons while simultaneously seeking negotiated agreements that would reduce, limit, or even eliminate the weapons to be deployed. That imperative was spelled out forcefully in the Caribbean sunshine by the one allied leader who would not, and could not, accept any of the new missiles himself, because his country did not participate in the military command of the alliance. French President Valéry Giscard d'Estaing held an informal summit meeting on Guadeloupe with Carter, Schmidt, and British Prime Minister James Callaghan during the first week of January 1979. While Schmidt was the leader who had first sounded the alarm over a nuclear imbalance in Europe, it was Giscard who suggested joining deployment to an arms-control initiative.

The idea had an immediate appeal. The key West European proponents of modernization were disillusioned not so much with arms control as with the performance of the U.S. government at that time. They were worried that Soviet-American strategic arms control had been artificially divorced from what ought to be the goals of "Euro-strategic" arms control. Here was a way of recoupling the U.S. with Western Europe in both diplomacy and defense. While arms control was in some disrepute in the U.S., particularly among the Carter Administration's critics and challengers, the enterprise had a growing allure in Western Europe. That was because it was seen as a way to lessen the danger of war and to salvage the near-defunct policy of détente from which West Europeans felt they were deriving tangible benefits, such as trade with the East and the reunification of families across the Iron Curtain. If a way could be found to make the new deployments seem not just compatible with, but necessary to, the pursuit of arms control, then it might be easier for the governments to keep their constituencies and their own political opposition in line.

The Carter Administration more than just accepted Giscard's suggestion; it adopted the idea as its own brainstorm, and saw itself as performing a clever sort of therapy on its schizophrenic allies. As Zbigniew Brzezinski later put it:

> We felt we were responding to the European desire in shaping [the decision to proceed with the new missiles for NATO], but we were also very conscious of the fact that the Europeans were ambivalent. As a result, one track of the NATO decision was designed to satisfy those Europeans who felt that their insecurity ought to be reduced by some offsetting deployments giving the West an intermediate [-range] capability of matching the Soviets; the other track was designed to satisfy those Europeans who felt that it was important to match any security efforts by a new arms-control initiative.

As 1979 unfolded, the attempt to reconcile and coordinate rearmament and disarmament was institutionalized in the structure of NATO and ultimately consecrated in a formal decision by the allied leaders.

As NATO moved toward acceptance of the Pentagon's deployment package, a number of member states insisted that the process must not be monopolized by the defense ministries through the High Level Group. A second body, made up primarily of foreign-ministry officials, was created to study and promote arms-control initiatives that might do away with the need for deployment. This was the Special Group, which later became known as the Special Consultative Group, or SCG. It was conceived as a bureaucratic counterweight to the HLG, and it was a device for making sure that the military's bias toward proceeding with the new weapons would be offset by the diplomats' bias toward negotiations.

The High Level and Special groups went their separate ways, the former refining plans for putting the missiles in Europe, the latter for putting proposals to the Soviets, in spite of the fact that everyone involved recognized that the two exercises were supposed to be interactive rather than contradictory. In the fall, the U.S. National Security Council staff and the State Department took the reports of the HLG and SCG and in effect stapled them together. The result became known as the Integrated Decision Document, or IDD.

In December 1979, at a series of meetings in Brussels, the IDD went before the NATO ministers and emerged publicly—in the form of a truncated, sanitized communiqué—as the "dual-track" decision. The document contained a number of guidelines for the negotiations that would prove important, and troublesome, during the Reagan Administration. One was that the negotiations should concentrate initially on missiles, not aircraft. Another was that limitations should somehow deal with Soviet missiles outside Europe—that is, the Asian parts of the U.S.S.R.

There were two reasons for wanting some kind of U.S.S.R.-wide, or "global," coverage of the SS-20. One was that the Soviets might accept reductions in their European SS-20 force but instead of destroying the excess missiles would simply haul them eastward, out of range of NATO, to be moved back at any time. Thus, even SS-20s in Asia represented a threat to Europe. The other reason was that the SS-20s in eastern regions of the U.S.S.R. also represented a threat to the U.S.'s chief Asian allies, Japan and Korea, and to the People's Republic of China, with which the Carter Administration was normalizing diplomatic relations and hoping to develop what Brzezinski sometimes called a "strategic partnership," a kind of unwritten alliance against the U.S.S.R. The U.S. did not want, as a result of its effort to ease the anxieties of its friends in Western Europe, to frighten and anger its friends in the Far East. In 1979 State Department officials made a number of calls on the Japanese embassy with assurances that, whatever the outcome of the negotiations on the European nuclear balance, Japan's security would not suffer.

The alliance committed itself to proceed with the new American missiles along one track while the U.S. pursued reductions in Soviet missiles along the other. The connection between the two tracks was clear, at least in theory: if the Soviets were sufficiently forthcoming in accepting negotiated limitations on their intermediate-range forces, and in particular the SS-20, the West might not introduce all 572 of its own new missiles.

The Integrated Decision Document did not, however, encourage hopes that through successful arms control NATO could completely avoid installing at least some new forces. On the contrary, the document stated quite clearly that, while arms control might reduce the Soviet threat and therefore reduce the level of Western response, the arms-control track should not be expected to overtake the deployment track entirely. This point subsequently came to be overlooked and, indeed, contradicted by the Reagan Administration. The concept of a "zero solution"—total cancellation of the NATO program in exchange for total elimination of the SS-20s—was definitely not envisioned in December 1979. Quite the contrary. The predominant thinking at that time was that, in the unlikely event that the specific threat of the SS-20s disappeared, West European confidence in the existing American umbrella still needed bolstering because of the Soviet ability to attack Western European targets. Hence the goals of deterrence and recoupling would still require the U.S. to have more weapons capable of attacking Soviet targets from Western Europe. The SS-20 was the most obvious and pressing problem; but eliminating it would not reduce the uncertainties of extended deterrence completely. There was a widespread, though not unanimous, feeling among policymakers and strategists in Europe, and a general agreement in Washington, that the two-track approach should lead to *some* deployment and to *some* arms control.

For this to work, a number of things had to happen. The alliance had to remain committed to deployment. The Soviet Union had to be convinced that it would indeed face all 572 Pershing IIs and Tomahawks in Europe unless it cut back its SS-20s. And the U.S. had to find a negotiating proposal that would eventually yield an agreement acceptable not just to itself and the Soviet Union but to the Western allies as well.

As 1980 began, there was little ground for optimism on any of these points. Both the Pershing II and Tomahawk programs were having funding problems in the U.S. Congress and technical problems on the testing ranges. There were formidable political difficulties. The December 1979 communiqué had stipulated that the Special Consultative Group would follow the progress of future U.S.-Soviet arms talks. While the U.S.'s allies were not to participate directly in the negotiations, they had been granted more than their usual role of kibitzers. This new condition was sure to complicate American policymaking and negotiating strategy; as never before the U.S. would have to take account of its allies' wishes and needs, not to mention the vicissitudes of their electoral and parliamentary processes. The disadvantage for the U.S. was a potential advantage for the U.S.S.R. If the Soviets played the allies off against each other, fanned the hopes and fears of the West European peace movement, and exploited transatlantic tensions skillfully, they stood to win a double prize: a halt to a threatening American military program, and new political discord within NATO.

The Soviets' stand was accusatory and self-righteous: American and West European talk of disparities and imbalance was nothing but a smokescreen for NATO's ambition to regain superiority over the U.S.S.R. Moscow asserted that since the Tomahawks and Pershing IIs could reach into the U.S.S.R. itself, the planned NATO deployments would add a whole new layer of threat to the Soviet homeland. As such, NATO policy was "unacceptable." The Soviets used this word repeatedly, and from the beginning they issued an explicit warning that deployment would preclude negotiation. Within days after the meeting in Brussels, *Pravda* proclaimed that the NATO decision had "destroyed the basis for talks on medium-range weapons" in Europe.

Moscow had its own two-track, carrot-and-stick approach: an offer to freeze, and perhaps reduce, its own forces if NATO would give up on the new weapons, combined with an ultimatum to end the arms-control process and escalate the arms buildup if NATO went ahead with deployment. During a visit to East Berlin in October 1979, two months before the decisive NATO meeting, Leonid Brezhnev had made a dramatic attempt to head off a deployment decision by announcing, "We are prepared to reduce the number of medium-range nuclear [weapons] deployed in western areas of the Soviet Union . . . only in the event that no additional medium-range nuclear [weapons] are deployed in Western Europe." This seemed to mean that the Soviets were prepared to cut back on their missiles threatening Europe, or at least pull some of them back out of range of NATO targets, in exchange for cancellation of the Pershing IIs and Tomahawks. Brezhnev did not say, however, whether his offer applied to the only weapons that really mattered, the SS-20, or whether it was limited to the obsolescent SS-4s and -5s that were due for retirement anyway. The U.S. was in no mood to explore Brezhnev's proposal. President Carter was quick to dismiss the offer as "an effort designed to disarm the willingness or eagerness of our allies adequately to defend themselves."

However, the combination of Soviet threats and overtures did not fall on deaf ears in Europe. There was powerful parliamentary opposition to the deployment in Belgium, Holland, and West Germany, and the European anti-nuclear movement was beginning to build up steam in other countries as well, including Italy and Great Britain, which were also to be homes for the Tomahawk batteries. The U.S. did little to help matters. Reductions in European nuclear forces were to be negotiated as part of SALT III, but by mid-1980 it was doubtful that SALT II would ever be ratified.

Even Schmidt now seemed uncomfortable about the 1979 decision. When the Soviets floated yet another in their series of proposals for a permanent freeze on medium-range nuclear weapons in Europe, there were hints out of Bonn that Schmidt's government might welcome the idea. Schmidt had a slightly different freeze proposal of his own: "It would serve peace if both sides did not deploy for the next three years, and instead negotiated soon on mutual reductions." In other words, a moratorium on new deployments that would permit no new SS-20s in exchange for no Pershing IIs and Tomahawks at all.

While Schmidt's suggestion was limited to an interim measure and was intended to be consistent with the dual-track decision, it caused suspicion in Washington that he was weaseling out of the deployment half of the decision. When Schmidt went to Moscow to talk to Brezhnev in June 1980, Carter was persuaded by Brzezinski to send the Chancellor a stern letter warning him not to waver from the NATO line. Schmidt could barely contain his annoyance. Replying to the President in public, Schmidt said, in English, "You can rest assured that you can depend on the bloody Germans!"

In fact, there was little trust on either side of the Atlantic.

The Carter Round

Shortly before the 1980 election, Jimmy Carter dispatched a team to Geneva to meet with the Soviets and open the negotiating track of the December '79 NATO decision. It was a melancholy affair, and the participants could be forgiven for feeling that it was almost pointless. The American negotiators were led by Spurgeon Keeny, who was the deputy director of the Arms Control and Disarmament Agency. They were in Geneva when their President, the man who had authorized their instructions, was resoundingly defeated by Ronald Reagan. Like Carter, the U.S. negotiators were now lame ducks. They had agreed with the Soviets to a month of talks, and they stuck meticulously to that schedule, almost to the day. The Americans had been told by the White House to maintain an atmosphere that was "correct" but "not too cordial."

That was the Soviets' approach, too. Their delegation was led by Viktor Karpov, who had been his nation's chief negotiator in the final phase of SALT II. The Soviets were thus underscoring their commitment to consistency in arms-control negotiations generally and, more particularly, to the close connection between negotiations on strategic and European nuclear forces. In private, the Soviet delegates had difficulty disguising their curiosity and anxiety about the changes underway in Washington. But, when Keeny mentioned Reagan's victory in a more formal setting, Karpov replied rather brusquely for the record, "We're not interested in that. We're negotiating with the U.S. government, not with the Carter Administration."

The position that Keeny and his colleagues presented in Geneva was not so much a proposal as a set of guidelines based on the Integrated Decision Document drawn up by the NATO ministers at the time of the dual-track decision nearly a year before. Partly because it reflected a consensus of so many different parties, the position was extremely general. The American team in Geneva confined itself mostly, in Keeny's phrase, to "laying down markers" on certain goals for European nuclear arms control.

Most important was the proposition that there should be equal limits on both sides' long-range missiles. That meant the SS-4s, -5s, and -20s on the Soviet side and the Tomahawks and Pershing IIs on the American side. Equality, as defined and applied in an agreement, somehow had to take into account warheads rather than just launchers or missiles. The SS-20 was triple-MIRVed, while the other weapons in question were single-warhead. That meant each SS-20 had to count more than a single Pershing II or a Tomahawk. The proposition included no clear or unified idea on how that was to be done. SALT had been based on the expedient of counting and limiting missile launchers; warheads might be limited as well, but only indirectly, for instance by freezing the number of warheads per type of missile at the number already tested.

The other key proposition on the American side was that an agreement must somehow take into account the other highly troublesome feature of the SS-20, its mobility. In keeping with the IDD, the U.S. insisted that the negotiations must "consider the regional aspects" of the problem, and any agreed limits must be "worldwide in scope." Once again, the marker that Keeny laid down was not attached to any detailed proposal.

On the other side of the table, Karpov put forward a refinement of the Kremlin's freeze proposal: no new medium-range nuclear "means" in Europe. It quickly became apparent that the freeze meant the U.S.S.R. would stop, but not reduce, its deployment of SS-20s in exchange for NATO's cancellation of the Pershing IIs and Tomahawks. The Pershing IIs and Tomahawks were almost literally unmentionable. The Soviet negotiators did not want to grant any legitimacy to the notion that such missiles might be deployed in Europe. Therefore, in their formal statements, they confined themselves to urging a blanket freeze on the basis of the status quo. Soviet statements referred to the "existing balance" and the "principal arms under discussion," but barely mentioned the prospective NATO missiles. They were, as Keeny noted, "the ghosts at the table." In less formal discussions, Karpov let references to the Pershing IIs and cruise missiles pass his lips, but he made clear that these weapons "should never exist," and "a freeze by definition precludes things that don't exist."

While both sides had a long way to go in fleshing out their positions, the basic outlines of the disagreement between them were already apparent, and that disagreement was very stark indeed. The U.S. was looking for a settlement that would permit at least partial deployment of the new NATO missiles; if there was to be a reduction in the level of deployment, it would have to be in exchange for a reduction in the SS-20s. The U.S.S.R. was leaving open the possibility of some reductions on its side, but seemed to be foreclosing the possibility of a treaty that would sanction any new NATO missiles.

2 The New Regime

By the time the Reagan Administration came into office, both tracks of the December 1979 decision were subject to second thoughts all across the American political spectrum. Support for the arms-control track was shaky for a number of reasons: arms control in general had aroused hostility on the right and disillusionment on the left; and with the apparent collapse of SALT, negotiations on nuclear weapons in Europe alone seemed neither very promising nor necessarily wise. The deployment track, too, was criticized by liberals as well as conservatives, and on military as well as political grounds. Paul Warnke, who had been Carter's first director of the Arms Control and Disarmament Agency and principal SALT negotiator, argued that the ability of the Pershing IIs and Tomahawks to cover Soviet targets already covered by U.S. strategic warheads was not necessarily alliance-coupling or deterrence-enhancing; it was merely redundant: "Five hundred and seventy-two warheads [the number envisaged in the NATO plan] is less than what is aboard two Trident submarines; they represent a tiny fraction of our 10,000 or so strategic warheads, all of which can hit targets that will be covered by the [Tomahawks] and Pershing IIs." McGeorge Bundy, who had been John F. Kennedy's and Lyndon Johnson's special assistant for national security affairs, and was now devoting himself to the study of nuclear-weapons issues, asserted, "If the West Europeans' willingness to deploy these essentially irrelevant weapons becomes a test of alliance solidarity, we'll be handing the Soviets a splendid bludgeon with which to split the alliance."

Similar doubts were in the minds of some of the new President's advisers. Caspar Weinberger's principal aides, Fred Iklé and Richard Perle, both felt that the dual-track decision was a mistake. Iklé could see that the Tomahawks and Pershing IIs might reinforce a weak spot in Western defenses and that they might complicate, in a cautionary and therefore deterrent way, Soviet planning for an attack. But in his view those benefits were outweighed by a number of disadvantages. Both the Tomahawks and Pershing IIs were mobile, to be sure, and, according to the rules of nuclear war-gaming, "mobility enhances pre-launch survivability." But were they sufficiently mobile and therefore sufficiently survivable? Or would they simply draw enemy fire? With just that worry in mind, many Europeans were turning against the new missiles. In Iklé's view, deployment promised to be more trouble than it was worth.

Perle expressed "misgivings about the cost/benefit wisdom" of the Tomahawk and Pershing II. He scoffed openly at the idea of "paying billions of dollars for a mere 572 weapons." (The cost he had in mind included the total cost of developing as well as deploying the Pershing II and Tomahawk ground-launched cruise missile.) "That's a hell of a price tag for a marginal military fix." Perle had another objection, too—one that reflected his distaste for arms control as it had been practiced in the past. He blamed SALT for the very existence of the SS-20 and therefore for the need to counter it. He was a firm subscriber to the notion that the Soviets had consciously designed the SS-20 in order to take advantage of the loopholes in SALT, thus violating its spirit. He also blamed SALT for the West's misguided response to the threat of the SS-20s. The Carter Administration had reluctantly acceded to the December 1979 deployment decision—"a lousy decision, if ever there was one"—largely in order to allay West European anxieties that SALT had sold their security short. "The whole sorry story," remarked Perle, "is a classic example of how so-called arms control, far from controlling arms, has had the effect of driving the deployment of new weapons."

With liberals like Warnke and Bundy questioning the dual-track decision from outside the government and Perle and Iklé attacking it from inside, the State Department saw its job as one of making sure that the Reagan Administration did not repudiate its predecessor and upset its allies by abandoning the decision altogether. It was the strong conviction of Secretary of State Alexander Haig and his associate Lawrence Eagleburger that, whatever legitimate questions there might be about the wisdom of the NATO decision, the U.S. was stuck with it. The consequences of reversing course would be far worse than those of going forward. They realized that the new Administration was coming into office with a reputation for excessive hawkishness. If Reagan were to back away from the 1979 decision, it would be taken as proof of his antipathy to arms control, his insensitivity to the allies, and his disdain for even a modicum of continuity between administrations.

For a while the bureaucracy stewed over the problem. Finally, Eagleburger decided to bypass the interagency process. British Prime Minister Margaret Thatcher was coming to Washington for an official visit at the end of February. Eagleburger arranged with James Rentschler, a foreign-service officer who was working on West European affairs for the National Security Council staff, to insert a clear-cut endorsement of the dual-track decision into the text of remarks that Reagan would make during a public appearance with Thatcher.*

Now the President himself had committed his Administration to following through on both tracks. The debate in the bureaucracy no longer mattered. Nor did Iklé's and Perle's opposition. Eagleburger took some satisfaction in having, on that occasion at least, outmaneuvered the Pentagon. Doing so entailed putting words in the President's mouth—getting him to say something neither the background nor the significance of which he more than vaguely understood. This would become a recurring means of settling, or at least postponing, disputes in the Administration as time went on.

An Administration Divided

For Eagleburger, dealing with the allies was already turning out to be easy compared to dealing with his colleagues in Washington. He went off to Brussels in late March for a meeting of the Special Consultative Group, the first since the Reagan Administration had come into office. Eagleburger represented the Administration as chairman of the SCG, Perle as chairman of the High Level Group. But Eagleburger quickly discovered that Perle's point of view was not confined to the Pentagon; it had adherents throughout the government, including inside the State Department building and within Eagleburger's own entourage at the SCG.

Eagleburger was accompanied to Brussels by Michael Pillsbury, a protégé of a group of right-wing senators who was serving as acting deputy director of the Arms Control Agency. Pillsbury considered it his mission to serve as a one-man truth squad on behalf of his patrons on Capitol Hill. Eagleburger would not be allowed to "give away the store" to the allies, Pillsbury vowed on the eve of his departure; he must not be allowed to commit the new Administration to anything that smacked of continuity with arms control of the past.

During the SCG meeting, the West Europeans did, as expected, press for some reassurance that the new American leadership would resume negotiations. They did not ask for a firm date, but they wanted, at a minimum, a public statement that the arms-control process would continue—not someday, but soon, and not from scratch, but picking up from where it had left off in the previous Administration. Eagleburger was prepared to grant them

---

*Emerging from talks with Thatcher on February 26, Reagan said, "We're determined to consult closely with each other and with the rest of our allies on all matters involving our common security. In that connection, we affirmed our support for the alliance's decision of December 1979 to modernize long-range theater nuclear forces and to pursue arms control efforts at the same time, in parallel."

that much; Pillsbury was not. Eagleburger insisted on a paragraph in a press statement that said, "This meeting represents an important step in continuing implementation of the arms-control approach. . . . The U.S. and its Allies place great importance on Alliance consultations as a step toward resumption of U.S.-Soviet exchanges."

Pillsbury argued hard with Eagleburger, and then threatened him. The Senate had yet to confirm Eagleburger as Assistant Secretary of State for European Affairs. Pillsbury had influence with a group of senators who could hold up and perhaps prevent Eagleburger's confirmation. If Eagleburger did not relent on inclusion of the noxious paragraph, Pillsbury warned, "Your ass is grass."

Eagleburger was dumbfounded. He was also contemptuous. And he got his way. The paragraph he wanted went into the press statement, and Eagleburger made sure the story about Pillsbury's attempted blackmail got around back in Washington. Not long afterward, Eagleburger was confirmed, and Pillsbury was asked to leave the Arms Control Agency as soon as Eugene Rostow took over as director. To replace Pillsbury, Rostow brought in as his deputy Robert Grey, a career foreign-service officer who had worked for him years before in the Johnson Administration. Pillsbury went back to Capitol Hill to work for the Steering Committee, a caucus of right-wing senators. From that position, for years to come, he waged a vendetta against the State Department and the Arms Control Agency. He fought against the Administration's arms-control policy in all its manifestations, against Grey, Eagleburger, and anyone else at the State Department who qualified as a "crypto-arms-controller."

Another emissary from the Administration, Caspar Weinberger, traveled to Brussels in early April. The occasion was a meeting of the alliance's defense ministers, who made up the Nuclear Planning Group. Like Eagleburger, Weinberger sought to reassure the West Europeans—but on his terms, not theirs. Knowing that détente was still a cherished goal on the continent, he told an audience in Bonn, "If the movement from Cold War to détente is progress, then let me say we cannot afford much more progress." Far from echoing Eagleburger's promise about a quick resumption of arms-control negotiations, Weinberger underscored the new Administration's commitment to rearmament now, disarmament later, if ever. Richard Perle, who was traveling with the secretary, said on a number of occasions that the U.S. should not enter any negotiations with the Soviets until it was "ready"— meaning rearmed—regardless of pleas from the West Europeans. Fred Iklé, who was also along, delivered a number of lectures on the danger of Soviet "breakout"—the use of loopholes in arms-control treaties to prepare for a sudden surge in military force, confronting the West with a drastic shift in the balance of power.

Weinberger also sought to secure the allies' endorsement of a version of linkage whereby progress in arms control and other diplomatic business between the superpowers should be directly contingent on the Soviet Union's showing restraint toward third countries. The issue of the hour was Poland. The independent trade-union organization Solidarity had the Polish regime on the defensive. The Kremlin was clearly angry and apprehensive. There was a widespread expectation that a Soviet invasion might come at any time. If that happened, Weinberger said, arms talks could not possibly begin. The allies agreed. At the end of the meeting, Joseph Luns, the Secretary-General of NATO, issued a statement saying that the assembled ministers had "agreed that the Soviets would gravely undermine the basis for effective arms control negotiations if they were to intervene in the internal affairs of Poland." At a press conference, Weinberger said, "The date [of resumed negotiations] depends entirely on Soviet conduct in the next few weeks and months." Again Luns backed him up.

But Weinberger did not stop there. He wanted a written statement from the Nuclear Planning Group reiterating its endorsement of linkage. The other ministers were not willing to go that far, but Weinberger seemed not to hear what they were saying. On the next leg of his trip, he told the reporters traveling with him that the NPG had linked the resumption of negotiations to the threat, rather than the actuality, of a Soviet invasion of Poland. Back in Washington, Weinberger said at a press breakfast that the NPG had linked resumption to the Soviets' easing of pressure on Poland. The NPG had done nothing of the kind and had no such intention.

So, instead of consolidating American leadership over the alliance, Weinberger had deepened doubts among the West Europeans about whether they really wanted to be led by the U.S. down the road that he seemed to have in mind. He had intensified suspicions about whether the new Administration was going to buckle down to negotiations with the Soviet Union or look for excuses to avoid doing so. Moreover, inconsistency between Weinberger's expressed opinions and Eagleburger's called attention to the divisions within the Administration.

Pressure began to build from across the Atlantic for the U.S. to commit itself to a date for the resumption of talks. It was coming particularly from the two governments on the continent that were holding firm to the deployment schedule, West Germany and Italy. Schmidt sent word to Washington that he absolutely must have a starting date for the negotiations or he could not keep his government on the deployment track. Deployment itself was still not scheduled to begin until late 1983, but in the meantime all sorts of preliminary steps were necessary: the location and preparation of sites and the building of an infrastructure to support deployments. These required in West Germany a cooperative, or at least not openly mutinous, Social Democratic party, parliament, and populace. The Italians, too, made clear that the

U.S. must send a "signal" of willingness to resume talks with the U.S.S.R.

The State Department, with Eagleburger's European Bureau taking the lead, argued in Washington that the U.S. would have to make a commitment, if not to a particular date then at least to a time frame, such as before the end of the year. The place to make such a commitment would be at the NATO foreign ministers' meeting in Rome in early May. Haig pressed the case at National Security Council meetings, in a number of personal calls on the President, and at his regular breakfast talks with Weinberger. The Secretary of Defense objected to the notion that U.S. policymaking should be driven by solicitousness toward the West Europeans. "What the alliance wants, or at least what it needs," said Weinberger in early April, "is leadership, not compromise." He also argued that the U.S. need not make any commitments at all until the Soviets showed more willingness to talk about meaningful reductions.

Weinberger was usually accompanied at these sessions by Deputy Secretary of Defense Frank Carlucci and by Fred Iklé, but Richard Perle's presence was often felt. It was he who designed the principal tactic on which Weinberger relied to oppose a timetable. Instead of giving the Europeans a commitment to open talks with the Soviets by the end of the year, the Administration should put together what Perle called "a work program." It would involve "an update of the threat assessment and a review of NATO's requirements." The review would take place in Washington, at NATO headquarters in Brussels, and in the allied capitals. Haig should tell his European counterparts in Rome that the resumption of negotiations would be "contingent on the completion of the work program."

Haig argued against this with some vehemence: "If we emphasize the contingent nature of our commitment to begin negotiations, people [in Europe] will say, 'Now you're attaching preconditions and trying to get out of the talks!' "

"Al," said Weinberger, "if you agree, as I'm sure you do, that a lot of work is necessary, and if you agree that we've got to work closely with the allies, and if you know the allies as well as you must, then you've got to see that we can't predict how long it's going to take to get ready intellectually for what we ought to do."

This dialogue went on over a period of weeks. Haig found it difficult to contain his fury at the meetings and did not even try to do so with his staff. In the midst of one explosion, he slammed his fist down and blurted, " 'Work program,' my ass! It's a *make work* program, that's what it is! It's the oldest stalling tactic in the book!"

The Pentagon was not Haig's only problem. The environs of the White House, and particularly the National Security Council staff, were already becoming unfriendly territory in the bureaucratic guerrilla war that was now heating up. When Haig would visit the White House and make some extremely cautious, syntactically contorted statement to the press about the importance of "consultations with our partners in Europe" and the eventual need for "preliminary talks with Soviet representatives with a view toward having negotiations ultimately that would seek to achieve the objective we're committed to," Richard Allen, the President's National Security Adviser, would undercut him with a press briefing—not for attribution to him by name—warning that "we won't be stampeded" into talks. In the months and years to come, this phrase would become a kind of battle cry for hard-liners in the Administration.

Allen and his aides felt the U.S. did not need to sit still for "blackmail" and "pressure tactics" from the West Europeans, particularly from the West Germans. "Two can play this game," said Sven Kraemer of the NSC's defense policy staff: the U.S. could tell Schmidt to "take his demands and stuff 'em." So what if Schmidt's party and coalition partners and constituents turned against him? So what if his government fell? There was much to be said in favor of the Reagan Administration's doing business with a conservative Christian Democratic government instead. General Robert Schweitzer, the director of the NSC's defense policy staff, had once worked for Haig, but was now, along with Kraemer, one of his old boss's harshest critics: "Al's been taken over by the striped-pants types; he's been co-opted by the softies."

The issue came to a head at a National Security Council meeting on April 30, on the eve of Haig's departure for Rome. It was Reagan's first NSC meeting since his recovery from an assassination attempt on March 30. He was still on a limited schedule, but he felt he should be in the chair for this meeting since his secretaries of State and Defense were now publicly perceived to be at odds, particularly on the issue of arms control. Haig made a personal appeal in advance of the meeting, and it worked. The President could see that the U.S. had to appear accommodating to the West Europeans. Haig was authorized in Rome to commit the U.S. publicly to beginning negotiations by the end of the year.*

The communiqué released on May 5 by the ministers at the end of their two-day meeting said the allies "welcomed the intention of the U.S. to begin negotiations with the Soviet Union on [European nuclear forces] within the SALT framework by the end of the year." This phrase was repeated verbatim and prominently in another communiqué released later that month after Schmidt called on Reagan in Washington. Schmidt pressed Reagan to give him some ammunition to rebut charges from within his own party at home that the new Administration was not serious about the arms-control track

---

*While in the hospital recuperating from his bullet wound, Reagan had written out by hand a five-page letter to Leonid Brezhnev expressing his horror at nuclear war, his hopes for peace, and his willingness to move toward progress in arms control. Haig made good use of the letter in Rome.

and that therefore the Federal Republic should not feel bound to stay on the deployment track. He suggested that the U.S. accelerate the timetable for negotiations. Reagan was not willing to go that far, but he publicly assured Schmidt that the U.S. would be in a position to begin the talks between mid-November and mid-December.

The U.S. was now obligated, by a presidential promise, to resume negotiations in the near future, and to do so in a way that implied some degree of continuity with the recent past—that is, with SALT.*

However, the Rome communiqué also threw a bone to the Pentagon: "These negotiations will rely on an updated alliance threat assessment and a study of functional requirements for NATO [regional] nuclear forces to be undertaken within the framework of the Special Consultative Group and the High Level Group as matters of immediate priority." So Perle's "work program" would be conducted after all. Much of it would take place under the aegis of the HLG and therefore under Perle's chairmanship. To the extent that Perle could keep the HLG one jump ahead of the SCG in Brussels, he would be better able to outflank Eagleburger within the bureaucracy back in Washington. Eagleburger had to be constantly on the alert against Perle's maneuvers through the summer and fall.

In the summer of 1981, the Pentagon began pressing for a revision of the Integrated Decision Document (IDD), which, said Perle, was no longer an adequate basis for preparing a negotiating position that would deal prudently with the greatly enhanced Soviet threat. Perle wanted to distance the U.S. as much as possible from the formal document in which that decision was enshrined. He soon got some help.

Richard Burt, the director of the State Department's Bureau of Politico-Military Affairs, was trying to stake out a position halfway between the traditionalists of the State Department and the revisionists of the Pentagon. In July, he established a committee of outside experts to conduct a supposedly secret review of the December 1979 decision. He selected as the chairman Seymour Weiss, a former State Department official who was a well-known critic of arms control and a close friend and political ally of

---

*Having imposed an explicit acknowledgment of the connection between European arms control and SALT on the Administration and using it to reassure the allies, Haig had only to get the Soviets to accept it. That proved harder than he expected. When Haig met with Foreign Minister Andrei Gromyko in September at the United Nations, Eagleburger sat down with Gromyko's deputy, Georgi Kornienko, to work out a joint statement. Eagleburger naturally suggested including the phrase "in the framework of SALT." To the American side's surprise, Kornienko refused. When Perle learned what had happened, he felt a certain "I-told-you-so" smugness. Not even the Soviets appeared to join the State Department's "cult of reverence" for SALT, as Perle saw it. In fact, Soviet objections were based on a concern that the U.S. would use the SALT precedent as an argument against including British and French weapons in any new agreement covering nuclear forces in Europe.

Perle's. In his own opening remarks to the panel, Burt warned that he was inviting them to "shake up thinking around here," but not to the point of recommending that the dual-track decision be scrapped altogether; such a recommendation, he said, would be "unhelpful" and "a waste of time."

Nonetheless, the hard-liners in the group closed ranks behind a devastating critique. It had been a mistake, they felt, to let the allies be partners in a decision on the deployment of American weapons; the 1979 decision had set the scene for a situation in which the Europeans could more easily push the U.S. around—and the Soviet Union could more easily push the Europeans around. There was talk about letting the West German government go "cold turkey"—either shut up and deploy its allotment of the new missiles or bear the responsibility for the collapse of NATO. As for the IDD, it was, in Weiss's phrase, "a real bummer."

When West European diplomats found out about this exercise, they were aghast. Here was a panel—a "commission," as it came to be called on Embassy Row—that was convened at the invitation of the State Department; its chairman, Weiss, was picked by the director of the Bureau of Politico-Military Affairs yet was known to share many of the views of Perle, who in turn was known to take a very jaundiced view of arms control. Eagleburger was also dismayed. It confirmed his belief that any modification in the IDD would further jeopardize the already shaky support for the dual-track decision in Europe.

But officials at the Pentagon and the NSC were unchastened. They complained that Eagleburger and his aides were again showing symptoms of "acute clientitis." They were "more European than the Europeans," said Sven Kraemer. Richard Allen's refrain during this period was, "Just because Helmut Schmidt is in a hurry and keeps telling us to hurry doesn't mean we're in a hurry." There were a number of testy exchanges in both Washington and Brussels in which Perle reminded his European and State Department colleagues, "We are happy to consult with our European friends, but we are not subject to European veto over our negotiating position."

In the end, the Europeans and the European Bureau at State were able to stave off any formal revision of the IDD, largely because they had the calendar on their side. The Rome communiqué had set a deadline for negotiations to begin before the end of the year. Aside from being crucial for satisfying the West Europeans, a deadline was the only thing that would force the U.S. government, and eventually the President, to overcome the inertia of a divided bureaucracy. Without a deadline, there was a real question whether the U.S. would ever have a position to negotiate.

The Negotiator

There was also, through much of 1981, the question of who would do the negotiating. Here arose another of those ironies with which the history of the Reagan Administration's conduct of arms control is rife. Paul Nitze, one of the best-known students of national-security affairs and one of the most experienced practitioners of national-security policymaking, was chosen for the job over the objections of Alexander Haig and the European Bureau of the State Department on the one hand and despite the misgivings of Richard Perle on the other. Thus he was the choice of neither the moderate nor the hawkish wing of the Administration. His appointment came about for reasons having more to do with bureaucratic politics than with ideology or the substance of policy.

In an Administration that would be dominated largely by young, relatively obscure officials like Richard Burt and Richard Perle, Nitze was a notable exception. He had just turned seventy-four. That made him roughly twice the age of Burt or Perle. In the 1940s, when Burt and Perle were infants, Nitze already had a successful career on Wall Street behind him and had embarked on a long series of jobs in government. He had held high posts in the State and Defense departments in every administration from Franklin Roosevelt's to Richard Nixon's. His last job in public service had been as a member of the SALT I negotiating team. He had resigned rather than stay on to help negotiate SALT II because he feared that Nixon, whose power was being eroded by the Watergate scandal, would sacrifice sound arms control to domestic political exigencies.

Nitze was not dovish enough for the Carter Administration and was passed over for a major job. He ended up having considerable impact on the debate over nuclear arms control in the late seventies from outside the government, as the principal theoretician and technical expert of the Committee on the Present Danger. In 1977, he testified against the confirmation of Paul Warnke as director of the Arms Control and Disarmament Agency. Nitze argued that Warnke, with whom he had served in the Pentagon during the Johnson Administration, was dangerously blind to the Soviet military challenge. In the event, the Senate approved Warnke, but by a narrow margin. Two years later, Nitze was the single most effective critic of the SALT II treaty.

He radiated experience, self-confidence, authority, and intellect, as well as remarkable health and energy for a man his age. His physical appearance alone—silver hair, chiseled features, firm gaze—went far to create the impression of a paragon of Yankee virtues of a rather old-fashioned and patrician sort. Yet, had it not been for his leadership of the crusade against SALT II, Nitze would almost certainly never have come into the Reagan

Administration at all. As it was, he entered with the reputation among liberals as an archvillain precisely because of his role in the downfall of SALT II. His appointment was widely interpreted as the ultimate example of letting the fox into the chicken coop—proof that the Reagan Administration was determined to kill arms control. But within two years, he had recast himself in the eyes of many of these same liberals and moderates as a hero, albeit a tragic one. It was apparent that he was far more interested in getting an agreement with the Soviets than was the Administration—and that he was willing to risk a great deal to do so.

Nitze got his job because of Richard Allen, hardly an advocate of arms control himself. Allen had been instrumental in picking Eugene Rostow over Edward Rowny to head the Arms Control and Disarmament Agency as a counterweight to Haig. Rowny got the job of chief negotiator of strategic arms control as a consolation prize. Rostow almost immediately began thinking about Nitze as the man to take charge of the European nuclear negotiations. Like Rostow, Nitze was a Democrat with a record of bipartisan government service and with good hawkish credentials. Rostow also saw Nitze, like himself, as a seasoned senior statesman, who should be a steadying influence on the youngsters around them. Nitze was an experienced negotiator. What was more, Nitze was a distinguished public figure, a proud and powerful personality and a veteran infighter. All these qualities would help him to help Rostow in his rivalry with Haig.

On just those grounds, Haig was against giving Nitze the job, but he required a less personal reason for opposing him. Eagleburger and his principal aide, David Gompert, suggested one: Nitze had not made a secret of his feeling that the December '79 decision had been defective in both its political and its military aspects. When Rostow first approached him about the chief negotiator's job, Nitze expressed reluctance largely because he had disapproved of the dual-track decision. At the same time, however, he said he thought it would be "disastrous to go back on that decision since it would appall the Europeans and confirm the impression that the U.S. can't be counted on for anything."

Thus, in a way Nitze represented both sides of the debate that had gone on that spring. His lack of enthusiasm for the NATO decision paralleled the Pentagon view, while his conviction that the U.S. must nonetheless stick by the decision was thoroughly consistent with the view of Haig himself and the State Department. Nevertheless, Eagleburger warned, Nitze's "notorious hawkishness might scare off the allies." The department had its own candidate for the job: Maynard Glitman, a professional diplomat with experience in NATO affairs. But try as it might, State could find no evidence that Nitze had ever come out flatly against the 1979 decision in public, and Glitman stood no chance of getting the job in any event: the White House was interested, as Allen put it, in "a well-known heavy-hitter, not a utility infielder." Allen was sold on Rostow's choice of Nitze; Glitman could serve as Nitze's deputy.*

Haig continued to argue that Nitze's appointment would be bad in view of European "sensitivities." Rostow made clear that he was prepared for a showdown. "I insist on prevailing," he told Haig and the White House; Nitze's appointment would be "the best possible signal to the Europeans and the Russians alike that we take these negotiations seriously." Haig considered taking the issue to the President, but Burt and others talked him out of it; Haig would weaken his position at the White House if he appealed for presidential intervention too often. In the end, Haig himself telephoned Nitze to offer him the job.

While accepting, Nitze insisted that he indeed be allowed to negotiate "seriously," and that there be an understanding in the government that a final agreement would perforce be lopsided in favor of the Soviet Union because of the sheer numbers involved. There was no way, given the advantage that the Soviets already possessed and given the shakiness of the alliance, to restore complete equality in the European nuclear balance. The best that could be achieved, and therefore the best that should be sought, was to reduce the imbalance that already existed and to meet the West European demands for an arms-control effort parallel to rearmament. That would be Nitze's goal if he took the job. The first condition put him in opposition to those in the Administration who regarded European arms control as essentially an exercise in keeping the deployments on track, and the second condition put him at odds with the alliance's professed commitment to equality.

Richard Perle observed this episode with a sense of deep personal ambivalence and rising apprehension. Paul Nitze had played a key role in his life. Perle had come to Washington in the late sixties to work for Nitze in keeping the anti-ballistic-missile system (ABM) alive despite public and congressional opposition. It was while assisting Nitze that Perle had met Senator Henry Jackson. But Nitze had, for some time, been the object of Perle's reservations and growing mistrust. The man, he said, was an "inveterate problem-solver." Perle used the term pejoratively, to mean someone who would seek solution of a problem for solution's sake, even if the problem was insoluble and should be accepted as such. Having helped secure congressional passage for the ABM program in 1969, Nitze had gone on, as a member of the SALT I delegation, to negotiate, almost singlehandedly, large parts of the 1972 treaty limiting ABMs. For all his doggedness in criticizing the

---

*For Nitze's publicly expressed view that it would be difficult to reach a meaningful and acceptable compromise in the European arms-control negotiations before the deployment deadline in 1983, see his article "Strategy in the 1980s," *Foreign Affairs,* Fall 1980, p. 98.

final SALT II treaty, Nitze was at heart, in Perle's view, an arms controller.

Nitze seemed destined to be respected by hawks and doves alike, but always with strong reservations. The hawks would never entirely forgive him for his role in bringing about SALT I; the doves would never entirely forgive him for his role in bringing down SALT II.

Nitze knew that, before he was through, he would have to struggle as hard with his colleagues in the government as with his Soviet opposite number. And he suspected that the principal struggle would be with his former protégé, Perle. But first he had to have an opening proposal. That in itself promised to entail a long and acrimonious struggle.

3 Shades of Zero

It was Helmut Schmidt's Social Democratic party that originally came up with the concept of the *Null-Lösung,* the "zero solution." The idea was that the removal of all the offending weapons on the Soviet side would make the American deployment unnecessary. The concept was originally floated as a means of dampening internal strife within the party and gaining West German public support. It caught on quickly elsewhere on the continent, but not in Washington. To many in the U.S., the very phrase "zero option" was suspect. Like "ban the bomb," "zone of peace," or "a nuclear-free Europe," it was one of those distinctly and distastefully European euphemisms for avoiding unpleasant political realities.

In early and mid-1981, while the new Administration was wrestling with various options in Washington, hundreds of thousands of West Europeans were taking to the streets in a movement protesting the spread of nuclear weapons. A new and disagreeable stereotype appeared on American television screens: disorderly legions of students, joining hands with clergymen, burghers and housewives, marching along the boulevards of Brussels, Nottingham, and Düsseldorf. Most of their chanted slogans and banners were impartial in denouncing nuclear weapons of both superpowers, but the overall tone and the accompanying message to their elected representatives in various parliaments were distinctly more anti-American than anti-Soviet. The crude caricatures of Reagan as a cowboy with rockets in his holsters made Brezhnev and his bushy eyebrows look grandfatherly by comparison. The Soviet rockets at issue were at least deployed on Soviet territory and thus easier to regard as defensive, while the American weapons would be far from home on West European soil. Besides, the Soviet missiles were familiar fixtures on the political landscape, part of the status quo; the American ones were something new, menacing, in prospect—and therefore might be stopped. The demonstrators were for peace and an "end of the madness" of the arms race. They were against a "new round" to that race, which meant the Pershing IIs and the Tomahawks.

Officials of the Reagan Administration described what was happening in Europe as appeasement, pacifism, or neutralism, and the zero option seemed to be part of its vocabulary. In a speech before the Conservative Political Action Conference on March 22, Richard Allen observed that only "pacifist" elements in Europe "believe that we can bargain the reduction of a deployed Soviet weapons system for a promise not to deploy our own offsetting system. Common sense tells us this is illusory." Allen succinctly expressed the Administration's contempt for the zero option, but his statement also contained an unintentional preview of the proposal that Reagan would make to the Soviet Union nine months later, in November 1981.

Those nine months saw the Administration come a long way. The State Department and Pentagon both ended up endorsing the zero option, although their preferences were for significantly different versions. Alexander Haig wanted to accommodate the Europeans by adopting the spirit of the zero option, but modifying it in a way that would make deployment politically more palatable within the alliance. In that sense, Haig wanted to maintain the dual-track approach on which NATO had embarked in 1979.

Richard Perle, by contrast, had never had any use for the NATO decision, and he felt no compulsion to see it vindicated or implemented. He had no particular quarrel with the analysis on which Allen had based his rejection of the zero option back in March: the zero solution was indeed, as Allen had said, "illusory." But then, in Perle's view, so was arms control, at least as it had traditionally been practiced. Yet it was an illusion that many Europeans, and many Americans, too, insisted on keeping alive. Many Europeans were calling for the zero solution. So why not give it to them? Then, when it failed, they would be party to the failure, just as they had been party to what Perle saw as the folly of the December 1979 decision.

The State Department: Up from Zero

Alexander Haig was acutely conscious of his vulnerability to the charge that he was too solicitous of the Europeans. He heard that Weinberger had told James Baker, one of the President's closest aides: "Al seems to think that every time Schmidt's got a problem, it's automatically our problem." Weinberger also complained to Reagan about "Al's automatically siding with the West Europeans all the time." As he began to think about the way to approach the European nuclear arms negotiations, Haig wanted, if possible, to avoid playing into the hands of his critics. He was, therefore, not in the least predisposed to embrace the zero option—a European idea—when he set off for West Germany in September 1981.

In Bonn, he was asked what the Soviet Union would have to do to make the zero option possible. "I think," replied Haig, "clearly it is rather ludicrous to debate an issue in which we are faced with some thousand warheads already deployed in SS-20 missile systems versus some contemplated and less numerous corresponding systems on the part of the West." Amidst all this forbidding syntax, the word "ludicrous" leaped out in the German press. Haig was widely reported as having dismissed the zero option itself as "ludicrous." His hosts, Chancellor Schmidt and Foreign Minister Hans-Dietrich Genscher, were acutely unhappy with the misquote and were eager for their guest to correct the record. At a farewell press conference, Haig said that while it would be "premature" to make a definitive statement, "I think I can affirm that we have not rejected this zero option proposal, and under ideal conditions, such a proposal might be very worthy of exploration and consideration."

Haig intended the comment as a gesture of support for Schmidt and Genscher rather than a blessing on the zero option. Still, some of his aides back in Washington felt it made their work easier as they set about developing a proposal that would accomplish the twin goals of getting negotiations started with the Soviets and bolstering support for U.S. policies in Europe. By paying lip service to the ideal solution of zero, the U.S. could hold the high ground in the propaganda war with the Soviets even as it set about negotiating toward a realistic goal—perhaps something in the neighborhood of 600 American warheads against the same number of Soviet ones.

If the Soviets could be squeezed down to, say, 200 triple-MIRVed SS-20s and held there, they would have 600 warheads. That would mean deploying approximately 600 new American warheads. In these calculations, the figure 572 single-warhead Pershing IIs and Tomahawks that had been established by NATO in December 1979 made sense. The original dual-track decision, after all, had rested on the assumption that some new Western deployments were going to be necessary in any event, no matter what the outcome of the negotiations. A true zero solution, if it was attainable, would actually be inconsistent with the December 1979 decision, for the new NATO missiles were not intended to match the SS-20s on a warhead-for-warhead basis. Rather, they were meant to enhance the credibility of NATO's deterrence of a Soviet conventional attack.

Before Haig's visit to West Germany, his aides had not cared so much whether U.S. declarations actually mentioned zero, so long as U.S. policy implicitly left open that possibility as a sop to the West Europeans. The phrase that had gained currency within the State Department by late summer of 1981 was "reductions to the lowest possible equal level." However, once Haig had, in Berlin, publicly endorsed the lowest of all possible equal ceilings—zero—"under ideal circumstances," and thereby cheered his German hosts by saying the magic word, Haig's deputies realized that now zero had to figure explicitly in the American proposal.

Burt, Eagleburger, and Gompert amended their phraseology accordingly. They added references to zero in their deliberations and memos. The new stock language became "lowest possible equal ceilings, including, ideally, zero," or "with the ultimate goal of zero."

The Pentagon: Down to Zero

Weinberger was convinced that, however much the U.S. might regret the impulses toward drastic disarmament then throbbing in Europe, it had to take them seriously. What was needed was a negotiating position that would redirect those impulses from defeatist panic into support for American policy and deployments. Unlike Haig, Weinberger was not especially sympathetic to the West Europeans. In private, he spoke of being fed up with European "hangups" and "moaning and groaning." He sometimes described the task facing the U.S. as a combination of therapy and trickery: "We've got to make them think that what we're doing is good for them. Not just that, but we've got to make them think that they're going to *like* it, and that it's what they've been asking us to do."

How to do that was a matter that Weinberger delegated to Richard Perle, who began to formulate a version of the zero option that differed importantly from the one then taking shape at the State Department. Perle decided to treat the option not just as an ideal but as the true, sole, and immutable goal of the negotiations, and to settle for nothing else. If anyone told Perle that the zero option was a gimmick designed to deal with a short-term political problem within the alliance, he would reply that the same was true of what the allied ministers had done in 1979. Only they had had less excuse. They had been starting from scratch. They had had real choices. He was simply trying to make the best of a bad inheritance, to limit the damage caused by his predecessors—and his colleagues at the State Department had compounded that damage by arranging for Reagan to endorse the dual-track decision during Margaret Thatcher's visit in February.

Perle was co-chairman, along with Richard Burt, of the Interagency Group charged with preparing for the talks. At a meeting in late August, Burt made a presentation, the nub of which was that the State Department was closing ranks behind a U.S. proposal for lowest possible equal ceilings on warheads. Perle did not like what he was hearing. He could see that the State Department position was intended to point the negotiations in the direction of an agreement whereby the West would end up with approximately 600 new warheads to compensate for the Soviets' being allowed to keep at least that many SS-20 warheads. Perle went home that night and sat up late in his study drafting a memo to Weinberger laying out his misgivings.

At Perle's direction, the Pentagon's analysts had been running studies for some time about the probable impact of various permutations and combinations of Pershing IIs, Tomahawks, SS-20s, and other missiles on the military balance in Europe. Those studies concluded that there were 250 to 300 vital military installations in Western Europe—air bases, nuclear storage sites, and ports. Thus, even if the Soviets had only 100 SS-20s, each triple-

MIRVed, that would give them 300 warheads, or enough to cover all the important NATO targets. A deal that let the U.S. go ahead with its Pershing IIs and Tomahawks in exchange for leaving the Soviets not 100 but 200 SS-20s, with 600 warheads, hardly seemed to Perle like a bargain. That would be twice as many warheads as the U.S.S.R. needed to threaten a comprehensive strike against the alliance. "Only as you approach zero," Perle concluded, "do you reduce the Soviet threat to those targets."

In his memo to Weinberger, Perle argued that the State Department's position was based on sloppy analysis. It failed to consider the military consequences of the diplomatic initiative then taking shape. "Considerably more work needs to be done," he warned. The interagency process to date had turned up "too many questions and too few answers." This was to become a standard Perle ploy: accuse the rest of the Administration of shortsighted impatience; warn against being "stampeded" into hasty decisions; call for more work, which would naturally take more time; encourage delay in the name of thoroughness.

Perle challenged the State Department's conviction that the Soviets would not give up all their SS-20s, or at least significant numbers of them. "The easy assumption that the Soviets would resist reductions is imprudent in the extreme," he wrote. "They might actually propose such cuts." Since the Soviets had far more SS-20 warheads than there were major targets in NATO, a large number of those warheads were "surplus to their military needs and can therefore be expended to achieve political needs." (On this point, Perle was prescient. The Soviets did probably deploy more SS-20s than their original program called for; and they did eventually offer to trade down on the surplus—although not, of course, to zero.) So, he concluded, instead of seeking an agreement that did little or nothing to improve NATO defenses—and instead of leaving the Soviets an opportunity to surprise everyone by proposing a cutback in SS-20s on their own—why not come forward with a bold, simple American initiative that would solve both the military and political problems at hand?

Perle saw another, strictly political advantage in what he was proposing. A no-nonsense, all-or-nothing American embrace of the zero option would steal a march on the Soviets in the propaganda campaign. Much more than the State Department's half-hearted acknowledgment of zero as the ideal outcome, an American commitment to achieving zero as the only acceptable outcome would "put the Soviets on the defensive" and keep them there. To judge from public-opinion polls, parliamentary debates, and demonstrations in the streets, the Soviets had been achieving alarming success with claims that their proposal for a moratorium proved their commitment to disarmament, while the U.S. was hellbent on loading the continent up with new missiles and starting a new arms race. Now the U.S. would be able to shift the onus back onto the Soviets: if they were serious about halting the arms race and easing the anxieties of their neighbors, why shouldn't they do away with precisely those weapons that had forced NATO to move toward modernization?

The next day, Perle sent his memo, under the heading "A Defense Proposal," to Weinberger by way of his immediate superior, Fred Iklé, who welcomed the idea. Iklé had commented on a number of occasions when the subject of the Europeans' advocacy of the zero option came up, "We already chose a 'zero option' as our own deployment mode in Europe back when we took out our Jupiters and Thors in the early sixties. Anything above zero is forced upon us by the other side."

Iklé was also one of those in the new Administration who advocated arms-control agreements that were simple—easy to explain, easy for audiences at home and abroad to understand. One complaint about SALT II, from some liberals as well as conservatives, had been that it was too complicated. Iklé felt that the goal of effective presentation was best served by the zero option in its simplest, starkest, most straightforward form. He also believed that Perle's approach would be "more responsive to, and in harmony with, what our allies wanted," since they were looking for an excuse to get out of accepting the new American missiles, and here was a proposal that held out that possibility.

Zero Plus Versus Zero Only

But the allies were not likely to take comfort from a proposal like that forever, or even for long. As soon as a zero proposal was made, everyone would see that achievement of the zero solution was an impossibility. If observers in the West were slow to come to that realization, the Soviets could be counted on to make the proposal's unacceptability to them quite plain. Then everyone would start asking what other solution the U.S. might settle for. It was partly in anticipation of a Soviet rejection that the State Department argued against letting the Administration get "locked in" to the zero solution. State called its position "zero plus," as opposed to the Pentagon's advocacy of "zero only."

By early October, this argument, refined and intensified, had acquired a ritualistic quality and had come to dominate the discussions of the Interagency Group. The debate was carried on primarily between Burt and Perle. The disagreement boiled down to whether the U.S., in its opening move, should assert not only its preference for zero but also its willingness to consider a negotiated compromise higher than zero. Burt felt it should; Perle felt it should not.

Burt was now the key figure in the State Department's handling of arms control. He had more expertise and interest in it than Eagleburger. On the question of how to make the best of the December 1979 dual-track decision he was not just skeptical about the chances of reaching an agreement before deployment; he was absolutely certain that there was no chance at all. The military imbalance in favor of the U.S.S.R. made a diplomatic solution in the interests of the West impossible. The task facing the Administration was what he called "alliance management." That phrase connoted a combination of therapy and trickery not unlike what Weinberger and Perle were after. The object of making a proposal and undertaking negotiations was damage limitation, public relations, and getting the new NATO missiles deployed with a minimum of anguish and recrimination inside the alliance. Burt's disagreement with Perle over the zero option was a matter of how to attain that goal.

Burt kept reminding his colleagues that "the purpose of this whole exercise is maximum political advantage." The zero option would serve that end only if it was flexible and perceived to be so. By telling the Soviets and the world that the U.S. would like to eliminate, or "zero-out," missiles in Europe but would listen to proposals for other ways of achieving a balance of nuclear power, said Burt, "we can have our cake and eat it, too; we'll get credit for a breathtaking initiative while avoiding the connotation of refusal to entertain other possibilities for significant reductions."

Perle turned that argument on its head. He contended that the State Department was recommending a recipe that would spoil the cake altogether. If followed, the recommendation would deprive the U.S. of both the political and the military benefits everyone agreed were desirable. By making it obvious to the Soviets that the U.S. was not serious about zero and would settle for something higher, the Administration would be guaranteeing that the Soviets would ignore zero, insofar as it figured in the American proposal at all, and set their sights very high indeed—high enough to preserve all their current deployments and future plans.

Perle cited the Pentagon studies that he had designed to prove his contention that any significant number of SS-20s at all, even if they were matched by Pershing IIs and Tomahawks, left Western Europe in jeopardy and undercut the credibility of NATO deterrence. His reasoning was that the SS-20s were far more potent and menacing weapons than the still undeployed American weapons. For the U.S. to assume in advance that zero was unacceptable would be to bow to the Soviets as arbiters of what was acceptable. By pressing this point every chance he could, and by pressing it with his own special blend of righteous wrath and sweet reason, Perle managed to make it seem like an act of political and intellectual cowardice for anyone to mention negotiability as a criterion.

Carried to an extreme, Perle's position would preclude genuine and productive negotiation. The key officials of the State Department's European Bureau and, to a lesser but growing extent, of its Politico-Military Bureau believed that was just what Perle intended.

Paul Nitze, meanwhile, was keeping his mind open and his powder dry. He agreed that "zero only" had the advantage of simplicity, of giving the Europeans what they professed to want, and of shifting the propaganda onus back onto the Soviets. Nitze shared another concern of Perle's: that zero plus had the political liability of looking to the West Europeans like a trick to proceed with deployment of the 572 American missiles in NATO. He also found the State Department's formulation fuzzy. Nor did Nitze have any patience with Burt's talk about "alliance management" as the sole purpose of the negotiations. Nitze had not taken the job simply "to be part of a charade." He did not intend to prejudge the possibility of reaching an agreement. He wanted an opening position that was clear and simple.

At the same time, Nitze had long been a believer in leaving a delegation considerable flexibility for exploring areas of compromise. One of his many criticisms of Henry Kissinger, from his experience as a member of the SALT delegation a decade earlier, was that Kissinger insisted on trying to run negotiations taking place in Vienna and Helsinki by remote control from Washington. This, Nitze believed, had led to mistakes and missed opportunities. Rostow had persuaded Nitze to accept the job as negotiator for the European arms-control talks with repeated promises that he would have a strong hand in writing his own initial instructions and in amending them as the negotiations progressed.

So Nitze remained above the fray, taking the attitude that whatever decision the interagency process in its wisdom produced he would dutifully accept and try to make work. He appeared content to go along with Perle on the opening position and hold his own fire for fights later on over how that opening position might have to evolve during the course of the negotiations.

A Question of Range

No sooner did State and Defense square off against each other over the most presentable version of the zero option than they plunged into a thicket of subsidiary disputes. One concerned the "scope" of the proposal. What weapons were to be covered by the proposed agreement? The Soviets, not surprisingly, included in their calculation of the nuclear balance in Europe every NATO weapon that they considered capable of reaching the U.S.S.R. This meant counting existing weapons, like carrier-based aircraft and British and French forces, as well as new weapons like the Pershing II and the Tomahawk. The Reagan Administration was solidly committed to the proposition that the only weapons on the NATO side that were eligible for limitation were the new American missiles. But the Administration was divided over what to count on the Soviet side. The division was predictable: State wanted a proposal of narrower scope that would concentrate on SS-20s, while Perle wanted to broaden the scope to include other Soviet missiles.

Burt made his case on the grounds that a less comprehensive proposal would be more "plausible" to the Europeans. Plausibility had replaced the more traditional, but now discredited, criterion of negotiability. A plausible proposal was one that would appear negotable to those who were naïve enough to think that an agreement was possible (or, for that matter, desirable).

Perle argued his maximalist position on grounds of logic and history. Logic told him that mobile, land-based Soviet missiles with ranges shorter than that of the SS-20 were potentially as dangerous as SS-20s themselves and should, accordingly, be limited by an agreement. He did not accept the distinction between long- and shorter-range Soviet missiles if their launchers could be moved. He felt their very mobility should be figured into any calculations of range. A missile whose launcher could be rushed forward in a crisis had an effective range much greater than the distance it could actually fly. History told him that past arms-control agreements had been flawed by the American penchant for arbitrarily exempting Soviet weapons that should have been limited. The classic examples were the Backfire bomber and the SS-20 itself, which Perle felt had come to haunt the U.S. because of the failure of SALT to achieve real arms control.

The SS-20 had a number of short-legged cousins. Of these, the most important were the SS-12 and SS-22. There was also yet another missile just coming into service, the SS-23. The SS-22 was a modern version of the SS-12, much as the SS-20 was a modernization of the SS-4 and -5. The SS-20 and SS-22 were both technologically advanced, relatively accurate, mobile missiles, but the SS-20 had multiple warheads and a nearly intercontinental range of as much as 5,000 kilometers, while the SS-22 was a single-warhead weapon with a range of less than 1,000 kilometers.*

Perle's original memo to Weinberger setting forth the hard-and-fast zero option had urged that the U.S. present at the outset of the negotiations a plan whereby both sides would reduce to zero the number of missiles with ranges greater than 800 kilometers. This would preclude deployment of the

---

*Here, as so often, the NATO system for designating Soviet missiles makes a complicated subject all the more difficult to follow. The SS-4, -5, -20 series has a considerably greater range than the SS-12, -22, while the SS-22 has a greater range than the SS-23. SS stands simply for surface-to-surface. The numbers 4, 5, 12, 20, 22, and 23 indicate the order in which Western intelligence saw various weapons emerge; they do not represent a comparative assessment of how large or formidable the weapon is, and they have nothing to do with range. To give the whole problem yet another twist, the Soviets often dispute Western designations and data. For example, NATO differentiated between the SS-12 and -22, attributing to the latter a somewhat longer range, greater accuracy, and a smaller warhead. NATO claimed that there were about a hundred deployed launchers for the SS-12, -22 series. The Soviets admitted to only about half that number and denied that there were two separate types of missile at all. What the U.S. called the SS-12 the Soviets said did not exist as such. They considered it a variation, or test model, of the SS-12. The SS-23 was the latest addition and was often labeled by NATO the SS-X-23, "X" standing for experimental.

Pershing IIs and the Tomahawks on the American side while forcing the Soviets to eliminate all their SS-20s, plus the older, single-warhead SS-4s and SS-5s that the SS-20s were meant to replace, plus the shorter-range SS-12s and SS-22s (Perle was using the Pentagon's maximum estimate of their ranges). In congressional testimony later in the year, Perle warned that "a failure to limit" shorter-range Soviet missiles "would leave an agreement eliminating the Soviet SS-4, SS-5 and SS-20 missiles hopelessly vulnerable to circumvention; for the fact is that the Soviets can cover some 85% of the NATO targets assigned to the SS-20 with the shorter-range SS-22 if they are deployed in sufficient numbers and moved forward on Warsaw Pact territory." The Pentagon believed that, once the SS-23 was in service, it could strike "as much as 50 percent of European NATO."

Almost everyone saw the technical logic in Perle's position, and opposed him nonetheless on grounds of intra-alliance politics. The documents amplifying the December 1979 two-track decision referred to long-range Soviet missiles—i.e., the SS-4, -5, -20 series—as the principal disruptive factor in the European strategic balance, and therefore the principal items on the agenda for the proposed negotiations. The NATO ministers had made it clear they would not back any proposal that seemed to go significantly beyond the guidelines set in December 1979.

At meetings of the NATO Special Consultative Group in Brussels in the late summer and fall, Lawrence Eagleburger notified his foreign-ministry counterparts that the Administration was concerned about the shorter-range systems and hoped to find a way of dealing with them in the talks. The allies were not willing to go as far as Perle in subjecting shorter- and longer-range missiles to equal treatment. Rather, they wanted to treat shorter-range systems as separate from, and less important than, the longer-range ones. The SS-20s would be counted and limited under the "central aggregate" established by the agreement, and there might be accompanying, less-stringent rules, called collateral restraints, that would prevent the Soviets from deploying additional SS-12s and -22s which might be able to cover some of the same targets as the SS-20s. The State Department, the Arms Control and Disarmament Agency, Paul Nitze, and the Joint Chiefs of Staff all lined up with the Europeans, against Perle.

The Chiefs had their own very characteristic reason for opposing the inclusion of shorter-range Soviet weapons within the zero option proper: they were afraid that, if the U.S. insisted on treating SS-12s and -22s along with the SS-4s, -5s, and -20s, the Soviets might have a stronger case for including shorter-range Western missiles, notably the Pershing Is already deployed in West Germany, in whatever limits or bans were finally negotiated to cover the Pershing IIs and Tomahawks. Here was an instance of what had long been, and would now again become, a recurring tension within the U.S.

government and within the Pentagon itself. On the one hand, there was a desire, personified by Perle, to include as many Soviet weapons as possible in whatever restrictions were to be proposed. On the other hand, there was anxiety about what one member of the Joint Staff called "the boomerang effect: if we throw at the Soviets a proposal aimed at limiting a maximum of their stuff, they get all the greedier in trying to limit ours—and by the logic of our own position, it's that much harder for us to resist them." The Chiefs had a tendency to worry about what would happen if the U.S. proposal was ever accepted. That was not a big concern of Perle's. He saw his proposal not as a means to an end but as an end in itself.

A Whiff of Blackmail

The Chiefs were also worried that the more comprehensive a proposal the U.S. put forward in the talks, the harder it would be to fend off the inevitable Soviet counterproposal covering American aircraft. The Soviets had always maintained that limits on aircraft must be included in whatever agreement was finally reached. What they had in mind was limits on American bombers that were not covered by SALT but that could drop nuclear bombs on the Soviet Union from "forward bases" in Western Europe. These were primarily F-111s in England and FB-111s back in the U.S. that could be moved to Europe on short notice, as well as F-4 Phantom fighter-bombers and A-6 and A-7 attack bombers on aircraft carriers in the Mediterranean and North Atlantic. Keeping aircraft off the agenda of arms-control negotiations was an obsession with the Chiefs. They would examine almost any option advanced within the bureaucracy, not to mention any proposal likely to be advanced by the Soviets at the negotiations, with a keen and suspicious eye for some hidden, delayed-action feature that might require them later to accept limits on aircraft.

Their resistance to any such limits was not as parochial or as unreasonable as their civilian detractors sometimes made it seem. Aircraft were a tricky subject for arms-control negotiations because of their versatility. Versatility carries with it ambiguity. Whereas almost all ballistic missiles were nuclear-armed, bombers could just as well be armed with conventional weapons as nuclear ones. The same plane could be used in a relatively restricted geographical area, or it could operate over great distances. For example, during the Vietnam War, B-52s based in the Philippines flew a short way to drop conventional bombs on North Vietnam; yet the same aircraft, with modifications, could also serve the Strategic Air Command as intercontinental "delivery vehicles" for attacking the Soviet Union with thermonuclear weapons.

Perle was well aware of the intensity of the Chiefs' concern and considered it legitimate, up to a point. In his August memo to Weinberger, when he first advanced the zero-only option, Perle had warned that extending the negotiations from missiles to bombers would at some point raise the question "Do we want to count F-15s in St. Louis when we get around to counting aircraft?" But he also knew that the Soviets had more "aircraft of comparable characteristics" than the U.S. and therefore would feel more of a pinch if aircraft were added to the negotiations. Widening the talks to include aircraft would be a way to call the Soviets' bluff. Soviet fighter-bombers were generally less capable than American ones, but they were more numerous, and presumably any agreement that limited U.S. fighter-bombers like the F-111 and the Phantom might also very well constrain the Soviet Sukhoi-24, code-named Fencer by NATO, and the MiG-27 Flogger. More important, it would constrain the Soviet Backfire bomber, which had so bedeviled the previous Administration's attempts to negotiate and ratify SALT II.

But, as with shorter-range missiles, the Chiefs worried what would happen if the U.S. proposal ended up being accepted in some form. They knew American aircraft were better fighting machines than Soviet ones, and they did not want to see Phantoms being traded off in simple-minded numbers games against Fencers or even FB-111s against Backfires.

Perle was prepared to indulge his uniformed colleagues at the Pentagon in their reflexive and obsessive opposition to any limits on aircraft, but only for something in exchange. He made no bones about the Chiefs' obligation, as he saw it, to him. He would let the Chiefs have their way on aircraft only if they supported him on the zero-only option. At a series of meetings with military officers, including Rear Admiral Robert Austin, the Chiefs' representative on the Interagency Group, Perle stressed the need for "a coordinated position in this building." He made clear that, while he would like the Defense Department to present a united front against the State Department on every issue, he absolutely insisted on it with regard to the zero-only option. Just to make sure this message got across at the highest level, Perle had Weinberger lay down the law to General David Jones, the chairman of the Chiefs.

Yet the Chiefs hesitated. At an Interagency Group meeting in early November, Richard Burt reviewed the various points that had been agreed by the group, including exclusion of aircraft, and then mentioned the two principal points of contention that remained—zero plus versus zero only and whether shorter-range Soviet missiles should be covered by zero. Admiral Austin spoke up in a way suggesting he and the Chiefs were leaning toward the State Department's zero-plus option.

Perle had thought the Chiefs were with him, and he countered Austin's unpleasant surprise with one of his own. "Well," he said, "maybe we should revisit aircraft."

Burt was incredulous. "What do you mean 'revisit aircraft'?"

Austin knew exactly what Perle meant: he was prepared to reopen an issue that everyone thought had been closed, and argue once again for inclusion of bombers in the U.S.'s opening position at the talks. Austin sensed a whiff of blackmail in the air. Perle, a third-level civilian official, could make this threat credible to Austin by invoking both of their bosses and by implying strongly that he was underscoring a threat that Weinberger had made to General David Jones. As the meeting was breaking up, Perle took Austin aside and told him that any "backsliding" by the Chiefs in their support for the zero-only option was "unacceptable," since it contravened "what has been worked out by the Secretary [of Defense] with the Chairman [General Jones]."

In the days following, Perle and Weinberger met separately with Jones and the other Chiefs to make sure there was no lingering misunderstanding: if the Chiefs failed to support them on the zero-only option, Perle and Weinberger would "reserve judgment" on the issue of aircraft. Just to show how serious they were, they added the issue of aircraft to the agenda for an upcoming National Security Council meeting.

What the tactic lacked in subtlety it made up for in effectiveness. General Jones broke the news to Eagleburger and Burt that the Chiefs would not be joining the State Department in support of zero plus. The Chiefs were the Administration's only high-level holdovers from the Carter period; they had endorsed SALT II; they were acutely conscious of being the odd men out, relative doves in an extremely hawkish Administration. By backing Weinberger and Perle on the zero option, they thought they might be able to build a better working relationship with the civilian side of the department. They were to be disappointed. Perle came away from the episode convinced that the Chiefs were not only living in the past in their devotion to old-fashioned arms control, but that they were, as he put it to a colleague, "push-overs and patsies for whoever leans on them the last, the longest and the hardest." He resolved to do the decisive leaning himself in the months to come.

A Global Problem

The mobility of Soviet missiles raised questions not just of which ones to count but of where to count them and how to make sure that all were accounted for. An SS-20 launcher set up in Siberia or Central Asia and aimed against a target in China could be loaded on the Trans-Siberian Railway, moved west of the Ural Mountains, and pointed at Britain or Italy. Therefore every SS-20 launcher, no matter where it was deployed, represented a potential threat to NATO. Yet the Soviets contended that only those SS-20s actually deployed as part of their defenses against NATO should be discussed in the negotiations and covered by whatever agreement was reached.

At the preliminary round of negotiations in October-November 1980, the U.S. delegation had made a vague proposal for limits that would be "worldwide in scope," thus covering all SS-20s wherever they were deployed, but that would "consider the regional aspects [of deployment] as well." When the Reagan Administration came into office, the Interagency Group chaired by Burt and Perle decided that the only way to tackle the problem of mobility was head-on—with a "global" limit covering all of the Soviet Union, and, as Perle put it, "none of this nonsense about regional sublimits." The idea of such a global limit had much to recommend it in the atmosphere of the new government. For one thing, it was simple, straightforward, bold —all virtues to which the Administration aspired for its arms-control proposals.

As in so many other instances, however, boldness was inversely proportional to negotiability. If anything was more important to the Soviets than fortifying their western flank against NATO, it was defending themselves against China. It was almost surely easier for the Soviets to imagine the U.S.S.R. under attack from the East than from the West. The notion of the West Europeans invading Russia must have strained the credulity of even the most paranoid worst-case planners in Moscow; the danger that China might, in some future xenophobic frenzy, hurl its huge army against the Soviet Union was less farfetched, at least from the Soviet standpoint.

Also, the Soviet Union feared an eventual Asian military alliance joining China, the U.S., and perhaps Japan and South Korea as well. One way to head off that possibility was for the U.S.S.R. to keep its European and Far Eastern options open and independent of each other. The Kremlin wanted to take advantage of diplomatic and arms-control opportunities in the West without letting down its guard in the East. Not only would that approach ensure maximum military flexibility, but it had the political benefit of sowing discord and distrust between the U.S. and the most important countries in Asia. Neither China nor Japan was happy about the possibility that Soviet-American arms-control agreements might have the effect of freeing Soviet weapons from Europe so they could be deployed in the Far East. It was very much in the Soviet interest to keep the Chinese and Japanese unhappy on just that score. If the Kremlin should ever agree to an American insistence on global ceilings, it would be enabling the U.S. to go to its Chinese and Japanese partners and say, "See? We've been looking out for your security as well as that of our European allies in this negotiation of ours with the Soviets." That was a boast the Soviets did not want the U.S. to be able to make.

Restricting Refire

U.S. intelligence had concluded that the Soviets were manufacturing twice as many SS-20 rockets as launchers. That meant there was a powerful presumption that the system was meant to have a "rapid reload/refire capability." On the grounds that the Soviets would not waste such a capability, Perle and others felt prudence required assuming that each launcher in the field could have a refire missile in a camouflaged vehicle nearby or perhaps even stored within the body of the launcher itself. If the zero option was accepted, refires would not be a problem, since all Soviet launchers would have to be destroyed. But if the State Department got its way and some Soviet SS-20s were permitted under the American proposal, Perle wanted that proposal to include a ban on refires. The only way to verify such a ban would be by frequent on-site inspection of Soviet missile factories and storage areas. That meant knowing the location of all those sites and securing Soviet agreement to station inspectors at each one, or at least being able to have a look at short notice. Few believed the Soviets would accept on-site inspection of their most sensitive military production and storage facilities.

Perle seemed to be staking out a position that would serve at least two broader purposes: it would make the overall American proposal more resistant to internal U.S. pressures for compromise; and it would strengthen the case he was simultaneously making on the unresolved question of which version of the zero option to propose. In his original memorandum to Weinberger laying out the zero-only option, Perle wrote that it would have the advantage of "simplifying verification problems, which at levels higher than zero are probably insurmountable," and it would "simplify the problem of refire, which at levels higher than zero will perpetuate." An absolute ban would be easier to monitor and enforce, since to discover so much as a single SS-20 rocket or launcher would be to catch the Soviets in a violation of the treaty. In addition, the Soviets would not be able to carry out any tests on a weapon that was prohibited rather than merely limited; and flight tests of ballistic missiles are virtually impossible to conduct clandestinely, so compliance with the ban would be easy to monitor.

Perle's proposal was not just internally consistent but also internally self-reinforcing. The arguments for zero buttressed those for a ban on refires, and vice versa. Thus, on every issue he had taken a position that was extreme, but that was also simple and compelling as long as one did not dwell on the question of negotiability.

On the big question, whether to go with the zero-plus or zero-only version of the zero option, the interagency process had not been able to generate an agreed Administration position. On other questions, the maneuvering and horsetrading back and forth across the Potomac had yielded uneasy truces that produced the illusion of a united position for the moment but would lead to ambushes, skirmishes, and pitched battles months later, when negotiations with the Soviets were underway.

4 All or Nothing

By late October, the Europeans were more restless than ever about the Reagan Administration's handling of arms control. The Administration had recently embarrassed itself, appalled the allies, and considerably set back the prospects for the deployment of new weapons in Europe with a spate of ill-considered public statements about nuclear war. Now more than ever it was important to get the European missile talks started with an American proposal that had the backing of the allies. At a National Security Council meeting, Caspar Weinberger followed closely a set of talking points that Richard Perle had prepared for him: zero only was bold; it was simple; it was what the allies wanted.

Alexander Haig responded by summarizing the State Department's concern about an excessively rigid negotiating position. He contended further that the zero option would not be in the interests of the West even if it were negotiable: "We wouldn't want it even if we could have it." By this he meant that the cancellation of the NATO deployments, even in exchange for elimination of the SS-20s, would risk decoupling the American nuclear deterrent from the defense of Europe. For just that reason, the NATO foreign ministers had envisioned, in their December 1979 decision, some Western deployments no matter what the outcome of negotiations.

The President's counselor, Edwin Meese, was more impressed by Weinberger's presentation. Meese asked the Secretary of Defense for a paper elaborating the rationale for zero only before the next meeting of the NSC.

At Weinberger's request, Perle drafted one. Both he and his boss were then traveling abroad, so the memo went from Stockholm to the White House by cable. Before sending it, Weinberger was not able to resist adding a few grace notes. He suggested that he, Meese, and Reagan get together to discuss the issue in person on his return from Europe. Then he inserted the suggestion that, if the Administration took advantage of the opportunity before it in the dramatic way the Pentagon was urging, the President would very likely be a candidate for the Nobel Peace Prize.

Meese had expected that any paper he got from Weinberger would be part of a campaign on behalf of zero only, but the notion of a three-way get-

together, excluding Haig, went a bit far; it looked like an attempt to circumvent not just the State Department but the National Security Council as a
whole. So Meese decided to rein in Weinberger and Perle. He sent a copy
of the memo to the State Department via the White House's most trusted
man there, Deputy Secretary William Clark. As Meese expected, Clark
showed the memo to Haig, and, also as Meese expected, Haig threw a fit.

The President, in His Fashion, Decides

On their return to Washington, Weinberger and Perle resumed their fight
for a hard-and-fast zero proposal. They had hoped that by the next National
Security Council meeting Weinberger would have persuaded Reagan and
Meese to accept the Pentagon position, and that the President's decision
would be a fait accompli. But Haig and Burt had moved to prevent that from
happening. The NSC meeting, they suggested, should be strictly "informational"; it should not attempt to produce a decision. Haig and Weinberger
would review for the President those matters that the Interagency Group
had already resolved, then seek to focus attention, "in a constructive way,"
on the few issues that were still under contention. Haig was trying his best
to act as the model senior cabinet member, guarding the orderly processes
of the National Security Council against the byzantine maneuvers of a
Pentagon cabal.

A little more than a week later, the pieces of the Administration's policy
and its proposal finally fell into place in an imperfect compromise. The
Pentagon got its way on the zero-only option: the U.S. would propose the
elimination of the long-range Soviet missiles capable of being targeted
against Western Europe (the SS-4s, -5s, and -20s) in exchange for NATO's
cancellation of its decision to deploy the Pershing IIs and Tomahawks. The
State Department got its way on shorter-range systems: the SS-12s and -22s
would be excluded from the main part of the proposal and dealt with as a
side issue, by some sort of separate numerical ceilings, perhaps a freeze at
existing levels.

The decision was made after a National Security Council meeting in the
evening of November 12. Haig made the case, one last time, for the zero-plus
option: The U.S. should go into the negotiations proposing equal ceilings at
the lowest possible level, preferably zero. Weinberger argued, yet again, that
if the U.S. preferred zero it should propose zero, period. Eugene Rostow had
favored the zero-plus option throughout the interagency wrangling, since it
gave his man, Nitze, more negotiating flexibility; but during the meeting he
struck the pose of the elder statesman.

"You know," he said soothingly to Haig and Weinberger at one point,
"we're not really all that far apart." But neither secretary was interested in
Rostow's mediation.

To no one's surprise, Admiral Thomas Hayward, sitting in for General David Jones, sided with Weinberger, though without much enthusiasm, and thus kept the Chiefs' half of the understanding whereby they would support the zero-only option if Weinberger would help them keep aircraft out of the negotiations. The Pentagon had come through with the united position Perle wanted. But it was not so much the sponsorship that impressed Reagan as the neatness and simplicity of zero only. The trouble with the zero-plus option, said the President at one point, was that it was a bit too much like playing a poker hand by laying all one's cards on the table. Zero plus would risk inviting the Soviets to dismiss the stated U.S. preference for absolute zero and negotiate for a numerical ceiling that allowed them to keep what they had.

As for the State Department's concern about negotiability, Reagan seemed to feel that the Administration could overcome Soviet resistance by the sheer force of its determination and eloquence. He dipped into his repertory of favorite Hollywood anecdotes to make the point. The actor Paul Muni was once in a play in the role of an idealistic union organizer up against a stubborn employer. At the end of the second act, the script called for Muni to make an impassioned appeal for concessions to the union, but to no avail. His adversary was to respond, "I will give them *nothing!*" But Muni's peroration was so powerful that the other actor forgot himself, and his lines, and blurted out, "I will give them *everything!*" The curtain fell to thunderous applause, although the company had to improvise a new opening for the third act.

The State Department, Reagan was implying, was proposing the same stale old script that the U.S. had followed in the past. Perhaps if the U.S. departed from that script and came forward with a blockbuster proposal, the Soviets might forget their usual lines and surprise everybody, including themselves, by accepting.

Reagan did not actually pronounce judgment on the question that had divided his two principal cabinet secretaries for so long, but the more he said, the clearer it became that he had made up his mind. "What I was thinking," he said, as though offering his own compromise on the spur of the moment, "was why couldn't we do it this way?" He then offered a rather fuzzy, rambling paraphrase of the case Weinberger had already made for zero only.

A number of people in the room, including some who had lined up with Haig, realized that the outcome was almost inevitable. The zero-plus option had been a diplomat's dream. It was subtle, flexible, and creatively ambiguous. But Reagan was not a diplomat, he was a politician, and the zero-only option was a politician's dream. It was easy to understand, easy to make attractive to the allies and the U.S. public. Reagan could far more readily imagine giving a Paul Muni–like speech that would bring the house down about the zero-only option than the zero-plus alternative.

Knowing he was beaten, Haig made a passionate plea for proposing the zero-only option in a way that avoided any implication of an ultimatum. Otherwise, he argued, the Soviets would adopt a propaganda stance of injured reasonableness, and the Europeans would sympathize with them. Reagan assured Haig that the U.S. would negotiate "in good faith" and would do everything it could to be perceived as negotiating "in good faith." He used the phrase a number of times. Haig picked up on it as a kind of consolation prize after his own defeat; he would repeat it many times, with the insinuation that the rigidity of zero only could not really be construed as "good faith."

Reagan did side with Haig against Weinberger on the issue of shorter-range missiles: only the long-range SS-4s, -5s, and -20s would be subject to the zero option, not the SS-12s and -22s. The U.S., he said, must not be "too greedy." Here Reagan was motivated by two desires: first, to keep the goal of the talks and an eventual agreement, if there ever was to be one, as simple as possible; and second, to accommodate as much as possible West European wishes in the process of pursuing American interests. Given both these objectives, Reagan felt that the inclusion of shorter-range missiles in the zero option itself could prove complicating, distracting, and divisive in NATO.

After the main decisions had been taken, Haig said he wanted to launch a major diplomatic offensive to sell the package to the allies. He recommended blitzing Western Europe with cables extolling the zero option as a triumph of allied cooperation and sending his principal assistants, Eagleburger and Burt, to Europe right away to make the case in person.

Weinberger objected: Reagan himself should unveil the zero option in the splendor of a major address; the prelude should be suspenseful, and the substance of the speech a surprise. Sending diplomats scurrying about in advance of the speech would only steal the President's thunder.

Haig slammed his fist on the table and reminded Weinberger angrily that it was the Secretary of State's *job* to send diplomats around the world to prepare the way for major policy statements. It was also part of his job to see that the U.S. avoided, whenever possible, surprising its allies, especially on matters in which they had such a keen interest as this one.

Reagan tried to be conciliatory, saying there was surely a way to lay the ground for the speech without diminishing its dramatic impact. In the end, Eagleburger and Burt were dispatched as Haig had wanted, but the secretary's outburst did nothing to help his standing among his peers or with his boss.

It is an old adage of bureaucratic politics that no decision is final except to those who like the way the decision came out. Perle liked the President's acceptance of the zero-only proposal, so he considered it final. He did not like the exclusion of Soviet weapons other than the SS-4, -5, -20 series from the zero proposal, so he did not consider that final. He was still very concerned about the narrow scope of the proposal and determined, if possible, to broaden it later on. "If we're not very careful," he warned, "we run the risk of an agreement that limits the SS-20 but that does not limit other systems that might serve as a substitute for the SS-20."

The bureaucratic follow-up on the November 12 NSC meeting was sloppy, partly because the NSC staff, which was responsible for it, was in disarray. The press was full of news stories about a federal investigation into Richard Allen's conduct in receiving a $1,000 honorarium and three wristwatches from a Japanese women's magazine as compensation for setting up an interview with Nancy Reagan at the very beginning of the Administration. Allen's days as director of the NSC staff were numbered, and his effectiveness, which had never been great, was approaching nil.

The paperwork coming out of the meeting did not fill in all the blanks in the paperwork coming into it. The President had stated his desire to apply the zero option only to the SS-4, -5, -20, but that decision was not clear in the National Security Decision Directive, or NSDD, assembled by the NSC staff after the meeting. Thus, the paperwork that circulated through the government, which constituted the only formal record of the President's decision and the basis of Nitze's negotiating instructions, did not explicitly foreclose an effort by Perle to shoehorn the SS-12s and -22s into the zero option at some point in the future, an effort that Perle promptly began.

Putting Words in the President's Mouth

Ronald Reagan would sometimes consult with Henry Kissinger. These occasions caused a certain amount of heartburn among those in the Administration and Congress who could never forgive Kissinger for détente. But others who were concerned with the President's political welfare beyond the confines of the far right, such as James Baker in the White House and Howard Baker, the Senate majority leader, felt it was good public relations to have Reagan seen to be seeking advice from the nation's acknowledged master of geopolitics. Kissinger, for his part, welcomed the invitations. It had not been easy to sit on the sidelines during a Republican restoration; nor had it been easy to learn that old enemies like Perle were now wielding immense influence, repudiating Kissinger's legacy and waging vendettas against such former associates as Eagleburger. So there was a touch of vindication in a summons to the White House. Even though Kissinger knew perfectly well that he was being used, he was still flattered.

And yet, on a number of these occasions, Kissinger noticed something unsettling about the President: Reagan seemed strangely uninterested in international relations as such. He displayed little knowledge or even curiosity about the interaction of states and forces in the world arena. Even more disturbing, he seemed remarkably blasé about U.S. foreign policy. It was as though long-term strategy was something other people were paid to worry about. Kissinger found that, when he advised Reagan on what the government ought to be doing, the goals it should set and the methods it should employ, Reagan seemed to tune out. The best way to get Reagan's attention was to suggest to him what he personally should say publicly about a foreign problem or a policy. Then the President would sit up, and his eyes would come back into focus. What he cared about was speeches—particularly his own speeches. He knew that his smooth delivery and easygoing, winning manner were huge assets. He would work at fine-tuning a speech with an enthusiasm that he rarely devoted to other duties.

It was this aspect of Reagan's approach to the presidency that led him to see the announcement of the proposal as an end in itself. If the speech worked as a speech, then the policy must be a good one. If the speech came off, the policy could be sustained.

The original impulse to have the President make a major address on arms control had come mainly from the State Department's European Bureau. Eagleburger and his aides were alarmed at the Soviets' increasing success with their propaganda in Western Europe. The Soviet "peace offensive" was building to a climax in Leonid Brezhnev's visit to West Germany in November. That trip was intended to give Brezhnev a chance to make his case personally against the introduction of new NATO missiles on the very eve of the scheduled opening of Soviet-American negotiations in Geneva on November 30. In mid-October, one of Eagleburger's deputies, Mark Palmer, wrote a memo for Haig saying that the U.S. needed to make a dramatic gesture in the manner of John F. Kennedy's famous "I am a Berliner" speech. Haig liked the idea, passing it along to the President later in October, and Palmer began work on a draft of the speech.

Most of the rest of the government supported the idea, although for widely varying reasons. Weinberger and Perle saw a major presidential address as a way of making sure that their preferred version of the zero option bore the presidential seal of approval and was therefore less vulnerable to the moderating—or, as they saw it, softening—pressures sure to be applied from Western Europe and Foggy Bottom.

Nitze saw it as a way of elevating the American negotiating position from the bureaucracy to a loftier plane, and setting it in the context of overall policy. The speech would necessarily skim over the tricky, technical points that had generated such passion among the experts. Nitze was reasonably confident that the President's political instincts would prevent American policy from getting locked into too rigid a position, and that Reagan's natural impulse toward striking the pose of a reasonable man and a conciliator would induce him to couch even the least-flexible form of the zero option in the most flexible-sounding terms.

The State Department deliberately did not send a copy of the Palmer draft to Perle, but he quickly got wind of it anyway. He did not like what he heard. The words that the European Bureau hoped to put in Reagan's mouth had a familiar and disagreeable ring to his ear. Instead of offering a rallying cry for a new, tougher approach to arms control, the speech seemed designed to reposition Reagan in the mainstream of U.S. arms-control policy over the past two decades. That, in Perle's view, was pure apostasy. He particularly objected to favorable references in the Palmer draft to continuity with the past and, worse, to continuity with the SALT process; this sort of "continuity" deserved only repudiation. Perle and Fred Iklé also objected to a passage in Palmer's draft that proclaimed a fairly elaborate-sounding arms-control "program" for the Administration. Here was a snare that the European Bureau had set for the President: get him to utter vague but positive noises on various arms-control negotiations now and soon he would be under pressure to deliver initiatives—and concessions. Any old hand in this business knew that presidential speeches were often not just ways of announcing a particular initiative but of foreshadowing future policy as well.

With the President's speech only days away, Perle sat down at home and wrote an alternative draft. His only reference to SALT and the heritage of previous administrations was to express frustration with the disappointments and raw deals of the past; his only reference to the future was a weary willingness, despite all that frustration, to try again. Perle's draft joined Palmer's in the President's in-basket. So did a third, prepared by the staff of the National Security Council. Increasingly frustrated by his lack of influence on policymaking, and now in the throes of what would be his final undoing, the scandal over the Japanese watches and the honorarium, Richard Allen was desperate for some way to insert the NSC staff, and thus himself, actively and usefully into the process.

Reagan took all three versions up to the White House living quarters with him the night of November 12 and read them over before going to bed. He preferred the State Department version. The Pentagon and NSC drafts had a harsh, combative ring to his ear; he wanted something that made the U.S. position sound more forthcoming—a genuine offer rather than an ultimatum. After a weekend of hunting and rest in Texas, Reagan made the trip back to Washington aboard the customized Boeing 747 that would serve as his airborne command center during a nuclear war. In those melodramatically appropriate surroundings, the President settled down to tailor the White House redraft of the speech to his own preferences for pace and emphasis. This was his métier; he involved himself in the speech as he had never involved himself in the assembly of the zero proposal itself.

·   ·   ·

In Washington, in another, less apocalyptic crisis center, the Situation Room in the basement of the West Wing of the White House, a final drafting session by Reagan's subordinates was under way. Iklé was still fighting hard against the Palmer draft. He had written a memo to Meese urging, among other things, that Palmer's reference to an arms-control "program" be changed to "agenda," on the ground that an agenda was more clearly a list of topics for future discussion and was less likely to suggest that the U.S. had clearly-thought-out plans ready to unveil any day. It was this kind of meticulous attention to detail and nuance that had led Iklé's detractors over the years to compare him to a Swiss watchmaker. (One official of the Reagan Administration, who had also served with Iklé during the Nixon years, remarked that he had "an unerring instinct for the capillary.")

In a passage about the danger of nuclear war, Iklé was adamant about deleting the word "annihilation" and a reference to "the threat of incineration hanging over the people of Western Europe." He complained that such language was "lurid" (meaning that it might resonate all too harmoniously with the rhetoric of the disarmers). He also continued to argue for taking out all explicit references to SALT in order to make clear that "we're making a clean break with SALT" and "going to go well beyond SALT II." As a result of these editorial interventions by Iklé, the final draft referred only to "the dread threat of nuclear war," and instead of saying, "We can and must benefit from the work done over the past decade in SALT," it talked generally about the need to "build on the work of the past" and proclaimed the President's intention to pursue a "new approach and therefore I call it START," for Strategic Arms Reduction Talks.*

The American name of European arms control also changed—from TNF (Theater Nuclear Forces) to INF (Intermediate-range Nuclear Forces). Since the issue of European-based nuclear missiles had first come sharply into focus during the Carter Administration, the terminology had been politically tricky. The Americans had talked about long-range theater nuclear forces, or LRTNF. In military jargon, "theater" refers to the zone of combat and communications involved in a war, extending to the larger area that may be directly affected by the fighting. The word "theater" conveyed a sense of something self-contained; it obscured what Helmut Schmidt and others wanted to believe was the organic connection—or coupling—between American and European defense interests and also between strategic arms control and the regional talks about to begin.

Paul Nitze took seriously Schmidt's concern with terminology. He also had some reasons of his own for disliking the reference to theater. One was

---

*The origin of the term "START" is explained in Chapter 11.

the suggestion that the weapons to be covered in the talks were exclusively those deployed in or against the European theater. The American objective of global limits on the SS-20 made it advisable to drop the word "theater."

By October, the Swiss government needed to be notified about the designation of the forthcoming negotiations in Geneva. At an Interagency Group meeting, Nitze suggested formally dubbing the subject for the talks "intermediate-range nuclear forces"—INF. He pointed out that this new name would make clearer than the old one had that the weapons under negotiation had nothing to do with intercontinental or battlefield missiles. The new term would sharpen the focus on SS-20s, at least in Western eyes. The proposal appealed to others in Washington simply on the ground that they were discarding a Carter-era phrase and coining one of their own.

The Soviets, however, were not willing to accept the new American term any more than the old one. They were holding out for some designation that referred to Europe, since they wanted to preserve just those geographically restrictive implications that Nitze wanted to avoid and those politically disruptive, alliance-splitting or "decoupling" ones that Schmidt wanted to avoid. The Soviets also liked to mention the word "Europe" frequently because it underscored their contention that they were the only Europeans who would be at the negotiating table; Europe was their home, not the Americans'; these were to be talks on European arms control; the goal, in their view, was to keep the U.S. from imposing alien—that is, non-European —weapons on the continent. The Soviet side wanted to specify the subject of the upcoming talks as "medium-range systems in Europe." The Soviets would not agree to any joint designation that failed to mention Europe, while the U.S. would not agree to any that did.

So a full year after the preliminary round of November 1980, talks were now about to resume with the two sides even further apart on the elementary questions of what they were about and what they should be called.*

Two Cheers

Reagan unveiled the zero proposal at the National Press Club on November 18, 1981. The place and time had been chosen to assure the maximum audience in Western Europe. He began speaking at 10 A.M. It was late afternoon across the Atlantic; Europeans coming home from work would

---

*As it turned out, there was even disagreement on how to number the rounds. The real first round of Soviet-American negotiations on intermediate-range (or theater) nuclear forces had been the one conducted by Spurgeon Keeny for the U.S. and Viktor Karpov for the U.S.S.R. in the fall of 1980. The Soviets, therefore, wanted to call the resumption of talks more than a year later Round Two. But the Reagan Administration, wishing to emphasize the new departure of the President's speech, and the discontinuity between its policies and those of its predecessors, insisted on calling it Round One.

be switching on their television sets. The U.S. International Communication Agency* paid for live satellite transmission to the European Broadcasting Union.

Almost everything about the speech was simple—the portrayal of the Soviet menace, the alarm on behalf of Western interests, and, of course, the zero proposal itself. Reagan and a number of his principal aides had often said that they were looking for arms-control proposals that could be stated in a single sentence. They had found one. "The United States," said the President, "is prepared to cancel its deployment of Pershing II and ground-launched cruise missiles if the Soviets will dismantle their SS-20, SS-4 and SS-5 missiles."

The initial reaction, on both sides of the Atlantic and across a wide spectrum of political opinion, was positive. Helmut Schmidt welcomed it as "the American peace strategy," demonstrating "a specific consideration for the political, strategic and even psychological needs of Europe." The speech contained "what we Germans had to ask for or would have wished." Paul Warnke, who had been the chief SALT negotiator during much of the Carter Administration and the object of vilification by the Committee on the Present Danger, called the speech "a stroke of genius" that was "totally unassailable from an arms-control standpoint."

But a few skeptics wondered whether the proposal would indeed prove to be part of a grand strategy, as Schmidt had declared, or turn out to be a tactical mistake. Walter Slocombe, Perle's predecessor in the Pentagon, who had been deeply involved in arms-control policymaking during the Carter Administration, agreed with Warnke that the speech was "politically and substantively brilliant. It's a classical opening bid. It identifies genuine problems for the U.S. and offers a genuine solution to them. It would be good for all concerned if it were to be accepted, and if it doesn't collapse at the first rejection." But Slocombe went on to wonder whether it might not represent too much of a good thing in that regard: "There's a school in this Administration that hopes the proposal is so brilliant that the Soviets will never accept it and that rather than advancing the negotiations, it will stop them." He was referring to Perle.

Other doubts were more pronounced. As William Hyland, a veteran of arms control from earlier administrations and an occasional, informal adviser to the State Department, warned at the time:

Reagan's proposal is a clever tactic that buys about six months, but it puts the U.S. on a negotiating slope that will end in disaster. It's a propaganda ploy that looks good in November '81 but will come back

---

*Subsequently, this organization reverted to its original name, the U.S. Information Agency, or USIA.

to haunt the U.S. in May or August of '82. It shifts all the issues to a propaganda treadmill. Six months to a year from now the U.S. will be preparing missile sites in Europe. If the U.S. had made a proposal that allowed for the deployment of some missiles, then we might have been able to get away with preparations to install some of them. But thanks to the zero option, the preparation of even one site for one missile will make a mockery of zero, and the Soviets and the disarmament demonstrators will have a field day.

The Europeans did not wait six months to start raising objections. Within a few weeks of the President's speech, regional conventions of both the Social Democratic and Free Democratic parties in West Germany—which comprised the governing coalition—passed resolutions rejecting the planned deployments of the American missiles. Euphoria in the Administration over the President's initiative quickly gave way to annoyance with the allies. Perle gave an interview suggesting that the anti-nuclear-weapons movement in Europe was a manifestation of "Protestant *angst.*" Reagan himself later said that the European demonstrations were "all sponsored by a thing called the World Peace Council, which is bought and paid for by the Soviet Union." No one doubted that the Soviets were abetting the West European peace movement in any way they could—with propaganda, with diplomatic overtures tuned to what the Europeans wanted to hear, and with covert financial and organizational help. But Reagan's comment did nothing to counter the Soviet campaign. The sweeping accusation sounded like transatlantic McCarthyism.

Preparing and Preventing Fallbacks

The most basic question that the President's speech raised was the extent to which the zero proposal would be negotiable. If the Soviets came back with a counterproposal that represented some movement from their own starting position, such as a willingness to accept reductions in the deployment of SS-20s, would the U.S. then move off its own starting position, possibly to meet the Soviets halfway? The State Department and Arms Control Agency participants in the policymaking process felt the answer was clearly and emphatically yes. That answer, they assured themselves, was implicit in the President's promise to Haig, during the November 12 meeting, that the zero-only proposal did not represent an ultimatum and would be the basis for the U.S. to negotiate "in good faith." As Eagleburger put it in a meeting at the time, "It's a foregone conclusion that we'll have to fall off of zero sooner or later. It's only a question of when, where, how and in exchange for what."

The European Bureau was driven by the conviction that an agreement was possible. Richard Burt still disagreed; he was convinced that the Soviets would never voluntarily give up the advantage they had established in Europe. Nevertheless, he felt it was important to proceed with the talks and to preserve the appearance not just of a reasonable, flexible American position but of guarded American optimism as well. Otherwise the allies would see the whole exercise as a sham. In Burt's view, it *was* a sham—but a justifiable, indeed an unavoidable and vital sham, one necessary for keeping the alliance together.

Paul Nitze was still avoiding taking sides. He managed not to get too closely identified with the positions of any of the other participants. He certainly did not see the negotiations as doomed. He would not have taken on the job of chief American negotiator had he shared Burt's unequivocal pessimism about the chances of an agreement. This was one of the causes of growing friction between the two men. Nor did he want the American proposal loaded down with features, and couched in terms, that effectively precluded progress. He was asked a number of times, by a number of different people with different political credentials—hard, soft, and in between—whether he thought there was any chance at all the Soviets would accept the President's initiative. His answer was always some version of the same cautious formulation: "It's hard to conceive that they'd accept it fast. But that's not the appropriate criterion for judging the proposal. The appropriate criterion should be, and is, 'Is it a solid basis for continuing negotiations?' And the answer to that is yes."

It was implicit in his carefully worded answer that during the "continuing negotiations" the American position would have to evolve; no matter how "solid a basis" the zero option might be as an opening proposal, it was not the basis of an agreement.

Perle was having none of that. He was against the European Bureau's outright advocacy of negotiability; he was against Nitze's guarded, implicit advocacy of the same thing; and he was against Burt's wish to preserve an appearance of negotiability for the sake of alliance management. He resisted the twin notions of inherent flexibility and inevitable retreat from the opening American position, arguing that any admission of flexibility—and any talk about the need to retreat—would simply undermine the credibility of the zero option.

When asked skeptically if the zero option was credible, given the near-impossibility that the Soviets would ever agree to dismantle all their SS-20s, Perle replied:

I don't think we can be sure about what's realistic until we get into the negotiations. Any agreement ought to be militarily significant, not just cosmetic. We believe the proposal will produce an agreement that is militarily significant if we can get it, but in the meantime will deal effectively with the Soviet political offensive. The Soviets will have to decide whether keeping their SS-20s is worth losing what they've tried to accomplish politically in Western Europe.

Perle seemed to assume that if the Soviets did not respond positively to the zero proposal they would lose the gains they had made with West European public opinion. But that assumption was not necessarily valid. If they played their cards right, the Soviets might very well be able to keep all or most of their SS-20s *and* their political gains in Europe.

Perle's critics felt that by downplaying or discrediting considerations of negotiability, he was seeking, cleverly but cynically, to rationalize a negotiating position that was intentionally *non*-negotiable. That was the nearly unanimous view of the European Bureau at the State Department. Eagleburger and Gompert felt that if Perle could be thwarted, and if flexibility could be preserved in the negotiations, there was still a chance of reaching a compromise along the lines of what they had envisioned all along—a trade-off between SS-20s and NATO missiles under an equal numerical ceiling on warheads. Perle's fear was their hope: zero plus might yet, in the course of genuine negotiations, prevail over zero only.

Haig continued to pound away at the three words that Reagan had used at the November 12 NSC meeting. "The proposal is being forwarded *in good faith,*" the secretary said at one briefing. "We want a Soviet reaction to it. We are prepared to listen." That led Perle to complain that "Haig's going around giving his own speech, and it's different to the point of insubordination from the President's."

Perle felt compelled to counteract the damage he believed had been done by Haig's statements and a spate of stories in the press that emanated from the State Department and hinted at flexibility in the U.S. position. For example, on the day that the negotiations were to begin in Geneva, November 30, the *Christian Science Monitor* reported that "a fallback position would include sharp reductions in, rather than elimination of, the Soviet SS-20 missiles in return for equally sharp reductions in the planned deployment of new American missiles in Europe." The next day, Perle testified before the Senate Armed Services Committee. He stressed that there was no middle ground between the zero proposal and full deployment of the 572 new American missiles in NATO:

> When one recalls that it took a full ten years to get the Soviets to honor their wartime treaty obligation to withdraw the Red Army from postwar Austria, it is clear that in dealing with the Soviets patience and resolve have their own rewards.

Perle then reviewed for the senators what he considered the disgraceful history of more recent negotiations, particularly SALT, in which the U.S. had retreated steadily from its opening positions:

We will not repeat that mistake. We have gone to Geneva with a proposal that we can defend; and defend it we will. There has been speculation in the press that Paul Nitze has left for Geneva with a fallback position to be tabled in the event that the Soviets do not embrace the President's proposal. I can assure you that these reports are false. We have learned from bitter experience that nothing would so dash our hopes for the successful negotiation of our proposal as a briefcase full of positions to which we are ready to fall back.

To that statement Nitze had no objection. He agreed it was tactically unwise to hint at compromise before a negotiation had even begun. But Perle went on to conclude by reading from the memoirs of Samuel Hoare, the British statesman whose reputation as an appeaser in the thirties kept him out of the wartime cabinet. Perle quoted Hoare reflecting ruefully on Neville Chamberlain's meeting with Adolf Hitler in Munich in 1938:

I had been caught up in the toils of a critical negotiation. The longer it went on and the more serious the issue became, the more anxious I grew to see it succeed. This is almost always the course of negotiations. As they proceed, the parties in them become increasingly obsessed with the need to prevent their final failure. If they are to continue, it is necessary to make concessions, and one concession almost invariably leads to another. The time comes when the question has to be faced: Is the substance being sacrificed to the negotiation, and is it not better to admit failure rather than to make further proposals and concessions? Throughout the Munich discussions I often asked myself whether the slide into surrender had not started.

This was strong stuff. Perle seemed to be putting his longtime mentor on notice that if Nitze became the Administration's principal advocate for compromise, he would be open to the charge of appeasement.

The Soviet Numbers Game

With his November 18 speech, Ronald Reagan had stolen a march on Leonid Brezhnev, who was due in Bonn a few days later. Not that Moscow was taken completely by surprise. On the basis of hints that had been leaking out of Washington for some time, the Soviets anticipated something like what Reagan proposed. About two weeks before the speech, Brezhnev had given an interview to the West German magazine *Der Spiegel*, in which he asserted that the zero option failed to take account of unfair Western advantages and that it was designed to be non-negotiable. In its coverage of Reagan's address, the Soviet news agency TASS said: "The reasoning in this speech can be summed up as the elimination of the U.S.S.R.'s existing defense potential in Europe, while the American forward-based systems and submarine-based missile complexes and nuclear bombers of Britain and France will be preserved." The U.S. Ambassador to Moscow, Arthur Hartman, got much the same message in private from Foreign Minister Gromyko.

The American proposal was of course overwhelmingly political, aimed at the West Europeans—and against the Soviet Union. And there was truth to the accusation that some of its authors were hoping that the negotiations would buy the U.S. time to build up Western defenses. But, while Soviet grumbling was possibly justified, Soviet self-righteousness was not. As Walter Slocombe commented when he heard Reagan's speech, "If you think our proposal is one-sided, wait till you see theirs!"

The Soviets had persuaded themselves that the composition of NATO gave the U.S. unfair advantages and that the U.S.S.R., as a co-equal superpower, was entitled to various kinds of "compensation." NATO, in Soviet eyes, represented triple jeopardy: first, the U.S. was a threat in its own right, because of its strategic forces that Washington vowed to use in a European conflict; second, the U.S. had additional weapons for use against Soviet targets stationed on European territory; and third, France and Britain were not only covered by the American umbrella, but had their own nuclear weapons as well, weapons that could reach into the U.S.S.R. The Soviets' claim to compensation for the strategic threat they faced from the long-range British and French nuclear forces was to remain one of the principal sticking points in INF.

The standard American rebuttal was that INF was a bilateral negotiation, therefore the weapons of third countries by definition could not be on the agenda. Moreover, the French weapons were not assigned to NATO at all, and while some British nuclear forces were so assigned, their real purpose was to deter a Soviet attack on Britain itself, just as the French weapons existed solely to defend France. They were not, in their principal purpose or to any significant degree, part of NATO's collective defense. The British and French governments did not want the U.S. to negotiate on their behalf, and certainly not to negotiate away their rights to their own defenses.*

The Soviet negotiating position was designed to avoid, or at least minimize, reductions in the SS-20s while at the same time preventing NATO from

---

*Another, more esoteric argument against including the British and French nuclear forces in INF derived from the negotiating record of SALT. On two occasions, in 1972 and 1974, the Soviets had tacitly acknowledged that certain numerical disparities favoring them constituted implicit compensation for the British and French nuclear forces. Yet now Moscow was claiming compensation anew in INF. The Soviets, of course, could reply that they had every right to do so, given the Reagan Administration's low regard for SALT and the uncertainty about whether other deals made during SALT would stand up.

acquiring a "unilateral advantage" with the Pershing IIs and Tomahawks. In the Soviet lexicon, a "unilateral advantage" is something that only the perfidious U.S. pursues, while the U.S.S.R. goes about its patient, principled quest of "equal security." Therefore the Soviets had to package their intertwined desiderata of keeping the SS-20s and blocking the American missiles in a way that seemed compatible with their professed dedication to equality. The plausibility of their posture in the negotiations depended largely on their claim that a balance already existed, one that would be upset by the introduction of new NATO missiles.

The Soviets were pretending to engage in the highly technical exercise of counting weapons while actually engaging in a highly political one of asserting equality. This kind of fancy but often phony addition and subtraction had a well-established place in the history of arms control. SALT had been an exercise in reconciling competing approaches to the arithmetic of inventories. It was natural that haggling over what to count and what to leave out of various aggregates should carry over into the European negotiations. It was one of the puzzlements of the INF story that the two sides, working from what were, or should have been, the same data could come up with such wildly divergent measurements of the nuclear balance in Europe. What Reagan read as a six-to-one imbalance in favor of the U.S.S.R. Moscow professed to see as almost perfect equality.* The disagreement was a classic example of how one can prove anything with numbers.

The Soviet position when Reagan made his zero-option proposal was a call for a moratorium on deployments of intermediate-range missiles and other weapons until a treaty was concluded. The Kremlin had been urging this since 1979, and Brezhnev reiterated it at the Twenty-sixth Congress of the Soviet Communist party in February 1981. At the same time, Brezhnev declared, "We shall be prepared to agree on rather substantial reductions from both sides." At first there was no firm indication of what weapons would be reduced and by how much, but there were hints later.

Elaborating on Brezhnev's speech to the Party Congress, TASS issued a commentary that laid out the Soviet position in greater detail. TASS said the U.S.S.R. was prepared to agree on a genuine zero option, whereby both NATO and the Soviet Union would remove all weapons intended for Euro-

---

*The American tally of 3,825 Soviet weapons versus 560 American ones—hence, six to one—excluded allied systems and shorter-range American missiles, while it included all the Soviet Badger, Blinder, Fencer, and Flogger aircraft. The battle of the numbers became a battle of the booklets. In the autumn of 1981, the Pentagon published a paperback titled *Soviet Military Power,* filled with colorful charts, photographs, and artists' renderings of Soviet weaponry (including an SS-20 lifting off from its camouflaged launcher). Not to be outdone, the Soviets brought out, in tens of thousands of copies and several languages, their own book in December titled *The Threat to Europe,* with the U.S. cast in the title role, and later another one, *Whence the Threat to Peace.*

pean targets. This would create a nuclear-free zone in Europe. It would also leave the Soviet Union with a preponderance of conventional military power and the ability to bring its supposedly strategic, or intercontinental, nuclear weapons to bear on European targets at any time. Western Europe would be very much at the mercy of the U.S.S.R. and utterly decoupled from the U.S.

"If," said TASS—with an obvious dig at the Reagan Administration for all its talk about being interested in real arms control and deep reductions —"the West is not prepared for such a radical solution," then the U.S.S.R. would consider an agreement that would apply to all nuclear weapons with a "combat radius" of 1,000 kilometers or more that were deployed on land in Europe, in waters adjacent to Europe, or intended for use in Europe. That meant British and French nuclear weapons would be included. So would American carrier-based planes. So would American fighter-bombers that were based in the U.S. but, by Soviet lights, "intended for use in Europe." So would U.S. Poseidon ballistic missiles aboard submarines regularly as-signed to NATO, or at least so the Soviets were claiming until mid-1981.* During the negotiations, each side would abstain from additional deploy-ments, and existing deployments were to be frozen "quantitatively and qualitatively." In other words, no upgrading of aircraft and, more impor-tant, no introduction of Tomahawks and Pershing IIs.

On July 25, 1981, Defense Minister Dimitri Ustinov had renewed the Soviet offer to reduce the number of nuclear missiles aimed at Western Europe in exchange for cancellation of the NATO deployments. He did not say whether the reduction would be in the form of a pullback beyond the Urals (the rough dividing line between European and Asian Russia) or dismantlement, nor did he specify whether SS-20s would be affected along with the old SS-4s and -5s. Around the same time, however, authoritative Soviets meeting with American visitors in Moscow took the line that reduc-tions "might well include a draw-down of SS-20s."

By the Soviet count, each side had approximately 1,000 weapons in the category where a moratorium, followed by reductions, was proposed. The operative phrase was that the moratorium and reductions should apply to "units of similar arms at [each side's] disposal." It was in defining these terms—*unit, similar,* and *disposal*—and in adding up the numbers in a way

---

*The inclusion of Poseidon submarine-launched ballistic missiles (SLBMs) would mean counting them twice, since they were already covered by SALT. One of the few changes in the Soviet position as it evolved during 1981 became apparent when Senators Charles Mathias and Alan Cranston visited Moscow in August and met with Marshal Nikolai Ogarkov, the chief of the Soviet General Staff and an old SALT hand. As he walked the senators through the numbers on which the Soviets were relying, Ogarkov omitted mention of American SLBMs in "waters adjacent to Europe." They never reappeared in the Soviet count. One reason for dropping the Poseidons was probably that the Soviets were vulnerable to the same double jeopardy as the Americans: the Kremlin was counting only a handful of its own SLBMs as weapons adjacent to, or for use against, Europe.

that came out near 1,000, that Soviet arithmetic became most ingenious. A sample Soviet tally looked like this:

NATO		THE U.S.S.R.	
U.S. Pershing I missiles in West Germany	108	Land-based missiles (SS-4s, -5s, and -20s)	496
West German Pershing Is	72		
Fighter-bombers (F-111s, FB-111s, F-4s, A-6s, A-7s)	555	Submarine missiles (SS-N-5)	18
British Polaris SLBMs	64	Bombers (Backfire, Badgers, Blinders)	461
British Vulcan bombers	56		975
French land-based missiles	18		
French submarine missiles	80		
French Mirage-4 bombers	33		
	986		

One Soviet complaint about the zero proposal was that it sought to eliminate weapon systems "randomly chosen." No such charge could be made of the way the Soviets chose their own numbers. It was, as Russians say, "no accident" that the column on the Soviet side was so much shorter. The bottom line on that side of the ledger represented more subtraction than addition.

The Soviets had consistently claimed that a balance had existed in Europe since 1979, yet during the ensuing two years they had been steadily adding SS-20s to their side of the supposed balance at an average rate of approximately one new launcher a week.* There had been no comparable offsetting deployments by NATO. The Soviets were including the Pershing Is, both those under American command and those (minus warheads) in the West German armed forces. Moscow had carefully defined weapons subject to

---

*By the end of 1977, the year the SS-20 first became operational, there were ten launchers; a year later the number had grown to 70; by the time of the NATO dual-track decision in December 1979, that figure had doubled to 140; by the end of 1980, there were 200; and by 1981, when the Reagan Administration proclaimed the zero option, the number was over 250; a year later, the figure was well over 300; by the end of 1983, there would be 360 launchers operational and nine more in preparation. In their rebuttal to the charge that they were ahead and still not quitting, the Soviets claimed that the SS-20s were merely replacements for the old SS-4 and SS-5 missiles that were being retired and that some of the new SS-20s were in Asia, therefore out of bounds for European arms control.

limitation as only those with ranges greater than 1,000 kilometers, yet the Soviets were making an obvious exception for the Pershing I, which had a range well under 1,000 kilometers. Then they turned right around and did not count a hundred or so SS-12 and -22s, which had ranges considerably greater than the Pershing I. They were counting nuclear-capable tactical aircraft on the American side, such as the F-4 Phantom, yet they were excluding about 2,700 of their own roughly comparable fighter-bombers (the Su-17 Fitter, the Su-19 Fencer, and the MiG-27 Flogger). The Soviets were treating the Phantom as though it had a "combat radius" of more than 1,000 kilometers, while the U.S. insisted its operational range was only 760 kilometers. Their own Fencer, which was about twice as big as a Phantom and which U.S. intelligence experts believed to have a range of 1,140 kilometers, fell below the 1,000 kilometers cutoff in the Soviet count.

The phrase "intended for use" allowed the Soviets to include American planes on all six aircraft carriers of the U.S. Alantic Fleet, even though only one or two of those ships were normally on patrol off European shores at any one time. "Intended for use" also applied to FB-111 bombers back in the continental U.S., but not to Backfire bombers deployed in the Far East of the U.S.S.R. Even these prestidigitations still would have left the Soviets with too many Tu-22 Blinder and Tu-16 Badger bombers, which had ranges well in excess of 1,000 kilometers. The Soviets seemed to count only those Blinders and Badgers that were armed with air-to-surface missiles, as opposed to gravity bombs, thus bringing the sum down to the desired level.

All these contrivances made the Soviet position unacceptable, strictly on intellectual grounds, even before one addressed the thornier problems of how to cope with the mobility of SS-20s (not to mention Backfires), with the MIRV factor (a single SS-20 launcher threatened not one but three NATO targets), and with the British and French nuclear forces. Yet the claim that a balance already existed in Europe was to remain an immutable tenet of the Soviet position for the next few years, and it was the basis for the reductions proposal with which they countered Reagan's zero option.

Working backward from their utterly artificial starting point of approximately 1,000, the Soviets said they would be willing to reduce to 600 units on each side by 1985 and 300 by the end of 1990. And how would they reduce on their side? The main means, they said, would be destruction; but this would "not exclude the possibility" of withdrawing some armaments behind agreed lines. In their case, that could only mean they were holding open the option of taking Backfires and SS-20s out of Europe and redeploying them in Asia.

But at the bottom of all these complicated ploys, behind all the loopholes, was a core of simplicity: as on the American side, the most important number in the Soviet game was zero. However it might, in the course of bargaining, juggle the composition and disposition of its own forces, Moscow seemed determined not to sanction a single Pershing II or Tomahawk in Europe. Whatever else they accomplished in INF, the Soviets were bent on stopping the NATO modernization program in its entirety.

Brezhnev in Bonn

Leonid Brezhnev went to Bonn four days after Reagan's speech. In his talks with Schmidt, Brezhnev complained that the American proposal would leave the West with a two-to-one advantage over the U.S.S.R. He then laid out a slightly refashioned version of the standing Soviet proposal. It was in four parts: (1) an immediate moratorium on what the Soviets were calling medium-range (1,000–5,500-kilometer) weapons in Europe; (2) during the moratorium, negotiations toward "substantial reductions"; (3) the reduction to zero of all medium-range systems "threatening Europe"; and (4) the eventual elimination in Europe of virtually all so-called tactical or battlefield weapons and those with ranges below 1,000 kilometers.

Brezhnev, members of his entourage, and the Soviet media also played up an offer to make an initial, unilateral Soviet reduction of "hundreds" of missiles as a way of getting the talks started: "As a gesture of good will, we could unilaterally reduce part of our medium-range nuclear weapons in the European area of the U.S.S.R. We could, so to speak, reduce in advance as we move toward a lower level on which the U.S.S.R. and the U.S. can agree as a result of the negotiations. This is a new, essential element in our position."

Actually, it was not so new. Soviet officials, including Brezhnev, had been floating the suggestion of such a gesture ever since Brezhnev visited East Berlin in October 1979, when he had been trying to head off the NATO two-track decision. While "hundreds" was intended to sound like a lot, there were hundreds of obsolescent SS-4s and -5s that were overdue for retirement in any event. The Soviets had originally intended to replace them with SS-20s more or less on a one-for-one basis, but they may have rushed ahead with the SS-20 program and held back on the dismantling of SS-4s and -5s precisely in order to be able to "offer" as a political gesture what they intended to do for military reasons anyway. If the negotiations failed to produce an agreement before NATO's self-imposed deadline for deployment, continued Brezhnev, the reasonable thing, of course, would be to let the deadline slip: "In order to simplify the dialogue and to create a favorable atmosphere for it," he said, "both sides should, for as long as the negotiations last, refrain from stationing new medium-range systems in Europe and from modernizing already existing ones."

Brezhnev's call for deferring deployment of the new missiles received a sympathetic hearing within Schmidt's Social Democratic party, although not from Schmidt himself. Within days after Brezhnev's visit, Willy Brandt, the party chairman and former chancellor, said that by the time the deadline for deployment arrived in late 1983 "a situation might exist that would not yet yield the need for a decision." The party's parliamentary leader, Herbert Wehner, said it was "not inconceivable" that the 1983 deadline would be extended.

Schmidt and American officials were aghast. If the Soviets could get NATO to accept deferment, they would have succeeded in undercutting the 1979 two-track decision. They would merely have to string out the talks unproductively but indefinitely, and the Tomahawks and Pershing IIs would never arrive. Not only would the deployment be delayed, but most likely the West European willingness ever to deploy would quickly erode. And the longer the Soviets could get the West Europeans to procrastinate, the less bargaining leverage the U.S. would have in the negotiations. As Alexander Haig said just as the negotiations began in Geneva, "Progress depends not only on the skill of our negotiators but on NATO's resolve to continue its preparations to deploy the missiles that will offset Soviet advantages. These preparations are the incentive that brought the Soviets to the negotiations and that will encourage them now to take a serious position."

That was to be the assumption underlying American negotiating strategy for the next two years.

5 Down to Business

Alexander Haig, Caspar Weinberger, and Leonid Brezhnev had all discovered, and demonstrated, that the road to Geneva led through Bonn. Now it was time for Paul Nitze to follow them. Just before keeping his appointment with the Soviets in Geneva, Nitze stopped off in West Germany to meet with Helmut Schmidt. The Chancellor told him that there must be real progress in the negotiations by the fall of 1982. Otherwise, West European support for the Tomahawk and Pershing II deployments, and for American policy more generally, would crumble. Schmidt's exhortation, which Nitze took very seriously, stood in marked contrast to Nitze's last conversation in Washington with Perle. Perle warned that Nitze must be prepared to "tough it out for a long, long time," and that he must "resist the temptation of agreement for agreement's sake."

The danger of unseemly haste seemed small, since Nitze had left Washington without a complete set of negotiating instructions. The interagency process had yet to solve the numerous problems left over after the National Security Council meeting at which the President had decided on the zero option. Nitze and his colleagues had been working on a draft of an INF treaty for some time, and they continued to sharpen it after they arrived in Geneva. But they could not show it to the Soviets until it was approved by Washington. Approval, much to the frustration of the negotiators, was simply not forthcoming. Part of the problem was that there was still no formally constituted "backstopping" committee in Washington to serve as the delegation's home office, its principal point of contact with the policymakers.* And the Interagency Group was still arguing over what had been decided in the President's name on November 12.

Since Nitze did not have a treaty ready to present to the Soviets, he came prepared instead to lay out the rationale for the President's zero proposal

---

*The backstopping committee was a victim of Richard Allen's distraction and the disorganization on his staff. Partly because of his preoccupation with his own troubles, Allen did not get around to issuing the order that empowered the committee to do its job until December 19, two days after the negotiators in Geneva had recessed for the holidays.

in a series of opening statements at full-dress plenary meetings. But even the preparation of those statements had generated some tensions between him and Burt, who wanted them to be submitted for prior approval by the Interagency Group. Burt was protecting his prerogatives as the co-chairman of that group; he was also reflecting the State Department's general mistrust of the Arms Control Agency and the Rostow-Nitze partnership.

Nitze, however, with Eugene Rostow's support, had stood up for his own prerogatives. He felt his obligation to follow his negotiating instructions did not extend to a requirement that he have his every word cleared in advance by a slow-working, often contentious committee thousands of miles away. He did not want to establish the precedent for a procedure that, if applied to other major statements he would be delivering later in the negotiations, was sure to be cumbersome and a bit undignified as well. Soviet negotiators had to check virtually any substantive utterance in advance with Moscow; Henry Kissinger had kept a very tight rein on his negotiators during SALT. Nitze had witnessed the former and experienced the latter procedure a decade earlier when he was on the SALT delegation. Now that he was chief negotiator, he did not intend to be reduced to a mouthpiece. Nor was there anyone over his head in the Reagan Administration who commanded the authority that had once been Kissinger's. But, while Nitze resisted, Burt persisted. In the end, they had agreed on a compromise: Nitze would brief the Interagency Group on what he was planning to say in the opening statements before he left Washington, while they were still in the first-draft stage.

The statements themselves were expanded, refined, and polished by Nitze and his colleagues after they got to Geneva; they were played back to Washington only after they had been delivered in the opening plenary sessions. They elaborated on the rationale for extended deterrence, the exclusively defensive nature of NATO, the American determination to remain the bulwark of West European security, and the threat of the SS-20s.

Until there was a formal treaty to put on the table, the American negotiators were in the uncomfortable position of having to talk around the issue at hand. They could only give the Soviets an oral explication of Reagan's proposal and its "essential elements." They also confronted the Soviets both orally and in writing with the Administration's insistence on the concept of a global ceiling to cover mobile systems, which in the case of the SS-20 meant a global "ceiling" at the floor level of zero.

Opposite Numbers

The Soviets came to Geneva primarily to listen, to repeat what Leonid Brezhnev had said in Bonn, and to object to almost everything said by the Americans. The chief of the delegation, Ambassador Yuli Kvitsinsky, was, at forty-five, a rising star of the diplomatic service. He was, not by coincidence, a specialist on German politics as well as arms control. His background included service in the Soviet embassies in both East Berlin and Bonn. He was not above bragging about his precocious achievement of a senior post, nor above hinting broadly that he had very good connections back in Moscow and that he could even influence the Politburo's decisions on arms control. The Americans were at first skeptical. Kvitsinsky sometimes seemed a bit defensive and excessively polemical, as though he felt constantly obliged to prove his hard-line, iron-pants credentials. Nevertheless, Nitze soon established a good working relationship with him (although he never entirely mastered the difficult Slavic name, and habitually referred to him as "Mr. Quitsinsky" or, less formally, as "K").

Meetings alternated between the U.S. headquarters, a nondescript modern office complex called the Botanic Building because it overlooked Geneva's botanical gardens, and the Soviet headquarters, a villa that had once served as the Lithuanian mission to the League of Nations. The two chief negotiators agreed at the very beginning that their delegations would observe a gag rule—no statements, attributed or otherwise, to the press on the substance of the talks; no attempts to grandstand for the West Europeans. Generally, both sides observed this rule. Kvitsinsky joked with reporters that Nitze had "ordered" him to keep his mouth shut in public. Nitze was not amused. He felt it was critical that any agreements worked out between the two of them should be presented as based on mutual desires and deliberation, not initiated solely by one or the other or imposed one on the other. While the issue at hand was minor and procedural, Nitze could already imagine that the day might come when he would need to be able to invoke the principle again on much more important and sensitive matters.

Kvitsinsky's principal deputy was Nikolai Detinov, a general in the Soviet Army. He had accompanied Brezhnev to Vladivostok for the 1974 summit meeting with Gerald Ford during SALT II. The Army had responsibility for the Strategic Rocket Forces, which in turn included intermediate-range missiles like the SS-20 as well as intercontinental missiles. Detinov was clearly authorized to speak for the Soviet military establishment as a whole. He once remarked that he consulted with his colleagues from the Soviet Navy and Air Force "only when matters of special interest to them come up." That, he implied, happened only rarely.

Detinov and the other military men on the Soviet side were, on the whole, more businesslike and less polemical than the civilians. Nitze often found them a relief to talk to. The military representatives sometimes seemed almost embarrassed by their civilian colleagues' flagrant distortions of facts and figures. As Nitze put it, "You can't run a military operation if you think $2 + 2 = 17$." Detinov and his fellow officers reciprocated Nitze's respect. Early on, Nitze began making a point of using the word "objective" whenever he could. It was a favorite word of the Soviets, and they often employed it when making the most propagandistic, unobjective statements. "However much we might disagree with Ambassador Nitze," remarked Yuri Lebedev, another military man on the delegation, "he makes a real effort to keep objective reality clearly in mind."

During Nitze's SALT I days, his nickname among his fellow American negotiators had been "the Silver Fox." The Soviets had picked up the phrase, and they meant it as a compliment: they had been impressed not just by his cunning, but by his willingness to apply his wits to the task of finding ingenious ways out of impasses in the talks, and they were hopeful that he would do the same thing in INF. "We were struck by Nitze's saying almost on the first day, 'I came here to leave no stone unturned.' " That observation was made by Vladimir Pavlichenko, not a full member of the delegation, but rather an "adviser." He had held the same post during SALT II. He was listed as being under the auspices of the Academy of Sciences. His real affiliation had long since been revealed to be the KGB.* He was cocky, sometimes snide, but he was also extraordinarily frank. He could be helpful to the Americans by providing early warning of changes in the Soviet position and insight into the reasons for shifts.

The Soviets' proposal was an amplification of the four-point plan that Brezhnev had unveiled in Bonn. Two of those points had been added to the Soviet position in order to counteract Reagan's championing of the zero option: the suggestion that all medium-range weapons "threatening Europe" be reduced to zero, and that eventually all tactical and other shorter-range weapons be eliminated as well. But, until reductions could be negotiated, the Soviets kept insisting, there ought to be a moratorium. And a moratorium meant no Pershing IIs and Tomahawks.

The Soviet delegation presented a one-page document providing some detail on how the moratorium would work. Neither side would deploy "new" systems in Europe; there would be a freeze on deployment of existing systems; and the two sides would enter negotiations on permanent reductions. Kvitsinsky offered a two-sentence elaboration: the Soviets were prepared to reduce their medium-range systems, which they currently counted at a little less than 1,000, to 300 by 1990 if NATO—meaning the British and French as well as American arsenals—came down to the same level. As an interim measure, the two sides would have to come under a ceiling of 600 by 1985. The Soviets explained, as though it were a point of particular magnanimity in their scheme, that the British and French weapons, which

---

The New York Times had exposed Pavlichenko as a senior KGB officer in 1971, when he was living in New York, working for the United Nations public information office, and circulating among American intellectuals at the Pugwash Conferences.

numbered in their calculations over 250, need not be reduced at all, although of course they would have to count against the eventual ceiling of 300. The purpose here was to use the British and French forces as a fulcrum against which to apply leverage in prying virtually all medium-range American weapons out of Europe.

In response to the American call for "global ceilings," the Soviets professed outrage at the notion that they would have to count weapons deployed in the Far East, against China, as part of a European arms-control agreement. But there was a tantalizing indication that they might eventually be more flexible. In the less formal "post-plenary" conversations, when the delegations divided up into smaller groups, a number of the Soviets said, in what was meant to seem an offhanded manner, "If we could get closer to an agreement, we'd find a way to deal with this problem."

Sometimes the U.S. negotiators wandered, quite purposefully, into subjects that were officially not on the American agenda at all, such as aircraft. Nitze had known that it would be foolish for the U.S. to pretend to ignore aircraft since they figured prominently in every aspect of the Soviet proposal. He was careful to explain to Kvitsinsky that, while he was ready to "discuss" aircraft, he was not authorized to "negotiate" them. He noted that aircraft were difficult to equate with missiles for a variety of reasons: their dual role, their slower flight time and vulnerability to air defenses, and the very fact that they were manned. As Nitze pointed out, unmanned cruise missiles "can sustain much higher rates of attrition" than piloted aircraft. In that sense, he added wryly, the drones are "infinitely courageous." The Soviets bridled at even this touch of humor. They thought it contained an aspersion on the bravery of Soviet pilots or on the willingness of Mother Russia to sacrifice as many of her sons as necessary to defend herself. "We don't care about attrition," replied a military officer on the delegation, A. I. Ivlev. "That is not a factor for us."

Nitze stressed the additional problem of defining aircraft range. For one thing, unlike missile ranges, aircraft ranges assumed a return trip from the target area to the base. A one-way mission could, in theory, double the range, but the pilot would have to bail out or land in enemy territory—or crash kamikaze-style. And while hardly standard operating procedure, suicide missions could not be completely discounted, given Ivlev's boast. Also, the ranges of airplanes varied dramatically depending on how heavily armed they were; smaller bombs could be delivered over greater distances. Yet, to make the matter more complicated, a full load of conventional bombs tended to be considerably heavier than thermonuclear armaments. Finally, the problems of one side's verifying the capabilities of the other side's planes were numerous and difficult. For example, U.S. intelligence believed the Su-24 Fencer had been tested to a potential combat radius of well over 1,000 kilometers and was capable of carrying nuclear weapons. But, by leaving the

Fencer out of their total of "medium-range" systems, the Soviets were saying its range was under 1,000 kilometers.

By pressing this point early, Nitze was preparing the ground for what might become an important trade-off later in the negotiations—that is, the exclusion of the Fencer in exchange for the exclusion of the closest thing to an American counterpart, the F-4 Phantom.

He was also, however, straying from his rather restrictive negotiating instructions and setting himself up for a confrontation with his own government back in Washington. Sven Kraemer, one of the NSC staff members most hostile to the Arms Control Agency, the State Department, and all their works, had been warning that "once Paul Nitze gets hungry for a deal, all the instructions in the world won't keep him from trying to make any goddamn deal he thinks he can cut." When Kraemer saw reporting cables from Geneva that so much as contained the word "aircraft," he showed them to colleagues, saying, "See! He's getting ready to trade away our planes! Just wait!"

Nitze, however, was more immediately concerned with handling the Soviets. His own countrymen could wait. He was reasonably pleased with the opening weeks of the talks. He genuinely enjoyed what many would have found the tedious exercise of banging his head against the Soviet stone wall. For him, there was intellectual satisfaction every time he made a point that Kvitsinsky seemed at a loss to rebut.

In December, Nitze prepared to go home "marginally more optimistic" about an eventual breakthrough than he had been at the outset. Kvitsinsky was more guarded, both formally and informally. In his final plenary statement, he let loose with a propaganda tirade, blaming the U.S. for seeking "unilateral advantage" in the talks. At a cocktail party shortly before the negotiations recessed for the Christmas and New Year holidays, he remarked that the enterprise was still in its "political phase." That meant the two sides were jockeying for maximum political advantage in the eyes of their main audience, the West Europeans. The talks could not move into a "technical phase," when concrete problems would lend themselves to concrete solutions, until there was some sort of agreement "at the top," between the Soviet and American leaders. He said he was "hoping for a miracle" by the fall of '82, when Reagan and Brezhnev might meet and set guidelines for an agreement if not sign a final pact. That Kvitsinsky was hopeful at all struck some Americans who heard him as a good sign. That it would take the "miracle" of a Brezhnev-Reagan summit to fulfill his hopes was somewhat less encouraging.

As Nitze analyzed Kvitsinsky's remarks, he heard him to be hinting that Brezhnev wanted a summit and might be willing to move a long way off the Soviet negotiating position to get one, as long, of course, as Reagan would meet him at least halfway.

Trouble on the Home Front

Over the Christmas–New Year recess in the talks of late 1981 and early '82 the uneasy modus vivendi that had existed among Paul Nitze, Richard Burt, and Richard Perle fell apart once and for all. Nitze had known from the beginning that Burt and Perle were bound to be jealous of each other when it came to making policy and setting objectives for the INF negotiations. Therefore, he bided his time, reckoning that the interagency maneuvering over the Administration's opening position was not as important as what he called "the dialectical process" that would determine how that position was to evolve. The outcome of the negotiations would depend not so much on the details of the opening proposal as it would on changes in his instructions as the negotiations unfolded.

At issue were technical details of the sort that have so often touched off bloody battles, internecine as well as international, in arms control. On one, Nitze found himself at loggerheads with the government as a whole, but particularly with Burt; on another, he was squared off head-to-head against Perle. On both issues, Nitze lost.

The first concerned whether Pershing Is, the shorter-range ballistic missiles already deployed in West Germany, would be limited by the American proposal. Nitze favored a freeze at current levels of the Soviet SS-12s and -22s in exchange for a similar freeze on Pershing Is. This feature would demonstrate to the Soviets—and to the West Europeans—that the Reagan Administration was willing to live within any constraints it sought to impose on its adversary. As he said, "a reciprocal approach would foster an appearance of fairness" in the overall U.S. position.

But the main concern back in Washington was to avoid presenting the Soviets with additional opportunities to pursue restrictions on the nuclear forces of America's allies. In addition to the 108 U.S. Pershing I launchers already based in Europe, there were also 72 of the same missiles, without warheads, in the hands of the West Germans. These could, in a crisis, be fitted with American nuclear warheads: the U.S. would give the Germans the warheads and authorize their use.

The Pentagon and the State Department were worried that any American willingness to accept restrictions on the U.S.'s own Pershing Is might create what Richard Burt called a "slippery slope" down which the allies would slide when the Soviets pushed for restrictions on the West German missiles. That same slippery slope might also make it easier for the Soviets to secure eventual restrictions on the British and French nuclear forces. Besides, for reasons of simple geography, no country but the Soviet Union could circumvent limits (or a ban) on long-range missiles in Europe by moving shorter-range missiles farther forward. SS-12s and -22s rolled into Eastern Europe could serve almost as well as long-range SS-20s in hitting allied targets. The American Pershing I, by contrast, was already deployed as far eastward as it could go in West Germany, and even from there it could not reach into the Soviet Union itself.

Burt, Perle, and the others also had a presidential dictum on their side of the argument. Reagan had indicated during the deliberations at the National Security Council on November 12 that he did not want the Pershing I to be affected by whatever scheme was devised for limiting the shorter-range Soviet systems. Thus Nitze, the delegation, and the Arms Control Agency were outgunned. Orders went out from Washington that the draft treaty should be changed from proposing a bilateral freeze to a unilateral one that would hold only Soviet shorter-range missiles at the levels deployed as of the turn of the year.

Far more troublesome in Washington than the treatment of Pershing ballistic missiles was the delegation's proposed wording of the clause banning the other U.S. missile to be sacrificed as part of the zero option, the Tomahawk. A struggle arose over whether the draft treaty should exempt conventionally armed, i.e., non-nuclear, weapons from the draft treaty's prohibition on long-range ground-launched cruise missiles.

Such missiles had existed in the past. Nazi Germany's V-1 buzz bomb was a primitive version. By the 1980s no such thing as a conventionally armed long-range ground-launched cruise missile existed, nor did most military planners predict that such a thing would or should exist in the future. Given the extraordinary sophistication and high cost of developing a long-range cruise missile, the Air Force saw no rationale for arming one with anything other than a nuclear warhead. The Navy was interested in the possibilities of a conventionally armed sea-launched cruise missile, and the Army had studied the feasibility of using ground-launched cruise missiles as chemical-warfare weapons—not exactly "conventional," but certainly non-nuclear. That idea was not at all promising. The West Europeans were sure to raise a protest that would dwarf the controversy over the neutron bomb if the U.S. so much as hinted that it was considering arming its European-based cruise missiles with nerve gas or other toxic agents.

After carefully considering the case, the Joint Chiefs concluded that they would probably never need a conventionally armed ground-launched cruise missile. Their representative to the INF Interagency Group, Admiral Robert Austin, had even brought with him to a meeting at the State Department a document to that effect, signed by General David Jones, with the key sentence underlined for emphasis.

Still, the question arose: should the new treaty, which was to be of indefinite duration, ban conventionally armed long-range ground-launched cruise missiles forever? Or should the treaty be written in such a way as to keep open the possibility of that hypothetical weapon just in case, at some point in the future, the military planners changed their minds?

It came down to a matter of verification. There was not, and probably never would be, any reliable way for an opponent to distinguish with confidence between conventionally armed and nuclear-armed cruise missiles. The two weapons could appear identical on the outside. Two time-honored principles of arms control militated in favor of a blanket ban: one was that agreements should contain only provisions that could be independently verified; the other was that, once a certain type of weapon had been tested with a certain capability, all deployed weapons of that type should count as if they had the capabilities with which some versions had been tested (such as the ability to carry nuclear warheads). If the U.S. dropped this principle and agreed to a provision permitting conventionally armed cruise missiles in the final agreement, the precedent thereby established might come back to haunt the U.S. later. The Soviets might deploy a whole new generation of long-range cruise missiles of their own, proclaiming them conventionally armed and therefore exempt from the ban. The U.S. would have no way of knowing for sure what sort of warheads they actually carried until they were detonated during a war, when the fine points of treaty compliance would hardly matter. Nothing would stop the Soviets from deploying large numbers of genuinely conventional cruise missiles and storing nuclear warheads for them nearby, ready to be mounted on the missiles at short notice during a crisis. That would constitute "breakout." The Soviet Union would not even need to cheat on the treaty in order to exploit a loophole originally intended to benefit the U.S.

The counterargument, pressed by those who felt that the option should be protected anyway, also rested on what they considered a matter of principle: nuclear arms-control agreements should not, willy-nilly, limit conventional weapons.*

Nitze and the INF delegation proposed treaty language banning all long-

---

*This dispute was an example of how, with the coming of new administrations, old dilemmas are discovered as though for the first time, and old battles are refought with fresh passion. During the Ford Administration, and then the Carter Administration as well, the civilian leadership of the Defense Department had struggled hard against the State Department and Arms Control Agency to exempt conventionally armed air-launched cruise missiles from the SALT II limits, even though most uniformed experts in the military regarded the idea of a conventionally armed air-launched cruise missile as a "silver bullet" and a "million-dollar wonder." Carter at first came down on the side of the Pentagon civilians, Harold Brown and Walter Slocombe. The President's advisers persuaded him that Sam Nunn of Georgia and other influential senators who might be decisive in the fight to ratify the treaty shared the Defense Department's point of view. The issue became a major sticking point in the negotiations with the Soviets, and a particularly awkward one for the U.S. negotiators, since Paul Warnke and most of his colleagues did not agree with the position they were instructed to take by their President. Eventually, Carter and his advisers realized that they had exaggerated the importance Nunn and others attached to the issue, and that the Defense Department had overstated its case. So Carter reversed his earlier decision and authorized an American concession on the point, which triggered some important Soviet concessions in return.

range ground-launched cruise missiles, regardless of how they were armed, on the grounds that all such weapons must be presumed to carry nuclear warheads. When the draft made the rounds in Washington, Richard Perle insisted that the blanket ban be rewritten to specify that it would apply only to those that were in fact nuclear-armed. In a series of interagency meetings at the beginning of 1982, he made clear that this was to be a do-or-die issue for him. At first it looked as though he might lose. It was Perle against almost everyone else.

Perle first took his stand at an Interagency Group meeting in early January 1982. Nitze, who was about to return to Geneva, was sitting in. Perle launched into a lengthy exhortation for more care and foresight in order to make sure that the language of the draft treaty did not "come back to make us sorry later on." He cited the ban not just as an example of the potential problem, but as a concrete, important case where the U.S. must protect future options. Nitze, who prided himself as being nothing if not careful and foresighted in these matters, was visibly exasperated.

So was Richard Burt. He tried at first to deflect Perle's complaint by assuring him that the delegation's treaty language did not necessarily preclude conventionally armed cruise missiles. If such weapons could be developed and distinguished from nuclear-armed ones, the option would still be open. That was a question of verification, and on this, as well as numerous other such questions, the Administration had not taken a position and did not yet need to raise the matter with the Soviets.

Perle was not satisfied. Once a restrictive measure was "carved in granite," as he put it, both Soviet negotiators and American arms controllers could be counted on to give that measure the widest possible interpretation. Therefore he was adamant about making it clear from the outset that the new treaty would have no application whatsoever to anything but nuclear-armed cruise missiles. When it was obvious that Perle was not about to yield, Burt said, "Okay, let's take it to the President."

Perle called Burt's bluff and raised the bidding. "Fine," he said, "and let's also take to the President the other issues that are related to this one." He then ticked off a number of subjects on which the Interagency Group had, with some pain, already reached agreement. One was the duration of the treaty. The Interagency Group had already accepted Nitze's recommendation to give the treaty indefinite duration, but Perle now argued that if it contained a ban on conventionally armed long-range cruise missiles then an open-ended treaty no longer was in the national interest, since the day might come when the U.S. would decide it needed the banned missile after all.

This was bureaucratic hardball, the same sort of tactic he had used to pressure the Joint Chiefs of Staff into supporting him on the zero-only option a few months before. The matter of duration was particularly close to Nitze's heart. One of his most persistent criticisms of SALT II was that it had been due to expire in 1985, thus encouraging the Soviets to have a whole new family of weapons ready to deploy in 1986. In his view, treaties with limited durations virtually invited the Soviets to prepare for breakout the minute the treaty expired. Perle had only reluctantly yielded to Nitze on the desirability of indefinite duration. By threatening to rescind that acquiescence now, he made his erstwhile mentor very angry. The tensest moment in this already extraordinarily contentious Interagency Group meeting came near the end, when Nitze, most uncharacteristically, blew up. He accused Perle of "talking rubbish," of raising "phony" problems and of trying to "torpedo" the negotiations.

It was by far the sharpest outburst Nitze had ever permitted himself against Perle in front of other officials, and it showed that the split between the two men was widening. Perle adopted an expression of restrained distaste, shook his head wearily, and waved off Nitze's charges. For the moment, at least, Nitze had gotten the last word. But he knew that Perle was not going to give up.

Nitze and his allies suspected Perle of throwing a monkey wrench into the works in order to slow down, if not halt, the negotiations. Perle retorted that Nitze was the one reopening an issue that had already been satisfactorily settled: neither Perle, nor for that matter the interagency process as a whole, had ever formally agreed to constrain conventional armaments in these negotiations; now here were Nitze and the Arms Control Agency, with the support of the State Department, pulling a fast one.

Before leaving for Geneva, Nitze complained about Perle's "obstructionism" to Rostow, who appealed to the newly installed National Security Adviser, William Clark. Clark saw an opportunity to give the National Security Council staff influence over the interagency process in a way that might not only solve the problem at hand but that would restore some of the power the NSC had lost under Richard Allen. Clark called a meeting "to get this thing settled."

Burt could see perfectly well what Clark was up to: it was, as he remarked to his staff, "shades of Kissinger and Brzezinski—a power grab by the NSC." If Burt could possibly prevent it, he would not let an ad hoc NSC meeting with one of Clark's men in the chair usurp the prerogatives of the Interagency Group (IG), which Burt chaired. So he suggested instead that there should be a "principals-only IG" meeting, a rump session of the more senior officials involved. Ideally, he wanted to get Perle merely to agree that there was a very real problem of verification and that the status of conventionally armed cruise missiles should be postponed. Failing that, he toyed with the idea of giving up indefinite duration of the treaty and falling back to a ten-year term, in exchange for Perle's acceptance of a blanket ban.

The rump IG meeting was held at Perle's office in the Pentagon, already a symbolic concession to him. With Burt coming across the Potomac River to meet him, and also coming around to his side of the argument, Perle was now riding high. His principal opponent, Nitze, was back in Geneva. But the Joint Chiefs were still a problem. They reiterated their earlier belief that conventionally armed long-range ground-launched cruise missiles were not cost-effective and had no conceivable military mission that made them worth protecting from the strictures of arms control. Perle replied that the Chiefs' position was typically shortsighted. All one had to do was remember the case of Billy Mitchell—the Army colonel who risked his career in an effort to persuade the hidebound, backward-looking military establishment of his time that air power could be critical in modern warfare, especially against surface ships. Policymakers, said Perle, should discount the Chiefs' judgment about what weapons the U.S. might need a decade or more in the future. Here was an Assistant Secretary of Defense, a civilian, arguing that the arms controllers must not be allowed to hinder the development of a weapon that the military said it did not now, and never would, need. And he was making that argument in terms that could hardly have been more insulting.

The Chiefs' representative in the meeting, Admiral Austin, took this abuse with laconic stoicism. The incident tended to confirm the suspicion that the Chiefs would not buck Perle. Even some of Austin's military colleagues were disheartened at the ease with which Perle seemed to be riding roughshod over the Chiefs.

The meeting ended without a compromise on how the draft treaty should address cruise missiles and therefore no choice but to go to the full Senior Interagency Group. The SIG was made up of under secretaries, one rung up on the ladder from assistant secretaries like Burt and Perle. SIG meetings were rarely more than sterile rehashes of debates and deadlocks that had already occurred at the working level. This one was no exception.

With the interagency impasse now complete, the dispute would have to go either to the National Security Council or to the President himself. Ronald Reagan had demonstrated little interest in the big issues of arms control or understanding of them, and this was hardly a big issue.

Once again, Clark saw an opportunity to step in. Rather than convening a formal NSC meeting, which would simply replay what had happened in the Senior Interagency Group, he took the document laying out the options that the SIG had considered and turned it into a short memo of the sort Reagan liked. The memo briefly summarized the arguments for and against each option and specified which agencies backed each one.

The very process of producing this summary gave Perle one last chance to lobby directly with the White House. The NSC staff was dominated by people like Sven Kraemer, whose sympathies were with Perle and whose analysis was tilted in favor of Perle's position on this as well as most other issues. This bias was reflected in the NSC paperwork accompanying the options that went to the President. One of Clark's deputies phoned Iklé to clarify a few points regarding the Pentagon's preference; Iklé had Perle join in the conversation on another line, and Perle was able, in effect, to have a direct crack at formulating and sharpening the very language in which the Pentagon option would be presented to the President and to lobby on its behalf.

Not surprisingly, and without much deliberation, the President ticked the box next to the Pentagon position for a ban explicitly limited to "nuclear-armed" cruise missiles; implicitly, conventionally armed cruise missiles were exempt. Burt's reaction, when he got the news, was to slam his fist on his desk and mutter, "Goddamn it!" In Geneva, Nitze's reaction was to purse his lips, shake his head, and say, "Well, it's just one more hole we'll have to dig ourselves out of later on."

Nitze was, however, somewhat relieved that his new instructions, when they arrived from Washington, did preserve flexibility on one point. If Kvitsinsky asked whether the U.S. was really seeking to exempt cruise missiles that were not armed with nuclear warheads from the limitations of the treaty, Nitze was authorized to fend off the question as pertaining to problems of verification, which the negotiations had yet to address. Kvitsinsky did indeed ask. Even while he was flipping through a copy of the draft treaty in a private session with Nitze, he noticed the controversial definition and raised his eyebrows. He challenged the definition again after he and his staff had had a chance to study the draft treaty. Nitze replied by explaining that the qualification of "nuclear-armed" might apply only to a hypothetical future weapon, not to the long-range ground-launched cruise missile of immediate concern, which was the Tomahawk and which the U.S. was proposing to ban as its part of the zero option in exchange for elimination of the SS-20. "The subject matter of our negotiations is agreed to be nuclear systems," said Nitze in his carefully prepared response. "Whether or not it might be necessary to limit conventionally armed systems to support a prohibition on nuclear-armed ones is a matter of verification that would be premature to deal with at this time."

The wrangle over what should have been a minor detail, involving one phrase in the draft treaty, had all but ended lingering doubts in Nitze's mind, and others', that Perle was out to scuttle any chance of an agreement. Significantly, too, in Ronald Reagan's first attempt to play mediator and decisionmaker in INF without benefit of an NSC meeting, he had, in the end, sided with Perle against Nitze.

Word by Word

At the plenary session on February 2, 1982, the U.S. finally presented its draft treaty. In order to impress on the Soviets the seriousness of the proposal and the extent of preparation that had gone into it, Nitze read aloud the entire document. The next day, Leonid Brezhnev made a speech in Moscow offering to accept mutual reductions of "hundreds of units," cutting back by two-thirds all medium-range systems. Brezhnev coupled this latest version of his long-standing moratorium/reduction plan with the accusation that the U.S. was dragging its feet: the Geneva talks so far, he said, had shown "the obvious reluctance of the American side to look for a basis of mutually acceptable agreement."

Nitze protested to Kvitsinsky that Brezhnev's statements were contrary to the spirit of their understanding that the negotiations would proceed in a confidential and businesslike way, without grandstanding. Back in Washington, the White House launched a retaliatory blow, also in public and also from the highest level. Over the objections of the State Department, a statement was released in Reagan's name announcing that the U.S. delegation had, two days before, presented its draft treaty. The White House spokesman, David Gergen, said that the Administration not only "reject[ed] the accusation that the U.S. [was] stalling," but that it rejected Brezhnev's own proposal as well. "The Soviet balance is based on selective use of data and is not a meaningful basis for negotiations," said Gergen.

That same day, February 4, Kvitsinsky finally tabled a document called a "Statement of (or Accord on) Intentions," and on February 9, TASS published a 2,500-word dispatch reviewing it in great detail. Once again, the U.S. decided to strike back. This time it was the State Department's spokesman, Dean Fischer, who pronounced the Soviet position unacceptable. "This is not arms control," he said. The negotiators could only agree: INF was in danger of deteriorating into a Moscow-Washington shouting match.

The starting point of the Soviets' position was still the claim that a balance already existed in Europe and that any new weapons on the NATO side would upset that balance. The substance of their proposal followed directly and logically. The negotiations should produce an agreement that would nail down the Soviet version of the zero option: zero Pershing IIs and Tomahawks. All the secondary provisions—on the moratorium, reductions, et cetera—served to provide layer upon layer of protection for the core, which was the prohibition against new NATO missiles. By the Soviet count, there were just over 250 British and French bombers and missiles. Thus, under the U.S.S.R.'s proposed ceiling of 300 and the accompanying prohibition on new missiles, the U.S. would have to content itself with less than 50 aircraft in Europe.

In discussion, Kvitsinsky made clear just how eager the Soviets were to induce a U.S. pullout from Europe if at all possible and to get "compensation" (that favorite word again) for any and all French and British systems, even if the U.S. was out of the picture altogether. In addition, Kvitsinsky proposed orally that, if the U.S. agreed to take all its medium-range systems out of the territory in question, the Soviets would be willing to go down to whatever level the British and French found themselves: "If the U.S. really wants to go to zero, the U.S.S.R. is prepared to go to zero, too, retaining only what it needs to offset the British and French forces." This theme— that the U.S.S.R. wanted only enough long-range weapons to offset those of Britain and France—would acquire important variations later in the negotiation.

At the same time, there were some hints of flexibility. Long and often frustrating debates over the relative capabilities of aircraft provided additional indications that the Soviets would not let that issue stand in the way of a breakthrough. The Americans picked up fresh hints that the Soviets might be willing to split the difference and drop both the Phantom and the Fencer from the inventory of what should be limited by the new agreement.

For aircraft and missiles alike, the Soviets were using the arbitrary range or "combat radius" as the cutoff, thus eliminating their shorter-range ballistic missiles from the agenda. They rationalized this feature of their proposal on the ground that 1,000 kilometers was approximately the distance between "NATO Europe" and the boundaries of the U.S.S.R.; hence, shorter-range weapons need not be included. The American negotiators made fairly short work of that argument. They pointed out that the distance between Lübeck in the easternmost part of West Germany and Kaliningrad in the westernmost part of Russia was about 600 kilometers, and that two NATO members, Norway and Turkey, actually bordered on the Soviet Union—the "range" between them was zero. The Soviets seemed to realize that sooner or later they would have to give ground where range was concerned.

They also indicated that there might be some room for negotiation over what constituted European territory. In their earlier official statements, they had used the crest of the Ural Mountains as the dividing line. But Kvitsinsky said in a plenary statement that the Soviet Union would undertake to meet the American concern about SS-20s' being redeployed westward in a crisis. The American inference, supported by some further cryptic comments by the Soviets in less formal post-plenary exchanges, was that the U.S.S.R. might accept a "dead zone" between the Urals and Novosibirsk, in which no SS-20s would be deployed. The distances and amount of time involved in redeploying SS-20s westward by rail would assure detection by American satellites and provide the U.S. with time for countermeasures, such as rushing American planes and missiles from the U.S. to Europe.

According to the Soviet draft, the whole agreement would expire on December 30, 1990, which was also the deadline for the reduction to 300 systems per side. But Nitze had inculcated his colleagues, back in Washington as well as in Geneva, with a dedication to the goal of an open-ended agreement; and he and his fellow negotiators were therefore particularly sharp in their questions about the Soviets' proposal for an expiration date that coincided to the day with the deadline by which the two sides were supposed to have achieved the required reductions. The notion of an agreement that self-destructed even as it was consummated pointed directly to what Nitze and others suspected the Soviet Union was really up to: once the U.S. was safely out of Europe, the deal was off. The Soviets displayed some embarrassment on that score themselves. They made little attempt to rationalize that provision, and a number of them said it was "minor—we can work it out."

"It's nice to know," remarked Nitze to his deputy, Maynard Glitman, "that these fellows are not completely without shame."

Nitze returned home in late March to a rude reminder that there was still a strong predisposition in Washington to reject any suggestion that the talks might be getting somewhere. Eugene Rostow, Nitze's staunchest supporter in the Administration, accompanied him to the White House for a mostly ceremonial briefing of the President. Afterward, Nitze spoke to the press, claiming, among other things, that "we have, I think, made great, substantial progress so far in clarifying and dealing with, in a way, [a whole range of] secondary issues. . . . I consider myself a hard-line optimist, so that even though I can realistically see all the differences that remain to be worked out, still I think we are working at it constructively."

Rostow shouldered Nitze aside and contradicted him. The talks, he said, had actually been "disappointing." Then he reminded the press—and, it seemed, Nitze himself—that "Ambassador Nitze has agreed to keep the content of the talks confidential. So that any wider comments should be taken up by officials here." Nitze could barely contain his fury. His jaw was set so tight that blood vessels were pulsing visibly in his face. He had been contradicted and slapped down in public. On their way back to their car, he snapped at Rostow, "Well, you sure pulled the rug out from me in there." He returned to his own office in Foggy Bottom spluttering and threatening to resign. It took him a full day to calm down.

Nitze also found himself at the center of a new dustup over an old issue —the status of aircraft in INF. He wanted his delegation to have formal authority to use precise data about the number, disposition, and capabilities of aircraft on both sides as part of its rebuttal of the Soviet position in Geneva. If he could put forward figures to support his earlier claims about "objective facts," he would be able to ram the Soviets' own arguments down their throats with even more force.

On March 30, he took his request to the White House. The meeting, set up by William Clark, took place in the Situation Room, with Haig, Rostow, and Weinberger's deputy, Frank Carlucci. Clark and Carlucci worried that a more detailed discussion about aircraft might be mistaken by the Soviets as a signal that the Administration was preparing a "fallback" that would trade off limits on aircraft against limits on Soviet missiles. Nitze promised the group that he would disabuse the Soviets of any such inference. The sole purpose of the exercise would be just the opposite of signaling softness in the American position; it would be to expose, and put pressure on, one of the weakest points in the Soviet position.

The group seemed assured. Nitze, after all, enjoyed special status as the government's premier figure in arms control—in terms of expertise, experience, and bipartisan credentials. He was not someone to be trifled with; and he made clear that he regarded the question of whether he was authorized to raise the issue of aircraft not just as a matter of negotiating tactics but as a matter of principle, indeed a vote of confidence.

Nevertheless, Richard Burt decided to object. When Nitze, with the help of the Arms Control Agency's veteran technical expert, James Timbie, drafted his own negotiating instructions and circulated them within the bureaucracy, Burt came up with a competing, much more restrictive draft.

Burt's motives were complex, having to do with personal ambitions and intramural alliances unrelated to the issue at hand. He wanted to establish himself as a vigilant and effective guardian of two interest groups—the Joint Chiefs of Staff and the West Europeans (and the Europeanists in the State Department). He was cultivating the Chiefs because at that point in the spring of 1982 he was trying to enlist them on his side against Perle and the Pentagon civilians over what the opening proposal in the strategic arms talks would be. Burt was cultivating the Europeans and the Europeanists because he was Haig's choice to take over the Bureau of European Affairs now that Lawrence Eagleburger had moved from that job upstairs to replace Walter Stoessel as Under Secretary of State for Political Affairs. Burt wanted to show both these constituencies that he was willing to go to the mat with Nitze to prevent aircraft in general—and French and British aircraft in particular—from winding up on the negotiating table in Geneva.

Nitze complained he was being "treated like a lackey." He said that Haig had "poisonous" people working for him. The contest came to a head at an Interagency Group meeting in early May. Burt was not there. In keeping with a by-now fairly well-established pattern, he left the dirty work to be done by his deputies, and one of them, Robert Dean, was in the chair. Dean informed Nitze that he was under instructions from the Secretary of State to deny him the authorization he sought to give detailed data on aircraft to the Soviets. The encounter had the formal, confrontational flavor of the toughest plenaries Nitze had sat through with Kvitsinsky in Geneva. Yet his adversary in this case was a deputy director of a bureau of the State Department, some thirty-five years younger than he, who was acting on behalf of an even more youthful, absent bureaucrat.

"I'm not going to work in these conditions," said Nitze. The threat of resignation was clear. "If the Secretary of State has a problem with the position I'm taking," he added, "I expect to hear it from him." The next day he appealed to William Clark, who sought to reassure him. "Don't worry," said Clark. "I'll get it straightened out. Anyway, Paul, you're not the only one who has these problems with Haig." Clark was now very much on the White House's side of the running battle with Haig.

In addition to Clark's mediation, additional and unlikely aid came from Richard Perle. Perle had not been at the Interagency Group meeting where Nitze clashed with Dean. But he had stayed close to the problem as it grew increasingly contentious, talking almost daily to his deputy, Ronald Lehman. "You don't give someone like Paul Nitze instructions like that," said Perle. "It's unduly restrictive to tell him he can't make arguments that aren't concessions." Perle backed a set of negotiating instructions that permitted Nitze to use figures on aircraft in response to specific Soviet assertions; he could discuss the range of various aircraft only in approximate terms; if he needed to carry the debate into areas of greater specificity, he was obliged to request authorization from Washington on a case-by-case basis.

It was far from the carte blanche Nitze had been looking for. Nevertheless, the compromise instructions that Nitze was to take back with him to Geneva contained just enough ambiguity, and implied just enough flexibility, to make him give up his threat to resign.

It also enabled him to step up his attack on the logic of the Soviet position. Once he returned to Geneva, Nitze relished skewering the Soviets on their own arguments about aircraft, such as their contention that an INF agreement should treat practically antique British Vulcan bombers as equivalents of SS-20 missiles. Much to Nitze's satisfaction, Kvitsinsky quickly became confused and defensive, then suggested they designate a bilateral group of experts to tackle the problem.

Nitze appointed General William Burns, the Joint Chiefs' man on the delegation, to be the principal American representative in the group. This arrangement could not have suited Nitze better. His enemies in the bureaucracy would have less ground for accusing him of exceeding his instructions; the Chiefs were less likely to worry that their interests were in jeopardy; and the groundwork might be laid for some useful compromises later on. Burns and some of his colleagues at the Pentagon were already beginning to look ahead to the possibility of including within an INF agreement a ceiling on aircraft that would satisfy the Soviets' demand but would be set so high that it would not affect deployments on either side. In other words, a token ceiling. Nitze was thinking about the same sort of thing. Such gimmicks were going to be necessary if the negotiations were to be rescued from stagnation.

Dancing at the Edges

On May 25, the Soviets finally presented their own draft treaty. It was billed a supplement to the flimsier "Statement of (or Accord on) Intentions" that Kvitsinsky had presented to Nitze in early February. There were no big surprises but, once again, a few tantalizing shadings on secondary issues. One was the question of whether the agreement was to expire on a given date. Nitze noted with satisfaction that, contrary to the original Soviet statement, it was now proposed that the reductions take place over five years but that the agreement itself be open-ended.

The Soviets showed movement in another passage, too. European Russia was still designated as the zone of reduction and limitation, the area where the U.S.S.R. would be allowed to keep no more than its allotted 300 medium-range weapons, but Asian SS-20s would have to be outside a newly proposed dead zone, or "non-deployment area," that they had hinted at earlier. This zone would extend into the eastern portions of the U.S.S.R. for a distance equivalent to the Soviet estimate of the range of the SS-20 from the inner German border (between East and West Germany, and therefore between NATO and the Warsaw Pact).

The Soviets were claiming a range of 4,000 kilometers for the SS-20; the U.S. judged it to be closer to 5,000 kilometers. On the basis of the Soviet estimate, the zone of withdrawal would reach to 80 degrees longitude, a meridian east of Omsk and west of Novosibirsk, more than 600 kilometers east of the Urals. If, in subsequent haggling, the Soviets were to inch upward in the range they conceded to the SS-20, closer to the American estimate of 5,000 kilometers, their proposed zone of withdrawal might be stretched far enough east so that the SS-20 squadrons near Novosibirsk would either qualify under the European limit or would have to be moved even farther away from Europe. (The next SS-20 squadrons along the Trans-Siberian Railway were east of Lake Baikal, near the Mongolian border.) This was a potentially important refinement, for it was one more indication that the Soviets might eventually meet the U.S. halfway in its concern about the mobility of the SS-20.*

On another secondary issue—collateral restraints on shorter-range missiles—Nitze and Kvitsinsky went through what Nitze sometimes called a "dance" that he hoped might lead to significant movement later on. The U.S.

---

*Meanwhile, however, the Soviets were rushing to have as many SS-20s in place as possible, even if it meant straining their own publicly declared position. They said their moratorium envisaged "a termination of preparation for the deployment of missiles . . . including an end to the construction of launching positions." Yet they continued work on construction of four SS-20 bases in the European U.S.S.R. and on three additional bases east of the Urals that were within range of NATO Europe.

had proposed a unilateral freeze at then-existing levels of the SS-12s and -22s. Nitze and others in the Administration had wanted the freeze to be bilateral, so that it would apply also to the American Pershing Is already in place in Western Europe, but the majority in the government, with the backing of President Reagan, had ruled against any limits on the Pershing Is, at least in the opening U.S. proposal. The Soviets, for their part, were not including the SS-12s and -22s in their calculations about the nuclear balance or in their offer of a moratorium and reduction, since they had a range of less than 1,000 kilometers and therefore did not qualify as medium-range weapons.

However, in exploratory conversation, Kvitsinsky indicated to Nitze that the Soviets were willing in principle to negotiate a freeze or other limits on missiles in the 500–1,000-kilometer category, as long as American missiles in the same category—i.e., the Pershing Is—were subject to the same limits.

Nitze was careful in his reply. "I've put forward those collateral restraints that we think are necessary to protect us against problems we're concerned about. You're welcome to raise your own concerns."

The implication was that while the American proposal was for a unilateral freeze, the U.S. might, other things being equal, consider making it bilateral in response to a Soviet counterproposal. Thus, Nitze managed to stay within his restrictive negotiating instructions; he managed to justify the one-sidedness of the U.S. position even as he invited Kvitsinsky to correct the problem simply by proposing a more equitable compromise.

As in the earlier round, the British and French, while absent from the negotiating table, were a ghostly presence, forming one of the most difficult obstacles to progress. The Soviet and U.S. diplomats reviewed and refined their arguments for and against "taking account" of allied weapons in INF. At one point, Nitze spent most of a weekend at a chalet in the Alps drafting a detailed, tightly argued case for, as he put it, "clearing away once and for all this nonsense" about inclusion of, and compensation for, British and French systems. He then turned the document over to his advisers, urging them "to tear it limb from limb if necessary" so that it would end up being a sturdier rebuttal to the Soviet position. His staff took him at his word and reworked the talking points unmercifully. It was this kind of rigorous, collective rehearsal for their encounters with the Soviets that kept morale reasonably high among the Americans, despite the absence of much progress. Nitze was pleased with the result and set about using the paper to pummel the Soviets if not into submission then at least into silence. If he could not get Kvitsinsky to agree, at least he could get him to squirm.

Nitze enumerated for Kvitsinsky various "levels of error" in the Soviet claim that British and French systems should be covered by the agreement. One of these was particularly telling. If the Soviet proposal was to become the basis of a new nuclear order in Europe, and the British and French were to keep the approximately 255 weapons they already possessed, the U.S. would be left with a total of 45 medium-range systems at the end of the five-year reduction scheme that Moscow was now suggesting. Those 45 weapons would have to be exclusively aircraft; they could include no missiles capable of hitting the U.S.S.R. And they would be lined up against 250 SS-20s—each with three warheads—and 50 Backfires.

"Is that your idea of equality?" Nitze asked Kvitsinsky rhetorically. "If so," he continued, "then it illustrates an underlying problem. What you're demanding is nuclear forces equal or superior to the aggregate of nuclear forces of all other countries. That amounts to a demand for absolute security for yourselves, which means absolute insecurity for everyone else."

This point seemed to cause Kvitsinsky some unease. He denied that "absolute security" was what the U.S.S.R. was after; the Soviet goal, he said, was "equal security." That phrase was one of the more hallowed shibboleths of Soviet rhetoric in arms control, and it was usually accompanied by another: the need to "take into account geographical and other considerations." The unstated "other" considerations were political, as the Soviets made clear in their refrain: "We're surrounded by enemies, while you're surrounded by oceans and friends." The implication of this premise for European arms control was that the U.S. must pay a price for its advantages by undertaking to keep its weapons on its own side of the Atlantic Ocean and to make sure that its friends, the West European allies, did not rise above a certain level (300) in their own nuclear forces that threatened the U.S.S.R.

As with other issues large and small, Nitze enjoyed turning the Soviet argument on its head. He replied that in fact geography constituted a Soviet advantage against NATO, since the U.S.S.R.'s huge forces were sitting menacingly right there in Europe, while most of the American nuclear deterrent on which Western Europe relied was an ocean away. Better, therefore, for Kvitsinsky not to overdo all this talk about "compensation." If, as he asserted, the U.S.S.R. had 450 medium-range aircraft against 228 for NATO (or 2,500 against 800 if one included shorter-range aircraft as well) Nitze asked, "Why should you get compensation? *We* are the ones who should be compensated!"

Moving to another "level of error," Nitze told Kvitsinsky, "These are bilateral negotiations. Bilateral agreements have never dealt with third parties' forces. Neither side in these talks is authorized to negotiate on behalf of the United Kingdom or France. It would be politically impossible for me to do so. I'm under instructions not to negotiate on their systems. The British and French have made it crystal clear that they don't want to be limited by an agreement arrived at between the U.S. and the Soviet Union. They regard their weapons as an ultimate safety net. You must remember that ours is an alliance of democratic countries." In contrast, he needed hardly to add, to the Warsaw Pact.

Kvitsinsky must have regarded that as a cheap shot, so he took one of his own. "What you're saying, Ambassador Nitze, is that neither the British nor the French can count on you."

"What I'm saying," retorted Nitze, "is that in an alliance of democratic countries the members need fallbacks. They need their own deterrents."

That led Kvitsinsky to scoff at the idea that the British and French were capable of standing up to the mighty Soviet nuclear arsenal with their own, measly forces. Comparing British and French weapons to Soviet ones was, he said, a "sandbox exercise."

Nitze replied that Kvitsinsky's apparent contempt for America's allies made it even less reasonable for the Soviet side to persist in claiming that allied forces ought to count along with America's in a U.S.-Soviet agreement. Besides, it was clearly impossible for the U.S. to negotiate in a way that implied American infringement of the sovereignty of its West European allies. To do so would, as Nitze put it quite simply to Kvitsinsky, "break the alliance."

Kvitsinsky could understand that argument well enough; what he could not admit was that breaking the alliance was precisely what the U.S.S.R. had in mind—although he came very close. "You have no business in Europe!" the Russian blurted out, with some exasperation, in mid-June. Shortly afterward he backed off just far enough to recall that, under the terms of his own government's proposal, "We're prepared to let you have about 45 aircraft." Later in their dialogue, Kvitsinsky seemed to relent further, and to betray some doubt about whether it would necessarily be an unmitigated blessing for the U.S.S.R. if the U.S. were to pack up and go home, leaving Western Europe entirely to its own devices—and (the nightmare that always lurked in the background of Soviet calculations) to the devices of the Germans. Vladimir Pavlichenko went further still: he took a number of Americans aside one by one to reassure them that the Soviet Union wanted the U.S. to stay in Europe "in a constructive way—particularly with regard to your German friends." Thus Moscow's strategy in INF was not without its own contradictions: the Soviets wanted to reduce the American military presence in Europe to an absolute minimum, but they did not want to create a vacuum that any power other than their own might fill.

On the whole, the negotiations were businesslike, with relatively little posturing and gratuitous propagandizing. A lapse occurred in mid-June. Ronald Reagan had just been in Europe delivering vociferously anti-Soviet speeches to British and West German audiences. In an address to the British Parliament, he proclaimed a "crusade" against Soviet Communism. The Kremlin could barely contain its fury and launched a rhetorical counter-attack. Until this exchange of unpleasantries at the highest level, the two delegations in Geneva had done their best to keep their enterprise insulated from the frigid climate of Soviet-American relations. But the Soviet team apparently received instructions to engage in some atmospheric linkage, for at a plenary session on June 15, Kvitsinsky delivered a harsh warning that any agreement other than the one the Soviets were seeking would be "unacceptable." He used the word over and over again, until Nitze bridled and delivered a tart lecture of his own. He pointed out that there was plenty in the Soviet draft treaty that the U.S. could brand "unacceptable."

Fine, said Kvitsinsky, "Why don't you tell us what's unacceptable to you?"

"Because," Nitze replied, "I prefer to talk about objective realities and inequalities. It's not profitable to exchange charges of unacceptability. Besides, I've never believed in the wisdom of burning bridges." Then he added, "And I feel somewhat uncomfortable in the presence of pyromaniacs."

With that, the flare-up ended, and the negotiators got back to business, which was going none too well in its own right. If this had been a college debate or a courtroom trial, Nitze would have been the hands-down winner. But there was only so much he could do with forensic skill. There were signs of bargaining room around the edges of the Soviet position, but not at what Nitze called "the guts" of it: the proposition that the U.S. was not entitled to station so much as one new intermediate-range warhead in Europe.

"There hasn't been any real change in your proposal from the start," Nitze told Kvitsinsky. "You keep dolling it up, but basic things don't change: we wind up with no new missiles on our side plus radical constraints on our dual-capable aircraft, which means both our nuclear deterrent and our conventional forces are disadvantaged, while on your side you end up with large numbers of SS-20s in Europe and no constraints on what you deploy in the Far East."

Nitze felt on somewhat more solid ground when he was debunking the Soviet proposal than when he was defending his own side's. One of his frustrations with the zero option was that while it had all the virtues of being "simple, comprehensible, and expressible in a single sentence," and while it sounded wonderful to talk about "eliminating a whole class of weaponry," it did not lend itself to logical argument with the Soviets. One had to appeal to their self-interest. The requirement that they wipe out the entire SS-20 program simply did not meet that test. The SS-20 was, after all, a pride of the Strategic Rocket Forces. They had sunk billions of rubles into developing it, training its crews, and getting it in place. With its three warheads, its mobility, its solid fuel, and its presumed capacity for a reload missile with every launcher, the SS-20 was the ultimate in cost-effectiveness. Kvitsinsky made clear early in their exchanges that, whatever the details of a final agreement, it could have nothing whatsoever to do with the zero option.

Zero-zero was, he said, "a formula for unilateral disarmament by our side and, frankly, an insult to our intelligence."

Nitze recalled that on the eve of the opening of INF in November 1981 Helmut Schmidt had warned him that there must be progress by the fall of 1982. Subsequent talks in West Germany with Schmidt and leaders of the opposition party, the Christian Democratic Union, made it clear to him that the U.S. position no longer satisfied the West European need for serious negotiations. Nitze felt a breakthrough was required not so much for the sake of arms control, for which he was no great enthusiast, but for the sake of American political and military interests, particularly in NATO. He was not so much concerned about East-West relations as West-West relations.

Moreover, Nitze's continuing wrangles in Washington had already shown him how difficult it was to get any additional flexibility. Judging from the trouble he had had on minor issues such as the negotiability of aircraft, he could see that getting approval for a major change would be almost impossible. Yet a major change was necessary.

6 A Walk in the Woods

For some time Paul Nitze had been discussing very privately with Eugene Rostow and with the senior members of his delegation the need to begin exploring common ground between the Soviet and American positions. It had almost always been the pattern in nuclear-arms-control negotiations for the U.S. to make concrete proposals, whether new ones or fallbacks, and for the Soviets to respond in their own way, first sniffing, then haggling, but sometimes finally agreeing. This was a pattern to which Perle and others had objected, and which they were determined to break. Nitze was, in this respect, a traditionalist. It was part of the nature of the Soviet beast that, to make it move, the U.S. must lead the way.

Nitze's task was all the more delicate because Soviet tactics were beginning to turn nasty. The Soviets in Geneva had been hinting for a long time that they would pull out of the negotiations if the U.S. went ahead with plans to introduce the new missiles into Europe according to schedule in 1983. The KGB's man on the Soviet delegation, Vladimir Pavlichenko, in a conversation with his CIA opposite number, said that once Soviet intelligence picked up evidence that the U.S. was "taking practical steps toward the deployment" of the Tomahawk cruise missiles and Pershing II ballistic missiles in Europe in 1983, the U.S.S.R. would "walk out in indignation," not just from the INF negotiations, but from the strategic arms talks as well; moreover, the U.S.S.R. would take unspecified military "countermeasures." That might mean the deployment of additional weapons of their own, perhaps the new cruise missiles that they were feverishly developing. Pavlichenko's threat was echoed by Yuli Kvitsinsky to Nitze and by other Soviet negotiators to their opposite numbers, though only with regard to INF, not START. Kvitsinsky would not be tied down as to exactly what would constitute "practical steps," although Pavlichenko said it meant "when we first see missiles and launchers or their components arrive where they are going."

The U.S. was planning to deliver its launchers for the Tomahawks to Great Britain by the late spring or early summer of 1983. That would certainly fit the Soviet definition. If the Soviets decided to exempt Britain, then the deadline would be the fall of 1983, when the Pershing IIs were due to arrive in West Germany.*

There was disagreement on the American side over how to interpret the Soviet ultimatum. Some members of the delegation, as well as some of their colleagues back in Washington, sloughed it off as just another typically heavy-handed Soviet pressure tactic. Nitze, however, did not think the threat could be ignored, especially when Kvitsinsky seemed, however obliquely, to give it his own imprimatur. And, if it were taken seriously, it might serve to concentrate the collective mind of the Reagan Administration on the need for a breakthrough in the negotiations.

However, the Soviet tactic made Nitze's task all the more difficult. Ultimatums are, or ought to be, unacceptable in negotiations. Negotiators cannot be expected to conduct themselves with patience and prudence if they are being blackmailed by the other side. The Soviets, of course, could retort that the U.S. was imposing its own ultimatum and engaging in its own act of blackmail by threatening to begin deployment by the end of 1983 unless there was an agreement. The fact remained, however, that for Nitze to be proposing a compromise in INF would be politically risky under any circumstances. Doing so under the shadow of a Soviet threat of a walkout was potentially disastrous. It would smack of capitulation rather than compromise.

Therefore Nitze had to be especially careful in the way he broached the possibility of a new position, both with the Soviets and within his own government. He knew that if he went through channels and formally proposed a compromise within the interagency process the idea would get nowhere. It would encounter the concerted opposition of the Pentagon civilians, led by Richard Perle, and probably other interest groups as well. The European Bureau of the State Department would want to consult with the allies about it. That would virtually guarantee a paralyzing debate. Richard Burt could be expected to oppose it because he believed deployment must precede any kind of deal. The right wing on Capitol Hill would be up in arms over evidence that the Administration was going soft in the negotiations. There would be a huge, futile fight in the government, accompanied, inevitably, by massive and damaging leaks in the press.

Nitze decided he had to do something drastic, and he had to do it on his

---

*As the West German elections of March 1983 approached, the Soviets in Moscow began making a distinction between the United Kingdom and the nations on the continent, particularly the Federal Republic. This was partly in recognition of the special relationship between the U.S. and Britain, and partly in order to apply special pressure on the Germans. The Soviet line became: all NATO deployments are unacceptable, but some are more unacceptable than others, and the West German deployments are most unacceptable of all. Still later, in the summer of 1983, there was at least one informal hint from an experienced Soviet diplomat that the Soviet Union might, under certain circumstances, be able to tolerate a few cruise missiles in Britain. This incident will be recounted later.

own. That a distinguished, disciplined official with decades of experience as a policymaker and negotiator should feel it necessary to embark on such a venture was itself extraordinary. Nitze was motivated by two considerations: first, that failure to reach agreement would be far more costly to the West than to the Soviet Union, since European popular opposition to deployment in the absence of an agreement could traumatize and perhaps paralyze the alliance for years to come; and second, that the Administration he served was too shortsighted to see that danger and too divided to give him formal permission in advance to explore a negotiable compromise. Therefore, he would seek a compromise on his own and then present the Administration with a solution to its political and military problems in INF.

Needed: A Soviet Partner

During Nitze's earlier stint as an arms-control negotiator, when moments of comparable delicacy had arisen during SALT I and SALT II, Henry Kissinger had resorted to his famous back channel direct to the Soviet leadership, through Anatoly Dobrynin or Andrei Gromyko. But now there was no back channel available. Haig and Burt had hoped to open one, but Haig had departed from the government. A long-simmering feud with the White House had come to a boil during the summer, and he had resigned. Haig's successor, George Shultz, had yet to focus on arms control or to establish a close relationship with any Soviet official. Reagan's National Security Adviser, William Clark, was not well enough versed in the substance of arms control to conduct back-channel negotiations even if he had been so inclined. What was more, Nitze had always criticized Kissinger for failing to keep his back-channel negotiations coordinated with those going on in the front channel.

So Nitze decided to initiate a two-channel approach that would guarantee coordination as well as discretion, since he would be the principal negotiator in both channels. His choice of an interlocutor was both obvious and ingenious: Yuli Kvitsinsky. Since Kvitsinsky was his designated opposite number in the formal negotiations, there was nothing inappropriate or suspicious about Nitze's engaging him in exploratory conversations on the side. He would open a back channel within the front channel.

Kvitsinsky's own background included a potentially important precedent. In 1970, as a junior diplomat, he had played a key behind-the-scenes role during the Four Power Talks among the U.S., U.S.S.R., Britain, and France over the status of West Berlin. He had helped advance those negotiations by "reinterpreting" his instructions in informal contacts with his American counterpart, exchanging feelers about concessions that the two sides might make to break a deadlock. That episode suggested that he had both personal initiative and political protectors back in Moscow. Shortly after the INF talks began, Nitze had made a point of flattering Kvitsinsky by remarking that he was held in high esteem by Americans who had dealt with him eleven years before, particularly for "your helpful role in going somewhat beyond your instructions." Kvitsinsky beamed at this praise.

Helmut Schmidt and others had convinced Nitze that, if there was to be a breakthrough in INF, it would probably be because of Leonid Brezhnev's presumed desire to have one last summit before his health failed him. Brezhnev might be personally inclined to press for an agreement to an extent that his successor would not be. Brezhnev's infirmity was growing more apparent with every passing month. Therefore, Nitze decided to lay the groundwork for his approach by asking Kvitsinsky whether the Soviet government was "seriously interested in a well-prepared" summit meeting between Brezhnev and Reagan in the fall of '82.

"Yes," the Soviet negotiator replied emphatically.

Nitze then asked a leading question: "What subject matter is far enough along to serve as the centerpiece for such a meeting?"

Without hesitation, Kvitsinsky answered that only the subject of their negotiations fit that bill.

"If that's so," continued Nitze, "shouldn't we put our heads together and explore ways to contribute to that possibility?"

Kvitsinsky agreed that was the thing to do.

Well before Nitze began to reveal the other bits of bait he had assembled, it was the prospect of a Reagan-Brezhnev summit that lured Kvitsinsky to join Nitze in a bold, risky venture.

Nitze suggested that their conversations might be more productive than usual if they were more private than usual. He illustrated this suggestion by recalling, in some detail, an experience he had had during SALT I, ten years before. The talks had reached a sticking point on some excruciatingly technical questions about anti-ballistic-missile (ABM) defenses, which were to be limited by the SALT I treaty. Nitze's counterpart in those negotiations had been an elderly, highly sophisticated, cosmopolitan scientist named Alexander Shchukin, who clearly had a wider license than other members of the Soviet delegation.

Shchukin and Nitze shared a fondness for classical music. One day Shchukin took the unusual step of inviting Nitze to get together over lunch with their wives and listen to some records he had acquired. Each man told his chief about the encounter in advance. The chairman of the Soviet delegation, Vladimir Semyonov, underscored both the importance and sensitivity of the Shchukin-Nitze get-together by commenting only half-jokingly to the American chairman, Gerard Smith, "All those records they're going to listen to will be off the record." Nothing that transpires between Soviet and American negotiators is ever really off the record. What Semyonov was telling Smith was that Shchukin was authorized to pursue with Nitze possible ways of resolving the quandary one on one, outside the rigid format and often stultifying atmosphere of plenary and post-plenary meetings. Only if the informal brainstorming led to an agreement formally endorsed by the delegations would it become part of the negotiating history. It was in that sense that Shchukin and Nitze were to meet "off the record."

As expected, the six-course lunch went largely untouched, and the records unplayed. With their wives trailing farther and farther behind, Shchukin and Nitze set off for a walk in the woods. "Here we are," said Shchukin, gesturing theatrically at their bucolic surroundings. "No one can hear us." The Soviet scientist then recounted conversations about SALT he had had back in Moscow with Brezhnev, Prime Minister Aleksei Kosygin, and Leonid Smirnov, one of Kosygin's deputies, who was in charge of military procurements. This was not idle name-dropping. Shchukin was providing yet another indication that he had authorization from the highest level to clear away the obstacles standing in the way of an agreement limiting ABMs. "How would we solve this problem if it depended on just the two of us?" Shchukin asked. Some of the answers he and Nitze worked out became part of the basis of the ABM Treaty signed by Nixon and Brezhnev at their 1972 Moscow summit.

However, Shchukin and Nitze had been overruled by Semyonov and Smith on one exceedingly abstruse point. It concerned whether, as Nitze and Shchukin concluded, it was scientifically possible for monitors on one side to distinguish between those ABM systems on the other side intended to defend hardened ICBM sites as opposed to those intended to defend cities. In keeping with the ground rules of the Shchukin-Nitze exchange, the very fact that such a possibility had been considered and rejected was never even hinted at in the negotiating record.

By telling this tale to Kvitsinsky in such detail, Nitze was sending a number of messages at once. He was showing that there was precedent for informal exploration between individual members, for probing that did not necessarily commit their governments. He was also suggesting that such contacts could be a useful, sometimes essential, supplement to the formal negotiating process. It was pertinent to Nitze's purposes that in the earlier episode it had been Shchukin—the Soviet representative—who had initiated the private exchanges. Nitze wanted to coax Kvitsinsky into engaging in private talks under circumstances that would permit each side to claim that the other had initiated the negotiation-within-the-negotiation. That way, neither side could be regarded as having blinked first. Finally, the ending of Nitze's reminiscence about his walk in the woods with Shchukin was meant to assure Kvitsinsky that if their effort failed to produce a breakthrough it would, in effect, remain a non-event. Neither side would have to bear the onus of having tried and failed to break the impasse. Kvitsinsky did not know Shchukin, who was now living in retirement, but his deputy, Nikolai Detinov, was a close friend of Shchukin, so Kvitsinsky would be able to check the accuracy of Nitze's story if he wanted to.

Shortly after this, Nitze had dinner at Kvitsinsky's apartment in the Soviet mission. When the Soviet's wife and daughter left the room to tend to the coffee, Nitze handed Kvitsinsky a piece of paper he had prepared outlining a procedure whereby the two chief negotiators could hash out an exploratory package; then each could present it to his government as a trial balloon that the other had floated. After Kvitsinsky had looked over the paper, Nitze asked him if he had any changes to suggest. Kvitsinsky said he did not.

A few days later, there was some sign that Kvitsinsky was beginning to get cold feet. At a dinner for the two delegations, Kvitsinsky seemed depressed and nervous. He commented rather sourly that Nitze might be prepared to sacrifice his career, "but I'm not. I have my own ambitions."

Later in the evening, Kvitsinsky and Nitze stepped outdoors for some fresh air and privacy. Kvitsinsky had relaxed somewhat, but his attempts at being lighthearted still exposed both barbs and raw nerves. "How confident are you," he asked Nitze, with forced humor, "that everything we're saying isn't being overheard?"

Playing along, Nitze replied, "Pretty confident. But somebody may have put a listening device up there"—and he gestured to a rolled-up awning.

"Right," said Kvitsinsky. "Better to meet in the woods"—as Shchukin and Nitze had done during SALT I.

With the thinnest of smiles, Nitze objected: "But how could either of us be confident that the other didn't have a listening device in the sole of his shoe?"

Kvitsinsky's comeback was prompt, and it was exactly what Nitze wanted to hear. "If that happened," said the Soviet, "each would know that the other was responsible." That, of course, was a major point of the scheme that Nitze was proposing: each side could, if the plan went awry, "blame" the other for it. Kvitsinsky was especially concerned about reserving that option. He all but told Nitze so. "You know," he remarked, "we have two rules in my country. The first is: The boss is always right. And the second rule is that if you come to doubt the first rule, reread the first rule."

Nitze was less concerned about his bosses than Kvitsinsky was, but he did not feel he could, or should, operate entirely on his own. When Eugene Rostow visited Geneva July 11–14, Nitze told him of his intention to engage Kvitsinsky in what he called "exploratory" discussions off to one side of the formal negotiations. Rostow had some coy exchanges of his own with Kvitsinsky. When the two men met, the Soviet negotiator asked, "Well, Mr. Rostow, have you come from Washington with a solution to our problem?"

Rostow went through a pantomime of arching his eyebrows inquiringly and looking up his own sleeve, then said, "In fact, we can solve the problem quite easily. All you have to do is accept two propositions: first, that the world is round, and you can't get anywhere by exporting your surplus intermediate-range ballistic missiles to Asia; and second, as you're so fond of saying yourselves, while all nuclear weapons are equal, some are more equal than others."

Kvitsinsky replied, "Perhaps I could accept those propositions if you accepted one of my own. And that is that all [negotiating] instructions are perfect."

"Certainly they are," said Rostow, beaming his most beneficent smile and drawing out his words as though to give Kvitsinsky extra room to read between the lines, "but I've always had a special regard for ambassadors who have the acuity and foresight to propose changes in their own instructions from time to time." The two men understood each other perfectly.

Needed: A Package Deal

Helmut Schmidt and President François Mitterrand of France had begun publicly to signal their own vague interest in solutions other than zero-zero; they seemed to want the U.S. to agree in principle to start exploring alternative solutions. Nitze was not in the least tempted by that advice. If the U.S. even hinted at concessions, no matter how conditionally, the Soviets would, in one of Nitze's own favorite phrases, "grab the raisins out of the rice pudding and run away with them," accepting the American concessions without agreeing to any of their own. He was interested in a negotiated compromise in which the U.S. might give up its insistence on zero-zero (zero U.S. missiles and zero SS-20s), but only in exchange for Soviet acceptance of an agreement that was virtually complete and that would establish equal limits on both sides. "Otherwise," he told Rostow, "the Soviets will simply sit there and watch our position erode until we end up sliding into acceptance of zero-infinity [zero U.S. missiles and no limits on the SS-20]."

Even as Nitze stayed on the offensive with Kvitsinsky, hammering away at the inequities of the Soviet position, he dangled the possibility that they might, as he once put it, "cut the Gordian knot" with a single, bold stroke. "Now, I take it," he said at one point, "that you don't want to move off of any of the basic elements of your position unless you're sure of getting something in return that is both satisfactory and comprehensive. Otherwise you'd just weaken your trading position. Same with us and our commitment to zero-zero. So what we need to do is to work out something which could be a complete agreement." He would later refer to what he had in mind as a "package deal—all or nothing; you buy what's in it, you buy the whole thing."

For Nitze, one of the most daunting challenges to his powers of argument was the difficulty of convincing Kvitsinsky that, as part of a package deal, it was in the Soviet interest to accept a compromise that left the U.S.S.R. with some SS-20s but far fewer than they had already deployed. The elimination of the SS-20 program was unthinkable; drastic reductions in it were, for the same reason, going to be extremely difficult to achieve. Soviet military procurement had always been guided by the principle that more is better; Nitze had to try to persuade the Soviets that, in the case of the SS-20, as many as they had was too many for their own good, and that less would be better. The line of logic he came up with went like this:

The SS-20 program was an example of the Soviet penchant for too much of a good thing, deployment run amok, a defensively conceived weapon system turned so offensive in the eyes of its Western beholders and potential victims that it becomes counterproductive for the Soviets themselves. There were only a limited number of military targets in Western Europe "worthy of" the SS-20. Throw in the prime civilian targets, or cities, for good measure. Even according to the most massive, murderous scenario imaginable, there were only 300 targets that the Soviets could want to hit. Therefore, with three warheads per missile, only the first 75 to 100 SS-20s had any point at all.

To have SS-20s in excess of 75 to 100 was not only wasteful—it was costly: it provoked a Western military response in the form of Pershing IIs and Tomahawks. Those missiles, with 572 warheads, could cover a "very juicy target set indeed inside the Soviet Union." One Soviet tactic in opposing the new American deployments was to threaten that they would add more SS-20s to match the buildup in NATO. But by Nitze's reasoning the Soviets were already far beyond the point of diminishing returns. Additional SS-20s would not increase the threat to the West anywhere near as much as NATO, starting from scratch with its Pershing IIs and Tomahawks, would be threatening the U.S.S.R. Hence the incentive for the Soviet Union to trade down: fewer SS-20s for a smaller NATO deployment.

Nitze had been working out the shape of a package deal in his own mind over a period of months. On the Western side, there were three choices: a force made up entirely of Pershing IIs, entirely of Tomahawks, or a mixture of the two. There were economic and military arguments against a mixed force containing fewer than 572. That meant choosing one missile or the other.

The Pershing II was the obvious candidate for cancellation. Unlike the Tomahawk, which was to be deployed among five countries, the Pershing II was destined only for West Germany. Its range was sufficient to reach into the western regions of the U.S.S.R., making it extremely provocative to the Soviets and a tempting target for preemption. Yet at the same time it lacked the range to attack hardened Soviet command-and-control centers around

Moscow itself. While it might, for example, be used against main operating bases for Soviet aircraft, other American weapons already available were equally, if not better, suited for that job. The Pershing II was formidable enough to frighten and anger the Soviets; it was formidable enough to make the West Europeans worry about its presence in their midst; but it was not so formidable that it contributed greatly to the ability of the U.S. to wage nuclear war or pose a credible deterrent.

In private conversation with Nitze, Kvitsinsky had made clear that of the two missiles NATO intended to deploy, the Kremlin attached higher priority to stopping the Pershing II. The Soviets remained highly skeptical about its limited range. They found it difficult to believe that the U.S. would develop an intermediate-range ballistic missile for deployment in West Germany that was intended to strike targets in the Soviet Union, but couldn't reach Moscow. Nor could the Soviets be sure that the U.S. would not tinker with it in some way that would extend its range, and perhaps fit it with multiple independently targetable warheads as well. Then it would become a true counter-SS-20.

Nitze did not try very hard to talk Kvitsinsky out of his suspicions and anxieties about the Pershing II. After all, if the U.S. was going to give up the thing, better let the Soviets indulge in their worst-case fears about its value to the U.S. They would be more likely to pay a good price for its cancellation.

At the same time, Yu. V. Lebedev, one of the military men on the delegation, made clear that the Soviets were still very concerned indeed about the Tomahawk, especially in the long run. Cruise missiles were so cheap compared to ballistic missiles and so easy to hide that Soviet military planners had to worry about the day when Western Europe and the seas around it would be awash with them. Such fears gave bargaining leverage to the West. Ground-launched cruise missiles could be precursors to sea-launched ones. It seemed worthwhile to keep that fear alive in the Soviet mind by proceeding with a reduced force of ground-launched cruise missiles as part of an initial INF deal, in hopes that the U.S. and NATO could buy more concessions from the Soviets for additional limitations on cruise missiles, particularly sea-launched, in the future.

The more Nitze learned about the Pershing II, the more convinced he became that the U.S. would be better off sacrificing it as part of an agreement rather than deploying it in the absence of one. In a series of conversations with General William Burns, the Joint Chiefs' representative in Geneva, Nitze put himself through a review course on the strictly military rationale for the Pershing II program. Burns was an Army man, and the Pershing was an Army program, so service bias might have inclined him to want to keep the Pershing program alive. It was not that simple, Burns explained. There were Pershings and then there were Pershings. The old Pershing Ia was now to be replaced by the Pershing II, with its extended range, its maneuverable, extremely accurate warhead, its upgraded electronics, and other features that made it more reliable and easier to maintain. But there was another Pershing that could be deployed in West Germany, too—the Pershing Ib: it would have the range of the Ia but the radar-homing terminal guidance and the other technical improvements of the Pershing II. If under an INF agreement the Pershing II could be banned on the basis of its extended range (1,800 kilometers), the Pershing Ib, with its considerably shorter range—only 800 kilometers—could then be freely substituted for the older, less capable Ia.

Not only would the Ib be permissible under the terms of an agreement Nitze was beginning to work out, it might actually be preferable to the Pershing II from a strictly military point of view. If 108 launchers for Pershing Ia's that could reach 720 kilometers into Eastern Europe were replaced by 108 Pershing IIs that could reach 1,800 kilometers, a whole new target set had to be drawn up to justify the extended range of the new missiles. For every target added beyond the radius of the old missiles, NATO would have to give up a target closer in. Therefore, as Burns and Nitze could see, it made more military sense to replace the Pershing Ias with Ibs, the better to cover the "close-in" target set, and leave U.S. strategic ballistic missiles and deep-penetrating ground-launched cruise missiles to cover the Soviet Union itself.

After his briefings from Burns, Nitze settled on an equation that would allow the Soviets 75 SS-20s in Europe—a two-thirds reduction from their current levels—to be matched by 75 Tomahawk launchers, each with four cruise missiles. Thus, there would be 300 Tomahawk missiles to offset the 225 SS-20 warheads on the Soviet side in Europe (since each SS-20 had three warheads). If the Soviets were to have a monopoly in long-range ballistic missiles within that region, the U.S. would have an offsetting monopoly of long-range cruise missiles. There would also be a numerical advantage in American cruise missiles, to make up for the faster flight time of Soviet ballistic missiles and for the fact that cruise missiles, unlike SS-20s, would be vulnerable to air defenses. At the same time, the Soviets' monopoly in ballistic missiles would allow them to claim, to themselves at least, that they had achieved their cherished "compensation" for the ballistic missiles in the British and French arsenals. The U.S., Britain, and France, of course, would not need to accept that claim. The beauty of the deal was that each side would be able to assert that it had preserved its quite different principles and vindicated its quite different perceptions of equality.

Cruise missiles were already a chronic headache for arms controllers because of the difficulty in monitoring their numbers and verifying compliance with restrictions on them. The problems would be just that much worse when the Soviets had them. It would be a major accomplishment if an INF agreement could prevent this. Nitze envisioned an additional provision whereby the Soviets would not be allowed to develop any ground-launched cruise missiles with ranges greater than 600 kilometers.

The SS-20's mobility presented a problem that Nitze knew he must also somehow deal with in his scheme. What would prevent the Soviets from loading their SS-20 launchers in the Far East aboard the Trans-Siberian Railway and hauling them to within firing range of Europe in case of a crisis? The U.S. could, of course, reserve "offset rights," declaring its prerogative to fly extra Tomahawk launchers from the U.S. to Europe as a counter to any SS-20 launchers that the Soviets might redeploy from the Far East. But beyond that Nitze hoped to reduce, or at least to freeze, the number of SS-20s outside the European U.S.S.R.

Nitze also envisioned a compromise on aircraft, one based on the discussions that had already taken place, causing such dissension back in Washington. Each side would be allowed a total in Europe of 225 medium-range nuclear systems, meaning missile launchers plus bombers. For the Soviets, Europe would be defined to include the eastern slopes of the Urals, where there were some SS-20s. After allowing for 75 missile launchers (75 SS-20s with three warheads each against 75 Tomahawk launchers with four cruise missiles each), this would leave an aircraft ceiling of 150 for each side. For the Soviets, this would cover Backfires, Badgers, and Blinders; for the U.S., F-111s and FB-111s. The purpose of this feature was to sweeten the pot for the Soviets so that they would be more likely to accept the severe reduction of SS-20s. The ceiling of 150 was so high that it would not require the U.S. to withdraw more than a few bombers from Europe, and it was narrowly enough defined so that it did not apply to carrier-based and shorter-range American aircraft that the Soviets had been including in their own rigged counts. It was, in short, the sort of token ceiling that Nitze and General Burns had been thinking about as a way to satisfy both the Soviets and the Joint Chiefs of Staff.

The Walk Down the Mountain

The two negotiators had scores of private conversations before Nitze set forth the package deal as a whole. They took walks together in the Botanical Gardens across the street from the U.S. mission; they dined and lunched together in their apartments and at restaurants; twice they cruised along the shore of Lake Geneva aboard a tourist boat. But the climactic session occurred on the afternoon of July 16, 1982, in a setting that assured far greater privacy. Nitze's driver took him to the Soviet mission, where he got into Kvitsinsky's car for a trip to a pass in the Swiss Jura Mountains outside Saint-Cergue near the French border. Soviet diplomats often went there to ski cross-country. Nitze wanted to walk up the mountain; but Kvitsinsky, who was not in as good physical shape despite being thirty years younger, preferred to walk down, so his car carried them close to the summit and went back to wait for them at the bottom.

Except for confiding in Rostow, Nitze had been operating completely on his own. That was not true of Kvitsinsky. No Soviet diplomat who valued his hide, not to mention his career, could act with that kind of independence. Kvitsinsky told Nitze he had consulted with Andrei Gromyko, who authorized him to keep the private discussions going up to that point. Gromyko had also instructed Kvitsinsky to make clear that one thing on which the Soviet Union would not compromise was its insistence on compensation for the British and French nuclear forces.

"Well," said Nitze, "then we're back to square one. There's no point in talking further. There's no way I could sell, or would want to sell, such an agreement to my own government."

Kvitsinsky sloughed that off in a way suggesting that, in fact, there was some point in talking further. "Certain things are absolutely required for an agreement," he said.

"What things?" asked Nitze, interested to see if limits on the British and French weapons would head the list, or even appear on the list, after the tough notice Kvitsinsky had just issued.

Kvitsinsky answered that the Soviet Union could not accept the American zero proposal as it stood. Nitze, of course, knew that. That was the whole purpose of the talk they were having. But, rather than stating the obvious and thus implicitly accepting the role of the first party to yield, he decided to respond in kind. "Well," he said, "certain things are required from our standpoint, too. We can't accept any limitation on dual-capable aircraft which would constrain their ability to contribute to the conventional defense of NATO. And it's profitless to talk about limiting sea-based systems." This latter referred to the attack bombers based aboard aircraft carriers. "Also," he continued, echoing what Rostow had impressed upon Kvitsinsky shortly before, "you can't export the nuclear problems of Europe to the Far East." He then went on to urge that "within these parameters," the two sides should "explore a deal."

Once they got down to business, Nitze and Kvitsinsky were sitting on a log. It was starting to rain. Nitze had brought along a typed outline of an agreement, from which he began to read aloud. Kvitsinsky listened for a while, then suggested some modifications. Incorporating these changes would make it a joint paper. Nitze asked Kvitsinsky if he realized that. "Yes," replied the Soviet. "Let's go through the rest of it." Anticipating and hoping for just such a development, Nitze had brought along paper and a pencil so that Kvitsinsky could make a copy of the document to take home with him. Huddled over their work, sheltering their papers against the drizzle, they set about tinkering with the language so that they could exchange identical versions of the package. After amending the paper, Nitze came back to the preface that would protect both the authors and their home offices. He wanted to make sure Kvitsinsky had gotten it right: "a joint exploratory package for the consideration of both governments." It was, as Nitze emphasized, not an offer or a proposal by either government.

If that disclaimer had ever given way to formal endorsement by Washington and Moscow, it would have been a very good deal indeed for the U.S. The Soviet Union would have finally sanctioned the introduction of new U.S. weapons in Western Europe. In doing so, Moscow would have tacitly conceded that its SS-20 buildup had created an imbalance and that the West was entitled to redress it. The Soviets would have also set aside their claim to compensation for the British and French nuclear forces. A freeze on Asian SS-20s would have enabled the U.S. to assure China, Japan, and South Korea that European arms control was not being conducted at their expense. The U.S. would have ended up with more warheads on its cruise missiles than the Soviets had on their SS-20s in Europe, and the U.S.S.R. would have dropped any plans for long-range ground-launched cruise missiles of its own—a verifiable ban on a potentially unverifiable addition to the Soviet arsenal. All this would have been in exchange for one major American concession: the sacrifice of the Pershing II.

Nitze was adamant about the word "package" in the preface, since it carried the connotation of a deal that would be acceptable only as a whole, not in whatever isolated parts the Politburo and the Reagan Administration might find to their liking.

By Nitze's own estimation, the contents of the final product were 80 percent his own and 20 percent Kvitsinsky's. The deal was not, as some Soviets and American critics of Nitze would later claim, simply a matter of Kvitsinsky's rubber-stamping, or passing along to Moscow noncommittally, what Nitze had cooked up. Kvitsinsky participated actively with additions, amendments, and objections—and there remained in the package nothing to which he objected. For example, Nitze proposed a reduction in SS-20s in the Far East from 90 to 75 (a level equal to the proposed European ceiling). Kvitsinsky said there was no way he could get his home office to approve such a thing; reductions in Europe would be hard enough. So Nitze settled for a freeze on Asian SS-20s at 90, roughly the number then in place.

Throughout, Kvitsinsky's half of the dialogue made clear beyond any doubt that the principal Soviet interest in the deal was stopping the Pershing II program.

The written incarnation of their exchanges now existed in both a Soviet and an American version, symbolizing that responsibility was shared. But it still carried with it that prefatory disclaimer. The document was, in diplomatic parlance, a "non-paper," in that it could be disavowed. In trying to allay Kvitsinsky's obvious nervousness about what they were doing, Nitze reminded him, "You can blame this on me with your people." Kvitsinsky understood. "I'll tell them it's your scheme, and you tell them it's mine," he said.

"Maybe we'll both go to jail," joked Nitze.

"No American government would send Paul Nitze to jail," Kvitsinsky replied. "And I have no intention of going to jail myself."

At the end of their conversation, Kvitsinsky said the next step was for him to sound out the Soviet government. He asked where Nitze would be on his return to the U.S. so that he could get in touch with him. Kvitsinsky had a friend in the Soviet embassy in Washington, Oleg Sokolov, one of Ambassador Dobrynin's deputies; Sokolov could serve as an intermediary and would let Nitze know if there was any interest back in Moscow. Kvitsinsky was saying, in effect, "Don't call us; we'll call you." He asked Nitze to wait for a Soviet response before broaching the plan with the American government. Nitze let that pass. He had at least as much explaining to do in Washington when he got home as Kvitsinsky did in Moscow—more, in fact, since Kvitsinsky had already been in consultation with Gromyko. Nitze said he would soon be going to his vacation home in Maine. The Soviet embassy in Washington would know how to reach him. Kvitsinsky was imprecise about when he would be able to get a reply from the Kremlin; August vacations might slow down the workings of the Soviet government. But he left Nitze with the distinct hope that on this issue there might be a response quickly, perhaps in a matter of weeks. Kvitsinsky warned, however, that the package might well be "rejected altogether or severely amended" in Moscow. Nitze replied that if it was amended it would no longer be a package; besides, he added, he did not know what the response would be from Washington.

Nitze made two memoranda of the conversation. One recounted what he called the "broad externals." The reasoning behind the initiative, the way he had approached Kvitsinsky, the Shchukin precedent, the preliminary conversations both in Geneva and on the mountainside—all this Nitze explained to his own delegation and sent back to Washington. Those who read the memorandum knew that Nitze had engaged Kvitsinsky in an active search for a way out of the impasse in INF. They did not know, however, how far Nitze had gone, or how specific he had gotten, in defining the terms of a possible breakthrough. That was in his second memorandum, in which he recorded everything that he had put in the first, plus what he and Kvitsinsky had committed to paper. The numbers and the other specifics of the deal remained one of the best-kept secrets of the Administration for many months to come.

Nitze told a few of his colleagues in Geneva that there was a second memorandum but that he was not free to reveal its contents. They knew this meant that their boss had begun to explore around, and probably beyond, the edges of the formal negotiations. For the most part they were supportive. Nitze telephoned Rostow on a secure line and told him he had met with Kvitsinsky and would report in detail on his return to Washington a little more than a week later.

Negotiations in Washington

Rostow went to the new Secretary of State, George Shultz, and told him that Nitze had established the basis for what could be a breakthrough in Geneva. Shultz was, as he would be all that summer, deeply involved in a search of his own for a solution to another stalemate: in the Middle East. He was spending much of his time coping with the Israeli occupation of Lebanon and its ramifications for American policy. Shultz had Rostow report in more detail to Eagleburger. The top men in the State Department were learning, very much after the fact, that Nitze had made a major departure from the official U.S. negotiating position without the knowledge, never mind the acquiescence, of anyone in the department. For that violation of territorial prerogatives alone, Alexander Haig would probably have gone into a table-thumping, door-slamming fury. Shultz's reaction, however, was one of mild annoyance, tempered by an appreciation for Nitze's dilemma, respect for his experience and skills, and instinctive sympathy for what he was trying to accomplish. Still, even after Rostow's report, Shultz and Eagleburger had only a general idea of what Nitze and Kvitsinsky had worked out.

Shortly after his return home, Nitze reported to the INF Interagency Group, but he did not go much beyond the memorandum he had already circulated on the "broad externals" of his conversations with Kvitsinsky. In a private call on Richard Perle, Nitze mentioned that his exploration had reached the point where Kvitsinsky had worried out loud about the venture's jeopardizing his career, but he did not reveal that he had actually floated a concrete proposal. Instead, Nitze talked in the future tense about how it might become necessary for both sides to move off their opening positions.

Nitze was somewhat more candid with Richard Burt. There was not much love lost between the two men, but Nitze was counting on the State Department to back him up. In giving Burt the outlines of what he had been up to in Geneva, "just informally and ever so privately," Nitze also tried flattering him: "You're the only fellow in the government who understands these issues, Rick. And for God's sake, keep it under your hat."

Burt was cautious in his comments but obviously skeptical. "Watch your step as you proceed with this thing," he warned. He conceded that there were some "technically interesting and attractive" aspects to the plan, but it was politically flawed in that "it won't be perceived as moving the negotiations forward." Burt feared that introducing aircraft would be viewed in Europe as a new complication. If the West Europeans worried about a delay in an agreement, they were more likely to call for a delay in deployment. Insofar as Nitze's plan made the American position in INF more complicated, it became "less promising in terms of putting the U.S. on high enough ground to keep deployment on track." His first concern, as always, was with deployment.

Burt had another concern, too. West Germany was not due to get its Tomahawks until the end of 1986. Only the Pershing IIs were scheduled to arrive there at the end of 1983, and if the Pershing IIs were scuttled, then the Germans would get nothing. "If we let the Germans off the hook," remarked Burt, "we can wave goodbye to everyone else as they run for cover." He had in mind the British and Italians, who were scheduled to accept their allotment of Tomahawks by the end of 1983. This issue, which was to be brandished as one of the critical objections to the Nitze-Kvitsinsky scheme, was in fact not as compelling as it might have seemed: the timetable for Germany's own Tomahawks could have been advanced to coincide with the others so that the Federal Republic would be accepting new American weapons about the same time as Britain and Italy.

Nitze cared far less about Richard Burt's reaction than about Ronald Reagan's. Nitze and James Timbie, the Arms Control Agency's principal expert, laid out the plan for presentation to the White House. The document stressed that an agreement based on the compromise would transform the debate in Europe, defusing political opposition to deployment, and that a two-thirds reduction in SS-20s would be of major military benefit to the West as well. This paper was attached to Nitze's memorandum of his exchange with Kvitsinsky on the mountainside. Then he and Rostow took the plan to Clark.

After hearing Rostow and Nitze out, Clark told them not to discuss the plan with anyone else in the government, including Secretary of State Shultz. Clark felt it was important for the President to learn what was going on first. He was confident that the President would want the idea to be aired among the principal members of the National Security Council, and Shultz would be brought in then, but for the moment at least Clark instructed Rostow and Nitze to "stand down" and not to tell anyone. This was a bit awkward for Rostow, who had already briefed Shultz and Eagleburger, and for Nitze as well, since he was due to have lunch with Shultz the next day. Had Shultz come alone to the lunch, Nitze was prepared to talk frankly with him anyway; but the secretary was accompanied by aides. Nitze simply explained that he had been directed by the White House not to discuss his plan in detail until Clark had a chance to check it with the President.

Clark, meanwhile, was consulting with his deputy and eventual successor,

Robert McFarlane, who in turn brought in General Richard Boverie of the NSC staff. They regarded it as a favorable development that the Soviets now seemed to be signaling a willingness to consider concessions. But they were upset with Nitze for having made what McFarlane called a "private, unauthorized" departure from Administration policy. McFarlane and Clark were old-fashioned when it came to respecting lines of authority and abiding by rules. McFarlane was a former Marine and particularly devoted to discipline and an orderly chain of command.

In addition to what he saw as Nitze's breach of discipline, McFarlane also had doubts about the wisdom of giving up the quest for global ceilings, and he questioned whether a trade-off that left the U.S. with no ballistic missiles to counter the remaining Soviet SS-20s was in the American military interest. Briefing Reagan, he spelled out that concern, virtually assuring that Nitze's plan would encounter presidential resistance on its key feature—the cancellation of the Pershing II.

Here was an example of Reagan's decisionmaking in arms control. He relied heavily on the guidance of his aides, especially if the issue at hand entailed matters of military technology and strategy. After sitting through some tedious, sometimes befuddling debates over INF and START, the President had developed a few simple principles for himself. One was that cruise missiles were "good" because they were, by their nature, confined to retaliatory, second-strike missions; ballistic missiles were "bad" because they were capable of preemptive, aggressive, first-strike missions.* Yet here was Nitze proposing that the U.S. let the Soviets keep a reduced force of ballistic missiles in Europe, which the U.S. would counter with a force made up entirely of cruise missiles, canceling its Pershing II ballistic-missile program altogether. In the phrases that Reagan contributed to the terminology of arms control, the U.S. would be relying on "slow-flyers" to meet the challenge of Soviet "fast-flyers." So this feature of Nitze's package had McFarlane and Reagan against it from the start, and it was that feature alone on which Reagan focused.

In early August, Clark convened a special, secret session of the National Security Council, with Shultz, Rostow, Weinberger, Director of Central Intelligence William Casey, and General John Vessey, the new chairman of the Joint Chiefs (David Jones had retired)—everyone but the President and the Vice-President. Each of the principals was allowed to bring one deputy.

---

*Soviet spokesmen did not agree that cruise missiles were necessarily more benign than ballistic missiles. Typical was the comment in 1982 of Aleksei Arbatov, a specialist on nuclear weapons at the Institute of World Economy and International Relations: "So what if the [Tomahawk ground-launched cruise missile] takes some hours to reach its target. If we are the target, and we don't know it's coming until it explodes—which is the whole point of its deceptive means of approach, after all—then we have zero warning. In our judgments about what constitutes a first-strike threat, we care about warning time, not flight time."

The paper circulated in advance of the meeting stressed the extraordinary sensitivity of the subject, and Clark, in his capacity as chairman, issued an explicit injunction to those present that they were not to breathe a word of the plan to anyone else. Weinberger registered an oblique but unmistakable objection: eventually, he explained, he and others would require technical help from their staffs. Without saying so, he was thereby putting the group on notice that Clark's gag rule would not extend to Richard Perle, who was absent from the room but who would no doubt be most interested in what was going on there.

Perle was out of town. At the end of July, he had left for Colorado to attend the annual symposium on arms control sponsored by the Aspen Institute for Humanistic Studies in Aspen, Colorado. Also absent was Richard Burt, who was no longer in charge of the Politico-Military Bureau; his nomination to be head of the European Bureau was running into serious trouble from conservative senators. Part of Burt's problem with the right wing was that by their standards he was an arms controller. He had become a lightning rod for suspicion elsewhere in the government against the State Department as the soft spot in the Administration's hard-line foreign policy. Shultz himself was concerned about being criticized for relying on Burt too heavily. He also wanted to reduce Burt's exposure at meetings on the subject of arms control. Thus, both Perle and Burt, the two assistant cabinet secretaries who had been most intensely and contentiously involved in INF policymaking from the beginning, were, for the moment at least, cut out of the play. In both cases, their places were taken by colleagues with their own views toward Nitze's plan. Instead of Perle, Iklé was at the meeting; Burt's stand-in was Admiral Jonathan Howe, the new director of the Politico-Military Bureau.

Howe did not share many of Burt's objections to the plan. Shultz himself was not so much interested in the technical fine points of the package deal as in the very fact that Kvitsinsky had gone along with it. That, to Shultz, suggested that the Soviets were serious about reaching a compromise. It reminded him of his experiences years earlier as a consultant advising industry in disputes between labor and management: whenever one side allowed itself to be drawn into private, informal discussion of ways out of an impasse, it was usually a sign that a breakthrough was possible.

Iklé, too, was cautiously supportive of Nitze. Knowing that the Pentagon civilians would be by far the hardest group to persuade, Nitze had made a point of briefing Iklé in advance of the meeting. Iklé's initial reaction was that the package deal was "very cleverly put together," and that it showed, in his words, "a lot of intellectual savvy." He particularly admired the way the scheme not only compensated the U.S. for the Soviet SS-20s' being triply MIRVed, but actually would have left the U.S. with more Tomahawk missiles in its 75 launchers than the Soviets would have warheads on their

75 launchers. As he told Nitze, "I'll say this much, Paul: you've certainly met the MIRV problem and licked it."

Iklé's main misgiving concerned timing rather than substance. He did not share Nitze's sense of urgency. But he was leaning in the direction of favorable consideration, and he tilted his boss, Weinberger, that way just before the meeting.

Weinberger had become wedded to the idea that land-based ballistic missiles were a critical necessity in correcting what he saw as America's across-the-board inferiority. He was devoted to the new MX intercontinental missile as the centerpiece of the U.S. program of "strategic modernization." He was also reluctant to see the U.S. forgo the Pershing II in its NATO buildup. Iklé agreed with Weinberger that giving up the Pershing II program would be a very big price indeed to pay for arms control, but he gently, cautiously pushed the idea that it would not be prohibitively expensive if it was part of the package deal that Nitze had in mind. There were, he said, "some very significant benefits here for us in terms of what the Soviets would have to give up"—that is, a large part of their European SS-20 force, their right to deploy as many SS-20s as they might otherwise wish in Asia, and long-range cruise missiles. Also, the Soviets would finally be sanctioning the deployment of a new generation of long-range American missiles in Europe. For the moment at least, Weinberger was willing to keep his mind open. When the group gathered, Weinberger—to the great relief of Nitze and Rostow—said the proposal sounded interesting and deserved close, serious study.

The Joint Chiefs of Staff as a group had yet to be brought in on the deliberations. Neither formally nor informally had they considered Nitze's proposal among themselves. From his own conversations with Nitze in Geneva, particularly on the question of whether NATO might be militarily better served by the Pershing Ib than the Pershing II, General Burns was able to guess what Nitze had proposed to Kvitsinsky—and what Nitze would now propose to the Administration. While he, like McFarlane and Boverie, had misgivings about how far Nitze had gone without authority, Burns felt that recriminations over procedure should not get in the way of consideration of the plan on its merits. And its merits, in his view, were considerable.

That was also the view of Burns's boss, General Vessey. As an Army man, he had reason not to want to see the Army's Pershing program scrapped. But he bought the military argument in favor of the Pershing Ib over the II. At the same time, however, he was not ready to commit himself to an endorsement of the package deal. With Burns at his side, he went to the rump NSC meeting expecting a general, inconclusive, and highly confidential airing of the idea. He made a number of cautiously favorable comments without any expectation that they would echo elsewhere in the government or that he would be held to them later on in the process. This was naïve on his part, as he later admitted.

The inner circle agreed to set up a high-level working panel to explore the proposal further. Nicknamed "the mini-group," it was chaired by McFarlane and included the deputies who had attended the meeting, plus Timbie, who would represent Rostow and Nitze. This group drafted a paper assessing the initiative in fairly neutral terms. It noted, but did not dwell on, the disadvantage of canceling the Pershing II program. The only recommendation was that the plan be subjected to further analysis and that the President authorize Nitze to continue his private discussions with Kvitsinsky about a package of the general shape that Nitze had already suggested.

Exceptional secrecy was still very much in effect. No one except the designated deputies—one per agency—was supposed to know of the existence of the package deal. Jonathan Howe told no one on his staff what was going on and wrote out memos to Shultz on the subject by hand rather than let his secretary type them. Burns took similar precautions; he typed out his own messages to Vessey.

Perle Strikes Back

In the civilian corridors of the Pentagon, however, as Weinberger had warned it would, the circle of those privy to the secret quickly grew. Fred Iklé notified McFarlane that he needed help in preparing paperwork for the inner circle, then enlisted the services of Ronald Lehman and William Hoehn, both from Perle's staff.

Perle himself was still in Aspen. Hoehn almost immediately set about trying to reach Perle by phone to tell him what was going on. The message finally caught up with Perle while he was on his way to a concert with his wife, and he called Hoehn from a pay phone. Because of the sensitivity of the subject and the lack of secure communications, Hoehn gave his boss only a cryptic account of what was happening, but Perle got an idea of what Nitze was up to. He was very upset. He instructed Hoehn to have the Office of the Secretary of Defense adopt its familiar tactic: "Tell the White House we've got to resist any stampede toward a decision. There's got to be a much more careful review than would be possible before Nitze goes back to Geneva."

As he brooded on the conversation, Perle began to assemble in his mind a lengthy bill of particulars against the Nitze plan. By the time he returned to the Pentagon on August 12, he had honed his arguments further as he learned more about the details and background of the Nitze initiative. He felt Nitze had been deceptive, even dishonest, with his colleagues on the delegation and in the government, and had now put the U.S. in danger of being dishonest with the West Europeans as well. The front-channel zero-option proposal—which Perle still believed was by far the best—would have become a sham, a subterfuge, a cover for the real proposal that was being passed back and forth on scraps of paper in the woods. "This," he said to a colleague, "is a totally outrageous way of doing business." Perle had not previously been known to be so reverential about the sanctity of openness among colleagues in the government or of close consultations among the allies. He was in fact angry at what Nitze had done, not so much the way he had done it.

A key argument that Nitze was making in favor of his plan was that he had managed the approach to Kvitsinsky so that either side could disavow it and that neither could use it to increase its leverage on the other. Perle simply did not find that claim credible. It was a time-honored Soviet tactic to accept what they liked in a comprehensive American proposal and reject, or quibble over, what they did not like. Conversely, it was, in his view, a proven American weakness to give in to that tactic.

Once the U.S. endorsed the proposition that NATO could live without the Pershing IIs under one set of circumstances, it would be that much harder for the West German government to get the weapon deployed under another set of circumstances. A signal would have been broadcast that the Pershing II was expendable. Perle was quite sure that sooner or later the Soviets would mischievously leak the Nitze initiative. Once that happened, he could just imagine West German politicians saying, "See! The Americans were willing to eliminate the Pershing II. Why should we go ahead with it on our own?"

Perle said he could also imagine Helmut Schmidt howling in protest that the fickle and perfidious Americans had pulled the rug out from under him again, just as Jimmy Carter had done in the neutron-bomb affair. "Schmidt has been stalwart in fighting for the Pershing II against his own left wing," said Perle on a number of occasions. "We can't leave him high and dry, and at the mercy of his opponents, by reneging on our own commitment to deploy it." (Perle's role as defender of Helmut Schmidt's political interests was, to say the least, a new one.)*

He also objected to Nitze's willingness to abandon the quest for global ceilings. A freeze was a "copout," sure to cause trouble with America's Asian and European allies alike. In short, Richard Perle had nothing good to say about Nitze's initiative. The whole thing, he said, was "an act of intellectual and political cowardice."

---

*When Schmidt learned about the aftermath of the walk in the woods, he was indignant. He regarded the deal as sound on its merits and the arguments used against it in Washington as spurious. The notion that the Pershing II must serve as a test of West German fidelity to the alliance was downright insulting to him, especially since the Federal Republic had also agreed to accept cruise missiles and could have done so on an accelerated schedule under the terms of the Nitze initiative.

A Reprimand from the White House

Clark, McFarlane, and Boverie had continued to brood over the way Nitze had, as McFarlane put it, "wandered off the reservation," and the more they thought about it, the more convinced they were that they could not let it pass without "restoring discipline to the process." A slap on the wrist was in order. Clark sent Shultz a memorandum in the President's name on August 24. It was brief and contained no fire and brimstone. It did not even refer to Rostow and Nitze by name, merely to "senior officials" of the Arms Control Agency. It said that the President had become aware of arms-control initiatives that had been taken without prior consultations and without the full participation of the interagency system.

The memo also addressed—again, obliquely—an issue that had been sputtering between the State Department and the Arms Control Agency since the beginning of the Administration. Rostow had insisted that he had principal responsibility for arms control, and that he and his deputies should therefore chair the various interagency committees. As Clark understood him, Rostow also claimed the right of direct access to the President, bypassing not just the Secretary of State but Clark as well. Clark's memo pointedly noted that, since the secretary was the senior cabinet official charged by law with the direction of U.S. arms-control policy, the White House expected Shultz to monitor the activities of his colleagues in the Arms Control Agency more carefully, and run their initiatives through the system. Despite the low-key, elliptical quality of the memo itself, there was no question that Clark, in the name of Reagan, was reprimanding Rostow and Nitze for exceeding their instructions.

Rostow and Nitze were unchastened. They both regarded themselves as senior statesmen in an Administration overpopulated by pygmies in high places. On September 10, in a speech in Los Angeles, Rostow hinted that a compromise was possible and might even be in the works, noting, "It is clear that a potentiality exists for accommodating the analytic concepts used by both sides." The phrasing of this sentence was so excruciatingly crafted that a number of those who read the text of the speech back in Washington knew it could only mean that Rostow and Nitze were up to something. But the secrecy within the government held. More and more people outside the original inner circle were aware that Nitze and Shultz were seeking authorization to explore some sort of compromise, but the nature of it remained closely guarded. Nor, as Perle had expected they would, did the Soviets leak it. They were maintaining total silence. Nitze had hoped he might have heard from Kvitsinsky by now, but the Soviet end of the line had gone dead.

Meanwhile, the initiative was encountering skepticism that was less focused, sweeping, and expert than Perle's, but potentially more damaging.

The working group produced a rather bland assessment, approved by all the top-level principals, including Weinberger and Vessey. McFarlane gave the plan to Reagan, who took it off with him to Camp David for the weekend. The following Monday, Reagan handed it back to McFarlane with a question addressed directly and explicitly to the Chiefs. It was the question McFarlane himself had planted in the President's mind, and it concerned the fate of the Pershing II. Was it really equitable—and was it militarily prudent—to counter fast-flyers (ballistic missiles) with slow-flyers (cruise missiles)? "I'm puzzled about the Chiefs' view on this," said Reagan. "I'd like to know why the military has signed onto it." He said he was concerned about the potentially precedental impact on START.* "Also," he continued, "even if it's a good deal, should we grab it now, or can we get a better one by waiting? I'm not going to reach a decision until I have that information."

So McFarlane "tasked" the Chiefs to address the issue the President had raised. Were they prepared to commit themselves, as a group, to the proposition that the U.S. could live without the Pershing II in NATO?

Retreat to the Tank

That question aroused both consternation and suspicion on the part of the Chiefs. Here they were, the nation's top military officers, being asked to justify a weapons system that had always been primarily political, not military, in its assigned mission for Europe. What was the White House up to? Were the Chiefs being set up to take the blame in the political arena if the fallback touched off accusations of sellout and surrender from the right?

The Army Chief of Staff, General Edward Meyer, was especially upset about being asked formally by the President whether he could endorse Nitze's proposal to do away with the Pershing II. The intermediate-range ballistic missile, after all, "belonged" to the Army. (Intercontinental ballistic missiles, by contrast, were the Air Force's responsibility.) Meyer had only recently testified on Capitol Hill in support of continued funding for the Pershing II, despite its poor performance in test flights and the lingering doubts over both its political and its military rationale. He had stuck his neck out for the sake of a weapon that two Administrations felt was necessary for the sake of alliance solidarity. Now the White House was asking him whether he could just as well do without it. His answer, he felt, could only be a resounding "no."

---

*Reagan meant that even if it made sense for INF to balance off SS-20s with cruise missiles, there was a danger that the U.S. position would be weakened in START, where the Administration was trying to focus exclusively on ballistic missiles and to avoid or at least postpone limits on cruise missiles.

Meyer was well known for his volatility and bluntness, and these qualities came out during a number of meetings, including several in the National Military Command Center, known as the "Tank," the inner sanctum where the Chiefs held their most important and sensitive deliberations. It seemed to Meyer that not only were the Chiefs as a group and he in particular being put on the spot, but arms-control policy was, as usual, being made in a vacuum. Not only was there little regard to how arms control fit into national security, but one set of negotiations, INF, was being divorced from another, START, with which it ought to be intimately linked.

"There needs to be some clear idea around this government over what are the golden nuggets, what are the family jewels," lamented Meyer. "We're being asked to comment on one piece of the pie without seeing the whole pie." He was sick and tired of American negotiators going off and talking about their bright ideas with their Soviet counterparts before a comprehensive rationale for those ideas was "worked through the system." There was a degree of civilian improvisation and, at the same time, a lack of civilian-military coordination on the American side that surely never occurred on the Soviet side: "What is negotiable and what isn't, and in what overall context? Nobody's asking us or anyone else that. They're asking, can we live without this or that system, and the question changes every week. And they always want an answer right away, when data and analysis are incomplete."

Some recently acquired data concerned Meyer especially. It was extremely secret intelligence indicating that the Soviets were making considerable progress in the development of a "look-down/shoot-down" capability, an airborne radar system like the American AWACS that could, if perfected, make it much harder for cruise missiles to sneak deep into Soviet territory under anti-aircraft defenses. Given the distinct possibility that cruise missiles might not be "penetrable and survivable" into the 1990s, was it a "militarily viable tradeoff" for the U.S. to give up ballistic missiles altogether while letting the Soviets keep the SS-20? That was a tough problem, and not one that the Chiefs should be expected to answer "by next Monday." Now, trading the Pershing II for all the SS-20s in the U.S.S.R. —that was easy; that would unquestionably be a good deal. Perhaps it might not be negotiable, but at least there was no doubt it would be militarily desirable, and the Chiefs were in the business of making military calculations, not diplomatic ones.

Much of what Meyer had to say about the Nitze initiative was couched in terms of questions, some rhetorical and some merely skeptical, but they were put with considerable force, even passion. They suggested that the policymaking was in shambles and that the Chiefs were being put in an unfair and improper position. Vessey had had a lot of practice calming Meyer down. Before being elevated over Meyer's head as the dark-horse candidate to the job of chairman of the Chiefs, Vessey had been Meyer's deputy. Many a time he had patiently sat by while Meyer "went ballistic" in the presence of some ashen-faced subordinate or perhaps even a fellow chief. When Meyer's fury was spent, Vessey would sometimes play the role of conciliator and interpreter: "What General Meyer meant to say was . . ."

Vessey was by now persuaded that, while Meyer's concerns were valid, there had to be a bottom line, and the bottom line was that the Nitze package made a certain amount of sense. Still, he held back from arguing that position as forcefully as he might have among his colleagues. Vessey was new to the job (so, indeed, were his Air Force and Navy colleagues). He was painfully conscious of his responsibility to guide the group, if possible, to a consensus, and more than a little sobered by the outspokenness of his former boss, who was also a veteran of the bureaucratic wars of SALT as well as earlier campaigns in INF and START.

In the end, Vessey and the Air Force Chief of Staff, Charles Gabriel, adopted a view closer to the one that Iklé had held from the beginning: giving up the Pershing II was a large price to pay, but if by paying it the U.S. could buy a major reduction of SS-20s in Europe, a freeze on them in Asia, and the freedom to proceed with more Tomahawks than the Soviets would have SS-20 warheads targeted against NATO—that might be a good deal. The Chief of Naval Operations, James Watkins, sympathized with Meyer, although he ended up taking a more neutral position.

The Chiefs produced a paper in which they threaded their way delicately through various aspects of the plan, although bearing down heavily on the risks of abandoning the Pershing II. The paper stressed that precisely because the Pershing II was a ballistic missile much feared by the Soviets, it was the principal source of leverage for the U.S. in the negotiations. It should not be given up lightly, and no matter what giving it up accomplished, there were serious questions about whether a European nuclear balance composed of Tomahawk cruise missiles in NATO and SS-20 ballistic missiles in the U.S.S.R. could be said to be equal. Also, it was one thing to give up the 108 Pershing II launchers slated for deployment in West Germany in 1983. It would be quite another for NATO to give up the right ever to deploy long-range ballistic missiles in Europe. That would be unacceptable.

If the Chiefs had been the final arbiters, Nitze would have certainly had some tough negotiating ahead of him. But the basic plan he and Kvitsinsky had agreed to would probably have remained intact on the American side. By questioning the Chiefs as he did, Reagan had implied that their opinion was going to play a decisive role in the Administration's reaction to the plan. It would at the very least represent Pentagon thinking. But that was not the way things turned out, for the Chiefs were effectively shoved aside by their civilian colleagues.

. . .

In Perle's absence, his deputies Hoehn and Lehman had produced, on behalf of the Office of the Secretary of Defense (i.e., the civilian side of the Pentagon), a paper of their own. As Perle had instructed, they urged a careful analysis of the long-term military implications of the proposed trade-off between SS-20s and Tomahawks. That study would take more time than Nitze's request for quick authorization would have allowed. But they stopped well short of a firm recommendation on the basic question of whether or not what Nitze was proposing was a good deal for the U.S. Thus the paper they wrote was cautious and temporizing.

After returning from Colorado, Perle was asked by Weinberger to have a look at the two papers. Weinberger had already indicated on the Joint Chiefs' paper his agreement with their misgivings about trading away the Pershing IIs. In the margin of the Hoehn-Lehman draft, however, Weinberger had noted his impatience with their circumspection. That was all Perle felt he needed to blast away. He scheduled a meeting with Hoehn and Lehman to begin preparing a new memorandum that would presume to represent the Department of Defense as a whole. The meeting was listed on Perle's calendar as "Project X." When another member of the staff, tantalized by the designation, asked what was up, he was told, "Don't ask. If this ever gets out, there'll be lie-detector tests all over the building."

The outcome was a paper that went, under highly classified cover sheets, to Weinberger. It subsumed the skeptical points made in the Chiefs' paper but sharpened them up considerably and made quite a few additional points. While the Chiefs had been rather narrowly focused on the issue of ballistic versus cruise missiles and had raised questions about the Nitze initiative in that context, Perle's draft launched an all-out attack on it, reviewing most of the criticisms that had been forming in his mind since he first heard from Hoehn in Aspen. The paper was intended to speak for the entire Pentagon, and it claimed (inaccurately) that the Chiefs concurred in the views expressed.

The Chiefs had intended their own paper to go straight to the President, a direct response to direct questions. To the annoyance of some of them, Weinberger and Perle had intercepted the paper before it left the Pentagon and turned it to their own purposes—to stop Nitze in his tracks and kill his initiative before it went further.

"One Tough Son-of-a-Bitch"

Perle wanted to bring the issue to a head, preferably without further involving the President. On September 1, there was a meeting in the Situation Room at the White House. Most of those present were the second- and third-echelon experts who had constituted the working group set up after

Nitze first unveiled his plan within the government. Only now it was Perle, not Iklé, representing Weinberger.

When reminded that Iklé had been supportive of the Nitze plan at that earlier meeting, Perle waved the matter aside, suggesting that Iklé had been motivated more by his lingering skepticism about the wisdom of the NATO deployments than by any favorable analysis of the Nitze proposal on its own merits. That statement misrepresented Iklé and implied that Perle's own concerns were much broader and more germane than Iklé's. It also made quite clear that Perle was taking charge, pushing his ostensible superior out of the way. About this time Iklé began telling people that he was withdrawing from the field of battle on arms-control issues to concentrate on other things, particularly U.S. policy toward Central America.

Perle wanted Nitze's plan repudiated before word of it leaked and it thus acquired a life of its own in the public arena. At the meeting in the Situation Room, Jonathan Howe said, "Ambassador Nitze deserves more of a hearing than that." Perle snapped back, "Nitze doesn't deserve a damn thing." If there had to be a presidential decision, then let each agency submit its position in writing to the White House. Perle was quite confident that, even with the backing of the State Department and the Arms Control Agency, Nitze's position would not survive what he hoped would be construed as the united opposition of the Joint Chiefs and the Secretary of Defense. He wanted to duplicate the episode of the previous winter when the Pentagon had squared off, and won, against the State Department on the issue of protecting the option of conventionally armed cruise missiles in INF. In that instance, a simple menu of options had gone to Reagan, and he had checked the Pentagon's choice. Perle wanted to avoid a full National Security Council meeting, at which Nitze in person or Rostow and Shultz on his behalf might be able to out-argue Weinberger.

McFarlane, however, insisted that the issue should be aired in front of the President. He felt an NSC meeting was necessary if Reagan's own desires were to be clear in the minds of his advisers—and clearly reflected in subsequent directives and negotiating instructions. He had seen too many instances in which the President's wishes had been tendentiously reinterpreted by various contending officials and agencies after a decision had been promulgated. He wanted to avoid such "revisionism" this time around.

An NSC meeting was scheduled for September 13. Only the principal members and advisers, plus Nitze, were included. Nitze delivered a tightly argued brief on behalf of the plan, concentrating on why it did not make political sense to go with a reduced NATO force made up entirely of Pershing IIs and why it made neither economic nor military sense to preserve a mixture of Pershing IIs and Tomahawks at levels as low as 75 launchers. Shultz was supportive of Nitze. There was nothing unusual, or inherently impermissible, about what he called "sidebar" negotiations of the sort that Nitze had carried out, especially if they produced hints of flexibility on the other side. It was good negotiating psychology to respond favorably and flexibly when the other side indicated a willingness to move. The Soviets, by going along with the package deal to date—however tentatively— were making such an indication. It would be a mistake for the U.S. not to follow through.

On that score, the President agreed. Like Shultz, he had had some experience with labor negotiations. He recalled an experience he had once had in bargaining with the Hollywood mogul Louis B. Mayer on behalf of the Screen Actors' Guild thirty years earlier. The negotiations were at an impasse when Reagan received a private, informal tip from someone that if the union made a certain adjustment in its offer "I think Louis will buy it." On the strength of that "unauthorized" intervention from the sidelines, the union and the studio had been able to reach an agreement.

But Reagan was still obsessed with the distinction between "slow-flying" and "fast-flying" weapons. He was unenthusiastic about putting the full onus of countering the SS-20s on the slow-flying Tomahawks. He liked the idea of keeping Pershing IIs because of their virtues as fast-flyers.

Nitze told Reagan that those virtues were exaggerated and even somewhat illusory; the President ought to be aware that there were serious questions about the strictly military need for American ballistic missiles of the range, in the numbers, and in the basing pattern envisioned for the Pershing II. Nitze said he thought the President was entitled to an objective assessment of the military requirement for the Pershing II, given the fact that the Pershing Ib was in a number of respects better suited to the targeting mission.

Reagan was somewhat taken aback; he seemed to be hearing this for the first time. It had been an almost unquestioned article of faith with him that the Pershing II was indispensable to the credibility of American deterrence and the execution of American war plans. The distinction between the military and political reasons for deploying the Pershing II had not been impressed upon Reagan, and had long since been blurred in any discussions in which he participated.

Vessey had little to say—surprisingly so in the face of Nitze's critique of the military justification for the Pershing II. The chairman was not prepared to defend the Pershing II on military grounds; it was a political weapon, after all. He and his fellow Chiefs had already addressed themselves as best they could to the President's question on the matter. He was upset at the way Weinberger and Perle had prevented the Chiefs' paper from going directly back to the President. More generally, he was angry at the way Perle persisted in riding roughshod over professional soldiers, abusing them both behind their backs and to their faces. But he suppressed his anger. He certainly was not going to give vent to it during an NSC meeting. If the

Secretary of Defense was to speak on behalf of the uniformed military about military matters, then let him do so now in response to Nitze.

That is exactly what Weinberger did. He delivered a withering attack on the Nitze initiative, following closely the script Perle had prepared for him and that had been circulated in advance of the meeting.

The Defense Secretary's blast seemed to encourage Reagan to voice more of his own misgivings. He remained firmly attached to the simplicity and finality of his original proposal. Why, he asked, if the U.S. could live without its new missiles in Europe, couldn't the Soviets live without the SS-20s?

Because, quite simply, said Nitze, there was a big difference between not deploying a weapons system still under development and removing one already perfected and in place. It was inconceivable that the Soviets would ever accept a proposal that required them to dismantle every last one of their most modern intermediate-range missiles; that was simply asking, and hoping, for too much.

The President was unconvinced. "Well, Paul," he said, "you just tell the Soviets that you're working for one tough son-of-a-bitch."

Nitze was doubly discouraged. He had been overruled by his President, and nearly two months after the climactic conversation with Kvitsinsky in the Jura Mountains he had still heard nothing from Kvitsinsky's friend and designated intermediary in Washington, Oleg Sokolov. He was beginning to conclude that the Kremlin's reaction to the package had been at least as negative as the White House's now appeared to be.

In the aftermath, there were, as usual, horsetrading, intrigue, and manipulative interpretation of what the President had supposedly decided. Rostow, Nitze, Timbie, and Howe made one last attempt to persuade the Pentagon to keep the package intact. But in a testy, confrontational meeting Weinberger made clear that he was not to be moved. The timing was all wrong for compromise, he said. The Europeans were satisfied with the zero-zero proposal as it stood; they would deploy on schedule; there was no need to change. Nitze looked more and more glum. He warned Weinberger that he was being too sanguine; it was a mistake to take the Europeans for granted; deployment might yet prove dicey, especially if the U.S. seemed to be stonewalling in the negotiations.

What Shultz Did Not Tell Gromyko

George Shultz was due to meet with Andrei Gromyko at the United Nations in New York, just before Nitze was to have another private session with Kvitsinsky in Geneva. To prepare for those upcoming encounters with the Soviets, McFarlane's staff drafted a National Security Decision Directive, which was cleared within the interagency process and issued over the President's signature on September 15.* It reiterated that zero-zero was still the Administration's preferred position, and it made clear that an alternative to zero-zero that allowed the Soviets to keep any SS-20s would have to permit the U.S. to deploy some intermediate-range ballistic missiles of its own, i.e., Pershing IIs. The Nitze package deal in its original form was unacceptable, and the Soviets should be told so at the next opportunity. The directive also made clear that the U.S. was not prepared to offer another proposal. The Nitze-Kvitsinsky back channel remained open, however, and the U.S. was prepared to consider any new proposal the Soviets might want to make. Nitze was authorized to sound out Soviet flexibility, but not to indicate any American flexibility. In that sense, the presidential directive was a step backward from compromise and a rebuke to the chief negotiator.

This document became the basis of a carefully prepared statement, or set of "talking points," that Shultz might use with Gromyko at the United Nations. If Gromyko raised the subject of the Nitze-Kvitsinsky discussions, Shultz was to give Gromyko an "American response," as though the proposal had not been primarily an American initiative to begin with. That response was to say that any agreement whereby the U.S. was allowed only cruise missiles and the Soviet Union was allowed ballistic missiles was not acceptable. However, if the Soviet Union had "other ideas," the U.S. would be happy to listen to them.

Gromyko did not raise the matter at their meeting on September 28 in New York, and Shultz deliberately avoided doing so himself in a way that would call undue attention to the Administration's disavowal of Nitze. Shultz had told his own aides in advance of the meeting that he wanted neither to "get into the substance of the negotiations," nor to "pre-empt or undercut Paul." Unlike Haig, Shultz did not feel threatened by Nitze; unlike Haig, Shultz was not enthusiastic about opening his own back channel via Gromyko and Dobrynin. So instead of reciting the talking points that had been prepared for him—which would have amounted to a vote of no confidence in Nitze and perhaps a signal to Gromyko that all future back-channel negotiations should be through Shultz himself—the secretary made a very general, low-key comment to the effect that, while discussions to date in Geneva had not resolved the problem, the channels established there remained open, and the U.S. was interested in hearing any fresh ideas that the Soviets might have on how to break the impasse. Shultz's written summary

---

*McFarlane already had considerable experience in the fine art of negotiating and drafting presidential directives, and he would have a lot more in the months to come. As Alexander Haig's counselor at the State Department in the first days of the Administration, McFarlane had helped prepare National Security Decision Directive No. 1, which set forth the responsibilities of the various agencies of the government in foreign policy and established the hierarchy of interagency groups.

of what he had told Gromyko was this: "While it remains to be seen what comes out of this procedure, the pattern of communication remains worthwhile."

Whether Gromyko interpreted Shultz's cryptic statement as a repudiation of Nitze and the Nitze-Kvitsinsky deal is a question that may never be fully answered. The Soviet Foreign Minister, whose dour, poker-faced visage had for decades been an emblematic mask of Soviet diplomacy, confined himself to listening carefully and nodding. His government had yet to respond, through any channel whatsoever, to the substance of the deal, and he offered no response on this occasion either.

Kvitsinsky Says "Nyet"

The Soviet response came soon thereafter, and there was nothing subtle or indirect about it. On arrival at the airport in Geneva on September 29, Kvitsinsky read a harsh attack on the U.S. position.

When the executive secretaries of the delegations met to fix the schedule for the talks, V. M. Grinin asked his American counterpart, Norman Clyne, "By the way, would Ambassador Nitze like to see Ambassador Kvitsinsky?"

"Naturally," said Clyne, thinking Grinin was referring to a routine heads-of-delegations meeting.

"No," explained Grinin, "I mean does he want to see him privately and take another walk?" (As so often, the Soviets were trying to maneuver the Americans into taking the initiative.)

During lunch at a famous restaurant outside Geneva, La Réserve, and in another stroll through the woods near Saint-Cergue, Kvitsinsky made clear his side's rejection of the package deal. Lest Nitze have any illusions that he was up against intransigent bureaucrats who needed only to be prodded toward flexibility by the top leaders, Kvitsinsky stressed that his instructions —of which he gave Nitze a copy—had been cleared by the Politburo itself. He claimed that his bosses had given him a very rough time even for playing the messenger for the scheme and for implying Soviet endorsement of it. He also noted wryly to Nitze, "I understand you had some trouble back in Washington yourself."

"I'm still here," Nitze replied.

Kvitsinsky's instructions reiterated the standing Soviet position in the starkest, most uncompromising terms. In addition to verbally shredding the document he and Nitze had exchanged in July, Kvitsinsky complained about the procedure they had followed. As a result of those exchanges, the American side had gained insight into the thinking of the Politburo itself on what sort of INF deal might be possible beyond the formal Soviet proposal. The Soviets, by contrast, had gained insight only into the thinking of Paul Nitze. Ever sensitive on such matters, the Soviets felt this was unequal. Kvitsinsky was instructed to put Nitze on notice that if their back-channel dealings were to advance further, Nitze would have to be speaking for Secretary Shultz as well as for himself.

"No more walks in the woods unless you're under instructions, too," said Kvitsinsky.

Nitze was now very much under instructions, which he proceeded to discharge. He "implemented" the presidential directive of September 15, telling Kvitsinsky that, contrary to what they had discussed in July, a package deal would have to include Pershing IIs.

Nitze sent two cables to Washington reporting the bad news, one through the regular State Department channel, another, more detailed, directly to Shultz by means of a highly secret channel, code-named Sphinx, that had been established especially to handle any communications regarding one-on-one exploratory discussions between the negotiators. Nitze noted laconically that Kvitsinsky "comes back from the U.S.S.R. with no flexibility."

The deputy American negotiator, Maynard Glitman, phoned the Politico-Military Bureau and said that the two chief negotiators had had "another walk," and it had not gone well. Glitman recommended that the allies be briefed on the Soviet rejection. Nitze had felt all along that, if his proposed compromise accomplished nothing else, at least it would help persuade the allies that the Reagan Administration was serious about getting an agreement and was interested in a deal toward that end. The willingness of the U.S. to accept a settlement other than zero-zero would put the lie to the Soviet accusation that the Administration was cynically using the negotiations as a cover for deployment.

But, while it was true that Kvitsinsky had rejected the deal flatly, it could also be said that the Reagan Administration had undercut Nitze and invited Soviet rejection. By repudiating Nitze on the sacrifice of the Pershing II, the U.S. was doing precisely what the deal had been designed to preclude, "pocketing the raisins" of Soviet concessions and reneging on the principal American one. This was far from the spirit as well as the letter of the original understanding.

Partly because the affair was sure to be controversial, the State Department and White House staff did not want Nitze to brief the allies in any detail on what had happened. They wanted the whole thing hushed up. When Nitze eventually did call on Helmut Kohl, the new West German Chancellor, and Hans-Dietrich Genscher, the Foreign Minister, they asked whether Nitze was getting anywhere with Kvitsinsky in their private conversations. "I've had lots of private talks with Kvitsinsky," replied Nitze, "and I find that I don't get very far with him in those either." And that was just about all he would say of the episode.

.   .   .

The closest thing to a leak about the walk in the woods appeared on October 22. An article by Ray Moseley in the Chicago *Tribune* datelined Paris reported that "the U.S. has conducted secret negotiations with the Soviet Union to try to break the impasse in the nuclear arms talks in Geneva, but this effort has failed for the time being." The story was attributed to "well-informed French sources," who in turn claimed that Rostow "conveyed this information to the West German government during a visit last week in Bonn."

Rostow had been given the strictest instructions on what he could and could not tell the West Europeans about the negotiations in Geneva. Under no circumstances was he to inform them about the Nitze-Kvitsinsky package deal.

But during his visit to Europe in October, Rostow disregarded the gag rule. He gave a number of his hosts, particularly the British, extensive briefings, including on the numbers involved and the key feature—the proposed sacrifice of the Pershing II. Whatever their opinion of the deal itself, the few British who knew about it were grateful to Rostow for keeping them informed. They were also appalled that the Administration had intended to leave them in the dark.

Rostow also confided in the Germans, who confided in the French, who confided in the Chicago *Tribune* reporter. Top officials in Washington held their breath. They feared the dam was about to break, and they were going to be deluged with leaks. At least one Pentagon official who was against the Nitze proposal hoped that would happen and dropped broad hints to tantalize a Washington *Post* reporter that he should dig further into the *Tribune*'s revelation. Rostow, who wanted the story out for different reasons—as evidence of Yankee ingenuity and good will—tried to get a nationally syndicated columnist to follow up on the article. But, largely because the *Tribune* appeared in Chicago rather than in Washington, its scoop remained an exclusive.

During his swing through Europe, Rostow also stopped off in Geneva and had lunch with Nitze and Kvitsinsky. "Some people in Moscow," said Kvitsinsky, "were relieved that your side rejected the package." The implication might have been that, if the Reagan Administration had backed Nitze up on the contents of his package as originally conceived, the Kremlin would have felt under considerably more pressure to negotiate on that basis, or at least not to reject the plan as categorically as it had. But, even if that was the impression Kvitsinsky meant to convey, there was plenty of reason to be wary of taking him at his word.

During their lunch at La Réserve on September 29, Kvitsinsky had offered a number of hints about the nature and origins of the trouble he had had in Moscow. He expanded on these in the months that followed. He had never really expected the deal to be accepted lock, stock, and barrel. Rather, the paper constituted a "string which could be played out in a useful way" —a string that he had hoped might be used to pull on Brezhnev's desire to cap his career with a last arms-control agreement, a restoration of détente, and a summit with Reagan. Kvitsinsky claimed he had never counted on Gromyko's endorsement of the plan, even though he had been operating on Gromyko's instructions back in July. He was hoping only that the Foreign Minister would support him sufficiently to bring the plan to Brezhnev's personal attention and to do so in private, bypassing the Politburo. Then perhaps Brezhnev, with a sweep of his hand, would have cleared away all the objections that had become so embedded in the Soviet position and overruled the almost certain opposition of Defense Minister Dimitri Ustinov.

Those hopes were dashed. There was powerful resistance to the plan itself, and there were also deep doubts in Moscow about whether the U.S. would be able to play out the string without a leak that would abort the deal. More important, there was suspicion about whether Nitze was "serious and sincere" in suggesting, at the time of his first approach to Kvitsinsky, that an INF breakthrough might lead to a "well-prepared summit." The Kremlin's "informants in Washington"—a phrase that probably meant Anatoly Dobrynin and others in the Soviet embassy there—had taken soundings of their own. They determined that the Administration was not serious about a summit. (The embassy had also picked up rumors about Nitze's having been reprimanded for exceeding his instructions.)

Kvitsinsky noted with regret and a touch of recrimination that Shultz had said nothing, during his meetings with Gromyko in New York, about the Nitze-Kvitsinsky discussions in the context of a possible summit. That was taken by Gromyko and others as confirmation of their suspicion that Nitze had misled them about an American interest in such a thing. The walk in the woods had taken on the look, in Soviet eyes, of a trap, with the false prospect of a summit as the bait for major Soviet concessions in the negotiations. The Soviet side, Kvitsinsky seemed to be saying, felt it had been tricked into tipping its hand, exposing its ultimate fallback in the negotiations.

Months later, once the episode did leak out into the press, the Soviets saw and seized an opportunity to work mischief around it. They did everything they could to fan speculation among Americans that the U.S., by making an offer and then withdrawing it, had doomed any chance that the two negotiators' walk in the woods might have led to an exit from the impasse in INF. In addition to coy hints of American culpability, they also put out flagrantly bogus versions of what had happened. For example, two senior diplomats in Washington claimed that Kvitsinsky had been under orders to do no more than hear out what Nitze had to suggest. Before they had begun,

Nitze had half-jokingly assured Kvitsinsky that one of the advantages of such private, exploratory discussions was that each negotiator could tell his home office that the other partner had initiated whatever plan they discussed. Kvitsinsky's home office was now exercising that option with a vengeance.

In a bizarre bit of symmetry, William Clark and Ronald Reagan engaged in almost identical—and even more disingenuous—revisionism about what had happened that day in the Jura. Clark, when asked what lay behind the press stories and rumors that Nitze had tried to cut a deal with Kvitsinsky, would look his interlocutor in the eye and say that Nitze had indeed had some informal conversations with Kvitsinsky, but that the initiative had been the Soviet negotiator's; Nitze's role had been solely that of conveying a Soviet trial balloon back to Washington; moreover, in no sense had Nitze been reprimanded for what he did. It was not clear whether Clark was deliberately distorting the truth, or whether he was engaging in what psychologists call cognitive dissonance (reshaping one's perception of reality to conform with the way one would like it to be). In any event, he stuck to this rather crooked line before a more complete version of the Nitze-Kvitsinsky episode finally came out into the open in early 1983. By then, it was no longer credible for anyone to pretend that Nitze had simply been "in a listening mode."

Yet that is exactly the way the President himself continued to try to explain the whole thing away—a minor, forgettable incident that had occurred at Soviet instigation. In a breakfast meeting with reporters on February 23, Reagan at first seemed puzzled when the columnist Joseph Kraft asked about Paul Nitze's "proposal" during a "walk with the Soviet delegate." Then, seeming dimly to remember something like that, Reagan told Kraft that Nitze had "referred to us a hint that had been dropped by the man he walked in the woods with, but nothing that he had said back." Once again, there was a question of whether Reagan was deliberately distorting what had occurred or, more likely, simply confusing what Nitze had been instructed to do in September with what he had already done on his own initiative in July. In any event, the President's candor and his memory served the truth better when he added that the Soviet side "might look more kindly on cruise missiles than on the Pershings. . . . I don't think cruise missiles alone would be a deterrent to the SS-20s." Reagan obviously remembered the incident well enough to recall why he had refused to back Nitze up on what had been—and would again be—the key feature of the plan: a willingness to sacrifice the Pershing II.

When news of this exchange reached Nitze in Geneva, he was dismayed. He sent a message to Washington asking for an explanation of what the President had had in mind by putting out such an upside-down, inside-out version, but he never got a satisfactory response.

. . .

The walk-in-the-woods episode remained as mysterious as it was controversial. The principal mystery concerned what had actually happened on the Soviet side—and, hypothetically, what might have happened if the Reagan Administration had quickly and unequivocally endorsed the package deal. There is not enough evidence to conclude, or even to speculate persuasively, that the Administration missed an opportunity to reach what would have been a very good agreement for the West, in both its political and its military consequences. On the contrary, it is at least as plausible that the package deal would have come apart and been repudiated in Moscow, regardless of how Washington responded. So Nitze himself, in his own post-mortem of the affair, came to believe. However, the American handling of the incident still vividly dramatized three things about the Reagan Administration's conduct of INF: a deep-seated mistrust of the West Europeans, who were seen as likely to abandon their remaining commitments under the December 1979 NATO decision if the Pershing II program were cancelled; a preoccupation with what should have been at most secondary military issues, such as the relative merits of cruise and ballistic missiles; and a shortsighted fixation on meeting the 1983 deployment deadline in all its aspects—come hell, high water, or a breakthrough in the negotiations that would entail sacrificing one aspect of the deployment program.

7 The Long, Cold Winter

Having lost the support of his government, Paul Nitze was also losing his principal backer. Eugene Rostow's position was becoming weaker all the time. He was still unable to establish rapport with the President, William Clark, and the other members of the inner circle. "Imperious," "arrogant," "pompous," "not a team player"—these were the complaints about Rostow in the White House, and they had their echoes in Foggy Bottom.

For months, the White House had been inflicting a kind of Chinese water torture indirectly on Rostow, directly on his deputy, Robert Grey—nearly two years after beginning work, he was still awaiting confirmation by the Senate. As 1982 and the session of Congress came to an end, it became increasingly clear that the White House was hoping that by letting the Grey nomination die it would force Rostow to quit. Rostow inadvertently encouraged his enemies to press ahead with this tactic. He vowed on a number of occasions that he would resign if he could not keep a deputy of his own choosing. And, if Rostow quit, what would happen to Nitze? In the fall, one of the Senate conservatives, Orrin Hatch, visited Geneva and asked Nitze if it was true that he would leave if Rostow was driven out.

"No one's talked to me about any of this," snapped Nitze. "I haven't expressed any such intention." On his return to the U.S. in December, he traveled to New Haven, where Rostow was recuperating from a hip operation, and urged him to withdraw his threat of resigning: "You quit over substance and principles, Gene, not over personnel matters."

It was apparent, however, that even if Rostow stayed on he was not going to do Nitze much good in the fights still to come. The only ally who could make a difference was George Shultz. Moderates inside and outside the government were counting on Shultz to rescue the Administration from itself in INF (and START, too). The contrast between Shultz's style and Haig's fed hopes that, whereas Haig had been his own worst enemy, Shultz might work magic. He was Ronald Reagan's kind of Secretary of State even if he wasn't one of Reagan's intimates or ideological soulmates. There was a widespread assumption inside the government and out, heavily tinged with wishful thinking, that one morning Reagan and the country would wake up and find themselves with a more traditional, middle-of-the-road foreign policy, including a more negotiable set of arms-control positions. And it would all be thanks to Shultz.

In one of his first private talks with the President, Shultz had found Reagan receptive in the abstract to the argument that sooner or later something would have to give in the U.S. position in INF. "I understand that in a negotiation naturally we have to negotiate, George," said Reagan. "And I know what negotiating means. I know we can't just plunk a proposal on the table and sit there." On another occasion, Reagan commented that back in his days negotiating on behalf of the Screen Actors' Guild he had a "heck of a good sense of timing about when to budge and when to hang tough."

Shultz's own instincts were beginning to tell him that the time had already come for the U.S. to budge in INF. But there had to be more orderliness and unity than the Administration had demonstrated in the episode over the Nitze initiative. He said on a number of occasions, "We've got to move, but we've got to move *together*." In an Administration with so many key officials so far apart, tugging in so many different directions, that could only mean waiting. And the longer the U.S. waited to adopt a new position, the more time the Soviets would have to play up the growing impression in Europe of American paralysis and intransigence. Lawrence Eagleburger kept looking for ways "to light a fire under some people's behinds." The behinds that mattered were Shultz's and Reagan's.

Eagleburger had David Gompert prepare a memorandum for Shultz. The secretary was to depart with Reagan on a good-will trip to Latin America at the end of November 1982. They would have some time for relaxed, private chats on Air Force One. Eagleburger hoped to nudge Shultz, who in turn would nudge the President, toward a realization that the time for compromise in INF had arrived—and that the time might be running short. The memo argued that zero-zero was no longer a solution. The longer the Administration stood pat, the less opportunity there would be to move to an adjusted package that would accomplish the U.S.'s political purposes and be compatible with its military interests.

As Eagleburger told Shultz just before the Latin American trip, "If anyone can carry the government forward, it's the Secretary of State." Shultz seemed to agree, but it was hard to be sure. He was undemonstrative to the point of being enigmatic, even to his own closest advisers.

The Burt Option

Eagleburger and Gompert's memo to Shultz reviewed "the structural problem," the inability of the system to produce new ideas in a way that allowed them to get serious, high-level attention before they were shot down by opponents at the working level of the government. The authors did not need to name Perle, who was perfectly positioned to intercept any recommendation for change as it worked its way up from the bureaucracy toward the President. What was needed was to turn the process on its head, so that initiative could come from the top down. That is how it had worked in the days when Henry Kissinger, with Eagleburger at his right hand, ran the National Security Council staff.

Not surprisingly, Eagleburger saw the State Department as the obvious institution, and the Secretary of State as the obvious personality, to fill the vacuum. But Shultz was still a newcomer, a cautious newcomer who had very little background in arms control and numerous other preoccupations, particularly the Middle East. Shultz's friend Kenneth Dam, whom he had brought in as the Deputy Secretary, was equally new to the subject. Like Shultz, Dam was a moderate, a low-key, nonconfrontational one. With White House approval, Shultz put Dam in charge of a new interagency committee that was supposed to oversee arms control. "I want Ken Dam to take the bull by the horns," said Shultz; but Shultz quickly added, "I think Ken can do that with a maximum of effectiveness and a minimum of friction."

It quickly became apparent that Dam himself was more interested in minimizing friction than maximizing effectiveness. In explaining what came to be dubbed "the Dam Group," its chairman said that the furthest thing from his mind was to "set up a new Administration organ." Rather, he conceived the exercise as "just a discussion group"—a combination of a seminar at which the principals would educate themselves on broader issues and a therapy group at which they would learn to know each other better and, presumably as a consequence, find it easier to reach agreements.

Perle was a member of the group, yet Eagleburger and the others hoped that it might still be used to limit his influence. Isolating Perle would require some collusion on the part of Iklé, however, and that proved impossible. Around the turn of the year, William Clark convened a meeting in the White House Situation Room to review Soviet-American relations in general and INF in particular. It was a cabinet-level assembly—Weinberger, Shultz, Casey, with Meese and Baker sitting in. Dam was also there; he was assigned to chair a working group that would make recommendations on where to go in the new year. The working group, which met a number of times in January, included Eagleburger as the State Department representative and Iklé on behalf of the Office of the Secretary of Defense. It was essentially, though not nominally, the Dam Group minus Perle. Iklé was even asked not to tell Perle that the meetings were taking place.

The non-Pentagon members hoped that Iklé and Perle were moving sufficiently apart that they could now be played off against each other. Even though Perle and Iklé were both members of the Dam Group, the hope was that Iklé could be included, and Perle excluded, at meetings when real business was transacted. Without Perle to argue otherwise, there was a loose consensus that the Administration ought to begin moving off the zero option.

But the State Department officials overestimated the extent and depth of the differences between Iklé and Perle, and they certainly deluded themselves in thinking that Iklé would let himself be used to undercut Perle. Perle soon found out about the "cabal," as he called it, and went into a fury. He launched into a tirade against the State Department. He was fed up, he said. He learned about the meetings from which he had been excluded at a time when he was depressed about his job and worried about the effect it was having on his family; he started telling associates he would leave the government in the early spring. The other members of the Dam Group wanted to neutralize and circumvent Perle, but they didn't want him to resign in protest, taking with him evidence of what he would denounce as U.S. concessions and capitulations. Dam moved quickly to reassure Perle that there was no State Department cabal against him.

While Perle proved impossible to keep out of the process, Richard Burt was, at least initially, difficult to include in it. Like Robert Grey, Burt was many months in legislative limbo. Alexander Haig had promoted him to be Assistant Secretary for European Affairs in May 1982, despite considerable resistance at the White House. A little more than a month later, Haig himself had resigned, and Burt was still awaiting confirmation by the Senate. Conservatives on Capitol Hill stepped up their campaign to block him. With Haig gone, Burt's surviving protector was Eagleburger, himself a suspect figure in the eyes of the right wing. Eagleburger urged Shultz to keep him on. In the end, Burt survived and Grey did not. One key reason was that Burt had the backing of Shultz, while Grey had to depend on Eugene Rostow.

While Burt's confirmation was still in doubt, Shultz kept him in the background and off to one side. Burt could barely contain his frustration. In an unguarded moment with some colleagues, he blurted out, "I want in! I want back in!" Like Eagleburger, Burt had now concluded that the interagency process had outlived its usefulness. It was "barely adequate to put together an opening proposal, but it's nowhere near capable of guiding negotiations." Besides, it was turning into "an orgy of freelancing." The principal offender, in his view, was Nitze, and the principal offense was the walk in the woods.

Burt had his own plan for a fallback in INF. Like the original zero option —and unlike Nitze's scheme—what became known as the Burt option was intended to keep the allies satisfied, and thus the alliance managed, while the countdown toward deployment took place. This plan would pick up on a number that the Soviets themselves were using in their own proposal: 300. That was to be the limit on medium-range launchers (bombers and missiles) allowed in Europe, under the Soviet draft on the table in Geneva. Under Burt's plan, 300 would be a ceiling on warheads (so each SS-20 would count as three), and it would apply globally, not just in Europe. At the same time, Burt hoped, the mere incorporation of the figure 300 into a new U.S. position would make the plan look like a conciliatory gesture to the U.S.S.R. Three hundred had the added "presentational advantage," he noted, of being approximately halfway between zero and the prospective deployment of 572 new NATO warheads. Thus, the U.S. would be offering to cut in half its original deployment package. But this was just a new numbers game.

Richard Perle opposed Burt's proposed fallback almost as strenuously as he had opposed Nitze's. He fought it in the Dam Group, in the Interagency Group, and anywhere else it came up. He had conceived and nurtured the zero-zero solution to be impervious to compromise, and now he set about to make sure it withstood the tests to which Nitze, Burt, and the West Europeans were subjecting it. Perle contended that, thanks to its embrace of the zero option, the Reagan Administration had coopted the European left; it had given the European anti-nuclear forces

> a stake in U.S. policy as long as we are negotiating toward a zero outcome. Once we give up zero and say we're willing to settle for something other than zero, we'd be saying, "If the negotiations fail, we'll deploy; and if they succeed, we'll deploy." At that point, the peace movement in Western Europe will be disheartened; their stake in our policy will evaporate. So will the short-term benefits of a compromise. The political situation will be worse. Therefore any compromise is almost sure to have a perverse political effect.

Perle made this case to Burt and also to Friedrich Ruth, the chief arms-control expert of the West German government, a frequent visitor to Washington and a persistent lobbyist on behalf of change in the American bargaining position. Burt and Ruth, who collaborated closely with each other, could hardly believe that Perle took his own argument seriously. The formulation "If the negotiations fail, we'll deploy; and if they succeed, we'll deploy" was exactly what NATO had committed itself to in December 1979. So why should the allies find that proposition repugnant now?

Perle was saying that the U.S. had to stick with zero lest it lose the European left. The U.S. had never *won* the European left in the first place. Nor had it tried to do so. Nor was there any point in trying to do so. Winning the left would be a mug's game. The left wanted no American missiles, period. It was the political center, not the left, that mattered in Europe, and the political center needed to be persuaded of American flexibility and sincerity in the face of Soviet intransigence, if it was going to support deployment.

Perle seemed to be proceeding under the impression that Europeans were all the same, and that they were all attached to the zero option. This risked playing right into Soviet hands. The stalemate that a zero-zero proposal seemed designed to perpetuate was one in which no new NATO missiles would ever be deployed in Europe, and no Soviet missiles would ever be removed. That was an even better outcome from the Soviets' standpoint than the one they were offering. In the view of Burt, Ruth, Eagleburger, and others, Richard Perle's real perversity was in arguing for an American policy that not only reduced the chances of an arms-control agreement, but that unintentionally made Western rearmament more difficult.

As it was, the Administration's program for an arms buildup faced growing troubles. Eagleburger had to spend much of his time trying to put out congressional and bureaucratic brushfires that might kill the Administration's already crippled arms-control policy. With deployment scheduled to occur in less than a year, the Pershing II was doing poorly on the test ranges. The cruise missile, too, was bothered by technical bugs and cost overruns. Congress was restless. It was looking for weapons systems to cut, both to help reduce the federal budget deficit and to put the Administration on notice that it had better start showing some results in Geneva.*

The Administration's response to these pressures was to say that it needed the weapons in order to exert leverage on the Soviets in the talks. "Negotiating wampum," Nitze called it in pleading with one senator who was threatening to withhold support for the cruise-missile program. Suddenly the weapons were being defended as less important to the cause of rearmament than to the cause of arms control. But the case was a difficult one for the Administration to make. Reagan had been in office almost two years, and his Administration had yet to achieve any progress in the talks.

Old Threats, New Twists

At Geneva, during the fall of 1982, it was apparent that the bottom had dropped out of the market in compromises. The two delegations settled into what quickly proved to be one of the most polemical, least productive

---

*The first two tests of the Pershing II fizzled spectacularly. A third test took place November 19, 1982. Three days before, the House Appropriations Subcommittee had cut from the Administration's request for defense purposes in the 1983 fiscal year $504 million that had been earmarked for production of the missile. The move was a warning that, if the Army could not get the thing to work, Congress might stop funding it altogether. Shultz was sufficiently concerned to ask to be notified immediately how the third test went. It was pronounced a success, much to his relief. A week later the Army put out a postscript admitting that actually the dummy warhead had fallen wide of its target. While technicians shrugged off these problems as the inevitable growing pains of a brand-new system, the politicians howled. The missile's chief selling points, after all, were its range and accuracy.

sessions of nuclear-arms-control talks in more than a decade. The chief negotiators felt compelled to recommit themselves to their formal positions, which were as far apart as ever. Nitze concentrated again on a recitation of the virtues of zero-zero, while the tone on the Soviet side of the table became one of hectoring, grandstanding, recrimination, and old threats with new twists.

The principal Soviet accusation was that, contrary to Reagan's promise, the U.S. was negotiating in bad faith; it was using the talks as a stalling tactic and camouflage for the onrush to deployment. The Soviets hammered away at this charge in public as well. On his arrival in Geneva to begin the round, Yuli Kvitsinsky made a statement to the effect that his nation welcomed negotiations with the U.S. as long as they were not a cover for "military preparations" on the American side.

The principal threat was that deployment would trigger a walkout and a new wave of Soviet military countermeasures. Kvitsinsky had once implied to Nitze's deputy, Maynard Glitman, that Moscow would recall its negotiators at least from INF if deployment went forward. V. N. Popov remarked on a number of occasions that the negotiations could not possibly continue past the spring of 1983 if there was no progress. Nikolai Detinov commented more than once that there would be "no point in continuing these talks" past the spring unless a breakthrough was achieved or NATO postponed deployment.

Vladimir Pavlichenko, who had first issued the ultimatum during the summer, elaborated on it now. The introduction of American missiles into Western Europe would, he said, be a violation of the twenty-year-old U.S.-Soviet understanding that had allowed John Kennedy and Nikita Khrushchev to end the Cuban missile crisis. Kennedy had removed U.S. Jupiter missiles from Turkey and Italy. One of the countermeasures that the U.S. might have to contend with if it persisted in its plan to increase the threat to the U.S.S.R. from Western Europe would be an increased Soviet threat to the U.S. from "Cuba and other Central American countries," a phrase which, at that time, could only mean Nicaragua. "How would you like to have missiles there?" asked Pavlichenko.

The menace in that rhetorical question was hardly credible. A deliberate replay of the Cuban missile crisis would have been reckless in the extreme on the part of the Soviet leadership, and very much out of character. But other, more plausible threats were harder to dismiss. A number of Soviets suggested that countermeasures to the Tomahawks and Pershing IIs might include a surge in the SS-20 program. Kvitsinsky said that his country would deploy additional SS-20s on a one-for-one basis for every Pershing II that actually arrived in West Germany. That would mean countering the new Western warheads on a three-for-one basis, since the Pershing II had a single warhead while the SS-20 was triple-MIRVed. There were also repeated allusions to an acceleration in the development of the U.S.S.R.'s own program to deploy a modern long-range ground-launched cruise missile, and to the deployment of sea-launched cruise missiles aboard Soviet submarines off the coast of the U.S.

It was the conclusion of most members of the U.S. INF delegation that, starting with Pavlichenko's warning during the summer, the Soviets had been "laying down an audit trail." That meant establishing a record or building a case they could later point to, and very likely go public with, to justify a walkout should they decide to exercise that option. Nitze believed that the Soviets had decided sometime during the summer that it would not be possible to do business with the Reagan Administration on arms control or anything else of importance, and that they were getting ready to present themselves as the long-suffering but not infinitely patient good guys if and when the negotiations collapsed sometime in 1983.

Later in the fall of 1982, however, the Soviet negotiators seemed to soften and shift their tactics a little. They began talking less about walkouts and more about prolonging the negotiations in exchange for delay in the deployment of the NATO missiles. What they objected to was the American insistence on "automatic deployment," a phrase that was semantically attuned to their broader purpose of making the U.S. look rigid in its adherence to the deadline for deployment. But now there was the implication that perhaps the U.S.S.R. would take its threatened military countermeasures and keep talking at the same time. Popov asked whether it would be possible for the U.S. to withdraw missiles from Western Europe once they had been positioned there, assuming an agreement was reached that required their removal. Kvitsinsky made a number of comments indicating that the Soviet Union might go forward with additional SS-20s and various cruise missiles —partly as bargaining chips, in order to trade them for the Tomahawks and Pershing IIs. "Maybe someday we'll be negotiating our paper systems against yours," he remarked tartly.

Brezhnev's death on November 10 in and of itself had no discernible impact on the negotiations. A four-day period of mourning was declared in Moscow. The U.S. delegation phoned the Soviet mission and asked if a luncheon meeting and walk in the park that Nitze and Kvitsinsky had been planning was still on. Absolutely, came the reply. Kvitsinsky played down the significance of Brezhnev's death, saying that he was prepared to continue his end of the talks uninterrupted. Yuri Andropov had been personally involved in formulating Soviet INF policy for many months before his accession to the top post in the Kremlin, said Kvitsinsky.

Andropov used his first major address to the Central Committee on November 22 to sound a number of peaceful notes, including a reiterated willingness for an "honest agreement" on arms control, based on "reciprocity and equality" rather than "unilateral [Soviet] disarmament," which, he implied, was what the U.S. was after. The Soviet Union was interested in a restoration of détente, although it was not going to make "preliminary concessions" as a means of improving relations. There was a sense that the changing of the guard in the Kremlin offered an opportunity for progress.

However, nothing in Andropov's pronouncements from on high, or in his negotiators' statements in Geneva, indicated that the Soviets were any more willing than before to countenance new American missiles in Europe. On the contrary, the conciliatory rhetoric seemed primarily intended to encourage West European hopes that an agreement might yet spare them having to go through with deployment and to contend with the Soviet countermeasures that would inevitably follow. In effect, the softer words were in the service of the same hard line, which was to block deployment—or, failing that, to punish it.

Silence Is Assent

Andropov would soon emerge as the principal spokesman for shifts in the Soviet negotiating position. In mid-November, by remaining silent, Kvitsinsky managed to provide a hint of what Andropov would have to say in late December.

The Soviets had been seeking all along a ceiling of 300 "medium-range nuclear means"—missile launchers and aircraft—on each side. The Western "side," in their view, included the 255 British and French weapons already deployed, of which 162 were ballistic missiles and the rest were aircraft.* That meant less than 50 slots left over for American weapons. Until now, the proposal had also left open the theoretical possibility that the Soviets might devote their entire allotment of 300 to SS-20s, each, of course, with three warheads. Not that they seemed to have any intention of doing so. They were counting their Backfire bombers in Europe as eligible for inclusion under the 300 ceiling. They already had more than a hundred of these aircraft and seemed on their way to building them up to nearly 150.

But the American negotiators used every opportunity to point out that the language of the Soviet proposal would permit the U.S.S.R. to trade in Backfires for even more SS-20s than it already had in Europe. All right, said Kvitsinsky with theatrical exasperation in a plenary statement: his side might be able to agree on a sublimit for ballistic missiles under the 300 ceiling. The American side's response, added Kvitsinsky, would be a "crucial test of your seriousness."

The Americans had little doubt what the new Soviet-proposed sublimit would turn out to be. It would be somewhere in the neighborhood of 150

---

*The British had 64 Polaris SLBMs, the French 18 land-based missiles and 80 SLBMs, totaling 162.

—the predictable, not-so-magic number that would allow the U.S.S.R. to have about 150 Backfire bombers, which seemed to be the number they were planning to deploy, and about 150 SS-20s, a figure that would approximately match the 162 ballistic-missile launchers in the arsenals of Britain and France, while forcing the cancellation of the new NATO deployment in toto.

On November 17, Senator Gary Hart was in Geneva to look in on the negotiations. Hart—an active supporter of arms control who had frequently visited Geneva during SALT II—had lunch with the two chief negotiators and asked how the talks were going. His role in the conversation was, as Hart later commented, that of a "hollow log." Nitze, seeing an opportunity to probe the latest Soviet move, suggested that he would review the bidding as he saw it, "and if Ambassador Kvitsinsky disagrees or feels I've made a mistake, he can correct me." He went through a fairly detailed, deadpan recitation of the two sides' positions, noting that the Soviets had recently made a proposal for a subceiling on missiles.

Nitze then ventured his own guess about what this subceiling might look like in more detail than the Soviets had yet provided. Each side might be allowed 300 "medium-range nuclear means," but of those perhaps something like 150 could be ballistic missiles. Nitze was careful to give Kvitsinsky a chance to amend or disavow his understanding of the form the Soviet position seemed to be taking. Kvitsinsky let it stand.

It is a time-honored, though by no means foolproof, device of diplomacy for one side to make a unilateral statement, either about its own position or about its understanding of the other side's, and then to take silence as assent. Nitze was using that device now, as he put it to his own staff afterward, "to smoke Kvitsinsky out" on the question of what the Soviets were up to in their new proposal for a subceiling on missiles.

The Soviet numbers had obviously been worked out very carefully with an eye to pleasing the West Europeans and putting the U.S. more on the spot than ever. A residual force of 150 SS-20s would mean 450 warheads (150 $\times$ 3). That would be fewer than the total number of SS-4 and -5 warheads that had been targeted against Western Europe in the sixties and seventies. By moving 100 SS-20s, or 300 warheads, to Asia and by dismantling 250-odd single-warhead SS-4s and -5s, the Soviets would be able to claim that they were withdrawing 550 warheads, almost as many as the U.S. was planning to introduce with the 572 Tomahawks and Pershing IIs. The crowning ingenuity of the scheme was that it managed to seem new and forthcoming while not in fact altering the substance of Soviet policy one iota. The essence of that policy had always been to block the NATO deployments, to keep as many long-range ballistic missiles in Europe as the British and French had, and to keep Asia free of European arms control.

On December 21, Andropov made it official. In a live television address, he offered to reduce the number of the U.S.S.R.'s medium-range missiles in

Europe to match the combined arsenals of France and Great Britain, if the U.S. would abandon its deployment plans. To the letter, the newly installed General Secretary of the Soviet Communist party followed the script that Nitze had written for him during the luncheon in Geneva with Gary Hart and Kvitsinsky. Coupled with this offer were renewed hints that the U.S.S.R. might dismantle and destroy some of the excess SS-20s in Europe rather than redeploying them eastward, and that it might make some accommodation to the Western insistence on taking warheads into account, rather than just launchers. Significantly, the principal recipient of these teasers was a visitor to Moscow from Bonn, Hans-Jochen Vogel, Helmut Schmidt's successor as standard-bearer of the West German Social Democratic party and the party's candidate to face Helmut Kohl in the elections scheduled for March.

The British and French governments were quick to dismiss Andropov's offer. They were not going to consent to the inclusion of their independent deterrents in a Soviet-American agreement. Moreover, they could see that the suggestion of counting warheads contained two traps. The Soviets were careful not to say they were speaking only of land-based ballistic-missile warheads; they were leaving open the possibility of counting bombs and air-launched missiles aboard dual-capable aircraft as well. Also, Britain and France were both planning to add multiple independently targetable warheads to their SLBMs, so the effect of the new Soviet proposal would be either to halt the MIRVing of British and French SLBMs or to entitle the Soviets greatly to increase the number of SS-20s in Europe as part of a future claim for compensation.

Those objections, however, were technical points apparent only to experts. To West European public opinion and to politicians eager for a breakthrough in INF, Andropov's ploy had the effect of making the Soviet Union seem genuinely in search of a compromise. By contrast, the Reagan Administration's zero option was beginning to look rigid, stale, and unreasonable.

"The House Is Burning Down"

Back in Washington for the year-end recess, Nitze plunged into intensive lobbying for more flexibility to respond with a coherent and quite specific counteroffer to the new Soviet ploy. He called on all the top officials of the government as well as the Joint Chiefs of Staff. He told a number of groups that he thought the odds of getting a deal were about one in three. But, even against those odds, Nitze was coming with reluctance but with conviction to the pessimistic view that the best deal the U.S. could hope for might be a version of what the Soviets seemed to be getting ready to offer: a reduction of European SS-20s from 243 to 162, a level equal to the number of British and French ballistic-missile launchers.

The alternative was an utterly one-sided version of the zero option: zero new long-range missiles in NATO while the Soviets kept all of their SS-20s and were free to add as many as they wanted. In Nitze's view, that might indeed be the consequence if the West Europeans—prompted by their own anxieties, their perception of American intransigence, and the attractions, however meretricious, of the new Soviet position—reneged on their commitment to deploy the Tomahawks and Pershing IIs, thus depriving the U.S. of its only bargaining leverage in the negotiations. It was a dismal prospect, but Nitze took pride in his ability to analyze a situation rigorously and to follow his logic wherever it led, even if the destination was unpleasant and unpopular. And in this case, he felt that he had on his side "a chain of propositions that cannot be disputed."

"We have a political problem in Europe," he said at a meeting in the State Department. "A considerable percentage of European public opinion is not satisfied with our zero-zero position and *would* be satisfied with an outcome that left us with zero on our side [no deployment]. There's another percentage of the European population that doesn't hold out any hope for zero-zero but might be satisfied if we seem to be exploring an equitable solution above zero. The first thing we've got to do is start exploring those solutions so that it becomes more likely that the requisite percentage will support deployment."

He had some quite specific percentages in mind, based on a public-opinion survey that the United States Information Agency had recently conducted. It showed that only about 6 percent of the population in the basing countries was "unconditionally" in favor of deployment; another 30–35 percent was "conditionally" in favor of deployment "as a means of getting an agreement." But a solid 25 percent was unconditionally against deployment. It was particularly the disparity between those unconditionally for and unconditionally against that worried Nitze. It confirmed his fear that, in the end, Helmut Kohl and Margaret Thatcher—despite their sympathy with Reagan and their loyalty to the alliance—could not overcome the opposition of their constituents.

That pessimism led Nitze to continue: "It is almost certain that the Soviets will not buy finite equal limits on both sides. Nor is it clear that a sufficient portion of European public opinion would be satisfied with an equal-limits proposal to permit deployment, other than at a political cost so great as to be potentially very damaging to the alliance. The prime U.S. interest has to be in maintaining the alliance. There is no point in deployment at the expense of the solidarity of the alliance."

Almost everyone with whom he dealt in Washington thought Nitze was being far too apocalyptic. Richard Perle adopted a solicitous tone: "Who's Paul been talking to over there?" he asked others in the government. "Whoever it is has really got the poor man in a state of despair." Jonathan Howe, with characteristic restraint, said, "Paul's overreacting a bit, I think." Just as characteristically, Burt said, "Nitze's utterly spooked; he's gone around the bend; he's panicking; he's falling apart."

Burt told Nitze to his face that he "fundamentally disagreed" with his assessment of the political situation in Europe. During one lengthy, heated meeting, Burt said, "Paul, the minute I think this process will tear the alliance apart, that's the minute I'll join you in a search for a cosmetic solution."

Burt, of course, had been pushing a cosmetic solution of his own for months; he had never believed that his own preferred strategy for the negotiations was anything but a smokescreen and holding action for deployment. "I'm nowhere near sharing your pessimism on how bad it will be once deployment starts," said Burt. "The trouble will die down once we get over the hump at the end of the year." Even Robert Grey, still hanging on to his job, and an admirer and ally of Nitze's, shook his head, lamenting, "Paul's lost his mind."

Nitze's response was blunt. "You're all preoccupied with how a new American position will play in Washington. I don't give a good goddamn what will play here. I'm concerned about what will play in Europe." He was convinced that it was the U.S. grip on NATO that was giving way, not his own grip on reality; Burt, Howe, Grey, and the rest were, he believed, whistling past the graveyard.

Nitze had at least one sharp exchange with Burt in front of others. It occurred at the offices of the U.S. Information Agency. Burt emphasized that U.S. policy remained a formal, public commitment to zero-zero, but couched in terms of willingness to consider new Soviet proposals. The principal purpose of the various official advertising campaigns on behalf of U.S. policy should be to do everything possible to make sure that deployment went ahead on schedule.

Public relations, Nitze responded, was no substitute for policy; policy required recognition that there was virtually no hope of getting the Europeans to accept deployment of the new NATO missiles. Policy also required looking behind the deployment deadlines to the consequences for the alliance of deploying in the face of massive popular opposition.

In private conversation with Charles Wick, a California friend of Reagan's and director of USIA, Nitze stressed that his views were based heavily on the agency's own polling in Europe. Nitze urged Wick, as a public-relations expert himself, to study those polls closely and "derive the obvious lesson that there just isn't enough swing in public opinion to make deployment in and of itself the prudent object of a go-for-broke policy."

Nitze could not prevail in Washington. His colleagues heard him out; they humored him. The polite diagnosis was that he was being "Spenglerian." The less polite one was that he was running around like Chicken Little.

Shultz was scheduled to visit Europe in December. The issue of INF was sure to dominate his meetings there. Nitze offered to go along, since the Secretary of State was new to the job and had yet to master the "awful nitty-gritty," as Nitze called it, of the negotiations. Burt argued it would be "preposterous" to let Nitze accompany Shultz, given the negotiator's gloom and doom. Nitze's pessimism might be infectious; better not to contaminate the Europeans with it. Nitze found this argument ironic, since Europe was where he had "caught" his pessimism. But Eagleburger supported Burt, saying, "Paul should be given a chance to cool down a little bit."

So Nitze stayed home and worked on two papers about how the U.S. should respond to the Andropov proposal, one on how to handle the back channel that was still supposedly open between himself and Kvitsinsky, the other on how to proceed in the front channel of the negotiations proper.

The back-channel paper came about as a result of a meeting with Kenneth Dam in early December when Shultz was already in Europe. Nitze went through his by-now-well-rehearsed assessment of the bleak prospects in Europe and how it was necessary for the U.S. to cut its losses. Dam, ever the good listener, said, "Paul, that sounds very serious; I think you'd better put it on paper, but no longer than three pages because the President won't read anything longer than that."

Nitze did so. He suggested that in private conversations with Kvitsinsky he should explore the possibility of establishing equal limits on intermediate-range missile launchers in Europe, along the lines of what he and Kvitsinsky had discussed the previous summer, with additional limits on launchers outside of Europe (in the U.S. and Soviet Far East), and very high ceilings on aircraft. Nitze called this Plan A. (This would, in time, become known as the Nitze option, in competition with the Burt option of 300 warheads per side.)

But, as he had been saying over and over, the chances of getting the Soviets to accept such a compromise now, with everything going their way in Europe, were almost nil. Therefore he included a fallback to the fallback —what he termed Plan B. If, as he feared, the Soviets would not sign an agreement that permitted the U.S. any Tomahawks or Pershing IIs in Europe, the Administration should be prepared to embrace the postponement option, with a few features borrowed from the various Andropov proposals and the Nitze-Kvitsinsky package. The Soviet and U.S. governments would issue parallel but nonbinding policy statements: The U.S. would suspend deployment of the Tomahawks and Pershing IIs, putting intermediate-range nuclear forces onto the agenda of the strategic arms talks. The Soviet Union would state that over a period of five years it would eliminate all the SS-4s and -5s and reduce its SS-20 force to around 160 in Europe, 250 throughout the U.S.S.R., thus matching the British and French missiles in Europe and freezing the Asian SS-20s at 90, as Nitze and Kvitsinsky had agreed in their walk in the woods.

For more than a year Nitze had argued strenuously against the increasingly fashionable idea of "folding INF into START." He had always believed, and continued to believe, that any chance of reaching an INF agreement would be destroyed if its substance became tangled up with that of START. He had also been convinced by the West Germans that they could not possibly sustain their domestic support for deployments if the U.S. seemed to be drawing out and complicating the negotiations by running INF together with START. As he put it at one point when asked about the possibility of a merger, "There's simply no sense whatsoever in merging the two negotiations—unless, of course, we've given up, in which case merger might be a way of saving face."

Now he had come to the conclusion that the U.S. must, at least as a contingency plan, get ready to give up and save face. The goal now, in addition to saving face, should be to get "some compensation for non-deployment" of the Pershing IIs and Tomahawks, and the compensation would be to take the Soviets up on their offer to reduce their European SS-20s from 243 to 162.

Toward the end of his European tour, on December 15, Shultz attended a meeting in London of U.S. ambassadors in the region. The secretary was to report to the envoys on his talks with the heads of government in the basing countries. He invited Nitze to fly over and join him. Shultz's briefing about his conversations with the three leaders whose nations were to begin accepting deployments the next year—Kohl, Thatcher, and Emilio Colombo of Italy—was very upbeat. Nitze then stressed that, however stalwart Kohl and Thatcher might be, there was growing parliamentary and public opposition to deployment.

During a private session with Shultz, Nitze elaborated on his pessimism. Shultz listened with some dismay, then said, "I hope you haven't put this on paper, Paul. That could be very dangerous. It'll leak."

Nitze said he had indeed done so, at Dam's request. He was also circulating a second paper intended to shake the U.S. free of zero-zero. This one bore the imprimatur of the INF delegation as a whole and concerned the official U.S. position in Geneva, as opposed to what Nitze might say privately to Kvitsinsky. It was in the form of a recommended set of negotiating instructions—the instructions the negotiators wanted the President to give them. The delegation proposed that it return to Geneva for the next round on January 27 and formally present a revised, geographically restricted version of the zero proposal. The Soviet Union would eliminate all its SS-20s (as well as SS-4s and -5s) from Europe in exchange for the U.S.'s not introducing the Pershing II and Tomahawk in NATO. Then there would be a ceiling on "worldwide" deployments of those missiles: the Soviet Union would be allowed a certain number in the Asian parts of the U.S.S.R., and the U.S. would have a symmetrical, offsetting number of its own missiles outside of range of Europe, but available for rushing into Europe if the occasion arose.

Nitze had no illusion that this scheme was any more negotiable than the more "global" version of zero-zero. He was trying to get formal authorization from the Interagency Group to set forth a new negotiating position that would satisfy the growing demand from the West Europeans that the U.S. match Andropov's flexibility. But even that turned out to be impossible.

The delegation forwarded its recommendation for new instructions to the Interagency Group, but there Nitze ran into another stone wall. He sent a copy of the instructions to Jonathan Howe, who was taken aback. Howe had been willing to give Nitze the benefit of the doubt the previous autumn on the walk-in-the-woods package deal, but that was when the President was still awaiting guidance on how to deal with Nitze's initiative. Since then, Reagan had made a decision: zero-zero was to remain Administration policy. Howe took the view that the Interagency Group had no authorization from the President or the Secretary of State to be considering anything other than the global zero-zero proposal.

At a meeting of the Interagency Group on January 10, 1983, with Nitze in attendance, Howe used his prerogative as chairman to preempt Nitze; he stressed at the very outset that "global zero-zero" was the only acceptable basis for the delegation's instructions. Nitze argued that it was self-deluding and self-destructive to pretend for one moment longer that the pursuit of zero-zero was a viable policy. But Howe did not budge. As far as he was concerned, it was not the viability of the policy that mattered but the sanctity of the chain of command. He and Nitze were under orders from their Commander in Chief to fight for zero-zero, not against it.

Nitze's frustration was mounting. Shortly afterward he exclaimed to one of Howe's deputies, "Good Lord, man! Don't you know the house is burning down? Do you want to wait until it burns to the ground before you do anything?"

Exit Rostow

Nitze complained to Rostow that, once again, he was being thwarted by the Politico-Military Bureau. Rostow sent a note to Shultz on January 12, asking for a meeting on the situation later that day. When Rostow arrived at the secretary's office that afternoon, still on crutches from his recent hip operation, he was prepared to discuss Nitze's negotiating flexibility. Instead,

Shultz informed Rostow that the President no longer had confidence in him and wanted his resignation. Stunned, Rostow went back to his own office and told his aides, "I've been sacked." He then sat down at his desk and wrote a brief *pro forma* letter of resignation.

Rostow had always been an outsider; his habit of treating the President and members of the Cabinet like not-very-bright law students made him a deeply resented outsider. Reagan and Clark did not like him. It was almost that simple. When Rostow did not quit over the lack of White House support for Grey's nomination, Clark suggested to Reagan "getting it over with and firing the guy." For once, the President's decision was crisp and clear: "Fine, let's do it."

Rostow, however, could not bring himself to view his downfall in such mundane terms. He minimized the extent to which his undoing stemmed from the incompatibility of his background and personality with Reagan's, Clark's, and the others', and he exaggerated the importance of substantive disagreements, particularly over how much latitude to give Nitze. In a farewell speech to his staff, he went public with the plea he had intended to make to Shultz: "If our people, our allies, and our friends lose faith in . . . both the firmness and intelligent flexibility of our arms-control efforts . . . it will be impossible to achieve worthwhile agreements with the Soviets and our alliance systems will be in grave peril."

Rostow also maintained that it was his own "zealous" championing of flexibility that had led to his downfall. As a case in point, word quickly got out from Rostow and his staff that he and Nitze had been partners in a bold but star-crossed attempt at salvaging INF the year before. *The New York Times* published an account of the Nitze-Kvitsinsky walk down the mountain. Other papers followed with more of the story. Rostow and some of his closest aides had convinced themselves that if the incident was known to the world the allies would appreciate how seriously he and Nitze had sought an agreement—and, by extension, how seriously Nitze could be expected to continue seeking an agreement.

By thus lifting the veil, albeit partially and selectively, from one of the government's best-kept and most-sensitive secrets, Rostow had—whatever his motive—inadvertently undercut Nitze even further. In addition to having been deprived of a staunch ally and denied the more permissive negotiating instructions he wanted, Nitze was suddenly exposed in public as a negotiator who had been repudiated and reprimanded by the White House. The very phrase "walk in the woods" became something of an in-joke, in both Washington and Geneva. Even the wives of Soviet INF negotiators would say to their American counterparts things like: "Let's get together for a nature outing. Perhaps if we take a walk in the woods, we'll accomplish more than our husbands."

Nitze was furious at Rostow, and uncertain about how much longer he should remain at his post. William Clark had told Nitze shortly before Rostow was fired that the President wanted him to stay on. Nitze agreed to go back for another round, but he was not sure whether to believe Clark. He could not help but suspect that Reagan and Clark might actually be trying to keep him on for a while longer, so that a decent interval could elapse after they dumped Rostow, and then they would dump him, too.

The response to Rostow's firing both in Europe and in Congress was one of dismay. Rostow had succeeded in transforming himself in the eyes of the West Europeans from a hard-liner, the personification of the worst that the Europeans feared in the new Administration, into a champion of—and now a martyr for—the cause of moderation. The dismissal seemed to offer further evidence not only that the Administration was in disarray but that the hard-liners were winning in the fights going on behind the scenes. Reagan and Shultz each felt compelled to make appearances before the press corps to deny that there was disarray and to assert that they were in charge.

Yet it was apparent to those inside the government that Shultz in particular was, if anything, even less in charge than before. After the White House had stopped supporting Grey's nomination as Rostow's deputy, Shultz had endorsed the choice of another career diplomat for the job. But William Clark had his own candidate: Kenneth Adelman, a thirty-six-year-old neo-conservative who had been serving as Deputy Permanent U.S. Representative to the United Nations, under Jeane Kirkpatrick. Clark's plan had been to put Adelman in the No. 2 slot at the Arms Control Agency, force Rostow out, and find a fairly senior person, more compatible to the White House, to take over as director. Among Clark's initial choices for director had been Seymour Weiss, the one-time director of the State Department's Politico-Military Bureau, who had become an opponent of SALT, a close friend of Perle's, and an outspoken critic of NATO's 1979 dual-track decision; and Fred Iklé. When Clark had sounded him out, Weiss declined on grounds of poor health; Weinberger wanted to keep Iklé at the Pentagon.

Adelman, who also had close ties to Perle, moved from being Clark's pick as deputy director to being offered the top job. Adelman had a charmed, precocious career, the result of energy, ambition, good connections, and luck. He had once been a student of Jeane Kirkpatrick's when she was a professor of political science at Georgetown University. In the mid-seventies he had also been an aide and protégé of Gerald Ford's Defense Secretary Donald Rumsfeld, who, along with Iklé, had helped to scuttle Henry Kissinger's last-ditch attempt at negotiating a SALT II agreement in early 1976. He had written extensively about the shortcomings of traditional arms control. Early in the Administration, Rostow had sounded him out for the job that went to Grey, so in that sense things had come full circle. Adelman was not, however, high on Shultz's list for any position, including the one he held. Some close aides to the Secretary of State strongly suspected Adelman of leaking to the press cables from Washington that were intended to make the State Department look "soft" in the war of words against the Soviets in the UN. It was, therefore, a double blow to Shultz when Rostow was suddenly fired and replaced, at Clark's initiative and with Perle applauding from the sidelines, by Adelman.*

Nitze, too, was deeply distressed about this latest turn in events. Among other things, it further diminished his hope that Shultz would assert himself in prying the Administration away from the zero option. Nitze was about to return to Geneva. After two months of dealing with his own colleagues and countrymen, the prospect of confronting Yuli Kvitsinsky was almost a relief. But he was returning with instructions only to sound out new Soviet proposals, not to advance any of his own. He had been, quite bluntly, forbidden to do so.

---

*As it turned out, the Administration had traded one kind of confirmation fight for another. Grey had twisted slowly in the wind because of conservative opposition on Capitol Hill and double-dealing on the part of the White House. The Adelman nomination touched off a furor among moderates and liberals in the Senate. Some senators opposed him because of his lack of experience; for others, he was a lightning rod for their impatience with the Administration's arms-control policies as a whole. The Foreign Relations Committee voted to send the nomination to the floor with a recommendation that he not be confirmed. Shultz and Dam distanced themselves from the White House's effort to save Adelman. The President, however, urged on by Clark, fought all the harder, and after intensive lobbying on his part, the full Senate did confirm Adelman, 57–42, on April 12.

8 The Interim Solution

In the Reagan Administration, only when arms control was a political exercise, either within the U.S. or within the alliance, did it capture the President's attention. So it was at the beginning of 1983, the make-or-break year for the negotiations, the do-or-die year for deployment. Eugene Rostow's ouster, the revelations of the abortive walk-in-the-woods deal, Paul Nitze's impending return to Geneva, a step-up in the Soviet peace offensive, and the approach of national elections in West Germany—all these made INF into an urgent political challenge.

The immediate issue was whether sticking with the zero option was the best way to assure that Helmut Kohl would be reelected and that deployment would proceed on schedule at the end of the year. The Administration could be forgiven some confusion over what the West German leaders wanted. Did they want the U.S. to stand firm on zero, or did they want it to lead the way to a new, more promising position? The signals from Bonn were, to say the least, mixed.

In public, Kohl himself held to an unequivocal endorsement of the zero option. An acceptable outcome in Geneva, he kept saying, would be the achievement of the zero-zero solution and nothing short of that. However, Kohl kept saying that mainly because he knew it to be Reagan Administration policy, and he did not want to appear to be wavering. He would have been glad, however, if the U.S. had taken the lead and adopted a more flexible approach in Geneva, especially if it brought the two sides closer to an agreement.

But in Washington there was a tendency to take Kohl at his word. His support for the zero proposal was used to justify the Administration's own adherence to it. That was especially true at the Pentagon, the birthplace and the last bastion of the hard-and-fast zero option. During an informal discussion of the INF conundrum at the White House in early January, the President said he was a bit worried about "getting too dug in on zero." Shultz raised the possibility of the U.S.'s "leaving zero behind us," and moving instead toward something along the lines of what Burt had been quietly promoting and refining since the autumn: 300 warheads on each side.

Weinberger, Clark, and Casey all favored holding firm, and they cited the West German political situation as a reason to do so. As Weinberger kept saying, "We don't want it to look like we're letting the German left push us around."

Anonymous official comments to that effect quickly filtered into the press, and the reaction in Bonn was dismay. Friedrich Ruth, the West German specialist on NATO and INF affairs, hastened to Washington to tell Richard Burt, Richard Perle, and Jonathan Howe that his government wanted the U.S. to demonstrate more flexibility. Howe and Burt made a point of asking Ruth, "Are you speaking for the Chancellor when you say this?"

"Yes, I most certainly am," replied Ruth.

What, exactly, would constitute flexibility? On that, the West Germans were uncertain. But, while they did not know precisely what they wanted, they knew what they wanted to avoid, and that was the appearance that the American leadership was gearing its policies for NATO to the upcoming German elections. Such an appearance would carry with it the implication that supposedly lofty decisions about grand strategy for the West were actually being made on the basis of German domestic politics, that a conservative American Administration was tinkering with nuclear diplomacy in order to help its ideological brethren win an election in the Federal Republic. A conservative West German government would appear to be in the pocket of a stubborn and hawkish American one.

That appearance was particularly unwelcome to Ruth's boss and Kohl's Foreign Minister and coalition partner, Hans-Dietrich Genscher. His Free Democratic party was to the left of Kohl's Christian Democratic Union and was therefore more vulnerable to the Social Democrats in the competition for votes in the upcoming election. As he campaigned around the country, Genscher began urging that if the U.S. and U.S.S.R. failed to achieve the zero solution by the time the deadline for deployment arrived they should adopt a *Zwischen Lösung,* an interim solution, whereby each side would set equal ceilings at levels higher than zero but lower than 572 on the NATO side. Another dramatic indication of the extent to which the zero option had become an orphan in its fatherland was its dismissal as "utopian" and utterly non-negotiable by Franz Josef Strauss, the conservative leader of Bavaria, who had ambitions to replace Genscher as Kohl's Foreign Minister after the elections. Thus, like the "zero option" in 1981, the catch phrase that would end up becoming American policy in 1983—the "interim solution"—was a translation from German, and from the language of West German domestic politics.

The concept, if not the exact phrase, of an interim solution found its way into English quickly enough, from the mouth of Margaret Thatcher. On January 18, she told the House of Commons: "The principle is a balance in order to deter. The best balance between the Soviet Union and NATO is zero. In the absence of that, one must have a balance between the SS-20s and the cruise and Pershing missiles. . . . That is the proposition before us. One hopes to achieve the zero option. But in the absence of that, we must achieve balanced numbers."

While Thatcher had been the most resolute supporter of Reagan Administration policy in Europe, the British Foreign Office had been skeptical about the zero option from the beginning, since it did not conform with the December 1979 NATO decision: whatever the diplomatic outcome in Geneva, some military modernization would still be necessary for the alliance. Thatcher was persuaded by what she called "the strategic logic" of the Foreign Office, but her decision to endorse the interim solution was fortified by domestic political considerations of her own. It now appeared that she might have to call a general election later in the year, shortly before the first Tomahawks were due to arrive at Greenham Common, outside London, where a group of women had set up a round-the-clock "peace camp" to protest deployment. The British nuclear-disarmament movement was gathering force, and the Labour party had made opposition to the new missiles one of its principal issues in trying to unseat Thatcher.

Bush as Front Man

At least part of the reason for the West Europeans' impatience and nervousness was that in his first few forays to the podium in 1983, President Reagan turned out to be something other than the Great Communicator, at least on the subject of INF. In a press conference on January 20, he tried to paraphrase the need for new missiles in Europe: "We claim that to continue to stand there with [the Soviets'] having enough warheads to literally wipe out every population center in Western Europe, with no deterrent on our side, and the NATO allies recognize this, and we have said at their request that we will provide a deterrent."

The sentence was not quite complete, but the meaning could be grasped: without the Pershing IIs and Tomahawks, Western Europe would have no nuclear deterrent. By implication, according to Reagan, if the U.S. failed to install the new missiles and the Soviets managed to keep even a substantial number of SS-20s (as Nitze, for one, now felt would probably be necessary), NATO would be naked; decoupling would have occurred; the U.S. would have folded up its nuclear umbrella and gone home. The President's statement ignored the thousands of American tactical nuclear weapons already in Europe and the thousands more strategic weapons committed to Europe's defense. Simply by saying such a thing, Reagan had further exacerbated the confusion and the shakiness of confidence within the alliance. Yet at his next press conference, on February 16, he repeated that if NATO failed to deploy the new American missiles "We would not have any deterrent force on our side."

On January 20, Reagan also inadvertently confirmed the widespread suspicion that the Administration regarded Andropov's various gestures as nothing but propaganda and intended to respond in kind. The White House had just announced the formation of a task force that would try to sell the zero option, Madison Avenue style, in Western Europe. Asked if the U.S. was treating it as a propaganda issue, Reagan replied, "The answer to that is not propaganda. It's public relations."

Watching from the back of the room or on television in their offices, officials throughout the Administration were wincing. So were the U.S.'s friends in Europe. Reagan was due to meet the next day with Nitze and a group of top foreign-policy and national-security advisers. It was decided that the President should not be allowed to put in another live, extemporaneous appearance on the issue of arms control on that occasion. Instead, the State Department drafted a statement to be released in Reagan's name after the January 21 meeting: "The coming round [of talks] is particularly important because our far-reaching proposals, combined with our defense modernization programs, provide a strong incentive for reaching agreements on *lower levels of forces.*" (Italics added.)

It was a new example of his aides' putting words in Reagan's mouth, although without the risk of letting the President himself speak the lines. This time the State Department had succeeded in writing the script. Richard Burt was now emerging as the director of Administration policy in INF. The phrase "lower levels of forces" was deliberately intended to sound a note in harmony with the sudden preference in Western Europe for an interim solution in INF at a level above zero.

After months in limbo, Burt had been finally assured of confirmation by the Senate as Assistant Secretary of State for European Affairs (the final vote came on February 16). He no longer had to hide in the background of the interagency process, although he would still work behind the scenes. He had a scenario for events during the year ahead ("the Year of the Missile") and the front man was to be Vice-President George Bush. Burt saw Bush as an old-fashioned all-American archetype, the sort of Gary Cooper figure, friendly and straightforward, whom Europeans tended to like. The Vice-President was restless in his largely ceremonial job in Washington and was eager to hit the diplomatic high road.

Shortly after George Shultz had replaced Alexander Haig the previous year, Burt had written the new Secretary of State a memo suggesting Bush as the best person to send on a barnstorming tour of the countries where the NATO missiles were to be based. The Bush trip was scheduled for the beginning of February 1983. As that date approached, Burt sent Shultz another memo, urging that the Administration move quickly to recapture the initiative from the Soviets by making a counteroffer to Andropov's proposal of December 21 to reduce European SS-20s to 162: Bush would proclaim once again American willingness to negotiate in good faith and set forth some criteria for what would constitute an acceptable INF agreement. Zero-zero would remain both the ideal outcome and the American negotiating position of record, but the criteria would be sufficiently flexible to embrace an interim solution at a level above zero.

The White House resisted the idea that anybody but the President should announce, or even suggest publicly, a formal change in the U.S. position. William Clark and other members of the Reagan inner circle were particularly averse to the idea that George Bush, whom they still saw as a potential usurper, should do so. Bush's role, as Eagleburger summarized it at a meeting of the Dam Group, would be to "reiterate zero-zero, but with lots of softness around the edges."

Bush was almost too successful in the way he played his part. During his tour, he invited suggestions, put the best possible face on the zero option, hinted at American gestures of flexibility still to come, and stressed that deployment would not necessarily be irreversible: missiles that went in on the deployment track could later be withdrawn if there was progress on the negotiating track. But the high point of his trip came on January 31, during a speech in West Berlin, when he pulled out an "open letter" from Ronald Reagan to the people of Europe. Avowing the Administration's commitment to "spare no effort to reach a fair and meaningful agreement that will reduce the Soviet nuclear threat," Reagan's letter continued:

> In this spirit, I have asked Vice President Bush, in the city where East meets West, to propose to Soviet General Secretary Andropov that he and I meet wherever and whenever he wants in order to sign an agreement banning U.S. and Soviet intermediate range land-based nuclear missile weapons from the face of the earth.
>
> I make this offer out of a conviction that such an agreement would serve the interests of both sides and, most importantly, that the people of Europe want nothing more. I urge Mr. Andropov to accept it.

Helmut Kohl himself led a standing ovation. The immediate reaction in Germany was generally favorable. Even Kohl's opponent in the upcoming elections, Hans-Jochen Vogel, remarked, "I think this is progress. It's the first time Mr. Reagan has offered such a step."

In fact, the letter did not advance or alter Administration policy at all. What Reagan was offering, through Bush, was the same zero proposal and the same conditions for a summit that had been U.S. policy all along. When

Reagan had signed the letter in the Oval Office just before Bush left for Europe, he had stressed that he was not calling for a summit in the sense of a meeting at which unresolved issues would be negotiated. He would only meet with Andropov if the negotiations were already completed on terms satisfactory to the U.S., and to him that still meant Soviet acceptance of zero-zero. But, by rephrasing an old, intransigent position in a new, more positive-sounding way, Reagan had, for the moment, regained some of the ground he had lost from Andropov in the propaganda war.

Edwin Meese and William Clark congratulated each other on how well the ploy had worked. They wondered if the lesson of the episode was perhaps that the U.S. needed only to concentrate on improving its "public diplomacy"—the new euphemism for public relations and propaganda. Perhaps there was no need, or certainly no urgent need, for abandoning zero at all.

Burt had foreseen the danger that the White House might take excessive consolation from the success of the Bush trip. He was afraid that there might be a similarly optimistic misreading of a Kohl victory in the upcoming West German election. While still in Europe for a Special Consultative Group meeting, Burt wrote warning memoranda to the Vice-President and to Shultz in Washington. The President's loudly applauded letter had given the U.S. some breathing space, but Kohl, Thatcher, and the Italian leaders were all saying that, having changed the tone, the U.S. must now change the substance of its position.

There were, in Burt's view, three ways of doing that: (1) to offer a concrete new position, with new numbers above zero; (2) to set forth the criteria for an acceptable compromise as though they constituted a new proposal, but hold back on the specifics; and (3) to ask the Soviets to come forward with a new proposal of their own that met the new American criteria. These were the principal choices considered at a National Security Council meeting on February 11, at which Bush reported on his trip. At that session and a number of subcabinet follow-up meetings, it was decided to inch toward a new proposal by setting forth the criteria first.

In a speech to the American Legion on February 22, Reagan laid out four criteria for a compromise that the State Department had been working on for months. Reagan repeated the words so often used as a kind of incantation by the State Department to dispel fears of American inflexibility: the U.S. was "negotiating in good faith in Geneva, and ours is not a take-it-or-leave-it proposal." He had instructed Nitze to explore "every proposed solution consistent with the principles to which the alliance subscribes." The implication was that zero-zero was just one of a number of possibilities, and the nod to the allies was explicit. Then came the four criteria: "equality of rights and limits," no compensation for the British and French forces, an agreement that was verifiable, and restrictions on Soviet forces in the Far East ("Soviet proposals which have the effect of shifting the threat from Europe to Asia cannot be considered reasonable").*

For Richard Perle, the speech came as an unpleasant surprise. "The State Department thinks it's really pulled a fast one," he said. "It thinks it's going to buy off the Europeans with this dance of the seven veils and all this talk about flexibility. But mark my words: the Europeans won't be satisfied. They'll just say they want more, more, more. They'll start chanting, 'Take it all off! Take it all off!' " In fact, the response in London and Bonn to the American Legion speech was that while the President's move was welcome, he must go further. He must now embody the criteria he had set forth in a new American proposal.

In the March 6 election, a coalition of Kohl's Christian Democrats, Genscher's Free Democrats, and Strauss's Christian Social Union took 55.7 percent of the vote. The Social Democrats lost ground, though the new, leftist Green party, which based much of its campaign on opposition to the new missiles, for the first time gained representation in the parliament. George Bush proclaimed the outcome a "magnificent victory" that would improve the U.S. negotiating position in Geneva.

Kohl and Genscher, who remained Foreign Minister, were for their part pleased to have Washington's congratulations. But they saw no reason for complacency about the INF. They hoped that their victory had convinced Moscow that they would stick to the deployment track and that they had impressive public backing for doing so. They now turned their attention and their powers of friendly persuasion on Washington in order to get the U.S. moving along the negotiating track.

In the first days after his triumph, Kohl told the U.S. ambassador to Bonn, Arthur Burns, and others not just that the Reagan Administration should make a new proposal, but that he was certain it would do so. By his lights, he was not pressuring; he was expressing a heartfelt conviction that "the inescapable logic of circumstances" made a show of flexibility by the U.S. "inevitable." He and the West German electorate had rebuffed the left and, in so doing, had rebuffed the Soviet Union. The U.S.S.R. would now give up on its hope of stopping the NATO deployment altogether by means of manipulating West German public opinion. That made an INF compromise possible. But it also meant that the U.S. had to make a move toward such a compromise. Now Kohl, too, was an outright proponent of the interim solution.

---

*During an official visit to Washington, the new Japanese Prime Minister, Yasuhiro Nakasone, gave Shultz a blunt lecture on how Tokyo did not want to see an INF agreement that allowed the Soviets to redistribute its intermediate-range nuclear forces from Europe to Asia. The Japanese had expressed such concerns before, but rarely with such force, at such a high level. On his own visit to Tokyo shortly afterward, Shultz assured the Japanese government that the U.S. "approached arms control on an international basis, with its global responsibilities in mind."

The week after the West German election, Friedrich Ruth was asked when the U.S. should make good on Kohl's prediction of a new proposal. "The sooner the better," said Ruth. Over in London, the principal official on INF at the Foreign Office, David Gillmore, was asked the same question. His answer: "Better today."

The message coming across the Atlantic was: Don't just stand there—do something. That message was received clearly at the State Department, where it resonated sympathetically with the institutional predisposition against standing pat on a proposal that was obviously going nowhere in the negotiations. Richard Perle's position, in his own wry words, was just the opposite: "We can't just do something; we've got to stand there—and stand firm."

At a series of interagency meetings in January and early February, he warned that the Administration was falling into a trap by "cranking out all this stuff about how arms control is our highest goal. We're just asking to be hoist with our own petard. What we should be saying is that we're in no rush, we're not going to be stampeded, we'll hold out for as long as necessary to get an agreement that's truly in our interests, and we're ready, indeed would prefer, to live without an agreement rather than settle for a bad one."

In two conversations with Weinberger early in 1983, Perle went even further. "The costs of deployment," he said, could "vastly exceed the benefits"; the U.S. should be prepared to live without deployment rather than settle for a bad agreement. If it ever came to the point where the only way the U.S. could keep the installation of the Pershing IIs and Tomahawks on track was to sign an imprudent agreement, Washington should be prepared to "terminate" the deployments. For example, it would not be worth having deployment in the context of an INF agreement that failed to preserve the distinction Perle had been fighting for over the past year and a half between nuclear and conventionally armed cruise missiles.

"The objectives of the alliance are being subordinated to arms control," Perle warned Weinberger.

These were familiar arguments. Weinberger had not only heard them from Perle before—he had agreed with them, and had backed Perle's determined fight in the interagency process on behalf of exempting conventionally armed cruise missiles from INF. But now Perle was using the same argument to prepare Weinberger for a still unlikely but not impossible showdown: there might be a breakthrough in INF, either in Geneva or in some back channel; the State Department and the allies would be clamoring for an agreement that included American concessions on relatively esoteric issues; and Perle would have the Department of Defense not just veto the arms-control deal, but urge that the U.S. abandon deployment as well.

Weinberger had shared, and been guided by, Perle's intellectually elegant and extremely articulate distaste for arms control. He had not, however, ever absorbed Perle's distaste for the deployment half of the December '79 NATO decision. Because of successful machinations by the State Department at the very beginning of the Administration, the President had been manipulated into an endorsement of the two-track decision before Weinberger was ever drawn into the bureaucratic guerrilla warfare over the question.

Now, all of a sudden, here was Perle saying that the evils of arms control (signing an "imprudent" INF agreement that, say, banned conventionally armed cruise missiles) were so great that the U.S. might have to forgo rearmament (proceeding with deployment in Europe) for the sake of stopping disarmament. Or as Perle put it, "We might have to look for ways to get out from under this very costly situation."

That was too much for Weinberger. For him, as for the Administration as a whole, getting the new missiles into NATO was the be-all-and-end-all of U.S. policy. He began putting some distance between himself and Perle. With strains developing between them, it became all the easier for Richard Burt to take command of INF policymaking.

Back to Zero Plus

The Europeans were clamoring for the U.S. not just to endorse the idea of an interim solution but to make a formal proposal for one. Nitze and Kvitsinsky were winding up the spring round in Geneva. The President wanted to be able to say he had instructed Nitze to make some move before the round ended. Big demonstrations against deployment were planned for Greenham Common outside London and various sites in West Germany over the Easter weekend of April 2–3. The U.S. Senate, when it returned from its Easter recess, would be using the still unresolved issue of Kenneth Adelman's confirmation to be director of the Arms Control Agency as a starting point for a general debate on the Administration's arms-control policies. The White House would be all the more on the defensive if it had nothing to show for itself in INF.

A National Security Council meeting was scheduled for March 18. Several ideas were floating. The Administration could stand pat on zero, although it might offer to let the Soviets come down to zero on their side over five years, at the rate of 20 percent a year. This was Perle's preference, and this option was set forth in the paper circulated in advance of the meeting. But Perle could see that it did not stand a chance, so the Pentagon offered an alternative: the U.S. could go ahead and deploy its missiles, then reduce to an agreed, equal level once it was in a position of negotiating from strength. One possibility would be for the U.S. to express, in advance of deployment, a willingness to stop at a given level of warheads if the Soviets would themselves agree to drop back to that level. Asked by a State Department official what would be the minimum feasible numerical ceiling above zero, Perle responded, "One warhead on each side." He and the Pentagon were giving up on zero only reluctantly, and they were giving up as little as possible. As part of his office's effort to salvage as much of zero-zero as possible, Weinberger argued against the use of any numbers at all and urged that Soviet acceptance of "an eventual zero outcome" be made a precondition of American willingness to accept any interim solution, no matter what the numbers eventually turned out to be.

Shultz argued that the U.S. should offer specific numbers right away in order to advance the negotiations and to satisfy the need of the allies, particularly the British, for a concrete interim proposal. The State Department had now formally adopted Richard Burt's scheme of 300 warheads on each side: 300 single-warhead American missiles against 100 triple-warhead SS-20s, with both ceilings to apply globally, so that there could be no more than 100 SS-20s deployed throughout the U.S.S.R. That would mean that the U.S. could build up to 300 Pershing IIs and Tomahawks while the U.S.S.R. would have to build down to 100 SS-20s.

Burt and David Gillmore of the British Foreign Office had been in constant, close touch with each other, and Burt worked hard at orchestrating what he called "echoes" of his own position from across the Atlantic. The British government let it be known that whatever version of the interim solution was adopted and whatever lip service was paid to zero as the ultimate goal, the interim solution must not be preconditioned on Soviet acceptance of zero. Otherwise it would look like a slightly disguised zero option, and as such would not appear sufficiently new and flexible. Thus Burt, through Gillmore, had effectively enlisted the Prime Minister of Great Britain as a lobbyist against the Pentagon.

An old pattern was then repeated. The President listened. He was uncomfortable with the disagreement among his advisers and uncertain about what to do. "Isn't there some common ground here?" he asked Clark rather plaintively after the NSC meeting. The next morning, March 19, an interagency group gathered again in the Situation Room, without the President in attendance. Neither State nor Defense budged. In the end, Reagan tried, with Clark's help, to split the difference. Rejecting the State Department's demand for a specific number and the Pentagon's demand for a link to the zero solution, Reagan decided to tell the world that the U.S. was proposing equal but unspecified levels of warheads above zero, and to tell his own aides that he had chosen a synthesis between the two agencies' positions.

There were attempts to find a virtue in the expedient. Richard Boverie of the NSC staff claimed that the absence of numbers increased the appearance of forthcomingness on the part of the U.S.: "By not including numbers, we're showing greater flexibility. It shows that even the numbers are negotiable. It shows that we're not going to stick a finger in their eye and leave it at that." Burt later stated publicly that the interim proposal permitted the U.S. to explore with the Soviets "their readiness to accept various specific levels for an agreement, starting with 50 warheads on each side, and going through 450 warheads on each side."

Reagan exchanged letters with Kohl, Thatcher, and other leaders to establish a record of consultation within the alliance on what he was about to do. On March 25, Burt flew to Brussels to preside over a secret session of the Special Consultative Group to brief the allied foreign-ministry representatives on the decision. (The following week, when Burt, Perle, Howe, and McFarlane briefed a group of newsmen, Perle commented with some asperity, "The secret meeting of the SCG was so secret that I didn't know about it until it was over. Ordinarily, that would concern me, except that the SCG has done such a superb job coordinating allied and U.S. opinion. And my colleague [Burt] has been tireless in that. I don't even worry when they keep a meeting secret." Burt's face reddened, but he remained silent.)

On March 30, Reagan and Shultz held a fifteen-minute meeting with Washington-based NATO envoys and told them about the decision, then stepped before the television cameras and microphones in the East Room of the White House and announced what the Administration billed as "a new proposal":

> When it comes to intermediate nuclear missiles in Europe, it would be better to have none than to have some. But if there must be some, it is better to have few than to have many. If the Soviets will not now agree to the total elimination of these weapons, I hope that they will at least join us in an interim agreement that would substantially reduce these forces to equal levels on both sides. To this end, Ambassador Paul Nitze has informed his Soviet counterpart that we are prepared to negotiate an interim agreement in which the United States would substantially reduce its planned deployment of Pershing II and ground-launched cruise missiles, provided the Soviet Union reduce the number of its warheads on longer-range INF missiles to an equal level on a global basis.

The word "interim" had passed the President's lips, but his statement did not change the essence of U.S. policy in any significant respect.* When

---

*One small refinement was that a fifth criterion had now been added to the four that Reagan had spelled out in his American Legion speech. In addition to the principles of equality, non-compensation for British and French weapons, global treatment of SS-20s in Asia, and verifiability, the interim solution must also avoid jeopardizing NATO's conventional defenses. The new criterion about conventional defenses was a hedge against eventual inclusion of bombers and fighter-bombers in an INF agreement. The Administration wanted to be on public record preemptively rejecting any limitation on dual-capable aircraft. Perle attached another meaning to the fifth criterion: he was

queried skeptically about what was new in all this, McFarlane explained, "Well, up until this time the President has said that there just hasn't been a serious proposal from their side. The point of today's announcement is that, out of frustration at their intransigence, and out of commitment to getting results, the President is saying that zero is not the only immediate acceptable outcome."

Of course, the President had never said that zero was the "only immediate acceptable outcome" in the first place. The willingness of the U.S. to accept an interim solution above zero had been implicit in U.S. pronouncements for months. All Reagan was doing now was making it explicit. Eighteen months after deciding on the Pentagon's zero-only option, he was now, in effect, adopting the State Department's zero-plus option instead.

Another "Nyet"

Two days before Reagan's announcement in Washington, Nitze and Kvitsinsky had lunch at a restaurant called the Hunters' Rendezvous, near the French border. Nitze gave Kvitsinsky a preview of the interim proposal. He stressed that zero-zero was still the best ultimate outcome, and that any solution above zero would involve increased problems of verification, but that the U.S. would consider equal ceilings on each side's intermediate-range missile warheads. Kvitsinsky told Nitze that his government would "carefully study" the new proposal, but would, he felt sure, "promptly and unambiguously" reject it. Nitze said he would regret that if it happened, since it was an important and constructive move by the U.S. The next day, March 29, during the final plenary session of the round, Nitze formally made the proposal, and Kvitsinsky presaged the Soviet response in more detail: there was nothing new in the U.S. position because it still treated the U.S.S.R.'s Asian-based forces as part of European arms control; it was posited on the acceptability of new American missiles in Europe; and it failed to compensate the Soviets for the British and French nuclear forces.

On April 2, the Soviets rejected the new proposal in public, at great length, and at the highest level. Gromyko held a press conference in Moscow, broadcast live to the U.S. In an hour-long opening statement, followed by a question-and-answer period, the Foreign Minister reminded the world that the Soviet Union had its own criteria for an INF agreement, and that the American interim proposal failed to meet any of them. The White House and the Kremlin were back in the business of trading proposals and rejections before their negotiators had even settled into their seats in Geneva.

---

determined to keep fighting for the principle (and the explicit provision in the draft treaty language) that any limitation on cruise missiles must apply to nuclear-armed ones alone; conventionally armed ground-launched cruise missiles, if there ever were such things, must be exempted from limitation.

Once the next round got underway in mid-May, the U.S. presented a new draft treaty embodying the interim-solution proposal. Another feature, added later as a sweetener, was an offer to make limitations on shorter-range missiles reciprocal—i.e., Pershing Is would be limited in the same manner as the Soviet shorter-range SS-12s and -22s (this was a gesture Nitze had wanted to make early on in the negotiations). There were a few amplifications and adjustments of the standing Soviet position. Some were marginal, token advances; others were more significant steps backward. In the first category, the Soviets extended their zone of withdrawal, the line beyond which they would have to pull back all the SS-20s in excess of what they could retain in Europe to compensate for the British and French forces. They declared out of bounds for the SS-20 northern Siberia, an inhospitable area where no SS-20s were likely to be deployed in any event.

At the same time, they clarified their position on compensation for the British and French forces in a way that was intended to seem forthcoming but in fact made it even less acceptable to the West. A series of statements, by General Detinov among others, indicated that the Soviets were going to match the British and French not just missile for missile, but warhead for warhead. This would mean an increase rather than a reduction in SS-20s as the British and French converted their submarine-launched missiles to MIRVs.

If the British and French completed the MIRVing of their SLBMs, they would, by Soviet calculations, have around 1,200 warheads. In that event, Detinov said, under the terms of the Soviet proposal, the Soviets were reserving the right to have an equal number of warheads—i.e., 400 SS-20s in Europe with three warheads each, an increase of more than 150 missiles over the existing level. That feature of the Soviet position was important, since, in its public posture, Moscow was already trying to make it look as though its willingness to match British and French warheads rather than launchers was a big concession that would lead to further reductions on their side. The small print was that those additional reductions were contingent on the cancellation of the British and French modernization program, just as the Soviet willingness to reduce in the first place was contingent on the cancellation of the American modernization program in Europe.

It was, altogether, an extraordinarily discouraging series of meetings. As part of his fascination with Russian diplomatic tactics and his determination to beat them at their own game, Nitze had been reading up on the history of the Jesuits' attempts to negotiate with Czar Ivan the Terrible on behalf of the Poles. Nonetheless, he was now finding it harder to derive even the compensatory intellectual pleasure of out-arguing the Soviets: the arguments themselves had become so familiar, tedious, and sterile; the Soviet position was becoming in some respects more subtle, in other respects more blatant, but in all respects more unyielding.

When Nitze and his colleagues tried to discuss what were intended as concessions on the American side, the Soviets replied brusquely that they would not "bless" the idea of any deployments at all. In one plenary statement, Kvitsinsky had said that the real nuclear balance between the superpowers in Europe was 10,000 to 0 in favor of the U.S. He meant that the U.S. and its allies had that many weapons (including presumably nuclear artillery shells that could reach Soviet forces in Eastern Europe), while the U.S.S.R. had no medium-range weapons that could reach the continental U.S. It was the *reductio ad absurdum* of the Soviet position and an indication of how polemical INF had become.

In late June, after the formal Soviet rejection of the interim-solution proposal in Geneva, Nitze traveled to Bonn for a private symposium on Western security issues sponsored by the Social Democrats. He put the full burden on the Soviets for the impasse that had arisen. George Shultz, on a trip abroad, tried to help Nitze out in a press conference in Manila. The latest U.S. offer, said Shultz, was "reasonable. . . . It is up to the Soviet Union to respond to that, and not simply say, 'We reject it. Try something else.' I think we are owed a responsible answer."

"The responsible answer," said Vladimir Pavlichenko in Geneva, "is no. You're going to have to learn to take that as the only answer you're going to get to this proposal or any other one like it."

9 Walking Out

With the deadline for deployment looming closer, the West Europeans wanted an agreement, not reasons to blame the Soviets for the absence of one. The leaders in Bonn were still committed to deploying the Pershing IIs if the talks failed, but they were looking, with an eagerness that bordered on desperation, for some way to avoid having to make good on the commitment. To them, the Nitze-Kvitsinsky walk-in-the-woods package was looking more attractive all the time, not least because it would have entailed sacrificing the Pershing II and thus spared the West Germans their own exclusive share of the West's collective obligation. They began sounding out both Soviets and Americans on whether the package deal might be resurrected.

The response from both Moscow and Washington was ambiguous. Kvitsinsky had asked Nitze whether their package of the year before would qualify as an acceptable interim proposal under the terms of the President's decision. Nitze was interested that Kvitsinsky would still be thinking in those terms, but his answer had to be no: the American interim proposal quite explicitly entailed global ceilings, while the Nitze-Kvitsinsky package had included regional ceilings and a freeze on SS-20s in Asia, and the U.S. was now reserving the right to deploy Pershing IIs.

Later Kvitsinsky told Egon Bahr of the West German Social Democrats, "It's clear that the U.S. insists on a mix between Pershing IIs and [cruise missiles], but that just won't do, because the essential thing about [the original package] was that there was to be no Pershing II." Bahr passed that comment along to Nitze, who asked Kvitsinsky if Bahr had quoted him correctly. Kvitsinsky shrugged and let Bahr's version stand. "Then can I assume," asked Nitze, "that the implication here is that if the package were to be put forward again in identical terms"—with the sacrifice of the Pershing II once again part of the offer—"your side would not turn it down?"

"No," said Kvitsinsky sharply. "You can't assume that."

The exchange was typical of the way the Soviets were now playing coy. The Chief of the Soviet General Staff, Marshal Nikolai Ogarkov, told a visitor to Moscow that the walk-in-the-woods formula had encountered stiff resistance from the Soviet military the previous summer because it would have permitted NATO deployments. In August, Ronald Lehman, Perle's former deputy who had moved to the NSC staff, visited Moscow and was told much the same thing by Kvitsinsky. Nitze had long since concluded that it was precisely this objection from the Soviet military, and not the American rejection, that had prevented the walk from leading anywhere.

However, on that same visit to Moscow, Lehman had an informal but intriguing chat with Alexander Bessmertnykh, Dobrynin's former deputy, who was now a senior aide to Gromyko. Bessmertnykh hinted that there might be certain unspecified circumstances under which the Soviets would relent in their categorical opposition to any American deployment whatsoever: a few cruise missiles in Britain might be permissible, he suggested. Lehman reported the exchange to Washington. Officials who favored the walk in the woods interpreted Bessmertnykh's comment as a deliberate, authoritative signal that the Soviets were prepared to accept a scaled-down NATO deployment package as long as it included no Pershing IIs.

In July, one of Ogarkov's deputies, Marshal Sergei Akhromeyev, received a congressional delegation and was asked by Congressman Thomas Downey whether the Nitze-Kvitsinsky scheme might be negotiable. The marshal replied in a rather offhand, elliptical way: the U.S. had never formally put forward such a proposal; were it to do so, it would be "considered." That same month, when Helmut Kohl asked Yuri Andropov himself about the walk in the woods during a three-hour meeting in Moscow, the Soviet leader turned the question aside; he did not endorse the package, but he did not echo Ogarkov's rejection of it either. Was this a polite put-down or a teaser? It may well have been both.

It was in the Soviets' interests to keep alive any West German hopes that an agreement might yet be possible, especially if it involved the cancellation of the Pershing II and a Western willingness to hold off deployment while the negotiators went on trying to reach a compromise. In Geneva, Moscow, Washington, and everywhere else, the Soviets kept probing for some indication that the U.S. might yet accept "the postponement option": defer the deployment, if only for a few months, to give the talks an extra chance. It need not even be an open-ended postponement; there could be a new date set for deployment.

On this point it was the Americans' turn to be unbending. Under no circumstances would the U.S. let deployment slip by so much as a single day or week. So said virtually every responsible American official at every level, on every occasion, to every audience, no matter how the question was couched. Postponement was tantamount to cancellation, and it would not happen. In a letter to Austrian Chancellor Bruno Kreisky, who advocated postponement, Reagan wrote, "A delay in our deployments would only encourage the Soviets to believe that NATO's resolve was faltering and that they could stretch out negotiations endlessly without addressing our legitimate security concerns."

Newspaper stories began to appear in the summer suggesting that continuing technical problems with the Pershing II might force a delay in their arrival in West Germany. Government officials denied this emphatically. The Pershing II still had its mechanical problems. But, come what may, the first ones would be where they were supposed to go by the end of the year, even if their engines and their guidance systems were still unperfected.

"We don't care if the goddamn things work or not," said Burt in a meeting with his staff. "After all, that doesn't matter unless there's a war. What we care about is getting them in." The comment was a perfect illustration (if any was now needed) of the essentially political—as opposed to military—purpose of nuclear weapons in general and the Pershing II in particular. The Soviets took little comfort from reading about the bugs that continued to afflict the Pershing II booster; they knew that sooner or later the bugs would be ironed out, and that once the rockets were in place in Germany it would be extremely difficult to negotiate their removal.

As the deadline approached, the ruling West German politicians joined the opposition Social Democrats in toying more and more openly with the idea of reviving the walk-in-the-woods plan. Early in June, after Nitze had reported to Kohl in Bonn on the negotiations (and a very pessimistic report it was), Kohl's press spokesman Peter Bönisch noted that the Chancellor had expressed "personal sympathy" for the way Nitze had conducted the negotiations. West German officials anonymously encouraged the interpretation that this was an oblique endorsement of the walk in the woods.

Nitze himself actively discouraged wishful thinking in West Germany and elsewhere. Later that month, visiting Bonn for the symposium with the Social Democrats, Nitze had a small, private dinner with the party standard-bearer, Hans-Jochen Vogel, and another Social Democratic official, Horst Ehmke. They tried to persuade him the U.S. could once and for all assure widespread West German support for deployment, including the support of the Social Democratic leadership, if only it were to come forward with the walk-in-the-woods formula as the new American proposal. The walk in the woods had credibility in a way that the vague interim proposal did not. Even if the Soviets rejected it, as they probably would, the U.S. would get credit for having tried everything, and the people of West Germany would reconcile themselves to the inevitability and rightness of deployment.

Nitze was highly skeptical not only about the negotiability of any agreement, but about the chances of reversing the growing West German opposition to deployment. Nevertheless, after the adjournment of INF for a summer recess, he returned home to try again to make the sacrifice of the Pershing II the centerpiece of a new, final U.S. offer for a comprehensive deal. On July 15, he arrived at his office in the State Department in Washington and, as he told an aide, set about "giving it one last shot."

Nitze had acquired an unlikely ally. During a dinner hosted by Kenneth Adelman, Perle told Nitze that he could now "live with" the sacrifice of the Pershing II as long as it was part of a package deal that would not be open for further bargaining. That, of course, had always been Nitze's intention, as Perle acknowledged publicly. Testifying before the arms control subcommittee of the House Armed Services Committee in mid-July, Perle was asked about the walk in the woods, and his reply contained kind words for the compromise that he had done so much to spike the year before:

> Mr. Nitze's offer was intended as a final agreement and not as a starting point for a process of further concessions. . . . It was intended as a way of producing a rapid result, resolving all issues at once, and it was offered as a complete package. Let me set the record straight, both because there is confusion in general and because I personally have been accused of frustrating the effort to produce a formula along those lines. When Ambassador Nitze returned to Geneva, after the recess that separated the walk in the woods from the resumption of talks, he was in a position to say to the Soviets that he was prepared to keep this channel open and to talk further about the proposal. And the Soviet Union categorically and emphatically rejected that proposal. One hears frequently that it was rejected by both sides. I think it is only fair to say that the United States was prepared to consider it further. There was no interest on the Soviet side.

Rather than setting the record straight, however, Perle was rewriting it. He now claimed that he had never opposed the package on its merits; rather, he had opposed it strongly in 1982 because he believed that the timing was wrong and because the allies, particularly Helmut Schmidt, had not been consulted on the desirability of the deal. Nor, of course, were they consulted on the Administration's decision, engineered largely by Perle himself, that the deal was *un*desirable. Now a year had passed, and Schmidt's successor, Helmut Kohl, seemed to want the offer, so why not give it to him? Perle's reversal caused some additional tension between himself and Weinberger. Having been persuaded, largely by Perle, that the sacrifice of the Pershing II was unthinkable, Weinberger was unpleasantly surprised to find his assistant now thinking about it with apparent equanimity. He called him on the carpet for doing so.

Nitze himself would only say, with a thin smile, "It proves you can't keep a good idea down."

Richard Burt had his own theory of what Perle was up to. He knew that Perle had never cared much for either the deployment or the arms-control half of INF. At stake on the Western side were only 572 warheads that, in Perle's view, cost too much money and caused too many political headaches.

What Perle cared about was holding the line against compromise in strategic arms control. The big, numerous, U.S.-based weapons, the ones that really counted in the nuclear balance, were on the table in START, not INF. Burt figured that Perle was lining up with Nitze in order to confound and outflank Perle's own critics. If Perle suddenly emerged as an ally of Nitze's in INF, it would be harder to tag him as an obstructionist—yet it would be easier for him to obstruct progress where it mattered and where, in Burt's view, progress was possible: in START.

Burt was dead set against a resurrection of the walk in the woods. He always had been, but the year before he had not been in a position to make the point strongly because of his difficulty in getting confirmed by the Senate. Since then, he had moved to the offensive. He was especially scathing during a visit to Brussels in late July for a meeting with allied foreign-ministry officials. The walk in the woods, he said, had been a "disastrous episode, with the potential of doing more damage than any other in the thirty-year history of the alliance." It was the result of "one vain man's insistence on exceeding his instructions." Nitze presented a "pathetic spectacle of panic."

When Perle learned of some of the things Burt had been saying, he complained about his "stringency and disrespect" toward Nitze. That gave Burt another chance to observe ironically that "Richard, like Paul, has gone soft on INF."

Burt had long since succeeded in turning Eagleburger and Shultz against the walk in the woods. Eagleburger now believed that the Pershing II was necessary to the "viability and credibility of the deployment package as a whole; if we concede the principle that we don't need the Pershing II, then we've conceded the principle that we don't need deployment." The Nitze plan, he said, was playing into the hands of Soviet propaganda. "We need to watch out," Eagleburger warned Kenneth Dam, "because the walk in the woods is acquiring its own mythology in Western Europe, and the Soviets are beginning to use it."

Shultz explained away his original support for the scheme by recalling that he had been new to the job and new to the issues; he had been supporting Nitze personally more than the plan on its merits. Now he saw the merit of the September 1982 presidential directive repudiating the walk in the woods: "I think the Pershings in some fashion are an essential part of our deployment package because their characteristics are different from [Tomahawks]." Was it a matter, he was asked, of not leaving the Soviets with a monopoly in ballistic missiles? "Of course," he said. Was he also concerned with the political factor of keeping the West Germans in their proper place in the order of deployment? "That's a point but not the main point. Presumably if that were the only point, you could manage to work around that by deploying other missiles or changing other patterns."

Every time a West German leader dropped a hopeful word about the revival of the plan, Eagleburger and Burt waved it aside like an annoying fly. They would claim that the West German was being misquoted, or that he had not meant what he said. They called in the West German ambassador to Washington, Peter Hermes, and inveighed against "all the mixed signals" coming out of Bonn. Over time, the signals had indeed been mixed, but by July and August they were coming through unambiguously: Foreign Minister Genscher and Chancellor Kohl both publicly endorsed a new American INF position based on the walk in the woods.

Nitze made a private call on William Clark, urging that the President authorize him to return to Geneva for the autumn round and tell Kvitsinsky that the U.S. was prepared to accept the walk-in-the-woods formula if the Kremlin was. In addition to being the President's National Security Adviser, Clark had also been made head of yet another high-level committee charged with coordinating arms-control policy. The Clark Group was supposed to succeed where the Dam Group had failed: it was to take control of the interagency process and make it, finally, proceed toward quick, decisive, and harmonious decisions.

The real difference between the Clark Group and the Dam Group was that Clark had access to the President, while Dam did not. That meant Clark could answer questions with authority, and his answer to Nitze was blunt and negative. Knowing what was on Nitze's mind, he told Nitze he had already taken the matter up with Reagan, and the President had "come down very firmly against it." Reagan's reasons for not wanting to sacrifice the Pershing II, according to Clark, were the same as before: there was a "gross disparity in capability" between the ballistic and cruise missiles; an agreement that left the Soviets with a monopoly in ballistic missiles would be "a one-sided deal and as such unacceptable."

Nitze replied that military considerations were not as important as political ones. A walk-in-the-woods offer would help "head off disaster" with European public opinion.

"Sorry, Paul," said Clark, "it's simply no go. The President's mind is made up."

Andropov's Last Word

Nitze then decided to press for a new American position incorporating all the ingredients of the walk-in-the-woods plan except the sacrifice of the Pershing II. That was more or less what Richard Burt had been intending to do anyway. For nearly a year, he had been working out his own strategy calling for a "step-by-step approach to demonstrating flexibility." As the deployment deadline drew closer, as the West Europeans clamored for new gestures by the Americans, and as the Soviets made gestures of their own, the U.S. would play out its cards one by one. One card would be for the U.S.

formally to discuss limits on aircraft, approximately along the lines of what Nitze and Kvitsinsky had agreed to the year before (a high ceiling on intermediate-range bombers, perhaps defined to include only the F-111 and FB-111 on the U.S. side).

Another involved the Pershing II. It was not available for discarding altogether, but after months of trying to fend off the West Germans on the issue, Burt thought up a partial concession: the U.S. would offer a "proportional reduction." If a settlement resulted in the U.S.'s reducing its overall deployment package by a third, the Pershing II component would also be reduced by a third. That way, the West German leaders would still have to accept some Pershing IIs, but they could console themselves, and quiet their critics, by accepting fewer than 108. They would be forced to share in the burden of INF deployment, but at the same time would be able to share in the easing of that burden, thanks to INF arms control.

There would also be a new proposed solution to the problem of Asian SS-20s, but it carried with it the risk of looking more like a trick than a concession, and a rather obscure trick at that. It was extremely complicated, and it took a long time to evolve. It was still being refined right up to the moment it was unveiled first to the allies, then to the Soviets, then to the world in late September. Nitze's agreement with Kvitsinsky had been very simple: the U.S. would stop trying to impose a global ceiling, and the U.S.S.R. would stop trying to exempt entirely its mobile weapons in Asia from European arms control; there would be a freeze on SS-20s in Asia. Anyone could understand a freeze. But Burt did not want to abandon what he called the "principle" of a global ceiling, and he particularly did not want anything in the new package that was lifted straight out of the walk-in-the-woods package.

So he finally settled on a complicated half-measure whereby the U.S. would declare the right to keep in reserve extra weapons outside Europe to offset those that the Soviets kept in Asia. If the Soviet Union would agree to reductions and limits "on a global basis," the U.S. would agree not to deploy in Europe all the weapons to which it was entitled under the agreement; it would hold back some outside of Europe—presumably in the U.S., and presumably equal to the number of warheads the Soviets had in Asia.

The fine points of this scheme were not easy to grasp. A U.S. official was dispatched to explain it to the Japanese, who were much concerned that an INF agreement not increase the SS-20 threat against their country. A Japanese Foreign Ministry representative listened attentively, then asked to have it explained to him again. This happened several times, until the Japanese finally gave up, apologizing that it must be his inadequate knowledge of English. Even when Burt himself was doing the explaining, the result was not always comprehension or harmony. After a briefing in Brussels, one West European diplomat came away shaking his head in despair and saying,

"This is the ultimate example of Rick's subtlety and ingenuity run amok. I still don't get it."

Friedrich Ruth questioned Burt skeptically on whether it would not be more straightforward simply to call the new proposal a system of "regional subceilings." Burt wanted at all costs to avoid that phrase, since it connoted abandonment of "globality." Ruth persisted, leading Burt to interrupt him and explode, "Fred, will you just shut up and listen to me!" Ruth turned a color close to vermilion, and commented later to a British diplomat, "This is Rick's idea of consultations."

Burt's temper was particularly short with the West Germans because he felt they were beginning to backslide on the delicate issue of British and French nuclear forces. As Ruth put it, "We cannot, of course, accept the principle of granting the Soviets compensation [for the British and French weapons] in INF; but at the same time, we should not say 'never' on third-country systems altogether. Somehow they should be kept in the arms-control perspective."

What that might mean in practice the Germans did not precisely seem to know, and Burt was not eager to find out; but he did not like the sound of what he called Ruth's "gobbledygook." "Once we put our big toe over the line on this issue," he warned, "we're on a slippery slope."

It was decided not to drop any vague hints about explicit compensation for the British and French, even in some unspecified forum other than INF. However, Burt's own offset scheme contained what could be the guise for an implicit compromise on the problem: since the scheme might have left the U.S.S.R. with more warheads than the U.S. would deploy, the Soviets would be in a position to claim that the excess was their compensation for the British and French.

At a National Security Council meeting in mid-August, Shultz made the case for giving Nitze the authorization to modify the U.S. position according to Burt's scheme. "The time has come," said the Secretary of State, "for us to show more flexibility." Weinberger argued for standing pat. "We're doing fine," said the Secretary of Defense. "Our position is already a good one. If it's not broken, let's not fix it."

The President did not agree. He was by now very conscious that he was in an almost personal contest with Andropov. He could not let the Soviet leader, as he put it, "out-flexible" him. The Soviets had their own version of the Burt strategy: offering cosmetic concessions one by one as the deadline approached, thus tempting the West Europeans with the possibility of an agreement if only deployment were delayed.

On August 26, Andropov publicly announced that the U.S.S.R. would undertake to "liquidate" all the weapons that its own INF proposal would require it to remove from Europe. That proposal allowed the Soviets to keep as many SS-20s in Europe as there were British and French ballistic missiles, or 162. Since there were already 243 SS-20s in Europe, that meant removing 81. Until now the U.S.S.R. had insisted on their right simply to transport excess SS-20s from Europe to Asia, although on the eve of the West German elections at the beginning of the year, there had been hints from Andropov and others that the U.S.S.R. might destroy a few of them. Now he appeared to be promising to destroy all 81. That, to Reagan, seemed like a significant shift, one that needed to be countered.

Shot Down in Flames

On September 1, Nitze was to fly from Washington to California, where the President was vacationing, to get his new instructions. From there he would fly to Europe to brief the allies and to Geneva for the resumption of the talks. However, on that very day there was a jolt of ugly news: a Soviet interceptor had shot down a Korean airliner that had strayed into Soviet air space, killing all 269 people on board.

There were protests around the world—condemnations, suspension of flights into the U.S.S.R., boycotts of the Soviet airline, Aeroflot. The Reagan Administration reacted with harsh words, but otherwise with restraint. Shultz put Burt in charge of an interagency task force to monitor the crisis and prepare options for the President to consider in response, and Burt realized that the U.S. should not overreact. Any thought of canceling the resumption of INF or START was promptly dismissed. The Pentagon recommended postponing a number of other, non-nuclear, arms-control negotiations, such as the Mutual Balanced Force Reduction Talks in Vienna and the forthcoming Conference on Disarmament in Europe, but that advice, too, was rejected.

Reagan denounced the Soviet attack on the airliner, but toward the end of his speech, he said it was important to keep arms-control talks going. He had come into office espousing the concept of linkage, vowing to hold arms control hostage to Soviet good behavior. Now he was making essentially the same argument that Jimmy Carter's Secretary of State, Cyrus Vance, had made four years before when critics urged him to suspend SALT in retaliation for Soviet abuses: precisely because the Soviet-American relationship was so prone to crisis and confrontation, it was all the more important that the search go on for means to control the most dangerous weapons.

Negotiations continued, but in an atmosphere more poisonous than ever. The brutality of the Soviet action made a deep impression on George Shultz, and the harshness of the American denunciation angered Andrei Gromyko. The two had an appointment in Madrid; it was to have been the first in a series that might lead to a Reagan-Andropov summit in 1984. There was to have been a follow-up meeting between Shultz and Gromyko a few weeks later, at the opening of the General Assembly at the United Nations. In the wake of the crisis over the airliner, however, the Shultz-Gromyko encounter in Madrid became the opposite of an ice-breaking session: it was the chilliest, most vituperative high-level Soviet-American session in decades. The whole experience made Shultz considerably more combative in the international arena; he was, if anything, even less inclined than before to champion concessions in arms control.

Nor were the Soviets in any mood to make amends by demonstrating fresh flexibility in Geneva. So Gromyko told Shultz in Madrid, and so his deputy Georgi Kornienko told the world at a press conference in Moscow. Andropov had already offered to destroy 81 SS-20s, and it was, said Kornienko, "wishful thinking" for anyone in the West to expect any further concessions; it was now the U.S.'s move. Shortly after getting to Geneva, Nitze cabled home asking urgently for the instructions that would let him make one.

Once the crisis of the downed airliner subsided, Burt picked up where he had left off. He drafted Nitze's instructions, shepherded them through the Clark Group, and took them to Brussels to brief the allies. The Pentagon continued to fight any change, but Burt was now firmly in control. The week after Nitze presented the new position in Geneva, Reagan laid it out before the UN General Assembly. As usual, Reagan gave a superbly crafted, smoothly delivered, flawlessly tuned speech. It elicited prolonged applause in the chamber—although not from the Soviet-bloc delegates. Asked why he had refused to clap, Richard Ovinnikov, the deputy Soviet representative, replied, "Why should we? It seemed to be a [speech on behalf of] sugar-coated deployment."

Ovinnikov's reaction to Reagan's speech was mild compared to Andropov's. On September 28, two days after the President spoke to the UN, the Soviet leader issued one of the most extraordinary statements in the history of the Soviet-American dialogue. The President's new proposals, said Andropov, simply preserved the spirit of the original zero option and were, therefore, unacceptable:

All they do is prattle about some sort of flexibility of the United States at the Geneva talks. Another aspect of this "flexibility" has now materialized, and the deception contained in it has become clear this time as well. Leaving aside details, the essence of the so-called new move by the United States, which is being advertised as munificent, again comes down to a proposal to have the two sides agree on the number of Soviet medium-range missiles to be dismantled and on the number of American missiles to be deployed in Europe in addition to the nuclear potential already possessed by NATO. In brief, we are being asked to talk about helping the NATO bloc upset to its advantage the nuclear systems in the European zone, and this move is being presented brazenly as something new.

Andropov's claim that a balance already existed in Europe was as dubious as ever. But his characterization of the American proposal was accurate enough: the U.S. was indeed asking the U.S.S.R. to negotiate reductions in existing Soviet weapons in exchange for an increase, albeit a scaled-down increase, in NATO weapons.

The conduct of arms control by means of public one-upmanship on the part of the top leaders of the two countries was by now well established. Both leaderships had long since gotten into the custom of exchanging proposals in public and at the highest level. But now Andropov was using his bully pulpit not to advance a new concession, but to denounce an American one and, in effect, to declare Soviet patience at an end. "Even if someone had any illusions about the possible evolution for the better in the policy of the present U.S. Administration," he said, "the latest developments have finally dispelled them."

Hedging Bets, Fudging Threats

Before the Andropov statement, most officials in Washington had clung to the assumption that, for all their bluster, threats, and protests of injured innocence, the Soviet leaders basically recognized and respected a tough new American line and were restraining themselves accordingly. Reagan and a number of his aides hoped that the presumed realism of the Soviet leaders would prevail over whatever umbrage they took at American rhetoric. Andropov, after all, was supposed to be the ultimate pragmatist. The hope was that the Politburo would shrug off the accusations in Reagan's UN speech about the Korean airliner and concentrate instead on the concessions, or "initiatives" as they were called, in INF.

In Shultz's view, the Soviet leaders must have realized that, for all its fire-and-brimstone propaganda in the wake of the Korean airliner affair, the Administration had abstained from more substantive retribution. He believed that the Kremlin leaders might be perceptive enough to credit him personally as the champion of moderation. The Administration had hoped that despite its dire warnings the Soviet Union would accept new American missiles in Western Europe and negotiate an agreement on some modified version of American terms. The Administration remained convinced that deployment would actually soften Soviet resistance and intransigence and thus facilitate an agreement in 1984, when Reagan would need one for domestic political purposes.

Eugene Rostow had often predicted that just before deployment the Soviets would suddenly start negotiating seriously in Geneva. Others, like Bush and Weinberger, had forecast that the real bargaining would begin only after the American chips were already on the table.

The Soviets, however, showed no sign of vindicating such optimistic

American predictions. The closer the deadline for deployment, the more the threat of a Soviet walkout from INF began to sound like a promise. Anatoly Dobrynin had been talking privately for months about the "near-inevitability of suspension" of both negotiations, INF and START as well, if the missiles went in on schedule. Georgi Arbatov—the best-known Soviet expert on American affairs, and believed to be a close adviser to Andropov—said much the same thing to a congressional delegation that visited Moscow in early July. So did Yuli Kvitsinsky and Vladimir Pavlichenko in Geneva.

In Washington, the Soviet threat of a walkout had been dismissed as pure bluff. Perle, Burt, and Eagleburger were all confident that the Soviets realized a walkout would backfire against them with European public opinion, making them appear to be the spoilers and thus improving the climate for deployment. "If deployment goes ahead," said Burt, "the Soviets will have sustained a major defeat; it's not in their interests to compound that defeat by letting it precipitate further defeats, such as the collapse of arms control with themselves clearly identified as the villains. So they've got a big stake in staying at the table. For our part, deployment will strengthen our hand. It'll demonstrate allied cohesion and refusal to be pushed around, coupled with a commitment to hard-headed détente and arms control. If we play our cards right, INF deployment could actually be a nice prelude to getting business done in other areas."

Until Andropov's statement of September 28, only Nitze had taken the Soviet threat of a walkout seriously. Making explicit what Andropov strongly implied, Leonid Zamyatin, the senior spokesman for the Central Committee, told an audience in West Germany in October, "We do not want to take part in negotiations leading to a situation in which powerful new missiles and warheads will be stationed in Europe." Asked if he meant that deployment would end the Geneva negotiations, Zamyatin replied, "You have understood me correctly." After those statements, Burt, Perle, and others began hedging their bets. Maybe the Soviets would walk out after all.

At the same time, the Soviets began doing some hedging of their own. Their walkout, spokesmen began saying, would occur in INF, but not necessarily in START, as Pavlichenko, Dobrynin, Arbatov, and others had originally predicted. Nor did the Soviets seem able to agree on a single party line about what exactly would trigger a walkout. In Geneva, Kvitsinsky and his colleagues pressed their American counterparts to tell them when precisely the first Tomahawks would arrive in Britain. Asked why they wanted to know, they replied, "Because we can't continue talks after that date." The cruise missiles were now due in Britain in mid-November.

At the end of October, Yuli Kvitsinsky was dining at Nitze's apartment in Geneva. He was seated next to Alice Clyne, the wife of the delegation's executive secretary, Norman Clyne. At the end of the main course, she playfully complained that the uncertainty over how much longer she was going to stay in Geneva was complicating her life. She had a cut-rate ticket back to the U.S. and wanted to know if she would be able to use it before it expired. She employed a Soviet tactic on Kvitsinsky, an ultimatum: gâteau d'orange was now being served, but he would not get any unless he told her when the long-threatened walkout would take place. Kvitsinsky replied that he did not want to miss dessert and that, besides, he felt he owed her "an open and honest answer." The walkout would occur between November 15 and 22. Those dates seemed to bracket the expected arrival of the Tomahawks in Britain and the virtual certainty that the West German Bundestag (parliament) would approve the Pershing II deployments after a two-day debate on November 21–22. He also promised to give her twenty-four hours' advance notice.

Kvitsinsky seemed to be more certain than his home office about the Soviet response to deployment. The signals coming out of Moscow were confusing, perhaps in part because of disarray and incapacity at the highest level. Andropov by now was obviously very ill, and his incapacitation seemed to be affecting the workings of the government. Instead of taking to the podium, Andropov was issuing proclamations in the pages of *Pravda* and on the tickers of TASS—or the collective leadership was doing so in his name.

A new Andropov statement of October 26 said that talks would continue if the U.S. "renounced the deployment of its missiles in Europe within the announced deadlines." Presumably the talks would not continue if deployment proceeded on schedule. A few days later, Horst Ehmke, one of the Social Democratic leaders, quoted the Soviet ambassador to West Germany, Vladimir Semyonov, as confirming that the Bundestag vote would end the talks. The next day, however, the Soviet embassy in Bonn released a clarification: it would be the "de facto stationing," not the Bundestag vote, that would "make the Geneva talks impossible." That would seem to buy a bit more time, but not much. The Pershing II engines were ready for shipment to West Germany; the transporter-erector-launchers (TELs), the mobile vehicles for the old Pershing Is, were being converted to use for the Pershing IIs. All that remained was for some additional components to be flown in from the U.S. and for the engines, warheads, and launchers to be "mated." The first "flight" of nine Pershing IIs would be operational sometime in December.

Last Cards

The betting in Washington was now on a walkout, if not by November 22, as Kvitsinsky had promised Alice Clyne, then by New Year's Eve. Administration officials began preparing to turn the event, if it occurred, to their own advantage. Reminders started coming out of Washington that the Reagan Administration had every intention of talking past deployment. The Administration also wanted to make sure that the Soviets were not only seen to be stomping away from the bargaining table, but seen as well to be turning their backs on yet another American attempt to break the deadlock. Entering its final stage, INF had become largely a matter of which superpower would make the last offer before the negotiations collapsed—and thus be in a better position to blame the other for the collapse.

As of the beginning of November, the Soviets were ahead in this respect. In addition to threatening a walkout, Andropov's statement of October 26 had also contained a new note of "additional flexibility" on the question of medium-range nuclear-capable aircraft, suggesting that the Soviets might amend their proposal so as not to impinge quite so heavily on conventionally armed NATO aircraft. But as explained in Geneva, the gesture was extremely vague, and it still applied to British and French bombers as well as American aircraft. Andropov also said the U.S.S.R. was prepared to freeze SS-20s in Asia once an agreement was in force. Here, too, there was a string attached: the freeze would be contingent on the "strategic situation"—i.e., there would be no increase in Asian SS-20s as long as the U.S. and its friends in the area did not build up their nuclear forces in the Far East. Most important, Andropov offered to reduce SS-20s in Europe from 243 to "about 140"; the surplus would be, as he had promised before, "liquidated" rather than moved eastward. The earlier level to which the Soviets had been willing to reduce had been 162, the equivalent of the number of British and French ballistic-missile launchers. As General Detinov had privately already indicated in Geneva, the Soviets had apparently decided to match the British and French forces on a warhead-for-warhead rather than launcher-for-launcher basis: approximately 140 SS-20s, or more precisely 144, each with three warheads, would nearly equal the Soviet count of the number of British and French warheads.*

---

*The Soviets were calculating 18 French land-based missiles with 18 warheads, 80 French SLBMs with 80 warheads, 16 British Polaris SLBMs with 48 warheads, and 48 British Chevaline SLBMs with 288 warheads—a total of 162 launchers and 434 warheads. Hence Andropov's offer: 144 SS-20s, with three warheads each, would be 432 warheads, approximately matching the British and French by the maximum count; 144 SS-20s would represent 16 squadrons of 9 launchers each.

The U.S. negotiators refused to be drawn under any circumstances into a discussion of British and French forces as part of INF. Had they replied to the Soviets, they would have made clear that they did not accept the Soviet calculations. The Polaris's three warheads, for example, were not independently targetable; hence, by Western reckoning, they should not count the same as SS-20 MIRVs. The Chevaline was a trickier case. It had reportedly been tested with as many as six reentry vehicles, which is why the Soviets attributed that many warheads, or "nuclear charges," to each missile. But the number of warheads actually deployed on the Chevaline was considerably less than six (two per missile, according to some reports), and while they were maneuverable in a way that allowed them to evade anti-ballistic-missile defenses, they were not independently targetable.

In October and November, there were unofficial hints out of Moscow that as a final, magnanimous concession, the U.S.S.R. might even be willing to cut back its European SS-20s all the way to 54 —that is, 162 warheads, with one warhead for each British and French missile. This card, however, was never played, and Kvitsinsky denied to Nitze that it was ever contemplated.

To the bemused American negotiators in Geneva, the good news in this was that the U.S.S.R. had come a long way toward conceding to the Reagan Administration the principle of counting warheads rather than just launchers; the bad news was a reminder that as the British and French went about modernizing—i.e., MIRVing—their SLBMs, the Soviets, under their own rules, would be free to increase their SS-20s in Europe substantially.

The U.S. now needed another card to play. It was essentially a matter of filling in the blanks in Reagan's September 26 initiative at the United Nations, particularly a proposed global ceiling on warheads. Nitze sent back a message to Washington urging a ceiling of 600 warheads on each side, half of which could be in Europe. That would have left the Soviets with 100 SS-20s in Europe (with 300 warheads) and allowed the U.S. to proceed with 300 Pershing IIs and Tomahawks. Burt objected that this was too much of a departure from the principle of global ceilings. Also, for cosmetic purposes, he wanted a global ceiling of less than 572, so that the West Europeans would be sure to appreciate American willingness to lower the level of deployment established in 1979.

The Administration settled instead on a global ceiling of 420 warheads (at the upper end of the 50-to-450 range that Burt and Nitze had earlier proposed for the interim solution). The choice of the 420 was almost totally cosmetic. That was the number of warheads on 140 SS-20s and was therefore supposed to sound responsive to, and compatible with, Andropov's latest offer to reduce to "about 140" SS-20s in Europe. But Andropov's proposal had been conditioned on cancellation of the NATO deployments, and Andropov had been talking about a reduction to about 140 in Europe alone, a drawdown of about 22 percent in the total SS-20 force. The latest U.S. counter-proposal would have limited the Soviets to 140 SS-20s throughout the U.S.S.R., a reduction of more than 60 percent. And the U.S. would have deployed at least as many warheads in Europe as the Soviets retained there. For example, if the U.S.S.R. kept 70 SS-20s in Europe, or half its global allowance of 140, the U.S. might deploy a minimum of 210 Pershing IIs and Tomahawks, since that would match the number of warheads on 70 SS-20s.

The U.S. formally presented what it called an "elaboration" of its position on November 15. That plenary session lasted a mere thirty-five minutes, by far the shortest to date. One reason for the brevity was that there was so little to negotiate. Nitze had already given Kvitsinsky a preview of the new numbers; the *International Herald Tribune* had already carried a front-page story spelling out the details of the plan; and TASS had already rejected it as "patently unacceptable."

The U.S. negotiators had come to the meeting expecting it to be their last. The day before, November 14, Michael Heseltine, the British Defense Secretary, had announced to Parliament the arrival of the first squadron of sixteen Tomahawks at Greenham Common Air Base outside of London. A half hour after that announcement, the Soviet delegation in Geneva sent its American counterparts a shipment of "end-of-the-round presents" (lacquered wooden bowls, a Russian folk-art product manufactured for the tourist market), and a supply of caviar and vodka (Moskovskaya brand—far from the best). The Soviets apparently believed they were about to be summoned home, and Kvitsinsky seemed to be giving Alice Clyne the twenty-four hours' advance notice he had promised.

But the instructions cabled from Moscow that night were to keep talking at least a while longer. At the plenary on November 15, Kvitsinsky said that the "consequences" his government had been promising for so long would ensue with the arrival of new American missiles "on the continent of Europe," especially when there were "short-flight-time systems on the periphery of the Soviet Union." Translation: the moment of truth was now a week away; the walkout would come once the Bundestag cleared the way for the Pershing IIs.

The Walk in the Park

The last days of INF were marked not only by the collapse of the formal negotiations but by unprecedented acrimony between Nitze and Kvitsinsky. Theirs had been an extraordinary diplomatic partnership. Despite the deterioration in the climate of East-West relations and the irreconcilability of their official negotiating positions, the two men had managed to maintain a high degree of mutual respect. During their walk in the woods in July 1982, they may even have come close to achieving a breakthrough against all the odds and against the resistance of their home offices. Therefore, as INF staggered to a close, it was especially sad to see the relationship between Nitze and Kvitsinsky fall apart. Ironically, the occasion of the rupture was a bizarre replay of the walk in the woods.

On October 26, Nitze and his wife had held a dinner party at their apartment for half-a-dozen couples, mostly Swiss, but including the Kvitsinskys. The moment dinner ended, Kvitsinsky, with evident urgency, took Nitze aside. *Pravda* had just published Andropov's offer to reduce European SS-20s to about 140. Kvitsinsky suggested that in fact the Kremlin might be willing to go even lower if the U.S. would respond to Andropov with a new counteroffer of "equal reductions on both sides." Equitable as this phrase sounded, what it meant in practice was that the Soviets would take 572 missile warheads out of Europe by retiring SS-4s and -5s and reducing SS-20s, while the U.S. would cancel its entire Pershing II and Tomahawk program; the bottom line on the American side of the ledger would still be zero.

This was an idea they had talked about before, not in the context of anything Nitze had ever proposed but, during the fall of 1982, in the context of an idea that had originated with Paul Warnke, the dovish former SALT II negotiator whom Nitze had bitterly opposed on many issues. In 1982, Warnke, in his capacity as head of a pro-arms-control group called the Committee on National Security, had publicly suggested a solution similar to the one Kvitsinsky was now floating. At that time, when Nitze asked him about it informally, Kvitsinsky had been contemptuous of Warnke's scheme, presumably because of the extent of reductions in SS-20s that would be required. But since then the Soviet leadership had considerably raised the price it was willing to pay in SS-20s for cancellation of the NATO deployment: from a freeze at 243, it had come down first to 162, then to around 140, and Kvitsinsky now told Nitze that, if the U.S. put forward the "equal reductions" proposal, the Soviet Union would be left with only about 120 SS-20s in Europe—half their current number.*

Nitze was interested in drawing Kvitsinsky out a bit to see if, in addition to lowering the SS-20 level, the U.S.S.R. might also be willing to raise above zero the level of permissible missiles on the Western side. Was there, he wanted to find out, enough give in the Soviet position for the Kremlin finally to sanction some NATO deployments? Nitze probed first at another of their private lunches at La Réserve on November 2, then again the next day at a reception at the Soviet mission.

"I'm still not quite clear what you have in mind," said Nitze. "Is it the principle of equal reductions you're after, or is it reduction on our side from 572 to zero and then reduction on the Soviet side of 572 warheads? Is there room in here for a reduction, say, of 472 that would permit us to have 100 weapons on our side?"

"No," replied Kvitsinsky. "It's 572 or nothing."

"Under those circumstances," said Nitze, "it's of no interest to us."

But Kvitsinsky wanted to keep the dialogue going. Their next encounter was at the Soviet mission on November 7 at a celebration of the Russian Revolution. "I've reported back to Moscow on our discussion of equal reductions," said Kvitsinsky.

"And I've reported to Washington on *all* our discussions," replied Nitze, implying pointedly that his own dismissal of Kvitsinsky's 572-or-nothing statement was very much on the record.

But the Soviet was undeterred. "My people are interested in your questions." That seemed to imply that there might after all be a possibility of a reduction by less than 572, as Nitze had hoped. Either that, or Kvitsinsky

---

*Back in the fall of 1982, when Warnke had presented his version of this suggestion, the Soviets could have kept 150–160 SS-20s in Europe. A large portion of the 572 warheads they would have been required to remove would have been accounted for in SS-4s and -5s. But since then the gradual retirement of the old single-warhead missiles had proceeded, so by the fall of 1983 the Soviets would have had to cut deeper into their SS-20 force in order to achieve a reduction of 572.

was trying to create the impression that Nitze might still give in to the Soviet insistence on a reduction of 572, all or nothing.

On November 12, a Saturday, Nitze received a phone call from Kvitsinsky at 10:45 P.M. requesting that they get together the next morning. They met at the entrance to the Botanical Gardens, across the street from the U.S. headquarters. The Soviet initiative had now become as official as it was urgent and unusual. As they strolled through the park, Kvitsinsky said, "As you know, I've reported back to Moscow our discussions and your questions, and I'm under instructions to give you the following message: if the U.S. government were to propose equal reductions from 572 to zero on your side and 572 from our side, my government would accept it." Then came what was intended as an added incentive: "The Soviet government would also claim the right to raise the issue of compensation for future increases in British and French levels of weaponry in an appropriate forum." That sticking point, in other words, could be deferred; it need no longer block progress in INF.

Kvitsinsky asked Nitze to transmit his message to Washington right away and to support it. Nitze said he would certainly transmit it, especially if "the heart of the matter is that the Soviet side is prepared to enter into discussion of a mutually acceptable formula." But he made clear that the formula Kvitsinsky was proposing was not acceptable, adding, "I'm certain that the U.S. government will not convert a Soviet proposal into an American one."

In sending back a detailed report on the conversation, Nitze appended a recommendation that the U.S.'s NATO partners, particularly the West Germans, be notified right away of what had occurred. On that score, at least, Washington took its ambassador's advice. U.S. officials notified the five deploying European governments on November 15 about the walk in the park.

Nitze and Kvitsinsky soon saw each other at another reception. The Soviet was anxious to know if Nitze had heard any word from Washington. Nitze said, "No, but I want to get something clear. What would happen to the provision in your [official, standing] proposal on the issue of compensation for the British and French forces?"

"We'd drop it."

"And what would happen to your treaty language defining the NATO side [to include British and French weapons]?"

"It would be completely rewritten."

"Then there'd be nothing in your draft concerning British and French systems?"

"Correct," said Kvitsinsky, "although we'd maintain our right to claim compensation for British and French increase in this or another forum." That meant in a follow-on INF negotiation or in START.

But while Nitze was concentrating on nailing down a partial Soviet concession, the Reagan Administration moved swiftly to reject the feeler outright. On November 16, Nitze received instructions to deliver a rejection to Kvitsinsky. Nitze felt that was a mistake. He sent another message back to Washington urging consideration of a counterproposal rather than a "black-and-white turn-down."

The counterproposal that he developed with the help of his delegation was for an equal reduction of launchers on each side that would produce a result very much along the lines of the walk-in-the-woods scheme. Among Nitze's critics back in Washington, it was taken as proof that he was, in Burt's phrase, "still off there in the goddamn woods with Kvitsinsky, cooking up deals to kill the Pershing II if not deployment altogether."*

Not only had Nitze never completely given up on the walk in the woods, but during the final weeks of INF he had tried in vain to get the Administration to consider a variant of his far more drastic Plan B proposal of a year earlier, whereby the U.S. would defer deployment in exchange for Soviet reductions and fold INF into START. Resorting to the highly secret Sphinx communication channel, set up after the walk in the woods, he had, shortly before the walk-in-the-park episode, conveyed to Washington his assessment that there was only one way to get a deal before deployment: he could approach Helmut Kohl and suggest a Plan B–type combination of Soviet reductions in SS-20s, American deferment of Pershing IIs and Tomahawks, and merger of INF and START. He would, he told Washington, give Kohl the impression that he was floating the idea entirely on his own authority. If Kohl supported it, then the U.S. would come forward with the plan more formally. Nitze was motivated, as before, by his conviction that the political

---

*Nitze's counterproposal was for equal reductions of 167 launchers on each side. The arithmetic would have looked like this:

U.S.	U.S.S.R.
224 Pershing II and Tomahawk launchers	243 SS-20 launchers
(108 Pershing IIs @ one missile &	− 167
116 Tomahawk launchers @ 4)	76
− 167	× 3 warheads per missile
57 cruise-missile launchers	228 SS-20 warheads
× 4 cruise missiles per launcher	
228 cruise missiles *or* a lesser number of warheads	
if the U.S. insisted on including Pershing IIs	

The U.S. would, in accordance with the Administration's directive, be preserving the right to go ahead with the Pershing II; but it would also, in accordance with Nitze's own preference, be penalizing itself for doing so, since Pershing II launchers would "buy" the U.S. only one warhead per launcher, while cruise-missile launchers would buy four. This feature of the plan would be an incentive for the U.S. to give up the Pershing II after all—and perhaps for the Soviets to regard it more seriously. There would also be a global ceiling of 528 warheads (meeting Burt's insistence on a number less than 572), of which 300 could be outside Europe and 228 in Europe. That would require the Soviets to reduce their Asian SS-20s to 100. Whatever its merits, the plan was quickly overtaken by events.

price the alliance was about to pay for deployment in the absence of an agreement would be higher than the price of missing the deployment deadline.

But now that the deadline was at hand, virtually all that mattered to the Reagan Administration was getting the deployments started on time. Once that challenge had been disposed of, the political trouble in Western Europe would die down and the Soviets, seeing that intimidation had failed, would start negotiating seriously. The Year of the Missile would have paved the way for 1984 as the Year of an Agreement.

Nitze's renewed suggestion that the U.S. consider deferring deployment caused consternation among his remaining defenders and admirers, outrage among his critics and enemies. Weinberger was especially upset, urging that "we blow the whistle on this guy once and for all; we should come down on him like a ton of bricks." The State Department, partly out of respect for Nitze but particularly out of deference to the Europeans' respect for him, blocked a reprimand. Kenneth Dam called Nitze and told him, in effect, thanks but no thanks for his suggestion.

When, a short while later, Nitze's cable of November 13 arrived reporting that Kvitsinsky had floated a proposal superficially similar to Plan B, insofar as it involved no deployment on the U.S. side and deferment of some issues to START, there was an immediate suspicion in Washington that Nitze had actually initiated it himself. In fact, regardless of recommendations he had made to his own government, Nitze had never indicated to Kvitsinsky that he or the U.S. would abandon deployment under any conditions except the zero solution. But the suspicion that he might have done so lingered at his home office and soon came back to haunt him.

On November 17, the plot took a twist that Nitze had feared and protected himself against: Soviet ambassadors in a number of NATO capitals fanned out with diplomatic notes asserting that Nitze had made a new proposal calling for reduction of SS-20s in Europe from 243 to 120 in exchange for cancellation of the entire NATO deployment package.

In another, particularly mischievous distortion, the Soviets implied that the Reagan Administration had refused to back Nitze up. It was a transparent attempt on the Soviets' part to make it look as though the walk in the park was a replay of the walk in the woods, to make it seem that once again Nitze had on his own hammered out a workable compromise only to be shot down as before by the hawkish, intransigent Reagan Administration. This impression, had it taken hold, might have wreaked havoc in the West German Bundestag just as it was about to vote on the Pershing IIs.

Had it not been for Nitze's prompt and thorough reporting of the November 13 Kvitsinsky initiative, there probably would have been a predisposition in Europe to give credence to the Soviet version. As it was, because of the Plan B incident the year before and Nitze's recent, top-secret attempt to revive the plan, there was already such a predisposition in Washington. But it was the European response that mattered, and the key leaders there, having been forewarned, treated the Soviet trick as exactly what it was. They were also able to exploit it. Helmut Kohl publicly remarked that the Soviet proposal—for such he knew it to be—"gives up a point that [the Soviets] have up to now considered essential: the inclusion of French and British weapons."

Now it was Moscow's turn to retreat in disarray and to undercut its negotiator. The Defense Minister, Dimitri Ustinov, published an article in *Pravda* repeating his government's insistence on compensation for British and French systems, and an accompanying TASS commentary described Kohl's public reference to a concession on that point as a "diversionary ploy" designed to calm anti-nuclear forces in West Germany.

Nitze was more upset than he had ever before been in INF. He half-jokingly talked about walking out of the negotiations himself, "beating Kvitsinsky to the punch." On November 19, Nitze summoned Kvitsinsky to his office and formally discharged his instructions to reject what he called pointedly "the informal Soviet proposal of November 13." Nitze said the U.S. could not accept an arrangement that left the Soviet Union with a monopoly in long-range missiles in Europe. He added, however, that the U.S. "noted with interest" Kvitsinsky's willingness to drop compensation for British and French weapons and was "prepared to study carefully" any new proposal the Soviets might have, but that a negotiated outcome should provide for "U.S.-Soviet equality."

Then Nitze turned stern. "Washington—and I personally—find unacceptable Soviet attempts, in direct approaches to our allies, to misrepresent the informal Soviet suggestion of November 13 as an American proposal." Kvitsinsky was unrelenting. It had been an American proposal, he insisted. "All this has been turned into a filthy thing by someone" on the American side, he said. "This was a plot by the U.S."

Thus ended their most acrimonious encounter in two years, with each man in effect calling the other a liar. As he hurried out of the American headquarters, Kvitsinsky said bitterly, "Everything's finished." He came back once again, for a formal plenary session on November 23, the day after the Bundestag approved the Pershing II deployments, and the same day that the first nine American missles reached a U.S. Army field artillery brigade at Mutlangen, near Schwäbisch-Gmünd. According to protocol, Nitze, as the host, welcomed the Soviet delegation and invited Kvitsinsky to make an opening statement. It was, in fact, a closing one: the Soviet side was discontinuing the negotiations without setting a date for their resumption.*

---

*As though acknowledging that INF had passed into history, Richard Burt had the U.S. government and NATO release publicly a fairly detailed but highly selective history of the negotiations in December 1983. It was in the form of a "progress report" to the NATO ministers, and it laid

.   .   .

As they prepared the way for their walkout, Soviet spokesmen kept harking back to a theme that Pavlichenko had sounded in Geneva the year before when he first issued the ultimatum: For just over twenty years, the superpowers had lived under an arrangement whereby neither side stationed long-range missiles in proximity to the other's territory; if the U.S. upset that balance, there would have to be both a political and a military response. The mention of twenty years was a reference to the Cuban missile crisis of 1962. When Pavlichenko originally raised the subject of Cuba, he had hinted darkly, and rather implausibly, that some of the threatened Soviet "military countermeasures" to the Pershing IIs and Tomahawks might take place in Central America or the Caribbean. But now it was beginning to look as though that was not the point. Rather, the Soviets were putting the U.S. on notice that they regarded 1983 as offering them an opportunity—indeed, imposing on them an obligation—to make up for 1962.

According to the Soviet version of events, John Kennedy had agreed to remove from Europe forerunners of the Pershing II, while Khrushchev removed from Cuba the forerunners of the SS-20. (The difference was that in 1962 the U.S. had been planning to pull its missiles out of Europe in any event, for its own political and military reasons, while Khrushchev had tried to introduce his missiles in Cuba and, naturally, had intended to leave them there.) In one of the most famous remarks of the era of brinksmanship, Dean Rusk had said, as Soviet ships steamed home with the rockets on their decks, "We were eyeball-to-eyeball, and the other guy just blinked." To the Soviets, that interpretation of the outcome rankled. "You Americans will never be able to do this to us again," Gromyko's deputy, Vasily Kuznetsov, had said sternly to his American counterpart, John McCloy. The episode clearly stimulated the Soviet Union's decision to undertake its twenty-year military buildup, of which the SS-20 program was one of the most visible and troublesome manifestations. Now the Soviets seemed bent on turning the Year of the Missile into a replay of the Cuban missile crisis, with the tables turned and the outcome reversed, at least in its symbolic dimension as a clash of wills between the superpowers. This time the Soviets had no intention of blinking. While this did not necessarily mean a return to the brink of nuclear war, it certainly augured badly for an agreement that would help secure nuclear peace.

---

the entire blame for the breakdown of the talks at the feet of the Soviets. The Soviet counterstrike came in the form of a pamphlet published by the Novosti Press Agency titled *Who Wrecked the Geneva Talks and Why?* Kvitsinsky and Nitze went public with their conflicting versions of what had happened during the walk in the woods and the walk in the park (see the *New York Times* Op-Ed pages of January 12 and 19, 1984).

Part Two
The Strategic Arms Reduction Talks

10 The Burden of History

While INF was largely an inherited dilemma for the Reagan Administration, its conduct of START—the Strategic Arms Reduction Talks—was beset by problems much more of its own making.

There were, however, rough similarities in the issues. In Europe, the U.S. was looking for a way to redress the imbalance created by the intermediate-range, triple-MIRVed SS-20s. In the realm of strategic weaponry, there was a perceived imbalance created by intercontinental six- and ten-warhead Soviet rockets. The principal concern in both cases was ballistic missiles. Whether—and if so, how—to limit aircraft and cruise missiles was a sticking point, within the U.S. government as well as in the negotiations with the Soviets, in both INF and START.

The cast of characters and bureaucratic battle lines were more or less the same. The struggle would pit those like Richard Burt, who wanted to preserve a degree of continuity with the past and had some hope of eventual progress in the negotiations, against those like Richard Perle, who wanted to use arms control as a way of making a clean break with the past and of dramatizing rather than ameliorating the Soviet military threat.

In both dramas, the President would step to center stage to deliver his lines in set speeches. But behind the scenes, where decisions were made and policy was set, he was to remain a detached, sometimes befuddled character. Even though he chaired sixteen National Security Council–level meetings on START, there was ample evidence, during those meetings and on other occasions as well, that he frequently did not understand basic aspects of the nuclear-weapons issue and of policies being promulgated in his name.

In both negotiations, the Administration's principal concern was to keep military programs on track—the Pershing II and Tomahawk missiles in INF and an ambitious "strategic modernization" program in START. That meant the Administration had to be pushed to the bargaining table by political forces. Pressure on the White House from the allies across the Atlantic built up more quickly than from Congress at the other end of Pennsylvania Avenue. That was the main reason why the Administration was slower to come forward with a proposal in START than in INF.

There were other important differences, too. One was the absence in START of anyone in the role that Paul Nitze played in INF by trying singlehandedly to save the Administration from itself. Nitze's counterpart in START was Edward Rowny. Like Nitze, he had earned a place in the Administration largely because he was associated with the opposition to SALT II; unlike Nitze, however, Rowny ended up being almost as much of an obstacle to the achievement of a new agreement as he had been to the ratification of the old one.

Diverging Paths and Widening Gaps

The impulse to pursue bilateral agreements on strategic weaponry hand in hand with unilateral defense had been part of the Soviet-American rivalry for at least twenty years. The 1962 Cuban missile crisis had provided an impetus both to an arms buildup and to arms control, and on both sides. The remembered humiliation of that showdown probably contributed to the Soviets' decision to embark on the sustained accumulation of every category of weaponry: conventional and nuclear, battlefield-range and globe-spanning, tanks, aircraft, surface ships, submarines, and, most of all, rockets.

But the close call over Cuba also spurred the U.S. and the U.S.S.R., together with Britain, to conclude a Limited Test Ban Treaty ten months later, in August 1963. The pact banned nuclear explosions above ground, under water, and in outer space. Testing was to be permitted only underground. It was a fitting, almost mythological metaphor for nuclear weapons themselves: if man insisted on perfecting the things, he would have to confine his experiments to the underworld; before setting them off to make sure they would work, he would have to bury the weapons that could bury him.

On the American side there was another impulse for the Limited Test Ban Treaty. People were growing anxious not only about the threat of a catastrophic war but about the danger that atmospheric testing in peacetime posed to their health. The suspense over Cuba and worry about strontium-90, a radioactive isotope in fallout that was poisoning milk, left the American body politic with a deep, visceral attachment to the idea of arms control.

Arms control has often been buffeted by the upheavals of American domestic politics. The foundation of SALT was laid late in the Johnson Administration, but the opening of those negotiations was delayed by the 1968 Soviet invasion of Czechoslovakia, which coincided with a presidential campaign in the U.S. A Democratic President whose foreign policy had been discredited by the Vietnam war gave way to a Republican President who had based his career largely on a reputation for implacable anti-Sovietism. Once in office, Richard Nixon circled the idea of SALT cautiously before deciding to make it his own. When he moved, it was with dispatch and skill, and with considerable respect to the groundwork he had inherited.

Part of that inheritance was an effort to limit the deployment, as opposed to the testing, of nuclear arms. The most promising and at the same time most urgent opportunity was in the area of strategic defenses—weapons that would shoot down other weapons. Late in the Johnson Administration, at a summit meeting in Glassboro, New Jersey, Robert McNamara, then Secretary of Defense, patiently tried to persuade Premier Aleksei Kosygin that it was in the interests of both countries to forswear large-scale anti-ballistic-missile (ABM) defenses, since a defensive arms race would only fan the offensive race already underway. Each side would feel compelled to increase the number and destructiveness of weapons with which to "penetrate" the defenses of the other. Eventually, during the first Nixon Administration, the Soviets agreed to limit ABMs in SALT I.

Meaningful limits on offensive weapons proved more elusive. The Soviets were not willing to consider such a thing until they felt they had caught up with the U.S., ending forever the massive inferiority from which they felt they were suffering. By the early 1970s, they finally could, and did, claim military parity with the U.S., and were ready to negotiate seriously about offensive weapons. To a degree this was a reflection of their own psychological state. The Soviet regime is insecure about its legitimacy in the eyes of both its own people and the rest of the world. For the men in the Kremlin, a well-founded assertion of equal status with the U.S. was reassuring and rewarding. It was all the more so when the U.S. explicitly accepted equality as a new fact of life and endorsed it as an enduring, acceptable state of affairs in the prologues to treaties and in communiqués released at summits.

Arms control made the Soviets feel more secure in concrete ways, too. Long before the idea of a freeze of the two arsenals became fashionable in the U.S., the Soviets were pushing their version of the concept. Since the late 1960s they had held an advantage in gross numbers of many kinds of weapons, including rockets, and they wanted to make their quantitative advantage permanent. In addition to the ABM Treaty, which was of indefinite duration, SALT I produced an Interim Agreement on offensive weapons, which was to last until 1977, by which time, it was hoped, a longer-lasting treaty would replace it. Both the ABM Treaty and the Interim Agreement were signed by Nixon and Brezhnev at a summit meeting in Moscow in May of 1972. SALT I held the U.S. to 1,710 launchers for ICBMs and SLBMs. That was about 700 fewer than the U.S.S.R. already had in place.*

SALT I also established the principle that launchers—ICBM silos and SLBM tubes—rather than the missiles themselves or the warheads on the

---

*For the history of SALT I, see John Newhouse's *Cold Dawn* (Holt, Rinehart & Winston, 1973); the first volume of Henry Kissinger's memoirs, *White House Years* (Little, Brown, 1979); and the memoir of the chief negotiator, Gerard Smith, *Doubletalk* (Doubleday, 1980).

missiles, were the appropriate currency for trading, or units of account, in strategic arms control. The main reason had to do with verification: one side could, with relative ease and certainty, keep track of the other side's launchers; counting missiles would be more difficult, because they could be hidden away, and multiple warheads more difficult still, since they were inside the top stage of a missile.

Also, multiple warheads were, in those days, an exclusive American specialty. The first MIRVed Minuteman III ICBMs had become operational in 1970, the first Poseidon SLBMs the following year. The U.S. felt a combination of self-righteousness and self-confidence about its pioneering of MIRVs—self-righteousness because they were initially justified as a countermeasure against the ABM system that the Soviets were putting up around Moscow, and self-confidence because American technological superiority seemed to assure the U.S. a permanent lead in this new category of weaponry.

But, by the time SALT I was signed in 1972, MIRVs were already beginning to look more like a problem than an asset for the U.S. The ABM Treaty made them no longer necessary to penetrate enemy defenses, and the predictable, very vigorous effort by the U.S.S.R. to develop its own MIRVs erased the American monopoly. The Soviets had larger rockets, so they were able to have more warheads per launcher. In the early and mid-1960s, the arsenals of the U.S. and the U.S.S.R. evolved in almost opposite directions. The U.S. moved away from behemoths like the Titan ICBM toward the much smaller Minuteman. The U.S.S.R., meanwhile, was vigorously developing its own titans like the SS-9, the first of the so-called heavy ICBMs. It weighed about seven times as much as Minuteman and was twice as long, and its single warhead was in the 25-megaton range, more than 12 times the explosive power of Minuteman.

These contrasting trends had nothing to do with arms-control agreements then in force or in prospect. Each side was following the logic of its own military tradition, geographical position, doctrine of deterrence, and technological fortes (or, in the Soviet case, weaknesses). The U.S. had come to rely on a strategic triad, in which the nation's retaliatory forces were more or less evenly divided up among three means of delivery—ICBMs, bombers, and submarines. ICBMs were part of a larger, diversified system that had the advantage of redundancy; if one leg failed or was knocked out, there were two others to back it up.

Also, the U.S. was far ahead of the Soviet Union in the development of solid-fuel propulsion and electronic miniaturization, both of which made for smaller, more compact ICBMs. The Soviet rockets employed bulky tanks of liquid fuel and relatively primitive electronics. Their rockets had to have more heft in order to get all that hardware off the pad and on its way. The U.S. had a further advantage in the accuracy of its warheads, which meant there was less reason to hurl extra explosives. If the purpose of a missile shot is to knock out a small but well-protected target that can only be destroyed by a nearly direct hit, and the side doing the shooting is confident of being able to strike the bull's-eye with a single, well-aimed bullet, there is no need for throwing a stick of dynamite. The Soviets, on the other hand, had to make up in explosive power, or yield, what their missiles lacked in accuracy.

Further, in trying to justify their investment in great big ICBMs, some Soviets argued that they were merely following a time-honored tradition. They were fond of pointing out that Russia was a land power (compared to the U.S., which was traditionally a maritime power and in modern times an air power), and that the Russian military had accordingly always worshipped artillery as the "god of war." ICBMs were the artillery of the nuclear age.

The trouble was that over time the Soviets closed a number of the gaps between themselves and the U.S. for which their advantage in very large missiles had supposedly compensated. Their submarines and submarine-launched missiles became better. So did their bombers (although they continued to lag behind the U.S. in SLBM and bomber technology). They developed MIRVs. They made breakthroughs in propulsion and guidance systems and, through a vigorous testing program, vastly improved the accuracy of their warheads. A single city killer, the SS-9, gave way to its MIRVed successor, the SS-18, with ten warheads; and the initial model of the SS-18 gave way to a newer, still more accurate multiple silo buster, which could theoretically threaten to take out ten Minutemen. The entire American force of a thousand Minutemen could be put at risk by a mere 100 SS-18s, or by 200 if one took into account that the U.S.S.R. would have to devote two warheads to each hardened target in order to make up for warheads that would go awry. Planners in the West began to worry about a crippling preemptive sneak attack, a nuclear-age Pearl Harbor.

Stability and deterrence have traditionally depended on each side's having confidence that sufficient numbers of its own land-based weapons would survive an attack and be able to strike back. Each must be exposed to retaliation if it should strike first, yet at the same time be free from the threat of a preemptive attack that would deprive it of its own retaliatory forces.

Even with the loss of its ICBMs, the U.S. would still have other means of retaliation, SLBMs and intercontinental bombers. As in the case of Pearl Harbor itself, the side that succeeded in launching a surprise attack would not necessarily win the war. Even after the Soviet buildup, the U.S. deterrent still had advantages of redundancy and diversification. Nonetheless, the prospect that even one leg of the strategic triad might become vulnerable has been unsettling to American experts and policymakers for a long time. The U.S. was the first to develop and deploy MIRVs (a breakthrough that some of its own authors came to regret). But from the American standpoint, the single most dangerous, or destabilizing, development in the recent round of military competition between the superpowers has been the seemingly open-ended acquisition, beginning in the mid-1970s, of more and more MIRVed ICBMs by the Soviet Strategic Rocket Forces.

The SALT I Interim Agreement on offensive weapons froze the Soviet Union's arsenal of heavy (SS-9, -18) launchers at 308. Part of the American challenge in the next round of negotiations, SALT II, was to narrow the MIRV gap, or at least to keep it from getting wider.

Weighing the Threat

Well before the SALT II negotiations yielded a treaty, they generated controversy within the Nixon and Ford administrations.

Henry Kissinger and the U.S. negotiators in SALT I considered it an accomplishment to have frozen the Soviet monopoly in heavy ICBM launchers at 308. But they had not achieved a definition of "heavy." Critics of SALT would never forgive this imprecision, for it allowed the Soviets to proceed with the development and deployment of an extremely powerful new missile, the SS-19, which was smaller than the SS-18, but technologically more advanced. The SS-19 had six warheads, twice as many as the MIRVed version of Minuteman. The Americans had tried to write into the SALT I agreement a definition of heavies that would limit new "nonheavies" to the scale of the U.S.S.R.'s old workhorse ICBM, the SS-11. The Soviets refused, indicating informally to U.S. negotiators that they had under development a successor to the SS-11 that was halfway between the SS-11 and the SS-9 in size.

Later, after the SALT I agreement had been signed, the U.S. unilaterally issued its own definition, which categorized the SS-19 as a heavy. The Soviets in turn ignored this American attempt to wish away the negotiating history. Ever since, SALT critics have talked about the "SS-19 loophole," suggesting that it came about as a result of Soviet deceit and treachery. In fact, though the SS-19 was an outgrowth of the Soviet affection for large missiles and of their refusal to let arms control stand in the way of ongoing programs, no deceit or violation of an agreement was involved.

In addition to the MIRV gap, which the SS-19 widened, the U.S. found itself on the losing side of a gap in ballistic missile throw-weight. This is a technical term, but central to an understanding of the problems that the Reagan Administration inherited and of the solutions it would attempt.

"Throw-weight" sounds as though it might be borrowed from the world of athletics—wrestling, perhaps, or track and field. Its meaning in the context of missilry is not self-evident. Journalists and government officials alike have often tried to avoid it, looking for a synonym that would be more meaningful and vivid. "Destructive power," "lifting power," and "payload" are three common substitutes, but none quite matches the precise definition of "throw-weight."

Throw-weight is the total weight of what can be carried by a missile over a particular range. It is the weight of the business end of the rocket, and it includes the armaments along with the hardware necessary to get them to their targets back on earth from the apogee of a ballistic trajectory, once they have been "boosted" to that height by the launch vehicle and after the other stages of the missile have fallen away. In the case of a single-warhead missile, like the old SS-9, throw-weight is mostly the weight of the warhead itself. But in the case of a multiple-warhead, or MIRVed, missile, like the SS-18, throw-weight includes the warheads plus the post-boost vehicle with its dispensing and releasing mechanism (sometimes called the "bus," because warheads get off along the way), plus the guidance gear aboard the bus, plus possible additional items, such as propulsion devices with their fuel and penetration aids (decoys or radar-reflecting chaff) that will help the warheads get through the other side's ballistic-missile defenses. Thus throw-weight includes a number of components that do not actually arrive, much less blow up, at the target.

Of all the many ways to measure strategic nuclear power, missile throw-weight represents the single largest advantage that the Soviet Union has over the United States. The Soviets get their throw-weight primarily from their 308 heavy missile launchers, as well as two other types of large MIRVed ICBMs, the recurringly troublesome SS-19 with six warheads and the less capable SS-17 with four. The SS-19 and -17 are about one-third the volume of the heavy SS-18, but still nearly three times the volume of the "light" Minuteman. The contrast between the superpowers in the sheer brute force of their rockets brought about the greatest single anxiety underlying defense planning and arms-control policy on the American side. It was the Soviets' long-standing advantage in missile throw-weight, combined with their more recent development of highly accurate MIRVs, that made the U.S.'s own ICBMs vulnerable, at least hypothetically, to preemptive attack.

The debate over the significance of Soviet throw-weight and what to do about it was already simmering in the Nixon Administration. Starting in 1972, the year that the SALT I agreements were signed and the SALT II negotiations began, Kissinger found himself facing two formidable opponents on the issue—his colleague within the Executive Branch, James Schlesinger, and, in the Congress, Henry Jackson. Richard Perle in those days was a close aide of Jackson's and a friend of Schlesinger's.

Schlesinger had been warning since the late 1960s that the Soviets' love affair with huge missiles could upset the balance of nuclear power. Shortly after the Soviets rolled out their first heavy ICBM, the SS-9, in a military parade in 1967, Schlesinger, who was then at the Rand Corporation in Santa Monica, California, told the Kremlin's leading Americanologist, Georgi

Arbatov, "That big new missile of yours is going to create serious problems, not just for us but for you, too." Schlesinger was looking ahead to the era of Soviet MIRVs: "The unrestricted growth of throw-weight on your MIRVed ICBMs is disadvantageous to both sides, since it increases our mutual vulnerability and therefore the instability of our relationship."

Schlesinger joined Jackson in criticizing Kissinger for failing to try harder to cap Soviet throw-weight in SALT. SALT I limited the number of missile launchers at then-current levels, which left the Soviet Union with more ICBMs than the U.S.; it froze the number of Soviet heavy missile launchers at 308. As the SS-9 was retired in favor of the SS-18, 308 huge warheads became a force potentially ten times greater—3,080 smaller but more accurate warheads.

Throw-weight plus MIRVs plus accuracy equal "breakout," a crucial concept in nuclear strategy and arms control. Possessing all that throw-weight that it no longer needed for high-yield, bulky warheads, the Soviet Union could, after an extensive series of test firings, transform its rockets into delivery vehicles for more numerous, smaller, independently targetable warheads. As a result, the U.S.S.R. would have succeeded in "breaking out" of the bounds of the threat as perceived by the other side, enormously increasing that threat. SALT and START alike may be seen as American attempts to cope with further threats of breakout posed by the combination of Soviet throw-weight, accuracy, and MIRVs.

When the Senate approved SALT I, it also passed an amendment, sponsored by Jackson, that called on the Administration to make sure that any future agreements "would not limit the U.S. to levels of intercontinental strategic forces inferior to the limits provided for the Soviet Union." It was widely accepted that Congress was putting the Executive Branch on notice that SALT II would have to limit launchers at equal levels. But Jackson went further: he made clear in numerous speeches at the time that as long as he had anything to say about how his amendment was interpreted, he would insist that throw-weight, too, be equalized.

In 1973, Schlesinger, by now Secretary of Defense, urged Kissinger to approach the Soviets in SALT II with a proposal that would require them to decrease the throw-weight of their ICBMs as they modernized their forces. As they acquired MIRVs, especially more accurate ones, the asymmetry in throw-weight could no longer be justified as compensation for various American technological and geographical advantages. The Soviets would have to trade in their own advantage in throw-weight. In practice this would mean that MIRVed successors to the older, single-warhead missiles (the SS-11 and -13) and heavy SS-9s would have to be much smaller rockets, with much less throw-weight, hence capable of "throwing" fewer warheads.

Schlesinger knew perfectly well that chances were slim of getting the

Soviets to reverse the direction in which their forces were evolving. As insurance against the likelihood that the Soviets would keep their big MIRVs, and as an inducement for them to think twice about the wisdom of doing so, Schlesinger and others concluded that the U.S. needed a new missile of its own to help close the gaps in ballistic-missile throw-weight and in a related measure of power, the ability to strike hardened underground silos on the other side very quickly. The idea of a larger, more heavily MIRVed replacement for the Minuteman had been around since the 1960s, but Schlesinger's concern about the need for such a program gave it a boost. The initials MX stood for Missile-Experimental. The missile itself would be a long time coming. Not until well into the Reagan Administration would the missile finally get a name (Peacekeeper) and would a prototype finally lift off on a test flight. The technical problems of getting the rocket into the air were nothing compared to the political problems of keeping the U.S. Congress from shooting it down.

Rescuing the MX from a congressional veto would become a major preoccupation of the Reagan Administration, one intimately tied up with Congress's attempt to salvage progress from stalemate in strategic arms control. The MX was seen as an answer to the SS-18 and -19, much as the Pershing II came eventually to be seen as an answer to the SS-20. Like MIRVs and cruise missiles, the MX was conceived largely as a bargaining chip. Schlesinger believed that the U.S. should make clear to the Soviets that it would prefer not to deploy the MX, but would be forced to do so if the Soviets refused to accept a reduction in the throw-weight of their next generation of ICBMs.

Kissinger grew impatient with what he considered Schlesinger's narrow-minded concern with Soviet throw-weight. He felt the problem was real but exaggerated. He was a believer in the concept of "offsetting asymmetries." Yes, the Soviets had their monster rockets, but the U.S. had its superior submarines and bombers. Moreover, Kissinger questioned whether throw-weight was a problem that was amenable to solution in arms-control negotiations. The U.S., he often commented, had long since decided to "go the small-missile, diversified-deterrent, low-throw-weight route"; the Soviets had gone the opposite way. It was asking a lot, probably too much, of the negotiators of a new SALT agreement to achieve stability as measured by throw-weight when the military planners and policymakers of successive administrations had chosen to downplay that particular measure for more than ten years. At a meeting of the National Security Council in January 1974, Kissinger commented with some acerbity, "Many people have insisted on absolute equivalence in throw-weight. I wish the same vigor were applied to our military programs as is applied to our SALT position."

As another Nixon-Brezhnev summit in Moscow drew near in the spring of that year, Schlesinger persisted in arguing that the SALT II agreement should include limits on what he called "MIRVed throw-weight"—that is, the aggregate throw-weight of all multiple-warhead launchers. Otherwise, he warned, the Soviet Union would end up within a decade (by the early to mid-1980s) with a five- or sixfold advantage in missile throw-weight and a three- or four-to-one advantage in large, accurate ICBM warheads. While Kissinger had initially found merit in this approach and some of his own staff had been urging the same thing, in the end he resisted what he saw as excessive emphasis on throw-weight. In his view, limitations on throw-weight might be desirable, but then so was the elimination of the Soviet Strategic Rocket Forces altogether. He believed that a SALT agreement based on equality in throw-weight was, quite simply, non-negotiable.

While Kissinger saw Schlesinger as hung up on throw-weight, Schlesinger felt that Kissinger was excessively concerned with what was negotiable and not enough with what was strategically desirable. He suspected that Kissinger was pandering to Richard Nixon's desperation for a SALT II agreement in 1974 as part of his campaign to deflect attention from the Watergate scandal. As it happened, Watergate swept aside the Nixon presidency and, along with it, any chance of a SALT II breakthrough at the Moscow summit in 1974.

When Gerald Ford took over from Nixon, and Kissinger was preparing for the new President's meeting with Brezhnev at Vladivostok later in 1974, Schlesinger resumed his advocacy of limitations on throw-weight. But Kissinger prevailed in getting Ford to accept the proposition that SALT II should be based instead on equal aggregates of launchers. The central feature of the Vladivostok accord, signed by Ford and Brezhnev, was that each side would be allowed an equal number of MIRVed missile launchers. There was nothing about throw-weight in the agreement. The Minuteman, with its three warheads, would count the same as the SS-19 with its six.

In challenging Ford for the Republican nomination in 1976, Ronald Reagan sharply criticized SALT II on the ground that the Soviets were being allowed to keep too many weapons. It was largely in response to the Reagan attack that hawkish defense intellectuals inside the Ford Administration, notably Fred Iklé, who was then director of the Arms Control and Disarmament Agency, and John Lehman, who was his deputy, succeeded in preventing Kissinger from tying up the loose ends of SALT II and getting an agreement in 1976. They believed that Kissinger, détente, and SALT had all become political liabilities to the President and that any deal Kissinger might make would be militarily disadvantageous to the U.S.

When Jimmy Carter came into office, he was convinced he could leapfrog over the unfinished SALT II. He did not like the idea of merely putting the finishing touches on Kissinger's handiwork. Also, Carter hoped to earn support from both left and right with a more ambitious agreement. After consultation with Senator Jackson, who in turn was relying for advice on Richard Perle, Carter approved the so-called Comprehensive Proposal of March 1977. The key feature was an American offer to cancel the MX if the Soviets would cut in half their SS-18 heavy missile force (from 308 to 150). The proposal bore a significant resemblance to the zero option that Reagan would put forward in INF: it would have achieved drastic reductions in the most modern existing Soviet weapons in exchange for the sacrifice of an American weapon that still did not exist.

The Comprehensive Proposal was rudely and categorically rejected by the Soviets. Secretary of State Cyrus Vance, who carried it to Moscow, was told flatly that the Soviet leadership did not have to start from scratch every time a new President arrived in the White House with a new idea. To the lasting resentment of Jackson and Perle, the Carter Administration retreated, regrouped, and came back to the Soviets with a proposal that preserved and improved on what had already been accomplished in SALT II. The result was the treaty signed by Carter and Brezhnev in Vienna in 1979, two years after the SALT I Interim Agreement on offensive weapons had formally expired.

In SALT II, the Soviets accepted equal numerical ceilings on broad categories of weapons, as Congress had mandated, but they retained a monopoly in the sub-category of heavy ICBMs. The Soviets continued to insist that their heavy missiles were a form of compensation for American forward-based systems in Western Europe and the nuclear-armed missiles and bombers of America's allies, Britain and France—precisely those weapons that would end up on the Soviet agenda for INF.

In exchange for what they gained at the negotiating table in SALT II, the Soviets made concessions. The SS-19 remained classified as a nonheavy, but the U.S.S.R. agreed that it would be the largest permissible nonheavy: in other words, no more "loopholes" for a new missile halfway between the SS-19 and the SS-18. While the U.S. would not be allowed to develop a heavy missile of its own (it had no such plans anyway), the MX, which was to be approximately the size of the SS-19, could have ten warheads, as many as the SS-18 and four more than the SS-19. That made it a counter to the SS-19 in size and a counter to the SS-18 in number of warheads.

Moscow also accepted a ceiling on the number of launchers for ICBMs with MIRVs close to the number they already had (820) and a freeze on the number of warheads per type of ICBM (10 for the SS-18, 6 for the SS-19, and 4 for the SS-17). Thus, while launchers remained the unit of account for strategic arms control, SALT II did indirectly put a cap on MIRVed ICBM throw-weight as well as on the number of warheads.

On the chronically nettlesome matter of the long-range but not-quite-intercontinental Backfire bomber, the U.S. failed to get it classified, and therefore limited, as a strategic weapon, but Brezhnev gave Carter a written statement in Vienna promising that the U.S.S.R. would not increase either the range of the aircraft or the rate at which it was being produced.

The treaty aroused opposition in the U.S. for a variety of reasons, some having to do with its terms, others with the political context in which its merits were debated. Many felt the cap was much too high to be militarily meaningful. SALT II's constraints on missile launchers and its freeze on warheads per type left the Soviets with an approximately five-to-two edge in land-based (ICBM) warheads and in ballistic-missile throw-weight. Edward Rowny, the general who had represented the Joint Chiefs of Staff on the SALT II delegation, resigned at the time of its signing to work against its ratification. He charged that SALT II had left open a "window of vulnerability."

Proponents of the treaty, who were by now very much on the defensive, pointed out that the window would have been opened much wider if it had not been for SALT. The agreement bounded the threat by limiting the number of MIRVed ICBM warheads the Soviets could have. At the same time, the treaty left the U.S. free to catch up with the Soviets in some categories of weaponry and to preserve its compensating advantages in others. When the Joint Chiefs of Staff gave their endorsement to the ratification of SALT II in 1979, they repudiated Rowny and called the treaty a "modest but useful step."

Critics on both the left and the right were not willing to go even that far. They stressed instead what the treaty did not accomplish. Liberals pointed out that it failed to stop, much less reverse, the arms race, while conservatives claimed it did not slow the Soviet military buildup and left the U.S. virtually standing still. One of the accusations with which Ronald Reagan campaigned for the presidency in 1980 was the charge that SALT II was "fatally flawed." His foreign-policy advisers and would-be members of his Administration were people like Rowny, Eugene Rostow, and Paul Nitze, who had spoken out against SALT II.

But perhaps the greatest liability—the real fatal flaw—of SALT II, especially for its opponents on the right, was its sponsorship. The treaty was the fruit of three administrations' labors, but the signature on the bottom of the last page, alongside Leonid Brezhnev's, was Jimmy Carter's. Inasmuch as SALT II was a symbol of Jimmy Carter's stewardship of American foreign and defense policy, it barely stood a chance. The Soviet invasion of Afghanistan in the last days of 1979 was the *coup de grâce*. In early 1980, Carter withdrew the treaty from consideration by the Senate, saving it from almost certain rejection but consigning it to a limbo where it would remain for years to come.

However, while repeatedly attacking SALT II both on its own terms and as a manifestation of Carter's "vacillation" and "weakness," Reagan also promised, in the last days of the 1980 campaign, that he would waste no time in seeking a strategic arms-control agreement that met his high standards: "As President, I will make immediate preparations for negotiations on a SALT III Treaty. My goal is to begin arms reductions."

11 The Ghost of SALT

SALT was dead. Long live SALT.

That, in a nutshell, became the Reagan Administration's unstated policy with regard to the much-maligned and unratified agreement of 1979. The Administration decided to keep SALT II informally in force until there was a new agreement to replace it. The President was ultimately persuaded that the U.S. was better off with SALT II regulating the competition than without it, until his Administration came up with something better. The search for something better became one of the principal tasks that the Administration set itself in its foreign policy. It took a long time for that search to get underway in earnest.

During 1981, its first year in office, the Reagan Administration came up with little more than a new acronym. That was the handiwork—indeed, it was one of the few contributions—of Richard Allen, Reagan's original assistant for national security affairs. He got the idea from Richard Pipes, a Harvard professor of Russian history who had been active in the Committee on the Present Danger and who had joined the NSC staff as its senior expert on the U.S.S.R. Allen and Pipes were thinking like advertising men with a new product to sell when they suggested substituting the word "reduction" for "limitation" in the despised initials. Part of the problem with the old product, SALT—one of its fatal flaws, in fact—was that traditional arms control had contented itself with the quest for mere limitations. That implied acceptance of the status quo, which, to their minds, was unacceptable, for it entailed Soviet superiority. The new product would feature reductions. That sounded more ambitious and appealing; it sounded more like real arms control and even like a step toward genuine disarmament. The nuclear stockpiles, and therefore the threat of nuclear war, were going to be not just limited, but reduced. As Allen said at the time, "Hardliners and liberals alike can identify with reductions. Everyone wants reductions."

Well before the new Administration decided on a proposal in strategic arms control, it was operating on the basis of a concept very similar to the one underlying the zero option in INF. The word "reduction" was central to that concept: the U.S.S.R. should be required to pay a price for its promiscuous arms buildup of the past two decades and for its essentially aggressive nature. The price would be a reduction of its forces. If the Soviet Union refused to pay that price, then its leadership, not the Reagan Administration, would bear the responsibility for the failure of arms control. Or so the Administration hoped.

Allen, Pipes, and their fellow veteran of the Committee on the Present Danger, Eugene Rostow, began using the term SART, for Strategic Arms Reduction Talks, in meetings.* It did not take hold. In one meeting, James Baker scribbled a note suggesting a catchier alternative and passed it to Allen: "How about 'Faster Arms Reduction Talks'?" Of course, faster arms reduction talks were just exactly what the new Administration did *not* want. It wanted to stall as long as possible and concentrate on a defense buildup, so that eventually, if and when the U.S. did resume negotiations, it could do so from a position of far greater strength if not superiority.

Those career foreign-service officers, arms-control technocrats, military specialists, and other professionals who were hoping that their new bosses might come around to reviving strategic arms control felt the change in acronyms was fine if the new name made Reagan and his men less hostile to the process. Eventually SART became START, a modification proposed by Pipes. The addition of a single consonant made all the difference. The President liked it. It meant something. It suggested a fresh start, a new beginning. He agreed to put in a brief plug for START by that name in his speech in November 1981 unveiling the zero proposal for INF.

In fact, there was no policy—no product, new or old—to go with the new brand name. Pressure from the West Europeans had forced the Administration to focus its attention on INF and led to the President's zero-option speech in November, but strategic arms control as yet had no such constituency or lobbying effort behind it. The subject did not loom large in the deliberations of the Cabinet, the National Security Council, or the President's more informal consultations with his advisers during 1981. Edwin Meese once remarked that strategic arms control "will be lucky if we let it get away with benign neglect."

---

*In fact, not even the acronym, to say nothing of the concept, of strategic arms reductions was new. Zbigniew Brzezinski, in his memoirs published in 1983, *Power and Principle* (Farrar, Straus, Giroux, New York), cited a lengthy memo he submitted to President Carter on April 30, 1977. The memo suggested ten "strategic priorities" for the Carter presidency. Number 4 on the list was "[t]o push U.S.-Soviet strategic arms *limitation* talks into strategic arms *reduction* talks . . . to have a completed and ratified SALT Treaty by early 1978, and thus be ready to seek a SART (Strategic Arms Reduction Treaty) by 1980."

To Adhere or to Undercut?

In practice, benign neglect meant leaving well enough alone. It meant continuing to abide by the SALT I treaty limiting anti-ballistic-missile defenses, which was still legally in force; the SALT I Interim Agreement on offensive weapons, which had formally expired in 1977; and the unratified SALT II treaty—while saying and doing nothing that could be construed as an endorsement of the political or military wisdom of those accords. Alexander Haig commented in one of his first meetings with his staff, "You can't beat something with nothing, and we don't have our own SALT policy, so we'd be nuts just to throw out the old one." He was concerned, too, about not further alarming the West European allies, who were already skittish about the militant anti-Sovietism of the new American leadership.

An instance of what Haig meant occurred at the very beginning of the Administration, when the Air Force was planning to launch a Minuteman as part of a training exercise for its crew. The test range ran out over the Pacific, far outside the territory of the U.S. SALT II contained a requirement that each side notify the other in advance of any such tests. This measure was meant to diminish the danger that the test launch would be mistaken for the beginning of an attack. At one of his first meetings with Weinberger, Haig argued forcefully and successfully for notifying the Soviets of the Minuteman test, as had been done before similar launches since mid-1979. It was important, Haig said, to signal both the allies and the Soviets that the new Administration was proceeding deliberately and cautiously, "without gratuitous disregard for continuity."

Continued adherence to SALT II was militarily painless, since it involved no immediate sacrifices or significant slowdowns in American weapons programs. In fact, it might well have been militarily painful not to continue abiding by the treaty. The Joint Chiefs of Staff were acutely aware that the Soviets could add warheads to their missile force far more rapidly and menacingly than could the U.S. if the SALT limits were to go by the board. That was the principal reason that the Chiefs had, during the previous Administration, testified in favor of ratification, albeit belatedly and without enthusiasm. Early in 1981, General Richard Ellis, the commander of the Strategic Air Command, told an interagency meeting that "the Chiefs want a continuance of the adherence regime rather than deal with breakout on the Soviet side."

But Ellis and the chiefs were holdovers; some of the newcomers at the Pentagon and on the NSC staff objected to the idea of an "adherence regime." They wanted SALT put out of its misery; they wanted it unambiguously dead and buried.

John Lehman, Iklé's former deputy in the Ford Administration and now the Secretary of the Navy, made the case publicly, in a meeting with reporters on March 3. He accused Carter of having "illegally" kept the U.S. in compliance with the SALT I Interim Agreement. The Executive Branch was under a statutory obligation to seek congressional approval of any arms-control agreement that affected U.S. military programs. Yet when the SALT I Interim Agreement expired in 1977, Carter had extended it by an exchange of unilateral statements between Washington and Moscow: both sides would continue observing its terms while they negotiated SALT II. That, said Lehman, had been illegal. "I have no hesitation at all," he added, "in recommending that we not comply with SALT I."

Lehman mentioned in passing that he was speaking personally and that the issue of SALT compliance "has not been taken up" by the government as a whole. The very next day Richard Burt was due to chair a meeting of the Interagency Group charged with taking up the issue. Burt was angry at this shot across his bow from the Pentagon. He responded with a State Department cable to American embassies in Europe, followed by a tart public statement released on March 4:

> This Administration is reviewing its overall SALT policy. No decision has yet been taken on our adherence to existing SALT agreements. John Lehman's statements on SALT, as reported in the press, were not authorized, nor did they reflect Administration policy. While we are reviewing our SALT policy, we will take no action that would undercut existing agreements so long as the Soviet Union exercises the same restraint.

That last, carefully written sentence was to be repeated many times over the next year. The awkward diction ("we will take no action that would undercut . . .") was boilerplate used in international law to define the obligation of a party to a treaty still pending ratification. It meant taking no action that would irreversibly contravene the purpose of the treaty—that is, an action whose consequences would be permanent; it did not mean obeying every provision of the agreement. The Soviets had adopted much the same posture: they did not feel obligated to reduce their strategic launchers to the level set by SALT II unless and until the treaty was ratified, but in the absence of ratification, they refrained from adding MIRVs to their SS-18, since that would have been an irreversible contravention.

But the tone of the State Department's formulation was also intended to stress the grudging, conditional nature of compliance and to discourage the inference that the department was saying anything good about SALT.

Nonetheless, Ronald Reagan expressed some curiosity, tinged with annoyance, at a White House staff meeting. Who at State was making these statements? And on what authority? Was it Haig? Was this the best thing to be saying? What did it mean? Meese, who was supposed to be supervising national-security policy, replied that it was just a case of "the bureaucracy sorting itself out."

At an NSC meeting more than two months later, in mid-May, the President departed from the regular agenda and asked, "What are we going to do about SALT anyway?" There was some shuffling of feet and a number of quick glances around the room. Then a free-form discussion quickly took on the character of a debate rehashing whether it was in U.S. interests to continue abiding by the old agreements. Haig and David Jones, the chairman of the Joint Chiefs of Staff, said it was; Weinberger and Allen said it wasn't. The Defense Secretary and National Security Adviser made a number of claims to the effect that SALT obstructed weapons programs the U.S. needed right away.

"Like what?" asked Jones.

The cruise-missile program, replied Weinberger.

"How?" asked Jones.

Well, said Weinberger, SALT prohibits long-range cruise missiles.

Jones explained that that prohibition was contained only in the protocol to the treaty; that it applied to ground- and sea-launched cruise missiles, not to air-launched ones; and that the protocol would expire at the end of 1981, before the U.S. had any long-range ground- and sea-launched cruise missiles ready for deployment. "There's not even a marginal military reason for exceeding the SALT limits," he continued. "If the TTB [Threshold Test Ban Treaty of 1974] disappeared, we'd test weapons over 150 kilotons [the limit set by the treaty for underground tests]. But if SALT II disappeared, there's nothing we'd do differently."

The question that John Lehman and Richard Burt had fought out in March was now obviously still wide open at the highest level of the government. Others at the table—Director of Central Intelligence William Casey, Eugene Rostow, and the President himself—shared Weinberger's and Allen's visceral dislike of everything about SALT. But in the end the group came reluctantly around to accepting Jones's assertion that nothing about SALT in and of itself was an obstacle to the Administration's rearmament program. As Rostow put it, "SALT doesn't hurt us for the next little while." Therefore, better to continue a policy of declared adherence to the old agreements while the various agencies joined in a thorough review of what Allen called "the comparative benefits of SALT versus no-SALT."

General Jones came away from the meeting discouraged. "These guys have got a lot to learn," he commented to a colleague afterward.

"A Rock-'Em, Sock-'Em Démarche"

Aside from the question of whether the U.S. should continue abiding by SALT in the future, there was sharp division over whether the Soviet Union had abided by it in the past. That debate would continue through the next four years and would assume significance far beyond the highly technical issues at hand. If it could be established that the Soviets had already systematically cheated on arms-control agreements, hard-liners would more easily be able to question the wisdom of any future agreements; and if, for political reasons, the U.S. had to keep up the appearance of seeking agreements, it would be all the more justified in insisting on the most intrusive, comprehensive inspection of military facilities in the U.S.S.R.

The State Department seemed to have prejudged the question. By asserting that the U.S. and the Soviet Union were obligated to continue observing (or "not undercutting") the agreements, it had implied that both had complied with SALT to date. A number of the more passionate critics of SALT in the Administration disagreed; they were also defenders of what they believed to be true Reaganism in the field of arms control. Their self-proclaimed champion was David Sullivan, an ex-CIA analyst and adviser to the right wing in the Senate. Early in 1981, he was acting counselor of the Arms Control and Disarmament Agency.

Tacked to the wall behind his desk was a quotation from President Reagan's first press conference, headed "Soviet Duplicity" and typed out in extra-large print: "So far détente's been a one-way street that the Soviet Union has used to pursue its own aims. . . . Their goal must be the promotion of world revolution . . . They reserve unto themselves the right to commit any crime, to lie, to cheat." Those words were gospel to Sullivan, and he hoped to convert his position as a member of the transition team to a senior job in the Administration of the President who had uttered them.

Sullivan was, in his own eyes and those of many on the right, Washington's most knowledgeable and outspoken expert on Soviet cheating under SALT. He kept a constantly expanding list of alleged transgressions. In all instances, Sullivan's case for the prosecution rested on the presumption of guilt. He would interpret a questionable activity as an open-and-shut violation. He resolved ambiguities, both in Soviet behavior and in the provisions of SALT, in favor of a judgment to convict. Many of the newly arrived political appointees were inclined to give him rather than the Soviets the benefit of the doubt.

To settle the question, James Timbie and a number of other career experts from various agencies, including the CIA, prepared a lengthy report examining in great detail the allegations of Soviet cheating. It ended up being a refutation of Sullivan. The U.S. had raised with the Soviets the subject of the questionable activities cited by Sullivan; the Soviets had either adequately explained what they were doing or discontinued the activity. In none of the cases could the U.S.S.R. be said to have been caught red-handed in an outright violation. There was some predisposition to dismiss any report authored by "holdovers and SALTniks" like Timbie as a whitewash, but the document was so much more persuasive than Sullivan's various briefs that it served its purpose of keeping the Administration from accusing the U.S.S.R. publicly of cheating on SALT.

Not that the Administration was about to give the Soviets a clean bill of health. While Sullivan went on distributing articles and congressional testimony detailing alleged Soviet violations to anyone who visited him in his office at the Arms Control Agency, Timbie's report received a code-word classification, higher than top secret, and was never issued even as an interagency paper within the government.

The issue of past Soviet compliance with SALT was in the purview of the Standing Consultative Commission (SCC). This was a permanent joint Soviet-American panel set up in 1972 under the terms of SALT I and extended in 1979 under SALT II in order to give each side a chance to question the other on matters of compliance. Both symbolically and substantively, the commission was an important accomplishment of SALT. It was a unique forum in which military officers, intelligence officials, and diplomats from the two sides could sit down with each other on a regular basis and talk about subjects that used to qualify as military secrets—and, in other contexts, still did.

The SCC was a vestige of SALT, and as such suspect in the new Administration. The commission was due to hold its first meeting since the Reagan inauguration in Geneva, starting on March 25, 1981. Richard Allen, Sven Kraemer, and Robert Schweitzer of the National Security Council staff looked forward to what Schweitzer called a "rock-'em, sock-'em démarche."

Richard Burt was all for putting the Soviets on notice that the new Administration was going to be more vigilant and demanding with regard to all arms-control agreements, not just SALT but those dealing with the underground testing of nuclear weapons and the development of chemical and biological warfare as well. But he did not think it wise for the U.S. to "charge in there like gangbusters" with sweeping accusations of Soviet cheating. That would be taken by the Soviets as tantamount to repudiation of the agreements in question. Also, the allies would be rattled. Besides, the U.S. was a long way from having an agreed, defensible set of charges to make. So Burt suggested that the Administration seek postponement of the meeting until the end of May. Lawrence Eagleburger, then still the Assistant Secretary of State for Europe, agreed. He saw that the alternative to postponement might be an SCC meeting "that the crazies will turn into a donnybrook, and an ill-prepared donnybrook at that."

Haig and Burt breakfasted with Weinberger and Iklé in early March, and agreed on postponement of the SCC meeting from later that month until May. Haig sent a "decision memorandum" to the White House, signed by himself. Later that day, at the opening meeting of the Interagency Group, Burt announced the decision as a *fait accompli.* Allen, Kraemer, Sullivan, and others were angrier than ever at Haig and the State Department for presuming to speak for the entire Administration. Allen took the matter to the President, arguing that postponement would be viewed with alarm by the West Europeans and pro-arms-control forces in the U.S. These were two constituencies for which Allen rarely showed much solicitude, and his intervention did not succeed.

Reagan ended up backing Haig, but because of the intrigue and indecision the U.S. did not get around to proposing a new date for the meeting until just before it had originally been scheduled to begin. There was, in other words, a delay in proposing a delay. The President himself was a latecomer. When asked why he had approved postponement, he said, " 'Cause that's what Al had already decided. Or Al and Cap, I guess." Then he shrugged. It was the appropriate gesture. A pattern was already developing in strategic arms control, as in INF and other areas, whereby the bureaucracy churned away furiously, bucking its disagreements upward to the White House. The President then acted less as a decisionmaker in producing policy than as a rather reluctant and uninformed arbiter. It was a process that produced constant squabbles, temporary truces, and permanent, institutionalized acrimony.

Putting the Soviets on Notice

Now that it had been decided that the U.S. would go to Geneva to meet with the Soviets in May, the Administration had to decide what to say when it got there.

Burt had fought hard to head off John Lehman and others in the Administration who wanted to dump SALT altogether. But, when a number of newspaper accounts described Burt in flattering terms as the key official who had thwarted attempts to kill SALT, he was upset. That sort of credit exposed him to suspicion and resentment on the right. For days, he insisted to everyone that he was "completely neutral" on the question of SALT compliance. He wanted to make a place for himself in the Administration as a pragmatist who could counterbalance the ideologues around him—but a pragmatist who yielded to no one in his toughness toward the Soviets.

As a step in this direction, Burt proposed that the Administration depart from standard SCC procedure whereby the American representatives would give the Soviets written notification of steps the U.S. was taking to remain in compliance with SALT I. By notifying the Soviets orally rather than in writing, suggested Burt, "We will deliver the mail on our intention to continue adherence, but at the same time leave some deliberate ambiguity about formal adherence." He acknowledged that the idea also appealed to him "as a compromise to satisfy those in the Administration who have been pushing for renunciation [of SALT]."

Richard Perle pointed out that this was no time to be sending the Soviets mixed signals. Nor was it a good idea to give them a pretext for accusing the U.S. of playing fast and loose with the rules and procedures of SALT, which the Administration, thanks to Burt, had now publicly vowed not to undercut. Perle, who prided himself on being far tougher than Burt when it mattered, relished this opportunity to appear more reasonable and moderate on an issue that was purely tactical.

Burt also found it necessary to deal with a suggestion that the Administration should reopen at the SCC the old issue of the SS-19 and the Soviets' refusal nine years before to categorize it as a heavy missile. As another of his compromises, Burt decided to "lay down a marker showing that the SS-19 episode is an example of how the Soviets have distorted the spirit of agreements," but to do so through diplomatic channels rather than at the SCC in Geneva. Off went a cable to the U.S. embassy in Moscow instructing the chargé d'affaires, Jack Matlock, to inform the Soviet Foreign Ministry that certain activities in the past would not be acceptable in the future. He had a list with a number of "points of example." No. 1 on the list was the SS-19 as a violation of the spirit of the SALT I provision on heavy missiles. The SS-19 affair, said Matlock, "shows how an activity that runs contrary to declared interpretations can undermine confidence."

Matlock's host, Deputy Foreign Minister Georgi Kornienko, was incensed that the U.S. would bring up this *dokhlyi vopros*—this "rotten, stinking question" (the adjective *dokhlyi* is often used of carrion).

That was that. However it may have smelled to Kornienko, the issue had been aired, and Burt congratulated himself on finding a way to do it that did not further foul the atmosphere of the Standing Consultative Commission.

The Typhoon Codes and Rusty Barrels

It was just as well that the American SCC delegation was spared having to drag up at the session in May any extraneous and provocative pieces of old business. There was plenty of other business that was fully appropriate to the commission's agenda. The most delicate problem concerned the Soviets' employment of codes in the testing of their latest submarine-launched ballistic missile, designated by NATO the SS-NX-20, for the new Typhoon submarine.

SALT II prohibited any use of codes that "impeded" the other side's ability to monitor compliance with the treaty. Codes were not, however, banned altogether, since the Soviet Union insisted it had a right to protect its military secrets; the U.S. should not be able to carry out espionage under the guise of verifying arms-control agreements. SLBMs, like the one for the Typhoon, were subject to fewer constraints than ICBMs. That meant, presumably, that SLBM tests could be more heavily encoded than ICBM tests.*

But the Reagan Administration was not satisfied either with SALT II or with Soviet conduct. It felt the partial ban on encryption was too ambiguous and that the Soviets were taking too much advantage of that ambiguity. Also, there was concern that by using codes so heavily in their Typhoon program the Soviets might be laying down a marker of their own about the amount of encryption they felt was permissible in general—and the amount they would use in testing new generations of ICBMs. A Soviet official in a conversation with an American around this time suggested as much. "We'd like for people who study these matters to understand," he said, "that we've been really very restrained to date [in the encryption of missile telemetry]; there are plenty of things we could do but are not doing [in ICBM testing] out of respect for SALT."

Since the Reagan Administration did not share the Kremlin's reverence for SALT II and had no wish to acknowledge its value by appealing to its provisions, how to treat the Typhoon issue posed a particularly tricky problem. The Soviet activity in question was, in the language of a government report, "ambiguous and troublesome, particularly in its possible precedental connotations," but not an open-and-shut violation. In the end, the American delegation raised the issue only obliquely, referring to submarine missiles in general rather than the Typhoon in particular. The chief Soviet representative, General Viktor Starodubov, did not miss the opportunity to note with heavy sarcasm that it was curious for the American side to be raising an issue of compliance with SALT II, given its refusal to ratify the treaty.

SALT I was less stigmatized than SALT II, partly because it had been signed by Richard Nixon rather than Jimmy Carter, and also because the SALT I treaty limiting Anti-Ballistic Missiles (ABM) had been ratified by the Senate in 1972 and was still formally in force. Therefore, the Americans could, and did, raise issues of compliance with the ABM treaty more straightforwardly than matters relating to SALT II. Once again, however, the forcefulness of the American argument was weakened by reports in the U.S. press of the Administration's belief that the 1972 ABM treaty had

---

*The issue of codes in tests, or "telemetry encryption," is one of the more complicated and fascinating in the history of arms control. It is mentioned only cursorily here and in subsequent chapters because the Reagan Administration did not make enough progress toward agreement with the Soviets between 1981 and 1983 for questions of verification to assume much importance in the negotiations. For background on the encryption problem, see the author's *Endgame* and *Verification and SALT: The Challenge of Strategic Deception,* edited by William C. Potter (Westview Press, Boulder, 1980).

outlived its usefulness and should be radically renegotiated or scrapped altogether.

As for the other part of SALT I, the Interim Agreement on offensive weapons, it had expired in 1977. Like SALT II, it was still being tacitly observed, but with John Lehman and others publicly arguing for a clean break with SALT I, the Reagan Administration was not in the best position to press the Soviets on fastidious adherence to its fine points.

The Interim Agreement required the destruction of all remaining launchers for two Soviet ICBMs deployed back in the early 1960s. These were the SS-7 and SS-8, dinosaurs of the nuclear age. The real monster of the two, the SS-7, was the ancestor of the first modern heavy missile, the single-warhead SS-9. Dismantlement meant tearing down the launchers, plus the racks on which fuel tanks had been stored, and removing the tanks themselves from the launch sites. The Soviets had been slow in fulfilling the last of these conditions. Over the years, American SCC commissioners had repeatedly complained that there were still old fuel tanks lying around launch sites—"rusty barrels," as they came to be called. The Soviets would reply with weary rolls of the eyes and shakes of the head, and a few more barrels would be taken off to be used, in some instances, on pig farms. In the wake of the last SCC session in the fall of 1980, there was one site left in Siberia with rusty barrels.

The American delegation was instructed to raise the issue and provide the coordinates for the site in question. The Soviets gloated over what one of them called the U.S.'s "undying penchant for trivia; we are glad to see that in this respect, at least, there is continuity between Administrations."

While the SCC was still in session, American spy satellites confirmed that the last of the barrels had been removed. The U.S. delegates pronounced their government "happy that this issue has finally been resolved." It was to be the first, last, and only achievement of the Reagan Administration in nuclear arms-control negotiations for a very long time to come.

12 The Eureka Options

Alexander Haig appeared before the Senate Foreign Relations Committee in early May 1982 to praise the Administration's opening proposal for strategic arms control, which President Reagan had outlined a few days before in a speech at his alma mater, Eureka College in Illinois. As usual, the Secretary of State came on strong. He was lavish in his claims for the START initiative and peremptory in his dismissal of alternatives, such as ratifying SALT II or negotiating a freeze on the superpowers' existing nuclear forces. He seemed thoroughly confident in answering almost every question put to him. Only once did he turn defensive and snappish. That was when he was asked why it had taken almost exactly a third of a presidential term to formulate the proposal. Perhaps, some of the senators suggested, the Administration had been deliberately dragging its feet and had finally come up with a plan only in response to political pressure.

"That's all wrong," said Haig sharply. "We moved as rapidly as we could, with professionalism and care, in a very active interdepartmental environment."

It was as close as Haig allowed himself to come in public to expressing his frustration with the squabbling that had preceded the President's decision—and that would continue for weeks, right up until the day, June 25, when Haig stalked out of office with Reagan and his men closing the door behind him. The Administration was slow in coming forward with a proposal for a number of reasons. One was that the military crackdown in Poland in late 1981 deepened the pall over Soviet-American relations. But by far the most important reason for the delay was intramural, not international; for more than a year, the principal activity in what Haig called the interdepartmental environment was bureaucratic warfare.

"Real Men"

In what seemed to the participants the unending struggle over START, one technical issue was more contentious than any other. Early in 1983, as the bureaucracy was tearing itself apart over questions that the President had supposedly resolved a full year before, hand-made signs appeared on office walls at the State Department: "Real Men Don't Need Throw-Weight." The slogan was the experts' way of laughing at an argument that had assumed immense political symbolism and that would not go away. Throw-weight had indeed become more than just a way of measuring the destructive capability of Soviet missiles; it had become, in the eyes of those who believed it was the only important measure, a way of separating the true Reaganauts from the crypto-SALTniks; it was an index of ideological virility.

The history of START was, on one level, the story of old battles from SALT refought with new intensity, with higher stakes, and with some of the original combatants, who had come back to fight again another day in new, more powerful positions. That is how the "rotten and stinking question" of the SS-19 loophole came to be dug up in early 1981. But that was a passing incident. The very lively issue of throw-weight, by contrast, would continue to polarize and sometimes paralyze the Administration's START policies.

From the beginning of the Reagan Administration, there had been two cardinal rules governing strategic arms control policy. First, START must be—and must be seen to be—very different from SALT. Second, the R in START, which distinguished the new initials from the old, stood for reduction as opposed to mere limitation. Whatever else START achieved, it must achieve reductions, the deeper and more drastic the better. But what should be reduced? Richard Perle had always believed that ballistic-missile throw-weight was what mattered most in the strategic balance, tipping the scale in favor of the U.S.S.R., and that throw-weight therefore ought to be the principal unit of account in strategic arms control. He had never been satisfied with SALT II's indirect and lenient limits on Soviet throw-weight.

In essence, as Perle saw it, the Soviet threat was a function of four interrelated excesses—too many warheads that were too large atop too many missiles with too much cumulative throw-weight. Initially, he was interested in finding a means of measuring, and then reducing, these excesses all together. There must be "some way of reducing the elements of strategic power to a single index that would enable us to limit each side to X number of units defined in terms of that index." He was looking for a way to reduce the variety of weapons on both sides to packages of explosive power, increments of death and destruction that could be regulated and traded back and forth. Much the same concept would emerge again in 1983, when Congress joined the Administration in revising the U.S. position in START. But in 1981 and '82, Perle gave up on the idea of a single index. He concluded it was artificial and would make the proposal prohibitively complicated. Better simply to recognize that "you can't reduce the relevant measures below two separate ones—throw-weight and warheads; those two capture the problem in its totality."

The throw-weight and warhead ceilings in START must be very low, since high ceilings would allow the Soviets to stay where they were while the U.S. was unlikely to spend the money and adopt the programs necessary to catch up. The Soviet reductions necessary to come down to those low ceilings would be phased over a number of years. The details would be worked out in the negotiations. Perle made no bones about how different those negotiations would be from SALT. In fact, he made a virtue of the difference: "If you approach the negotiations with a quite radical departure, as we're prepared to do, then it's a little bit easier to fend off the Soviet charge that we're simply soliciting a change in the previous bargain. We'd be confronting them with an entirely new and different concept." Why this breathtaking novelty should, in and of itself, make the proposal harder for the Soviets to reject was not clear.

By the time the National Security Council finally buckled down to START in the spring of 1982, Perle was advocating one ceiling of 4,000 ballistic-missile warheads (about half the number of those then on each side's ICBMs and SLBMs) and another of less than 2 million kilograms of ballistic missile throw-weight, just below the American level and more than 60 percent below the Soviet level.

The throw-weight ceiling was overtly one-sided; the warhead ceiling was less obviously so. The U.S. would be reducing its total number of missile warheads in any event as it replaced older, more numerous Poseidon missiles with Trident SLBMs. The Trident missiles had fewer warheads than the Poseidon but they had a longer range and were more accurate and more destructive. Perle's plan for START meshed with the U.S. military's plan for its own modernization while it simultaneously served to reverse the direction of Soviet modernization, and to penalize the U.S.S.R. for the modernization it had already accomplished.

Perle's proposal for START was even more audacious than his advocacy of the zero option in INF. In Europe the Soviets would have to dismantle all of their most modern intermediate-range ballistic missiles or bear the full brunt of the Pershing II and Tomahawk deployments. In strategic weaponry, they would have to remove about two-thirds of their most modern, MIRVed intercontinental-range ballistic missiles and still face a major American buildup, the centerpieces for which were the MX and the Trident II SLBM programs.

Perle regarded anyone sympathetic to a throw-weight limitation as an ally. One was Edward Rowny, the chief START negotiator. He too favored a set of ceilings on missile warheads and throw-weight, although both would have been higher than the ones Perle preferred. "Never mind," said Perle. "What matters, Ed, is that we're both in the same conceptual ballpark."

Another potential ally was Paul Nitze. He and Perle had only just begun to cross swords in INF. While Nitze had no formal responsibility for START, he happened to be the key architect of the Arms Control and

Disarmament Agency's START option. That was the result of a number of factors, among them his expertise and experience as a former SALT negotiator, his prestige as the leading critic of SALT II, and his close partnership with Rostow and Timbie. Another reason for Nitze's importance was the fact that Rowny enjoyed little respect around the corridors of the agency, including in the front office. The personal chemistry between him and Rostow was bad. His plodding, lugubrious manner made him ineffective in meetings. His opinions were largely discounted.

Nitze and Timbie came up with a plan for START that, like Perle's, featured a ceiling of 4,000 missile warheads, but, instead of a throw-weight ceiling, set an upper limit on the weight of individual warheads. Large warheads, Nitze said, were "the cutting, killing edge" of the Soviets' arsenal, and therefore they should be the focus of the proposal. The upper limit on the permissible weight of individual warheads would be reduced over time. That would have meant in practice that the Soviets could keep the SS-18 in service, but as they brought on new generations of ICBMs, they would have to reduce the size of their warheads. In the meantime, to comply with the ceiling of 4,000 warheads, they would be cutting down on the number of their ICBMs, including necessarily the heavy ones. The result would be a huge reduction in throw-weight. Rostow liked the plan, nicknamed the warhead-size limit "the Nitze index," and made it the key feature of his agency's option.

Once again, Perle's reaction was low-key and accommodating. He called Nitze's plan "quite similar to our own," and he predicted that the Office of the Secretary of Defense and the Arms Control Agency would end up with a "common position." Yet, when anyone questioned throw-weight, Perle turned combative and menacing. Downplaying throw-weight would defy what he considered a mandate from the U.S. Congress—the Jackson amendment to the 1972 SALT I Interim Agreement on offensive weapons. That amendment, requiring equal levels in future accords, had been drafted largely by Perle himself. He carried a loose-leaf binder around with him that contained the text of the amendment and excerpts from the floor debate, in which Jackson made clear that throw-weight was one of the most important elements in the strategic balance that needed to be equalized. He pulled the book out and quoted from it so often that it became known as "Perle's bible."

"The Launcher Boys"

Perle's tactics were aimed at the Department of State and, more particularly, at Richard Burt. Unlike Perle, Burt was not a passionate believer in the folly of SALT. Also unlike Perle, he wanted an arms-control agreement in Reagan's first term. He felt that negotiations toward an agreement might very well make or break the Administration's foreign policy. START, Burt felt, was the only forum in which the U.S. could get an agreement. This was because, in his view, rough strategic parity still existed. In that crucial respect, Burt distinguished START from INF. An INF agreement was not even desirable until deployment of the new American missiles was underway, since any deal that might be patched together before then would serve only to consolidate Soviet advantages. In START, however, there was still a chance for an agreement, and Burt set out to make sure that the U.S. took full advantage of whatever chance there was.

Like Kissinger in earlier rounds of this old battle, Burt was against making throw-weight a unit of account in the U.S. proposal, since doing so would make the proposal non-negotiable. He professed to support the goal of limiting it—"Any agreement worth getting has to deal with the asymmetry in the throw-weight"—yet precisely because the Soviets had such an advantage by this measure, Burt felt it would be a mistake to make it the coinage of bargaining. Any reduction of throw-weight on the Soviet side would cost the U.S. a great deal—very likely too much—in those currencies where the U.S. was rich (SLBMs, bombers, and cruise missiles).

Burt pointed out that, beyond the circle of experts, throw-weight did not mean very much. He recalled that during his days in the newsroom of *The New York Times* Washington bureau, his colleagues used to treat throw-weight as one of the sillier bits of nuclear jargon, the sort of word that was best left to one of the last paragraphs in a newspaper story if there was to be any hope of getting a reader past the headline. "I'll bet if the President's secretary came into the room during an NSC meeting," remarked Burt, "and was asked what throw-weight meant, she wouldn't know." The same point might have been applied to the President himself. Indeed, later in the Administration, Reagan confessed to a number of visitors that he had never fully understood what "this throw-weight business is all about."

In addition to "comprehensibility," Burt was worried about preserving what he called the "plausibility" of the proposal. He feared that the leaders of the resurgent movement in favor of arms control in the U.S., not to mention the West Europeans, would question the sincerity of an opening bid in START that came right out and asked the Soviets to give up 60–70 percent of their throw-weight virtually gratis. "People will say this proposal is designed to fail," warned Burt. As in interagency deliberations over INF, Perle would often chide Burt for hiding behind "plausibility" as a euphemism for "negotiability."

Underlying all of Burt's arguments was the contention that, because of the great improvements in the accuracy of Soviet missiles, throw-weight as such was a "military indicator of declining relevance." When a Soviet warhead could, in theory, score a bull's-eye on a Minuteman silo, it hardly mattered how big the crater was and how much of the surrounding countryside was obliterated. The target would be destroyed regardless of the explosive yield of the incoming warhead. Thus, accuracy had become a key ingredient in "destructive potential." Moreover, yield itself was not strictly a function of weight. As bombmakers perfected their craft, with the help of miniaturization and new techniques for squeezing maximum bang out of small amounts of explosive material, they could get a larger yield out of a smaller warhead. Yet neither of these factors, increased accuracy and improved yield, figured in Perle's proposed units of account for START.

Burt needed to do more than marshal arguments against Perle's proposal; he had to have an alternative. The one he came up with was similar to Perle's, Rowny's, and the Arms Control Agency's in one respect: it concentrated on ballistic missiles, rather than on cruise missiles and bombers, as the weapons where reductions were most urgent, and it contained a ceiling on strategic ballistic-missile warheads. But Burt's option was different in its other unit of account. Instead of placing explicit limits on throw-weight (or, as Nitze and Rostow preferred, the weight of individual warheads), he would limit the number of ballistic-missile launchers—the underground silos for ICBMs and the submarine tubes for SLBMs.

One reason that launchers had figured so prominently in SALT, and that Burt favored them for START, was that they could be verified readily. Whatever the unit of account for an arms-control agreement, the U.S. had to be confident of its ability to make an accurate count of the other side's inventory. Soviet ICBM silos were conspicuous and stationary, therefore visible to American spy satellites. SLBM tubes were as easy to keep track of as the submarines in which they were housed. Throw-weight was harder to verify. Monitoring throw-weight for a new generation of Soviet missiles would be especially difficult.

As of mid-April 1982, when the interagency process was preparing for the first meeting of the National Security Council on START, the intelligence community estimated that, even with the help of some new equipment and techniques, verifying a throw-weight ceiling of the sort that Perle and Rowny wanted could entail a factor of error nearly twice as high as verifying a limit on warhead weight of the sort Nitze favored. By contrast, the number of Soviet ICBM silos and SLBM tubes could be monitored with almost total certainty.

Perle's retort was that "Burt and his launcher boys are using a lot of hoked-up arguments to maneuver us back toward doing things the old SALT way, and if he succeeds, we'll deserve the lousy agreement we'll get, and the agreement will deserve the same fate as SALT." If a throw-weight ceiling was difficult to verify with old, SALT-type procedures, such as spy satellites and remote monitoring of Soviet tests, then, Perle continued, the U.S. would just have to insist on new ones.

Nesting Dolls

Under Burt's plan, limits on launchers were to be coupled with limits on numbers of warheads; those were "the things that kill people; they're understandable." He did not want to duplicate the complexity of SALT II. As someone who had followed the SALT debate closely and understood the treaty well, Burt knew that one reason it had attracted so much opposition was that it was too complicated, and therefore subject to misinterpretation and distortion (in some cases by people who were now his colleagues in the government). Hence Burt's refrain in meetings: "We've got to come up with a proposal that is understandable."

By mid-spring of 1982, however, the State Department had developed an option that was controversial on precisely the two points about which Burt was so sensitive: it was complicated, and it bore a disadvantageous resemblance to SALT II, both in its complexity and in its inclusion of launchers as a key unit of account. The principal designers were Burt himself and James Goodby, a career diplomat who had been designated to serve as Rowny's deputy and the principal State Department representative at the negotiations. Goodby had most recently served as ambassador to Finland; before that he had worked as a senior official in the bureaus of European and Politico-Military Affairs.

The State Department's START proposal resembled a Russian *matryoshka* toy, in which hollow dolls nest inside each other. Each side would have to stay under ceilings and subceilings on the number of launchers it could have and the number of warheads it could put on its launchers. There would be an overall ceiling on strategic nuclear delivery vehicles, including bombers, followed by a series of subceilings on strategic ballistic-missile launchers (ICBM silos and SLBM tubes) and on heavy missiles (i.e., the SS-18). These ceilings would be lowered over time, eventually reaching a point of numerical equality between the two sides.

Various levels were considered for the proposed ceiling that would cover ICBM silos and SLBM tubes. The one on which Burt eventually settled was to be around 1,200. That would mean a reduction in existing forces for the U.S. of about 400 and for the Soviet Union of more than 1,100. Not only would the U.S.S.R. be required to dismantle nearly three times as many ICBM and SLBM launchers as the U.S., but the more modest reductions required on the American side would conform neatly to U.S. military programs on land and at sea. As the U.S. modernized its strategic forces, it would need fewer launchers, since the new MX and Trident II missiles were to be far more capable than the existing land- and sea-based missiles they would be replacing.

The Soviets had shown no intention of retiring their SS-17s, -18s, and -19s as they brought new missiles into service. As far as Burt was concerned, that was just the point: START would force the Soviets to give up launchers that they would otherwise keep. He had a chart made up that used bar graphs to illustrate how the Soviet advantage in throw-weight would be diminished significantly after five years and eliminated altogether after ten under the State Department plan. This chart became Exhibit A in his campaign to drum up support for his position, since it demonstrated that he too had a remedy for the problem of Soviet throw-weight, albeit an indirect one: throw-weight would be "driven down and kept down," he said, as a consequence of launcher limits.

Under the accompanying ceiling on ballistic-missile warheads, there would be a subceiling whereby only half could be land-based, on top of ICBMs; the rest would have to be on SLBMs. This provision might at first glance have looked fair enough, since, like the launcher ceiling, it set equal limits for both sides. But it too was very one-sided in favor of the U.S. because of the differences in the two arsenals. The U.S. had nearly three times as many strategic missile warheads at sea as on land, while the Soviet deployment was the reverse: they had about three times as many warheads on land as at sea. Their ICBM launchers were much bigger than their SLBM ones. Thus Soviets had most of their throw-weight on land, so a subceiling on land-based warheads that cut deeply into Soviet ICBMs further bolstered Burt's claim that his plan would drive down throw-weight just as effectively as Perle's direct approach.

For about six months, Burt and his staff had been thinking in terms of a ceiling of 6,000 land- and sea-based warheads. Both sides had about 7,500 warheads. Thus, the U.S. would be proposing a reduction in the range of 25 to 30 percent, and that would qualify as deep enough to be in the spirit of the R in START. In March, Burt decided simply to round off the numbers to 5,000 for ICBM and SLBM warheads together and 2,500 for ICBM warheads alone, which looked and sounded neater and more dramatic. The President could say he was seeking a one-third reduction. The U.S. at that time had just under 2,150 ICBM warheads, while the U.S.S.R. had a force of around 6,000. That meant the U.S. would be proposing what was ostensibly a formula for mutual reductions, but actually the U.S. would have the right to increase its land-based warheads, while the Soviets would have to cut theirs by more than half.

By trying to make his option more acceptable within a government that was committed to the goal of drastically reducing Soviet MIRVed ICBMs, Burt made it far less acceptable to the Soviets themselves. He knew what he was doing. For him, the challenge of the moment was to sell his option to the White House. Dealing with the Soviets would come later.

If It's Got Wings, It Doesn't Count

Another feature of Burt's option that harked directly back to SALT II was its treatment of bombers and cruise missiles. These weapons had usually been regarded as equalizers in the strategic balance, the "offsetting asymmetry" that favored the U.S. The Soviets had about a three-to-one advantage in the number of nuclear weapons on ICBMs, but the U.S. had a vast qualitative and quantitative advantage in its intercontinental-range bombers, the B-52s of the Strategic Air Command. If throw-weight was broadened to include bomber payload, the much-vaunted Soviet advantage disappeared, and the two sides were roughly equal. A bomber is itself as much a launcher as an ICBM silo or a tube on a submarine insofar as it can be used to fire a short-range attack missile or long-range cruise missile at a Soviet target, or drop a bomb on it.

But a bomber or a cruise missile takes hours to reach its target, while a ballistic missile takes minutes. A missile warhead can be a bolt from the blue, while the Soviets would presumably have some time to watch an American bomber coming at them. They might be able to shoot it down en route. The Pentagon worried that, as the Soviets improved their air defenses by developing a counterpart to the American AWACS planes and a "look-down/-shoot-down" capability, cruise missiles, too, might some day have trouble getting through.

For all these reasons, it was dogma in the Reagan Administration that ballistic missiles—"fast-flyers," as President Reagan called them—were bad; they were weapons of aggression and preemption; therefore, they were the things to be limited. They also, not coincidentally, happened to be the Soviet specialty. Bombers and cruise missiles—"slow-flyers"—were good; they were instruments of retaliation and safeguards of deterrence. They were to be protected in START. Again, not coincidentally, they were American specialties.

The SALT II treaty had included bombers under a single ceiling on delivery vehicles along with ballistic-missile launchers; each side was limited both in the number of bombers it could outfit as cruise-missile carriers and in the number of cruise missiles per bomber. Burt and his colleagues intended to carry over limits like those into START.

Perle, however, was prepared to let START limit bombers only if they were in an entirely separate category from missiles. There must be no "freedom to mix," no opportunity for the Soviets to "buy" extra ballistic missiles by giving up some of their allotment of bombers. He was, moreover, definitely not willing to allow START to follow the SALT II precedent of imposing special limits on bombers armed with cruise missiles (as opposed to gravity bombs): "We wouldn't need cruise missiles on our bombers if we could be confident that the bombers themselves could penetrate Soviet air defenses." Nor was he willing to consider separate limits on air-launched cruise missiles (ALCMs) unless the Soviets accepted severe constraints on their air defenses. Assuming the Soviets would refuse to put anti-aircraft defenses on the agenda of negotiations about strategic offensive weapons, Perle wanted to abandon the SALT II limitations on ALCMs altogether.

There was also the question of sea-launched cruise missiles, or SLCMs.* Here Burt had to lock horns, as he had early in the Administration, with John Lehman, the Secretary of the Navy, plunging back into a controversy that had already bedeviled the government in INF: whether to "protect" conventionally armed cruise missiles from arms control. Lehman had plans to deploy conventionally armed cruise missiles at sea, primarily for use against other ships but possibly for striking targets on land as well. These would be indistinguishable from nuclear-armed ones. Western intelligence had already observed the Soviets testing a prototype of a long-range, sea-launched cruise missile that might eventually be used to attack targets on land, perhaps with a nuclear warhead. Despite the Soviets' moves in this direction, they were clearly so far behind the U.S. in guidance technology that they might jump at the chance to close down that lane of the arms race before it opened up. That meant cruise missiles were one of the U.S.'s principal assets at the negotiating table. Therefore, Burt and Goodby suggested to Haig that the U.S. proposal include a ban on sea-launched cruise missiles or at least a sharp limit on their launchers. This offer might make the Soviets more willing to make concessions on ballistic missiles.

But precisely because cruise missiles represented an area of American technological superiority and therefore potential military advantage, it quickly became apparent that Weinberger, Perle, Iklé, and John Lehman would do everything they could to prevent the State Department from trading them away. In the end, the Politico-Military Bureau gave up on the idea of proposing at the outset of START to ban or limit sea-launched cruise missiles.

Burt had been counting on cruise missiles as a principal bargaining chip in START. But now it was beginning to look as though all three varieties of the weapons were going to be unavailable for that purpose: GLCMs were key to the deployment program in Europe; Perle was holding out against even the very lenient limits on ALCMs contained in SALT II; and the Pentagon civilians, with the support of the Navy, were determined to keep SLCMs off the table altogether.

Veterans of arms control had a depressing sense of *déjà vu* in two respects.

---

*ALCM is pronounced "alkum," SLCM "slickum," and the ground-launched variety that figured so prominently in INF, GLCM, is "glickum."

Henry Kissinger had originally been interested in cruise missiles primarily for the bargaining leverage they would give the U.S. in SALT. He had to press for their development against the resistance of the military, which saw the drones as unwanted competitors with manned bombers for scarce defense dollars. Once cruise missiles had been developed, however, attitudes changed; the bargaining chips became family jewels, much too precious to bargain away, leaving Kissinger frustrated in SALT II.

There was also the worrisome precedent of MIRVs. Just as cruise missiles were justified largely as a hedge against Soviet anti-aircraft defenses, MIRVs had been seen back in the early 1970s as a way of countering anti-ballistic missiles. They were supposed to help induce the Soviets to give up ABMs in arms control, since an ABM defense was futile in the face of a MIRV offense. At that time MIRV technology was too advanced for the Soviets, as was cruise-missile technology now, but the U.S. failed to use MIRVs for negotiating leverage in SALT. Goodby and others found themselves wondering how far the parallel would extend, and whether future Soviet cruise missiles, particularly SLCMs, might someday make the U.S. sorry it had not banned them when it had a chance.

The MX Factor

Rather than pondering the ironies and neglected lessons of history, Burt was looking for new ideas. He needed to give the State Department option what he called "a little more sex appeal" in the intramural competition and also offer the Soviets some incentive to accept it. For a while he was in favor of the U.S. offering to cancel the MX program in exchange for Soviet willingness to eliminate their entire force of 308 SS-18 heavy missiles. This would be a zero option applied to the largest missiles on both sides—a Soviet system already deployed, in exchange for an American one in prospect—much along the lines of what Reagan had proposed as a solution to the European nuclear balance. Had this plan taken hold, it would have brought the perennially troubled MX program full circle, since James Schlesinger had conceived of the MX in the early seventies as a bargaining chip to be given up if the Soviets would accept meaningful limits on their own large-throw-weight missiles, particularly the heavies.

The ensuing episode was important not just because it harked back to SALT a decade before, but because a year later, in 1983, the intimate and troubled connection between the MX and START would become a major headache for the Administration and the basis for unprecedented congressional intervention into the conduct of arms-control negotiations. Also, the outcome of the incident—a decision not to trade away the MX—illustrated the extent to which the Administration was determined not to give up any weapon system in its strategic modernization program—fast-flyer or slow-flyer—even in exchange for the massive Soviet reductions it would be seeking in START.

The idea of trading the MX for the SS-18 owed a great deal to two former policymakers, Brent Scowcroft and William Hyland. They had been top aides of Henry Kissinger's in the Nixon Administration, then the No. 1 and 2 officials, respectively, on the National Security Council staff under Gerald Ford. Hyland had stayed on for the first nine months of the Carter Administration before retiring from the government. Primarily because of their close association with Kissinger, SALT, and détente, Scowcroft and Hyland had been left out of the Reagan Administration, but Burt made use of them as informal consultants.

In mid-March 1982, Burt told Scowcroft and Hyland that the preparations for START were bogged down and his own preferred option was encountering resistance in the government. It was also sure to run up against a Soviet stone wall in the negotiations even if the U.S. adopted it. Scowcroft and Hyland asked if he had thought about a straightforward swap of the MX for the SS-18. During his brief service in the Carter Administration, Hyland had participated in the planning of the March 1977 Comprehensive Proposal. He had been in Moscow when the Soviets threw it back in Vance's face, and he had then helped the Carter Administration pick up the pieces and assemble what became SALT II. The central feature of the ill-fated Comprehensive Proposal had been an offer to cancel the MX program in exchange for a 50 percent reduction in the Soviets' heavy missiles. So why not, in the spirit of the new Administration's approach to these things, propose trading the MX for a 100 percent cut in Soviet heavies? Everyone's scheme for a START proposal—Perle's, Nitze's, Rowny's, and Burt's own —was at bottom an attempt to force the Soviets to get rid of all or most of their SS-18s. Why not make a straight-out deal, using the only possible bargaining chip the U.S. had? The proposed trade would be simple, dramatic, reasonable-looking and, while it was under negotiation, might even save the MX.

Save the MX? Burt's attention was now thoroughly engaged. Haig had been urging him for some weeks to find a way of using START to shore up the MX program against opposition. In Haig's and Burt's view, a congressional cutoff of funding for the MX would have been disastrous, not least because it might give the West European allies an excuse to back out of the NATO deployments. By making the MX a bargaining chip in START, the Administration could put Congress in the position of not daring to end the program.

The morning after his talk with Scowcroft and Hyland, Burt had his staff prepare a set of charts showing the advantages of a combination of launcher and warhead ceilings, with accompanying illustrations to dramatize that with the added feature of an MX-for-SS-18 trade, the consequent reduction in Soviet throw-weight and land-based warheads would be so great that the U.S. would not even need to insist upon a subceiling limiting land-based warheads, which he knew would be one of the least negotiable features of his proposal.

When Burt presented the idea to Haig in late March, the Secretary agreed that it might help keep the MX alive on the Hill, and he would like to tell the President that the U.S. was going to go after the most threatening of all Soviet weapons in one fell swoop. But Haig worried that the idea might come across as too much of a gimmick. Some of his other aides, particularly Lawrence Eagleburger and David Gompert, did not like its similarity to the INF zero-zero proposal, against which they had waged a losing fight the previous autumn. Haig told Burt to undertake a "marketing survey" elsewhere in the government.

Once Perle learned of what Burt was up to and discovered that Hyland and Scowcroft had been pushing the same idea, he disparaged it as coming from "the old SALT gang." Perle had a more substantive objection as well, one that went to the heart of what later became a hard-and-fast policy of the Administration as a whole: the U.S. *needed* the MX in any event, even with a START agreement in effect. "If we give up the MX," said Perle, "we're giving up the right to modernize our ICBM force. We'd be saying that we're content to live with our ICBMs vulnerable to attack. It's not just the SS-18 that makes them vulnerable—it's also the SS-19 [the largest of the nonheavy Soviet rockets]. Even with the SS-18 gone, the SS-19 is just as formidable a weapon. The MX, in terms of throw-weight and what it can do militarily, is the equivalent of the SS-19, not the SS-18. It's false and misleading to compare the MX to the SS-18, which is what we'd be doing if we offered to trade the one for the other."

For reasons similar to Perle's, Rowny agreed. Like so many others in the government, he had as a central ornament in his office a set of plastic scale models of Soviet and American ICBMs. He would point out how the slim white model of the MX was dwarfed by the dark gray monster of the SS-18; the MX was much closer in size to the SS-19. That was the match-up that would matter if the SS-18s were eliminated. Besides, he was fond of saying that Soviet MIRVed missiles, particularly the SS-18 and -19, were like Thunderbirds compared to the Model A Ford of the U.S. Minuteman. "The Minuteman III, even with the Mark 12A [the latest MIRV], is not a modern system," he said. "It's obsolescent; it's no match for the SS-17, -18, and -19."

Few, if any, experts agreed with Rowny. The Mark 12A was generally regarded as at least the equal of the best Soviet warheads in accuracy. Nevertheless, while Rowny's suggestion that the Minuteman III and the Mark 12A belonged in a museum caused even his more hawkish colleagues to wince, his conviction that the U.S. had to have the MX in order to keep its arsenal up to date was widely shared in the government.

In order to create the impression that the U.S. was willing to make some sacrifices in START, Rowny frequently argued that a proposal along the lines of what he and Perle were advocating would "force" the U.S. to have fewer Trident II SLBMs than it could otherwise have. That was, strictly speaking, true. But in fact the warhead ceiling they envisaged would still allow the Navy to deploy as many Trident II warheads as its strategic modernization program called for. So the Trident II was not a genuine bargaining chip any more than the MX was.

By early April, with the first NSC meeting on START a few weeks away, members of the Interagency Group were openly discussing the MX-for-SS-18 trade and generally savaging it. Perle's deputy, Ronald Lehman, predicted that the Soviets would "laugh it right out of court." Burt replied that a proposal requiring the Soviets to reduce their throw-weight by about two-thirds was likely to be met with comparable derision. But he saw that the zero option for the MX and SS-18 was not "catching fire." By the time the NSC met to discuss START on April 21, the idea of trading cancellation of the MX for elimination of the SS-18 was barely alive.

A Friend in Court

In this cutthroat marketplace of ideas, bureaucratic allies were at least as important as substantive arguments, and logrolling was as important as brainstorming. Burt was short on allies. The Office of the Secretary of Defense, the Arms Control Agency, and Rowny were all committed to some form of direct limits on throw-weight; they all opposed the State Department's proposed launcher ceiling.

Up until the end of 1981, the National Security Council staff would have probably joined the pro-throw-weight, anti-launcher majority. But at the beginning of 1982 the NSC was under new management. Richard Allen had been replaced by William Clark, who had brought Robert McFarlane with him as his deputy and alter ego for arms-control policy. McFarlane had spent 1981 down the hall from Clark as the Counselor, or chief all-purpose troubleshooter, of the State Department. His background and orientation made him gravitate toward Burt in the debate over throw-weight. The two of them had cooperated at State, sometimes against Perle. McFarlane had once worked for Kissinger, and he remembered hearing Kissinger talk about his own frustration in trying to negotiate throw-weight limits with the Soviets in the early seventies. McFarlane regarded that as "an important bit of history that ought not to be repeated." He was also interested in negotiability, even though he, like Burt, was careful in meetings to talk instead about the "plausibility," "credibility," and "defensibility" of the proposal.

As a former Marine, McFarlane placed great stock in discipline and obedience. That was one reason he reacted negatively to Paul Nitze's unauthorized walk-in-the-woods initiative in INF. In START, however, it was Perle who had the look of a rogue platoon leader. McFarlane thought Perle was far too ready to blame arms control for the troubles afflicting American defenses. One result had been a virtual halt in the development of arms-control policy. The President had come into office promising to seek a strategic arms agreement better than SALT II right away, and Eugene Rostow had told the Senate during his confirmation hearings in early 1981 that the Administration would be ready for START in March 1982. In fact, it was nowhere near ready.

Congress was getting impatient. A number of trends in public opinion were beginning to coalesce. A wide variety of religious and academic leaders were questioning the wisdom of the Administration's policies. Their concerns were partly a backlash against a series of controversial statements the year before by high government officials, including the President himself, about whether a limited nuclear war could be fought and won. In addition to the troubles over the MX, there was rising sentiment in favor of a negotiated agreement with the Soviet Union to stop all further testing, production, and deployment of nuclear weapons. The White House's contacts in Congress warned that a number of liberal senators were considering resolutions in favor of such a freeze. The Administration had to overcome its own inertia if only to avoid seeing its defense policies swept aside by a potent new movement. In a memorandum to Clark around this time, Rostow urged that the White House "combine the decision about starting START with the problem of the 'freeze' resolutions."

In late February, McFarlane realized there had to be a "management impulse" from the White House, "an explosive charge to blast apart the logjam in the bureaucracy." He and Clark decided to issue an NSC directive giving the rest of the Executive Branch two months to come forward with a START proposal. McFarlane asked Burt, as chairman of the START Interagency Group, to submit "terms of reference" for the directive. Burt drafted a memorandum. With a certain amount of tinkering and amendation to accommodate the other agencies, these criteria would become a litany in speeches, background briefings to the press, and congressional testimony by Administration officials for months to come.

The watchwords were to be: *equality* (with the strong implication of restoring something that had been lost as a result of the Soviet thrust for superiority), *stability* (once again, something to be recovered by doing away with the vulnerability of American forces, and that meant doing away with many of the Soviets weapons that created this vulnerability), *reductions* (in contrast to the mere limitations supposedly achieved in SALT), *comprehensibility* (the proposal and an eventual agreement must be easy to understand and therefore able to attract public support), *deference to the concerns of the allies* (START must be compatible with INF), *verifiability,* and *sustainabil-*

ity. As Haig later explained this last term, "We needed to devise a sustainable position which would provide a framework for detailed negotiations and the basis for an eventual agreement, even in the face of initial Soviet resistance. . . . The position needed to be demonstrably fair, mutually beneficial and realistic." The Administration wanted a START proposal that would look good to the American public and Congress, however bad it looked to the Kremlin.

Another criterion was eventually added at the head of the list. A START agreement must permit the U.S. to proceed with those new weapons programs it deemed necessary to match whatever the Soviet Union had left after reductions were accomplished. In other words, the Administration demanded a START proposal that would not interfere with a U.S. modernization program just getting underway and would at the same time roll back the results of a Soviet modernization program that had already been accomplished. This meant, first and foremost, that START had to reinforce the rationale for the MX.

An NSC directive in early March set a calendar of deadlines for the various levels of the government. Final positions would have to be on the President's desk by May 1. Burt's role in preparing the directive remained a carefully guarded secret. Neither he nor McFarlane wanted the rest of the government to know that the Politico-Military Bureau was helping write instructions coming from the White House.

The President Listens

Reagan's first sustained exposure to the debate that had been churning for months came at the National Security Council meeting on April 21. Operating against the NSC-imposed deadlines, the bureaucracy had ground some thirty variations down to four options: (1) Perle's simple low-throw-weight ceiling combined with a warhead ceiling; (2) the Nitze index limiting the size of warheads; (3) a plan favored by Rowny that was similar to Perle's but more complicated and constantly changing; and (4) Burt's two-tier limits on launchers (at a level of about 1,200), ballistic-missile warheads (5,000), and land-based or ICBM warheads (2,500).

While Burt and McFarlane kept the extent of their collaboration quiet, it was plain to Perle that Burt wanted to control the interagency process that summarized and channeled competing options to the White House. So Perle in effect boycotted that process. He began sending Ronald Lehman in his place to Interagency Group meetings, with orders to listen, gather intelligence, and raise questions about other agencies' positions, but not to reveal the details of Perle's own proposal. That way the State Department would have as little opportunity as possible to develop counterarguments.

On the eve of the NSC meeting, Perle announced his position. He urged that START should depart clearly, in form and substance, from the SALT I and SALT II agreements in order to achieve real arms control. The way to do that was to couple a ceiling on ballistic-missile warheads with a ceiling on ballistic-missile throw-weight. The throw-weight ceiling should be slightly below the current U.S. level of just under 2 million kilograms and 40 percent of the current Soviet level of over 5 million kilograms. A warhead ceiling alone, he said, would offer the appearance but not the reality of significant limits on Soviet strategic power.

Attacking the opposition, he argued that a START proposal which would limit warheads and launchers alone would drive the Administration to a repetition of past mistakes. The principal failure of the SALT II treaty, he believed, was its perpetuation of a 2½-to-1 Soviet advantage in ballistic-missile throw-weight. So that no one could miss his point, Perle criticized the Department of State by name for opposing a proposal calling for equal throw-weight at sharply reduced levels. He reminded one and all of their duty to live up to the requirements for equal aggregates in strategic arms treaties as set forth in the 1972 Jackson amendment. A ballistic-missile throw-weight ceiling, he said, was the best way to enshrine the principle of equality.

The NSC gathering on April 21 was billed as an "informational" meeting, at which the President and his top advisers were to acquaint themselves with the issues, not to reach a decision. The meeting opened with a presentation by Burt. He reviewed the various options the Interagency Group was then considering, showing how they would affect the Soviet and American arsenals. Burt's role as the lead-off briefer caught Weinberger and Iklé by surprise: they had expected McFarlane. In their view, Burt no longer represented the Interagency Group; he was a promoter of one agency's position —the State Department's—against their own. For McFarlane to defer to Burt was evidence that the two men were in collusion.

Weinberger exhorted his colleagues to push ahead with a START proposal that would offer the Soviets a "challenge." He used the word a number of times. He seemed to be advocating an American ultimatum to the Soviets: either they accepted U.S. terms for a stand-down, or the U.S. would give them a run for their money in an arms race that would make their heads spin and their economy groan. Weinberger reminded the President of the success of his November 18, 1981, speech that laid out the zero proposal for INF. By choosing the boldest and simplest of the options before him in INF, Reagan had served the cause of arms control and struck a blow in the battle for public opinion. A proposal for a low throw-weight ceiling in START could do the same again.

In addition to extolling throw-weight as a unit of account for START, Weinberger disparaged the idea of using warheads as the measure, which he knew figured in the State Department option. He seemed not yet entirely familiar with the Defense proposal that Perle had prepared in his name; it too contained a ceiling on warheads.

Rostow gave what appeared to be a ringing endorsement of Weinberger's call for tough demands on Moscow. He then went on to present Paul Nitze's outline for a proposal that differed from Weinberger's primarily in its reliance on limiting the weight of individual warheads rather than total throw-weight. Rostow had a tendency to hold the floor, straying from the subject at hand and from his area of responsibility. To others, this often seemed like pontificating. On this occasion, he delivered a lengthy disquisition on what he called "the broader context" of START. There were other negotiations, the problem of the imbalance in conventional as well as nuclear weaponry, the adverse changes in the public mood—"an isolationist movement," he called it.

Reagan's attention flagged. He began to doodle. As the lines came together, the head of a horse took shape on the note pad in front of him. It was common for the President to doodle during long meetings on subjects about which he was less than passionate, and horses and cowboys were two of his favorite subjects. He was there primarily to listen, but he wanted to make his contribution to the proceedings. He said he agreed that START should be different from SALT II and that it should be based on the goal of deep reductions. He wanted to be able to deliver a dramatic speech unveiling a proposal before leaving for Europe in June. Then, as though repeating a lesson he had learned by rote, he delivered a short discourse on the strategic triad. Missiles were the big problem, he said. Bombers had the advantage of being capable of recall; you could get them into the air but call them back. Also, bombers could be shot down. As for submarines, they could be "sunk." Some members of his audience winced. Sunk? Weren't submarines supposed to sink?

What the President seemed to be getting at was a jumble of concepts: the offsetting vulnerabilities of American bombers to Soviet air defenses and of Soviet submarines to American anti-submarine warfare; the stabilizing nature of submarine-launched ballistic missiles as opposed to the destabilizing nature of land-based missiles, which are vulnerable and immobile; the retaliatory function of bombers and submarines as opposed to the first-strike capability of ICBMs. The others in the room understood that Reagan was, in his fashion, supporting an approach to START that would concentrate on limiting land-based ballistic missiles while virtually exempting the two other, supposedly more benign legs of the triad, bombers and submarines. But the words with which he struggled to make this point betrayed the President's basic innocence in this arcane world. For a long moment, there was a numb silence around the table. Two or three people attempted nods of assent, as though their Commander in Chief had put his finger on the problem.

Haig feared that a rickety sort of bandwagon might be underway. If the meeting continued in this vein, the NSC—and the President—might willy-nilly embrace the idea of a throw-weight ceiling. The Secretary of State reminded the group that their purpose in meeting was to air the issues, not to reach a decision. On the basic goal of limiting the most destabilizing Soviet systems, he said, there was no disagreement, and even on the question of how to do it, "We're not all that far apart."

But the rest of his presentation made clear how distant he was from the Pentagon. Haig warned that if the U.S. went forward with a proposal that was dismissed as cynical and implausible the result could be "a military and political catastrophe"—politically catastrophic because it would create a backlash against the Administration both at home and abroad and militarily catastrophic because it would cause a loss of support both in Congress and among the NATO allies for the Administration's rearmament program. Therefore, said Haig, his steely gaze on Reagan, the decisions he would be making with regard to START would be "the most important of your Administration."

Bureaucratic Courtship

Haig and Burt came away from the meeting discouraged. They could see all the more clearly how difficult it was going to be in the weeks ahead to stop the momentum building for a ceiling on throw-weight. Burt had developed a promising relationship with McFarlane, but it was a personal relationship, not an institutional alliance. The State Department needed not just a friend at the White House but a partnership with another agency.

The State Department's traditional ally, the Arms Control Agency, was firmly with Perle and Weinberger on the throw-weight issue. Doing his best to coax the agency back onto his side, Burt called on Rostow and, as Rostow took it, tried to flatter him into modifying his position. "There's no question," said Burt to Rostow, "that your approach to START [limiting warhead weight] is by far the best in town from an intellectual point of view. But this is a case where the best can be an enemy of the good." Burt asked Rostow to "keep an open mind" on limiting launchers. Rostow suspected Burt and Haig of being interested only in a quick fix of SALT II. "State wants to make three or four amendments in SALT, call it START, and get an agreement before the ['84] election," he said after listening to Burt's bid for cooperation.

As the May 1 deadline approached, some of Rostow's aides had second thoughts about how closely they wanted to tie themselves to the Pentagon. Robert Grey met with Burt a number of times and attempted some last-minute horsetrading: if the State Department was willing to raise the launcher ceiling from its suggested level of 1,200 to 2,000, the Arms Control

Agency would support it. Two thousand would still be lower than the existing Soviet level of 2,300 ICBM and SLBM launchers, so it would still mean a net reduction for the U.S.S.R.

Now it was Burt who played hard to get. Would the Arms Control Agency let the 2,000 figure cover bombers as well? Could there be an allotment of, say, 250 for bombers, leaving 1,750 to cover missile launchers? Grey said, yes, the agency could come down that low. But in the end Burt decided not to come up that high. "You'll have to come lower," he told Grey. "We can't," said Grey. Burt shrugged. "Then frankly, Bob," he said, "at this point I don't give a damn if you're with us or against us."

At issue was not a difference of a few hundred missile launchers. Rather, it was a question of whom Burt was more interested in having as an ally. Earlier, when he had courted Rostow, he had thought the Arms Control Agency might be the only candidate. But by now he had his eye on a much more potent and promising candidate for collaboration—the Joint Chiefs of Staff.

13 Good Soldiers

Of all the agencies and interest groups involved in the formulation of the START proposal, the Joint Chiefs of Staff were in the most difficult, delicate, and anomalous position. In early 1982, when the proposal was taking shape, the Chiefs were also the principal defenders of traditional arms control in the Executive Branch. They had been at their posts since the Carter Administration, and it showed in their attitude toward SALT and START alike. They shared neither Ronald Reagan's visceral distaste for the former nor his high hopes for the latter. They had endorsed SALT II, so they were highly suspect in the view of the more hard-line Reaganauts. Caspar Weinberger and Richard Perle made no secret of their disdain for the Chiefs' behavior with regard to SALT II during the Carter Administration.

"Secretary Weinberger thinks we capitulated to Harold Brown [Carter's Defense Secretary] by supporting him on SALT," remarked the Chairman of the Joint Chiefs, General David Jones, "so he thinks now all he has to do is make us capitulate to him on START." Jones was determined to prove Weinberger wrong on both counts: the Chiefs had supported SALT II because they believed that it was in the nation's military interest to do so, and they would not support anyone's proposal for START, including that of the Secretary of Defense, unless they were convinced that it met the same standard.

"The difference that matters in this Administration," Perle once said, "is whether you like SALT II or you don't. The Chiefs are up to their eyeballs in SALT II." One of his deputies dismissed them as "has-beens who haven't assimilated the political fact of life that SALT II is *ipso facto* bad."

Because they had not been appointed by Reagan, the Chiefs were destined to be replaced by him. The three most closely identified with SALT were all scheduled to retire in June 1982: Jones, the Air Force's Lew Allen, and the Navy's Thomas Hayward. Lame ducks as well as holdovers, they were doubly jeopardized. Yet, for all their disadvantages, the Chiefs ended up playing a decisive role in producing the Administration's opening START proposal. They did this by siding with the State Department, opposing the inclusion of direct limits on throw-weight and favoring a launcher limit. It was an ambiguous accomplishment, one that made the Administration's START proposal a bit more negotiable—or a bit less non-negotiable—than it might have been otherwise.

But in another respect the Chiefs contributed to the erosion of confidence in the Administration on the home front. The Chiefs were more responsible than anyone else for a ceiling on ICBM and SLBM launchers that was considerably lower than the one the State Department would have preferred. The launcher ceiling drew criticism from all across the ideological spectrum, and in the end opened the way for members of Congress and other outsiders to intervene directly in arms-control policymaking.

The story of how the launcher ceiling came about shows the extent to which parochial military concerns and bureaucratic politics were allowed to overwhelm strategic considerations.

START and the SIOP

That almost unbeatable alliance of the uniformed military and the State Department was a long time in coming about. The Chiefs' delay in taking a position was partly a result of their function and their organization. They represented the four armed services, each of which had a degree of autonomy and its own special concerns, including predispositions and prejudices where arms control was concerned. The Air Force, for example, was naturally protective of its intercontinental bombers and land-based strategic missiles, while it was less concerned about the impact of arms-control proposals on submarines and sea-based missiles. The Navy felt just the opposite. The Army tended to become most engaged when one of its own systems, such as the Pershing II or anti-missile defenses, was at issue.

The Chiefs had to operate by consensus. The chairman could not impose his will on his colleagues the way Haig or Weinberger could on his. Jones and his colleagues had to thrash out a common position among themselves before they could take a stand in the interagency process or at the National Security Council. Some delay, therefore, was unavoidable.

But the Chiefs' foot dragging was also tactical. They had learned some lessons from their earlier battles with the civilians in the Pentagon. During the interagency debates over the zero proposal for INF, the Chiefs let themselves be drawn too early onto the State Department's side against Weinberger and Perle. Perle had been able to force them to change sides, giving the Pentagon an irresistible common front against the State Department. This time around, the Chiefs moved much more slowly and secretively. They were going to pick and choose the issues much more carefully than before, and they were not going to let themselves be rushed into doing anything.

Just before the April 21 NSC meeting on START, Perle put in writing his case for a throw-weight ceiling and against the State Department's proposed limits on launchers. He titled the document "Defense Department View." In fact, it did not speak for the department as a whole; it spoke only for the Office of the Secretary of Defense. Jones and his fellow Chiefs resented this. They did not see it as their duty automatically to support any arms-control position taken by the Secretary of Defense, to say nothing of one of his assistants.

As the nation's highest-ranking soldiers, the Chiefs had to be sure that they could, if necessary, still fight a war with the arms left them after an agreement. They wanted to be able to carry out any military task assigned to them by the President; they had to judge any arms-control proposal from the standpoint of "military sufficiency." That meant reconciling START with the SIOP—the Single Integrated Operational Plan. One of the nation's most carefully guarded secrets, the SIOP is a set of contingency plans for World War III.

During the first half of 1982, when the rest of the national-security apparatus of the government was suddenly preoccupied with preparing for START and urging the Chiefs to join in doing so, General Jones and his four colleagues had another preoccupation: they had been assigned by the White House to undertake a major review of their requirements for the SIOP, making sure that the U.S. had the means to "execute" the widest possible range of "targeting options." Their duty was to bring to the President a new "master plan" answering the old question "How much is enough?" What sort of inventory did the U.S. need to ensure its security into the 1990s?

In addressing this question, they were expected to have certain very specific objectives in mind. The National Security Council had instructed the Chiefs to certify that any START proposal put forward in the negotiations and ultimately enshrined in an agreement would not interfere with what amounted to the new "strategic mission" for defeating the Soviets. These instructions were spelled out in the so-called Defense Guidance, signed by Weinberger, and in a National Security Decision Directive, signed by Reagan. These documents proclaimed that the goal of the U.S. was to prevail in a protracted nuclear war.

All administrations since the beginning of the nuclear age have been concerned with the problem of how to use nuclear weapons in a conflict. A war-fighting capability has been generally accepted as an essential, though distasteful and paradoxical, component of deterrent strategy. Deterrence is based on the threat to use nuclear weapons. It is an almost inescapable dilemma that, to be sure its weapons will *not* have to be used, a superpower must be sure that the other side believes that they *might* be used. For mutual deterrence to work, each side must have a credible answer to the question of how it would employ its weapons if war began.

The Reagan Administration's desire to update the SIOP was similar to efforts by earlier administrations to make deterrence more credible, although there was a difference in degree and tone: the political leadership of the Reagan Administration threw itself into the task of enhancing the U.S.'s war-fighting capability with an enthusiasm and self-confidence that made some of the Chiefs themselves, not to mention many outsiders, uneasy.*

All the options for START under consideration in the spring of 1982 featured deep cuts in the number of missile warheads. Yet warheads were the principal instruments for carrying out the SIOP. They were what the U.S. would count on in order to destroy targets designated as having the highest priority, such as Soviet missile silos, command-and-control centers, munitions storage areas, and bomber airfields. Many of these targets were "hardened"—protected by reinforced concrete—and therefore could be destroyed only with the most accurate and powerful weapons. The targets were also "time-urgent"; they needed to be taken out of action quickly. Therefore, they could be destroyed only with high-speed ballistic missiles rather than relatively slow-flying bombers or cruise missiles.

The Defense Guidance contained what one veteran military expert called, in the jargon of the subject, a "maximalist wish list of time-urgent hard targets." It therefore required a large number of warheads to cover all those targets. Since they were also being asked to certify a START option calling for large cuts in warheads, the Chiefs felt they were receiving conflicting orders. As one put it, "We were being told by our Commander-in-Chief to be ready, on a moment's notice, to destroy all the Soviet Union—everything, everywhere, of any conceivable consequence or time-urgent value. At the same time we were supposed to climb on board the reductions band wagon."

Something had to give: either the goal of reductions would have to be sacrificed to the goal of maximum overkill in the SIOP, or the Defense Guidance would have to be more discriminating in its designation of targets. The Chiefs favored a more modest START proposal *and* a more modest SIOP. They doubted that the Soviets would accept an ambitious, not to mention one-sided, START proposal, and they doubted that the U.S. Congress and public would support a national defense strategy that put too much emphasis on plans to wage a nuclear war.

The rejoinder from Weinberger, Perle, and Fred Iklé was that the Chiefs were selling short both the possibilities for disarmament and the needs for

---

*When General Jones retired in June 1982, he publicly warned against throwing money down a "bottomless pit" to prepare the U.S. for a limited, protracted nuclear war with the Soviet Union: "I don't see much of a chance of nuclear war being limited or protracted."

For the definitive, yet still highly readable, history of deterrence, see Lawrence Freedman, *The Evolution of Nuclear Strategy* (St. Martin's Press, New York, 1981); also, Peter Pringle and William Arkin, *SIOP: The Secret U.S. Plan for Nuclear War* (W. W. Norton, New York, 1983). And for the best analysis of the overall dilemma of nuclear weapons, see Michael Mandelbaum's trilogy, *The Nuclear Question* (Cambridge, 1979), *The Nuclear Revolution* (Cambridge, 1981), and *The Nuclear Future* (Cornell, 1983).

rearmament. A more "robust" defense program (that adjective had become one of the buzz words of the Reagan era) would induce the Soviets to accept the sort of reductions that the U.S. would seek in START, and those Soviet reductions in turn would allow the U.S. to get by with fewer weapons because there would be fewer targets to cover. The Chiefs never did find that logic persuasive. Toward the end of April 1982, with the White House's May 1 deadline for a proposal only days away, they were still balking.

At the Senior Interagency Group meeting on April 29, the Chiefs were represented by General James Dalton, their staff director. The Office of the Secretary of Defense (OSD) was represented by Iklé. The tension between the two was palpable. At one point Iklé referred to "the DoD [Department of Defense] view," the same phrase Perle had used. Dalton pointed out that Iklé was offering "not the DoD view but the OSD view."

On the question of how low a warhead ceiling the Chiefs could endorse, Dalton wanted to explain how various reduction schemes would affect the targeting master plan. So sensitive was that subject that this part of the meeting was held in restricted session, with only the principals present. Iklé criticized Dalton's briefing on the SIOP and said that it should not be given to the President; in their preoccupation with the master plan, the Chiefs were failing adequately to take into account the transformation in the "strategic environment" that would result from START. "The whole atmosphere would change," said Iklé. "The threat we would face would be different and diminished if START would be in effect. If we succeeded in reducing the Soviet capability for nuclear war-fighting, our requirements for deterrence would be less."

Dalton replied, rather tartly, "Not if we're going to carry out *your* strategic program, Dr. Iklé. It's not us setting these requirements."

Beheading the Hydra

It was largely out of a desire to reconcile START with the requirements of the Reagan Administration's war-fighting master plan that the Chiefs concluded that, if there was going to be a low warhead ceiling in the proposal, there would have to be an even lower launcher ceiling to go along with it. Their rationale was simple enough: Among the most important targets they would have to cover in the SIOP were Soviet ICBM silos and ballistic-missile-firing submarines. If START was going to leave the U.S. with fewer warheads, then there would have to be fewer Soviet launchers for the U.S. to "take out" in a war. Therefore, the outcome of START should be a high ratio of American warheads to Soviet launchers.

Virtually everyone else in the government wanted a warhead ceiling of some kind, but only the State Department wanted a launcher ceiling of any kind. Therein lay the basis for the partnership between the Chiefs and

Richard Burt that would prevail in the short run. But it was also the basis of a controversy that would haunt the Administration later on.

One reason why everybody except Burt—Perle, Paul Nitze, Edward Rowny, and Eugene Rostow—opposed a launcher ceiling of any kind was that they all favored an evolution in the arsenals of the superpowers in exactly the opposite direction from the one envisioned by the Chiefs. Instead of increasing the ratio of warheads to targets, they felt START should reduce that ratio. That meant fewer warheads on more launchers. Nitze and others believed that if strategic arms control had any future it must promote "de-MIRVing": each side must be induced to give up large, stationary, multiple-warhead ICBMs in favor of small, mobile, single-warhead missiles.

De-MIRVing had been acquiring support for some time among liberal as well as conservative experts. One of the shortcomings of SALT, it was said, had been that by directly limiting launchers rather than warheads, the agreements had in effect encouraged both sides to load as many MIRVs as they could on as few ICBMs, since it was the missile launchers, not the warheads, that counted against the ceilings.

At issue here was how to diminish the danger of each side's being on hair-trigger in a crisis. Big, heavily MIRVed blockbusters were not only offensive threats and potential first-strike weapons; they were attractive nuisances as well. If warheads were concentrated on a relatively small number of rockets, then the launchers for those rockets would offer a relatively small—and therefore relatively tempting—set of targets for the other side to shoot at in a showdown. It also followed that, if each side knew its own ICBMs were vulnerable in a crisis, it would be all the more likely to shoot first—to "use 'em or lose 'em." MIRVed ICBMs were doubly destabilizing in that they simultaneously threatened and invited a preemptive attack. Single-warhead missiles were preferable on both counts, particularly in their presumed survivability: they would be too numerous and too widely dispersed to present tempting targets for preemption, and, since they were small, they could be made mobile and thus all the harder to knock out.

According to this argument, a world without MIRVs would be better and safer. One way to get there would be through arms control that featured maximum penalties for the retention of MIRVs and maximum rewards for trading in MIRVed missiles in favor of a new generation of what Nitze sometimes called "little guys." Some liberal Democratic members of Congress, such as Albert Gore, Jr., of Tennessee and Les Aspin of Wisconsin, agreed with Nitze on the wisdom of making de-MIRVing a goal, if not *the* goal, of arms control, and of moving toward an ICBM force made up of small, mobile single-warhead missiles. That meant letting the number of launchers permitted under START "run free" by imposing no launcher limits at all. In theory, and perhaps someday in fact, each side could have 4,000 warheads on top of 4,000 missiles.

The launcher ceiling of about 1,200 ICBMs and SLBMs in Burt's plan for START was antithetical to the spirit of total de-MIRVing. Since each side would be allowed many more warheads than missiles, it stood to reason that most of their missiles would be MIRVed. Burt thought he was only being realistic. Whatever the attractions of an ideal world without MIRVs, the real world of 1982 was made dangerous by the presence of Soviet SS-17s, -18s, and -19s, American Minuteman IIIs, and MIRVed SLBMs on both sides. It was not realistic to think that START could stuff the genie of MIRVing back into the bottle from which it had emerged in the early 1970s.

Burt had little use for arms-control schemes that sought to transform military reality. And the operative military reality was that the Soviets had too many big, heavily MIRVed missiles. The function of START should be to reduce them in number, not to try to force them onto the scrap heap altogether. "It doesn't make sense to design a START proposal around a weapons system that we don't even have in our plans or on our drawing boards," he said. "And look at the politics of it. We can't get 200 mobile MXs deployed. Do you really think that we could get people to accept thousands of small mobile ICBMs running around the countryside?"

For the Chiefs, too, de-MIRVing was a chimera. The Soviets showed no interest in joining the U.S. in the quest for a de-MIRVed world. And, if perchance they did, the Chiefs would still have to worry about how to hit Soviet military targets, including those new, more numerous, albeit single-warhead ICBMs moving around the U.S.S.R. That, after all, was their job —being able to blow up those things in the Soviet Union that could strike the U.S. In a de-MIRVed world, the target set on the Soviet side would be bound to increase many times over.

But the Chiefs were not primarily concerned about negotiability or even about theories of strategic stability. They were thinking about the immediate problems of how to reconcile START to the SIOP—and how to use START to bolster political support for their own weapons programs. That is why, as they studied the "exchange ratios" that whirred through the Pentagon computers—the calculations about who would do what to whom in various scenarios for nuclear war—the Chiefs concluded that a requirement of reducing warheads available to the U.S. must be contingent on commensurate reductions in targets, or "aim points," on the Soviet side. Aim points meant silos. Silos meant launchers. That meant a START proposal with a low launcher limit.

How low? Low enough to reinforce the rationale for the weapons systems that the Chiefs wanted to see proceed, particularly the MX. For years, they had been fighting for the MX as a counterweight to the Soviet SS-18 and SS-19. Now Nitze and others were telling them that they should endorse a START proposal that would penalize the Soviets for keeping the SS-18 and -19—and would undercut the case for the MX as well.

The Navy had a similar worry. Nitze and others wanted to promote an evolution in the U.S. sea-based deterrent much like the one on land. Looking to the future, they envisioned a submarine force that consisted of more boats with fewer missile-launching tubes on each boat, a more dispersed and less vulnerable force. This concept flew in the face of the Trident II submarine and missile program much cherished by the Chiefs, and particularly by Admiral Thomas Hayward.

As far as the Chiefs were concerned, whatever the direction taken by START, either as a proposal or as an agreement, MX and Trident had to be protected. Unlike Burt, they were not ready to write off the MX's chances for survival in Congress, nor were they willing to support him on the idea of canceling the MX in exchange for elimination of the SS-18. Burt made a hard sell to the Chiefs on the plan. He did so discreetly in order to avoid a head-on clash with Perle—but not discreetly enough. One spring day Perle was coming down the escalator at the entrance of the Pentagon and spotted Burt just ahead of him with a stack of charts under his arm. Perle hailed him and asked what he'd been doing.

"Just seeing some people."

"About what?"

"Oh, a number of things."

"Aha!" exclaimed Perle, "I'll bet you've been briefing the Chiefs on START!"

Burt looked pained. He avoided a direct answer and was obviously all the more eager to get to his car. Perle went back to his own office and ordered his aides to find out whom Burt had been seeing. His suspicions were confirmed. Perle said to Jones he was upset to discover that the Chiefs were paying more attention to a State Department official than to Perle himself, who was, after all, an Assistant Secretary of Defense. Jones gave Perle a stony stare and told him to have a nice day.

Back to the Tank

Perle may have been angry at Burt's courtship of the Chiefs, but Burt himself was finding the experience exasperating. Trying to work deals with the Chiefs, he said, was like trying to arrange a dance with the social committee of a girls' school. McFarlane was impatient, too. He complained to Colonel Robert Linhard, an Air Force officer assigned to the NSC, who kept in close contact with the staff of the Joint Chiefs. The President was serious about the May 1 deadline, McFarlane said, and the Chiefs had better "stop hiding their heads in the sand." He knew this message would quickly find its way to the Pentagon.

Not until two days before the first NSC meeting on START did the Chiefs' staff first tip its hand. On April 19, Admiral William Williams, the

Chiefs' representative on the START delegation, submitted a proposal to a working group headed by James Goodby. The three key features of the proposal were: a limit of 850 operational ballistic missiles and launchers— about half of the number then existing on the U.S. side; a limit of 5,000 to 6,000 strategic ballistic-missile warheads; and separate, equal ceilings on bombers, with the proviso that, unlike in SALT II, the Soviet Backfire be counted as an intercontinental weapon. The Chiefs had never accepted Soviet protestations to the contrary, and they had been unhappy at Carter's willingness to accept Brezhnev's written assurances on the range and pro- duction rate of the aircraft instead of direct treatment of it in the treaty.

The Chiefs' proposed launcher limit was considerably lower than the State Department's preference of around 1,200, but there was no secret about why 850 appealed to the military: it was a number that made sense only if the American arsenal included large numbers of big MIRVed MXs and Trident IIs. Still, the concept and structure of the plan—the presence of a warhead ceiling and the absence of direct throw-weight limits—made it highly intriguing to Burt. The Chiefs had tended all along to think that the Administration should not waste time and negotiating capital in pursuit of low, equal levels of ballistic-missile throw-weight since throw-weight was, in their view, overrated as an index of Soviet power and non-negotiable for arms control.

Once again, however, hope gave way to frustration at the State Depart- ment. The Chiefs as a group would not endorse Admiral Williams's pro- posal, at least not yet. Therefore, Perle was able to prevent the plan from being included in the papers that circulated to the NSC. At the April 21 meeting, General Jones confined himself to warning that deep reductions in warheads might inhibit the U.S.'s ability to come up with a master plan that "supported the national strategy" set forth in the Defense Guidance plan. Jones said nothing about the Chiefs' own preference.

Burt and McFarlane were now both worried that the Chiefs might sit out the whole game. McFarlane had the White House put them on notice that they must make up their minds on START before an NSC meeting on May 3. The last week in April the five officers and key aides repaired to the National Military Command Center ("the Tank") for a meeting. By the end of that week, they had finally decided to endorse the proposal that Admiral Williams had floated in the lower levels of the bureaucracy ten days before. Emerging from the Tank, they were aligned, once and for all, with the State Department against Weinberger, Iklé, Perle, Rostow, Rowny, and Nitze.

On that weekend of May 1–2, there was a flurry of last-minute activity to prepare for Monday's session of the National Security Council. The longest and most important of the meetings took place in the Situation Room at the White House on Saturday. It went on most of the day. The purpose was to prepare a "common paper," representing an interagency consensus, that would serve both as an agenda and as a prearranged outcome for the National Security Council two days later. During the course of the May Day meeting, Jones's assistant, General Paul Gorman, revealed that the Chiefs had made up their minds against direct limits on throw-weight. This came as thoroughly bad news to Iklé and Ronald Lehman. At a number of points in the marathon meeting, Gorman and Admiral Williams would argue that throw-weight was the wrong measure of destructive potential, and the Pentagon civilians would scowl and mutter, "We'll have to talk about this later."

The Chiefs were sticking firm to their preference for a ceiling of 850 on missile launchers, while the State Department wanted 1,200. Burt and Goodby huddled with Gorman and Williams to see if the Chiefs would come up a bit and split the difference. But the military men contended that a U.S. missile force limited to 5,000 warheads could not handle a targeting set on the Soviet side that included more than 850 ICBMs and SLBMs. Finally, Burt agreed to 850, and the deal was sealed. The State and Joint Chiefs of Staff were now lined up behind virtually identical options.

Their only remaining disagreement was over the need for an additional subceiling on land-based (that is, ICBM) warheads. The Chiefs, particularly Jones and Lew Allen of the Air Force, had felt all along that such a subceiling was too much to expect the Soviets to swallow, since it would require them to reduce their inventory of ICBM warheads by nearly two-thirds, while the Americans made no reductions at all. On this point, of course, Jones and Allen were applying the criterion of negotiability rather selectively, since they had just rammed through a launcher ceiling that would require the Soviets to give up twice as many launchers as the U.S. —and that conformed neatly to American modernization and targeting plans alike.

In the end, for the sake of preserving a united front against the throw-weight lobby, the State Department indulged the Chiefs on the 850 ceiling on launchers (or "deployed missiles," a term that was meant to sound less like one borrowed from SALT), while the Chiefs agreed not to oppose State on the 2,500 land-based warhead ceiling. A year or so later, when the Administration began looking for ways to demonstrate its flexibility and strategic far-sightedness in START, the 850 was the first ceiling to be lifted, and the 2,500 was among the next to be considered for "relaxation."

14 A Delphic Decision

President Reagan's speech at Eureka College unveiling his START proposal on May 9, 1982, was much like the one he had made proposing the zero option for INF the previous November: it was an effective piece of rhetoric that betrayed very little understanding about the rationale for what the President was saying, or its implications. Seventeen months later, in October 1983, when his START policy was under attack from Congress, Reagan would acknowledge that he had not realized at the time of his Eureka speech that most of the Soviet Union's nuclear muscle was concentrated in large, land-based missiles; nor had he realized that his proposal for the Soviets to dismantle most of those missiles without similar concessions by the U.S. might be interpreted as one-sided.*

Also, as with the zero option, the presidential decision on which the Eureka speech was based was actually a highly unstable bureaucratic compromise. The President "signed off" on that decision, but he could not be said in any meaningful sense to have made it.

The Consensus Option

The hectic round of meetings over the May Day weekend was supposed to produce a single recommendation. Instead, it produced a firm alliance between the State Department and the Joint Chiefs of Staff and a still deeper and sharper split between these two bodies on the one hand and the Pentagon civilians, Edward Rowny, and the Arms Control Agency on the other. Unless something was done to bridge the gap, the President would be confronted with two incompatible approaches to START when the NSC met on Monday, May 3. So Richard Burt decided to float the idea of a

---

*Reagan made this admission to a group of congressmen who were urging flexibility in START, and his remarks were reported in *The New York Times.* Subsequently, some of his own aides cited the incident as evidence, in the phrase of one of them, that there were "holes in the pockets" of Reagan's understanding of nuclear arms issues. In an interview with *Time* at the end of 1983, Reagan was asked how he could possibly have been ignorant of such basic facts about the Soviet arsenal. He replied, "I never heard anyone of our negotiators or any of our military people or anyone else bring up that particular point" about Soviet reliance on large ICBMs.

two-phase approach, making their preferred ceilings on warheads and launchers the goal of Phase I, with Richard Perle's throw-weight ceiling as the goal of Phase II.

This idea had been brewing in the Politico-Military Bureau for some time. It gained new impetus after Burt's plan to trade off the MX for the SS-18 ran out of steam. Late one afternoon, after a particularly grueling day, Burt and his principal deputy, Robert Blackwill, were sitting around Burt's office with their feet up. "I really want to win this one," Burt said. The two of them lit upon the notion of making an equal, low throw-weight ceiling a long-term goal, off over the horizon of an actual agreement. They dubbed this the "compromise proposal." Burt later renamed it the "consensus proposal." The semantic distinction was important. Reagan would like the word "consensus" because it suggested that his advisers had come together around a united position, while he would resist a proposal labeled a compromise, because that might suggest a retreat from the bold ambitions and lofty principles he had espoused. McFarlane was naturally predisposed to any scheme that would break the impasse; consensus proposals were exactly what the NSC staff was supposed to elicit from the bureaucracy.

Toward the end of the disputatious and inconclusive meeting in the Situation Room on May Day, Burt and Goodby literally dropped the idea of the consensus option on the table, in the form of a stack of copies of the few paragraphs that Reagan might use to present the proposal in a speech. Iklé led the attack on the idea. He was worried that the State Department would try to make Phase I self-contained, securing a Soviet-American agreement incorporating the launcher and warhead ceilings while letting the objective of direct throw-weight limits slip away. That was exactly what the State Department had in mind doing. Rostow's deputy, Robert Grey, said that the whole notion of trying to please everybody and put together a package that lumped together all the principal options was "too clever by half"—a phrase often used about Burt and his schemes. Disgusted, Burt asked for the return of all copies of the paper, and the meeting broke up shortly afterward.

Burt persuaded Haig to "take the castle by storm" by presenting the consensus proposal to the President directly at the NSC meeting. Doing so would make Haig look both imaginative and conciliatory, while Weinberger might appear stubborn, even obstructionist.

At the President's regular half-hour morning briefing on May 3—the day of the NSC meeting—McFarlane reviewed the various agencies' positions in a way that subtly but effectively pointed Reagan in the direction of Burt's consensus proposal. McFarlane noted that the Pentagon civilians were still adamant about making throw-weight the unit of account. He reminded the

President of what throw-weight meant, how technical it was, how it included a variety of components in the top stage of a missile. Then he explained that the State Department had come up with the idea of a two-phase approach, concentrating on warhead reductions first ("getting a handle on the things that really kill people"), throw-weight reductions later.

"You know," the President said of throw-weight, "that's just an awfully tough thing to get across in terms that Americans can understand." However, he continued, "Cap has a point about the importance of the [throw-weight] problem, so that's why it's a good idea to have a Phase II. I think phases make sense because Phase I represents numbers people can understand, but Phase II allows us to get at throw-weight."

Reagan was interested primarily in a going-in position, one he would present in a speech and have to answer questions about in a press conference. He realized that the structure of the proposal would probably evolve in the face of Soviet counterproposals and hard bargaining, perhaps sooner rather than later. "I'm sure that what we find ourselves with after two or three months of negotiation will be a whole different ball game," he told McFarlane. Reagan was not giving much thought to what those changes might be, but it was significant that he too was beginning to think in terms of that dirty word "negotiability"—and of those even dirtier ones, "fallback" and "compromise."

"We're Running Short of Time"

From the outset of the May 3 NSC meeting, a number of participants had the distinct impression that the fix was in. McFarlane gave an introductory briefing that seemed to be an overture to the consensus proposal that Burt had floated the previous weekend and that Haig would now present again more formally. Listening to McFarlane's opening comments, Iklé scribbled a note and passed it to Grey. "He's either deliberately or inadvertently going for the State option," said the note. Grey read it, nodded, then scratched out the words "or inadvertently."

Weinberger made one last stab on behalf of his office's preference for a throw-weight ceiling. He did so by using a chart to refute the State Department's contention that throw-weight could be constrained indirectly by limiting warheads and launchers alone.

Reagan was noticeably perplexed by the Pentagon chart. Its message was that throw-weight could not be dealt with after all under the State Department proposal, contrary to what he had been told by McFarlane that morning. This was obviously distressing to him.

Haig said he was not against "codifying equal destructive potential, as Cap suggests." In fact, Haig was prepared to "accept Cap's throw-weight ceiling," as long as it was placed firmly at a "later stage in START." Haig explained that dividing START into two phases was "not a question of negotiability but of practicality," since "the sheer physical magnitude of rebuilding strategic force structures means that many years would be required to achieve it." Moreover, "the sheer physical impracticality of attempting to restructure Soviet forces in the near term and in the massive way required by a throw-weight ceiling at current U.S. levels" argued against such a ceiling in Phase I.

The strongest resistance came from Rostow. The State Department and the Chiefs, he said, were recommending "the unit of account used in SALT II." Haig pursed his lips and looked down at his notes. Rostow ridiculed the notion that START should limit launchers simply because the Soviets were accustomed to that unit of account and would be shocked by a shift to limits on throw-weight. "The Russians are not Pavlov's dogs," said Rostow, "reacting favorably to the word 'launcher' and unfavorably to the word 'throw-weight.' " Besides, a launcher limit of 850 meant "there will only be 850 aim points—a profoundly destabilizing fact. On the other hand, the ACDA and OSD proposals would influence the situation in a far more stabilizing direction—a larger number of smaller and more dispersed weapons. This is a formula for stability."

Rostow then zeroed in on Haig personally. He recalled that at the previous NSC meeting Haig had warned that limiting throw-weight directly would be a military and political catastrophe. That, said Rostow, is exactly the argument Haig had advanced against the zero-option proposal in 1981. "He was wrong then and is wrong now," Rostow said. He further recalled that Haig, at the previous meeting, had told the President that the decision he would be making on START would be the most important of the Administration. "I disagree with that view," said Rostow. START did "not compare in importance" with the Administration's response to the Soviet crackdown in Poland and the "effective restoration of the policy of containment and collective security." In the absence of a forceful and coherent set of policies on other issues, concluded Rostow, "Paul Nitze and Ed Rowny will wear out the bottoms on quite a few pairs of pants" negotiating in vain, and "what we are arguing about here will, in retrospect, look like an argument about rearranging the deck chairs on the *Titanic.* " Rostow was saying, in short, that the Administration lacked a strong and coherent foreign policy, and it was the Secretary of State's fault.

At first, Haig could barely contain his fury, but he slowly became more composed. He realized that Rostow might well be damaging himself above all, as turned out to be the case; it was performances like this that led to Rostow's ouster a few months later. Clark was visibly upset and at one point held out his hand as though to stop Rostow from going further. "We're running short of time, Gene," he interjected.

Another Back Channel

Among those sitting in on the meeting was James Baker, the White House Chief of Staff, the highest-ranking representative of the moderate wing of the Republican party. He saw himself as responsible for "domestic input where foreign policy is concerned." Baker cared little and knew less about whether direct limits or collateral restraints were the best way to reduce Soviet throw-weight. But he cared a great deal about creating an impression of statesmanship and of keeping open an opportunity for an arms agreement later in the Reagan term if one turned out to be necessary for the reelection campaign.

Baker was disturbed by the combination of Weinberger's stubbornness and Rostow's purism. He could easily imagine that an arms-control policy pursued by Weinberger and Rostow would land the President in trouble, stuck with a START proposal that failed the test of being "reasonable-looking." Baker was particularly worried in the face of the pro-freeze movement. Reagan shared these concerns. In talking informally about START with Baker and other close aides, Reagan had commented a number of times that he could not afford to subject himself to the accusation that "we aren't serious about wanting an agreement."

After the NSC meeting, Haig arranged for Burt to call on Baker. Sitting in the sunshine in a garden outside Baker's office in the West Wing of the White House, Burt argued that the State Department's consensus option was designed with the President's political interests in mind. It would be true to his avowed commitment to deep reductions; it would help close the window of vulnerability; yet at the same time it would meet the criterion of plausibility. By contrast, a decision in favor of the Pentagon's throw-weight ceiling would be disastrous; the President would be accused of making a cynical ploy, a proposal designed to fail. He would provoke both popular and official rejection of his leadership of the Atlantic alliance on the very eve of his upcoming trip to Europe. Baker listened quietly, then told Burt that the President was already moving in the direction of the consensus proposal.

Burt's lobbying of Baker remained a well-kept secret even at high levels within the government for some time, but there was widespread suspicion that somebody close to Haig had lobbied somebody close to the President. Rostow, particularly, was upset. He had gone directly to the White House, over the heads or around the backs of the State Department often enough himself, but now he warned Clark, "If we're not careful, we're going to backchannel ourselves to death, in a way that will make Kissinger's style look like child's play."

"Not in this Administration, Gene," replied Clark.

Rostow was not reassured.

The Secret Mandate

It was apparent in the immediate aftermath of the May 3 NSC meeting that the State Department, aided by the Joint Chiefs, had outflanked the Pentagon and the Arms Control Agency. While the winners were clearly pleased, they knew that it was unwise to gloat. In their briefings for the press and in their demeanor at meetings, they did their best to play good winners. The final decision, they said, had been a synthesis of the best elements available throughout the government. Their magnanimity was tactical: Burt and others knew that, while they had won a battle, they had not won a war. The alliance between State and the Chiefs could not last; Jones, Lew Allen, and Hayward were about to retire.

The first new battle was over the contents of a National Security Decision Directive spelling out what exactly the President was supposed to have decided. The process of interpreting and implementing the NSDD would provide Perle with an opportunity to refight, yet again, the battle of throw-weight and to recapture the ground he had lost as a result of the NSC meeting.

The morning after the meeting, the President met with Clark and McFarlane in the Oval Office and told them to prepare a draft NSDD right away so that he could sign it quickly and get to work on his Eureka speech. The President's signature was a mere formality.

When the NSDD was finished, McFarlane summoned Burt to the White House and sent him into the Situation Room with a copy so that he could draft the exact language the President might use in unveiling the proposal. Only then were representatives of the other agencies given their own first look at the directive. Not surprisingly, Burt seemed more familiar with the text than the others in the meeting; this led Rostow to comment wryly, "Rick, it seems you've seen this before."

But that did not mean Burt liked everything in the NSDD. One unexpected and unwelcome provision concerned the negotiability of cruise missiles. The directive seemed to rule out any American concessions on cruise missiles during Phase I, which was the phase that mattered to the State Department. The only slow-flying weapons that could be limited in Phase I of the negotiations were bombers, which would be frozen at roughly current levels, with the U.S. free, of course, to trade in old B-52s for new B-1 and radar-invisible Stealth bombers as they came into service. Limits on other slow-flying systems—cruise missiles—were to be put off until Phase II. That meant, at least as long as the directive remained in force, that the U.S. was not prepared to trade away sea-launched cruise missiles, or even air-launched cruise missiles aboard bombers, in exchange for Soviet concessions in ballistic missiles.

The NSDD contained another provision that was an even more unwelcome surprise for Burt and an even greater windfall for Perle. In addition to the Phase II goal of reducing Soviet throw-weight by two-thirds, the directive stipulated an internal and very secret objective for Phase I: the reductions in warheads and deployed missiles achieved in Phase I must have the effect of bringing Soviet throw-weight down to 2.5 million kilograms from its current level of more than 5 million kilograms (the U.S. level, by contrast, was just under 2 million). The 2.5 million figure was not to be explicitly prescribed in any agreement that might come out of Phase I. Rather, it was to be the result of the consequent arithmetic. This was McFarlane's attempt to reconcile the State Department and Pentagon positions, to build in a link between Phase I and Phase II of the proposal, and to accommodate the President's very vague comment that "Cap has a point" about throw-weight.

Throughout the long, acrimonious, confusing wrangle over units of account, the State Department had repeatedly argued that its combination of launcher and warhead limits would also serve to reduce Soviet throw-weight drastically, if indirectly. The Pentagon civilians challenged both the accuracy and sincerity of the State Department's argument. Perle, Ronald Lehman, and Iklé insisted that unless throw-weight was directly and explicitly limited the Soviets would be able to maintain their advantage. McFarlane suspected that in strictly analytical terms the Pentagon was right, and that the State Department was playing a bit fast and loose with the numbers.

McFarlane had Colonel Linhard run his own analysis of what sort of throw-weight the Soviets would be able to retain if they accepted the ceilings of 5,000 ballistic warheads, 2,500 ICBM warheads, and 850 launchers, but still kept the maximum-permissible large missiles, particularly the SS-18 heavies. Linhard's estimate was around 3 million kilograms. That was higher than the State Department's projections. So McFarlane added the objective of 2.5 million kilograms of Soviet throw-weight to the directive for Phase I in order, as he put it, to "keep the State Department honest."

The secret target figure for throw-weight turned out to be immensely problematic. For one thing, if it were to become public, it would raise precisely those doubts about the negotiability or plausibility of the proposal that McFarlane and the President were so anxious to avoid and that had contributed to their decision to consign throw-weight to Phase II. Partly to keep the 2.5 million kilogram figure from leaking, the directive was treated on an "eyes-only" basis. Even when it finally circulated, it was given the most limited distribution. Rowny, for example, did not even show it to his own staff.

But more troublesome than the potential embarrassment of revelation was the immediate question of implementation. Now the onus was on the State Department to provide collateral restraints that would force the Soviets down to 2.5 million kilograms in Phase I. Perle, Rostow, and Rowny were able to harden the overall proposal, bringing it more into line with their original preference. "The President," said Perle, "has given us a mandate to put some backbone into this thing."

The way to accomplish that, he felt, was to insist on an outright ban on heavy missiles: the Soviets would have to give up all 308 of their SS-18s, with no nonsense about the U.S.'s giving up the MX in exchange. "We're going to zero-out heavies," said Perle confidently after the May 3 meeting, "and if necessary, we're going to go back to the NSC to do it." Nor was he going to stop there: "Heavies are only part of the problem, so we may have to look at additional ways of getting at the overall problem of throw-weight." On top of the ban on SS-18s, he proposed cutting the second-largest of the Soviet missiles, the "medium" SS-19, from 300 to 200 launchers.*

After steady lobbying by Perle and Lehman, Rowny came to support a total ban on heavies. Shortly before leaving for Geneva to begin the talks, he remarked, "We have to achieve equality of throw-weight before we can have a ratifiable treaty. It's that simple. I'm not going to come home without one. There's no way for the Soviets to get to equality except by zeroing-out heavies. It's a tactical question of whether you make that explicit to them or not." It would be better, he said, not to beat around the bush, but simply to tell the Soviets outright that they had to eliminate the SS-18s: "I know those people; I've negotiated with them for years. They appreciate forth-rightness. They do not like their negotiating partner to come in with one proposal and then drop a second shoe later on. If we're determined to get them to lower their throw-weight in a way that requires them to get rid of their heavies, then let's be right up front about it."

Burt knew that a ban on heavies would render the proposal utterly non-negotiable, but he was also aware that his refusal to support specific reductions in heavies would render the State Department position untenable within the Administration. As a compromise, he put forward an option calling for a total ban on heavies in the second phase with a proportional reduction in the first phase. The Soviets would have to reduce their heavy missile force in proportion to the reduction in ballistic-missile launchers as a whole. They would be required to reduce their overall aggregate of ICBM and SLBM launchers from 2,300 to 850; therefore, they must reduce their heavy ICBM launchers from 308 to 110.

But after another set of calculations the State officials realized that even if the Soviets accepted the ceilings on warheads and launchers, plus the new

---

*SALT had distinguished only between heavies and nonheavies, meaning anything smaller than the SS-18; SALT II established that the SS-19 would be the largest permissible nonheavy. In START, the Minuteman and the old SS-11 were considered light ICBMs; the MX and the SS-17 and -19 were classified as medium ICBMs.

requirement of reducing their SS-18 force by two-thirds, they could *still* exceed 2.5 million kilograms of throw-weight by building up their SS-19 force. So they went back to their calculators. If the Soviets kept 110 heavies, they asked, what would be the largest number of SS-19s and -17s they could retain and still end up under the 2.5 million kilogram ceiling? The answer clicked out: 100. The Soviets would have to cut their SS-18 force to 110, their SS-19 force from 300 to 100, and their 150 SS-17s would have to be eliminated altogether. Only then would the collateral restraints have served the purpose of driving throw-weight down to a level that Perle persisted in pointing out was "set by order of the President."

The State Department option paper proposed that, under the principal ceilings of START, collateral restraints on destructive capability would allow each side no more than 210 heavies and mediums, of which 110 could be heavies. The reason for that cumbersome formulation had to do with the MX. The MX would qualify as a medium ICBM, like the SS-19 and -17, and the U.S. wanted to make sure that it would be allowed 210 MXs—one for every SS-18 and SS-19 the Soviets retained.

After weeks of horse-trading similar to the bargaining that had taken place earlier over the main features of the Eureka proposal, State managed to form a loose alliance with the Joint Chiefs of Staff and the Arms Control Agency. The department's option was approved by the President at an NSC meeting on June 25, the day that Rowny's delegation left for Geneva. Once again, Reagan was impressed that the uniformed military and the State Department were together, and he leaned in their favor. "We can't ask for absolutely everything," he remarked after the meeting.

His Administration, however, was still asking for a great deal. It was only when compared to the even more extreme measures favored by Perle that the State Department option looked reasonable. Now, in addition to requiring the Soviets to reduce their ICBM warheads from the approximately 6,000 they were allowed under SALT II to 2,500 and their total launchers from more than 2,300 to 850, the U.S. would be demanding drastic, specific reductions in the three most potent types of Soviet ICBMs. State's successful maneuver on the eve of the Eureka speech was beginning to look increasingly like a Pyrrhic victory. Conversely, while he had, for the second time, not received all he wanted, Perle was beginning to look like the real winner.

Hard Questions, Soft Answers

The President's Eureka proposal immediately raised three questions that the Administration would find itself trying to answer for a long time. Even if an agreement could be negotiated along the lines he had proposed, would that agreement contribute to strategic stability? In the event that an agreement could not be reached any time soon, what was the status of SALT?

What was in the proposal to give the Soviets any incentive to accept it?

The presidential directive promulgated after the May 3 NSC meeting was so closely held that Paul Nitze did not learn until some days later that the President was going to include the Chiefs' 850 launcher ceiling, which would, Nitze believed, push both American and Soviet strategic programs in exactly the opposite direction from de-MIRVing. In dismay, he called McFarlane and said "this is not a force structure we can live with." He then went to William Clark and warned that the launcher ceiling would "ensure instability." Any reference to it, he urged, should be deleted from the President's speech.

Clark deferred to McFarlane on the merits of Nitze's complaint, and McFarlane told him he was overreacting to the 850 ceiling. It was a good "going-in position," explained McFarlane, and it was certain to "evolve." Therefore, there was no need, in his view, to be "too rigidly attentive to force-structure calculations." Put plainly, there was no chance the 850 figure would survive the negotiations; whatever launcher ceiling was finally agreed upon would be considerably higher.

Perle was more blunt. He thought the ceiling of 850 deployed ballistic missiles on each side was "crazy," but, he added, "Fortunately we can count on the Soviets to bail us out simply by not accepting it."

Once the proposal became public, echoes of the de-MIRVing argument that had gone on in the government sounded from one end of the political spectrum to the other. Herbert Scoville, the president of the liberal Arms Control Association, wrote an article in *The New York Times* criticizing the Administration's initiative on the ground that increasing the overall ratio of Soviet warheads to American targets was a formula for disaster: "There [would be] an incentive for one side to get a punch in ahead of the other side." Colin Gray, a controversial proponent of the need for the U.S. to develop a nuclear-war-winning capability who was serving as a consultant to the Administration, made the same point: as a result of START, the window of vulnerability would be open wider than before.

Rostow wanted Nitze to write a letter refuting Scoville, but on this point Nitze agreed with Scoville. So Rowny wrote the letter to the *Times* instead. He conceded the theoretical point that a high warhead-to-target ratio was destabilizing, but he went on to argue that "the President's proposal for substantial reductions of weapons should not be side-tracked by arguments based on hypothetical ratios." That was a curious case for Rowny to make, since Administration policy in arms control and defense alike was driven to a large extent by precisely the sort of "hypothetical ratios" that were now being used against it. Such ratios were what the window of vulnerability, and attempts to close it, were all about.

Paul Warnke—the principal negotiator of SALT II during the Carter Administration, and the personification of what conservatives considered the bad old days of arms control—was fond of saying, "If the Russians accept Mr. Reagan's proposal, he will be forced to reject it himself." Warnke was echoing from outside the Administration the point Perle was making inside.

Nor did the belated emergence of a START proposal lay to rest bothersome questions from outsiders about the agreements of the past. The Carter Administration had obtained in SALT II a concrete Soviet commitment to reductions, albeit modest ones. The Reagan Administration had now proposed deep reductions, but there was little reason to believe that the Soviets would accept them any time soon, if ever. Unless and until SALT II was ratified, the Soviets were not obliged to make even the modest reductions set by the treaty. Generally, the Administration sought to downplay this awkward fact, but Fred Iklé felt obliged to acknowledge it in a meeting with reporters on May 14: "The situation is as follows: We are not in conflict in what we are doing with the provisions of the SALT I and II agreements. The Soviets, based on our observations and verification, are likewise not in conflict with these provisions, except, of course, for the dismantling that would have gone into effect after ratification only."

One reason that Iklé felt obliged to offer this clarification was that the day before, on May 13, Reagan had remarked extemporaneously at a press conference that the only parts of SALT that were being observed were those that had "to do with the monitoring" of weapons. As so often when Reagan was discussing arms control without the benefit of a carefully prepared script, he had his facts wrong. Pressed on why his Eureka proposal bore down so hard on land-based, as opposed to submarine-launched, ballistic missiles, he explained that SLBMs were less threatening because, like bombers, they could be recalled after they were launched. This came as news to the U.S. Navy.*

One reason for the President's dramatic unveiling of his START proposal was to fend off pressure that had been building to ratify SALT II. The tactic did not work. Commenting on the Eureka speech, Senator Sam Nunn, a Democrat who was widely respected on defense issues and who would be an increasingly important figure in the Administration's attempt to maintain support on the Hill for the MX, said he thought it was "a good start," but that Reagan should also "seriously consider taking SALT II and then

---

*Of all Reagan's misstatements about nuclear weapons, perhaps the most stunning came during some off-the-cuff remarks he made to a group of congressmen in October 1983. Commenting on the strategic triad, Reagan noted that the most destabilizing weapons were land-based missiles because they were "the biggest and most accurate." So far so good. But he continued: "Also, land-based missiles have nuclear warheads, while bombers and submarines don't." Even as he said these words, his voice dropped and wavered, as though he had forgotten his lines and knew there was something not quite right about his attempt to improvise.

proposing any amendments he thinks necessary." The Administration was having none of that. Shortly after the Eureka speech, Haig told the Senate Armed Services Committee that SALT II was "dead." Yet, the very next day, Haig's old boss Henry Kissinger gave a speech in the Netherlands saying that the negotiation of radical reductions would be "enormously time-consuming," and that he had "great difficulty understanding why it is safe to adhere to a non-ratified agreement while it is unsafe formally to ratify what one is already observing."

Even the President had questions. At a National Security Council meeting on May 21, he asked, "What is good about SALT II?" There was an awkward pause, followed by mumbling around the table about how some features of the treaty protected the U.S. against breakout. Admiral Bobby Inman, the deputy director of the CIA, who was sitting in for William Casey, had been scribbling some notes to himself. He spoke up.

"Mr. President," he said, "at least six good things about SALT II come to mind." He then ticked them off. The "counting rules" established by the treaty—particularly the rule whereby all missiles of a certain type were treated as though they had as many warheads as the maximum tested on that type—were valuable precedents for future agreements and made the CIA's job of verifying compliance much easier. While less than airtight, the restriction on the use of codes in tests was helpful to the U.S. in monitoring Soviet military programs. The freeze on "fractionation," or the number of warheads per type of missile, would, as long as it was in force, serve as a hedge against the Soviets' suddenly proliferating land-based warheads. So would the subceiling on MIRVed intercontinental missiles. So would the prohibition against the construction of new launchers, particularly heavies. It was advantageous to have the Soviets continuing to dismantle strategic missile-launching submarines that might otherwise remain in service. Reagan reacted as though pleasantly surprised, and as though he was hearing all this for the first time.

Inman had been an unabashed proponent of SALT II. He was also frustrated in the Reagan Administration and had already submitted his resignation so that he could look for a job in the private sector. Meanwhile, it fell to him to tutor the President on the most elementary aspects of the subject at hand. Reagan asked, "Isn't the SS-19 their biggest missile?"

"No," replied Inman. "That's the SS-18."

"So," said Reagan, "they've even switched the numbers on their missiles in order to confuse us!"

Inman smiled. "No, it's we who assign those numbers to their weapons systems in the sequence that we observe them, Mr. President."

Weinberger argued for a policy of declaring that the U.S. would adhere to those parts of SALT it considered in its national interest but would not feel bound by those that impeded the MX and any other weapons programs the U.S. felt it needed. This course would probably have been taken by the Soviets as tantamount to abrogation. But the secretary had three professional soldiers arrayed against him—Haig, Inman, and David Jones. They all felt it would badly serve the nation's military interests to follow the course Weinberger recommended.

In a Memorial Day speech at Arlington National Cemetery, the President declared, "As for existing strategic arms agreements, we will refrain from actions which undercut them so long as the Soviet Union shows equal restraint." The President's declaration was almost identical to the position the State Department had declared more than a year earlier. Aside from the wish list it had proposed for START, informal adherence to SALT was still the only strategic-arms-control policy the Administration had.

The President's proposal had also elicited skepticism about negotiability. What was in it for the Soviets? Fred Iklé, Eugene Rostow, and other officials made clear in public statements that, while the U.S. was of course willing to live under the numerical limits on warheads and launchers it was proposing in START, it had no intention of giving up its program to replace old systems with new ones—the B-52 bomber with the B-1 and Stealth, the Minuteman ICBM with the MX, the Poseidon SLBM with the Trident.

The desire to keep American modernization going strong while reducing the existing Soviet arsenal posed a challenge to the forensic ingenuity of Administration spokesmen. Why should the U.S. be allowed to keep its MX, for example, when the Soviet missiles that the MX was supposed to counter were slated for drastic reductions in START? Well, came the answer, perhaps the U.S. would need *fewer* MXs if its START proposal was accepted. What the Administration was offering, said Iklé in mid-May, was "a greater stability, a lesser need to build up strategic forces, securing peace for the long term and reducing the chances of nuclear war." The Administration was willing to let the Soviets keep a few of its hard-target-killing SS-18s and -19s, so it was perfectly fair for the U.S. to proceed with at least a scaled-down MX and Trident II program. After all, said Eugene Rostow before the Senate Foreign Relations Committee, "The sacrifice of future weapons is not really different from dismantling existing arsenals."

In his own testimony before the same committee, Alexander Haig added a new twist to Administration policy. This was a warning not to the Soviets but to the U.S. Congress. "The President's strategic modernization program and the Congress's support for it will make or break our attempt to negotiate a reasonable arms control agreement," said the Secretary of State. "How seriously they [the Soviets] will negotiate depends on their view of how the military and political environment will look without an agreement." And they would not view that environment as frightening enough to warrant compromise unless Congress approved the Administration's plans for rearmament: "If we fail to adopt the President's [strategic modernization] program, we will reduce not the nuclear danger but instead the chances of reaching an arms control agreement."

With that statement by Haig, the Administration began painting itself into a corner that would prove very tight two years later. The Administration was saying to its critics on the left and at the center: You must support us as we rearm, or else our attempts to negotiate with the Soviets will suffer. The trouble with this line of argument was that it would work only as long as there seemed to be some possibility of progress toward an agreement. Once Congress realized the negotiations were going nowhere in any case, the tables would be turned: then Congress would be in a position to hold the weapons programs hostage to an easing of the Administration's hard-line negotiating position.

15 No More Mr. Nice Guy

The man waiting for Edward Rowny in Geneva was a known but rather puzzling quantity. Like Rowny, Viktor Karpov was a veteran of earlier negotiations. He had served with apparent competence as principal deputy to the chief negotiator, Vladimir Semyonov, during much of SALT II, then as Semyonov's successor in the concluding stages of those negotiations, and most recently as the chief Soviet delegate to the preliminary round of the INF talks in the autumn of 1980. Karpov had logged nearly as much time in superpower negotiations as all the American START delegates put together, and that experience had given him self-confidence and skill. He had developed a reputation for considerable adeptness—as long as he was sober. During SALT II, he had been drunk on the job a number of times, including one spectacular occasion when he was practically falling out of his chair during a plenary session. In 1978 Karpov was sent home to dry out.

On another occasion, his pub-crawling led to a Rabelaisian scene in an underground garage. To the accompaniment of music from a car radio, Karpov was flinging off his clothes for the benefit of a girl he had picked up in a bar when some of his vigilant, stone-faced countrymen appeared out of the shadows and led him off into the night.

The Soviet system is normally unforgiving of such peccadilloes, since they are the stuff that scandals—and, worse, blackmail by imperialist intelligence services—are made of. Yet he survived that incident, too. The assumption on the American side was that Karpov found favor in Moscow not only because of his negotiating skills, but because of his good connections. By assigning Karpov to START, the Kremlin was doing more than just underscoring its confidence in him; it was reiterating its determination to preserve as much continuity as possible between START and SALT II, and as much of a connection as possible between START and INF.

If Karpov was known among the Americans as a bit of a rascal, Rowny was preceded to Geneva by a different sort of reputation. Soviets generally avoid *ad hominem* comments about American officials (if only to preserve the self-righteousness they display when the U.S. press makes unflattering personal references to Kremlin leaders); but they made an exception for

Rowny. Vladimir Pavlichenko, who had watched Rowny operate during SALT II, was particularly scathing about him. "We can understand the U.S. sending a hard-liner like Nitze over here," he told a visiting American, "but Nitze is a serious fellow. Rowny is just a stubborn, stupid man, and a rabid opponent of arms control to boot."

Karpov was more circumspect, but he told a number of diplomatic colleagues that he had been hoping for "more dignified competition" than he expected Rowny to provide. He had seen Rowny in action during SALT II, when he had been the resident spoiler on the U.S. delegation. Nitze, by contrast, was remembered from his SALT I days as an enterprising, independent, technically masterful negotiator, who had conducted fruitful, one-on-one bargaining with Alexander Shchukin. No doubt another reason that the Soviets preferred Nitze to Rowny was that they quickly perceived that Nitze was determined to get an agreement, even if it meant straining at the leash of his instructions and dragging his government along behind him; Rowny seemed to pride himself on being willing to outwait the Soviets.

Rowny hoped to impress on the Soviets, and the world, that he was a principled loner who had fought the good fight against the odds and against the soft-liners for years and who had finally joined the ranks of an Administration with which he was truly compatible. He liked to remind people, including the Soviets, that he was of Polish descent; the implication was that he had a considerable dose of anti-Russianism in his blood. His name in Polish, he said on a number of occasions, meant "equal, straight and true": he was going to make the Soviets join him in pursuing a straight course toward the achievement of equality in the true measure of strategic power, which was, he believed, ballistic-missile throw-weight. He enjoyed striking the pose of the old pro who is not about to be taken in by Soviet tricks. "I can almost write their speeches for them," Rowny told reporters. "When my Soviet counterpart gives me argument 33, I can just say, 'I've heard that before, and my answer is number 17.' My problem is that the Soviets come from a country that has a lot of patience and plays chess. I come from a country that has a lot of quarters and plays Pac Man." He would quickly let it be known, however, that he himself played chess.

Whatever the game, the Soviets set about to convince the Americans from the beginning that they were prepared to play for a long, long time. Shortly before the negotiations got underway, Senator Larry Pressler, a South Dakota Republican who was chairman of the Senate Foreign Relations Committee's subcommittee on arms control, visited Moscow to survey the prospects for START. Pressler met with Karpov and the head of the Foreign Ministry's American desk, Viktor Komplektov. Pressler remarked that President Reagan was hoping for a fairly quick agreement, perhaps within eighteen months. Komplektov laughed scoffingly, then turned to Karpov and said, "You've got a ten-year job."

. . .

Arms control during the Reagan Administration was hampered by both sides' tendency to conduct propaganda at the expense of negotiations. In INF, Reagan and Brezhnev had been playing to the gallery of Western Europe, trading proposals and counterproposals, as well as rejections and recriminations, before the negotiators even reached Geneva in 1981. That pattern would continue for two years, right up to the Soviet walkout in November 1983. Much the same thing happened in START.

A little more than a week after Reagan's Eureka speech, Brezhnev addressed the Soviet Young Communist League. "We would be prepared to reach agreement that the strategic armament of the U.S.S.R. and the U.S.A. be frozen right away," he said, "as soon as the talks begin, frozen quantitatively—and that modernization be limited to the utmost." This meant freezing the production, testing, and deployment of all strategic systems. The plan would have left the U.S.S.R. in possession of all the weapons the U.S. was trying to reduce and blocked the development of the new weapons the U.S. was trying to produce: the Stealth bomber, cruise missile, MX, and Trident II SLBM program. Just as his proposal for INF had deliberately resonated with the crescendo of protests against the Pershing II and Tomahawk deployments in Western Europe, so the timing and content of Brezhnev's proposal in START was meant to coincide with the appeals in the U.S. Congress for a bilateral freeze on nuclear weapons.

Foreign Minister Andrei Gromyko held a press conference in New York on June 22, 1982, a week before START was to begin. He put the U.S. on notice that, if the new Administration insisted on reopening the old question of heavy missiles, the Soviet Union would reopen the question of forward-based systems (FBS) as fair game for strategic arms control. FBS meant, among other things, INF. In the Ford-Brezhnev compromise of 1974, the U.S. had agreed to let the Soviets keep its monopoly in heavy missiles, and the U.S.S.R. agreed to drop FBS from SALT. Now the Soviets heard the U.S. saying it wanted to renege on that agreement, that it wanted to deprive the U.S.S.R. of most if not all of its heavy missiles at the same time that it deployed new intermediate-range missiles in Western Europe. The Soviets' counterproposal in START would seek not only to preserve their right to large ICBMs, but to extend limitations on bombers, submarine forces, and cruise missiles while seeking new limitations on forward-based American systems.

Red Pawn's Opening Move

Once the talks began, the Soviet negotiators wasted no time elaborating on Brezhnev's proposal and Gromyko's warning. The executive secretaries of the two delegations, Donald Tice and Vladimir Aleksandrov, met after the first plenary session to plan for the second, which was scheduled for the following week. Aleksandrov said his side wanted to meet again sooner than that, at the end of the same week.

"What are we going to talk about on Friday?" asked Tice.

"A freeze," replied Aleksandrov.

That tip-off allowed the Americans to prepare a curt, categorical rejection in advance. When Karpov presented the Soviet proposal at the Friday meeting, Rowny produced a piece of paper of his own, read it, and tabled it. Karpov was taken aback: "But you will submit our proposal to Washington and get a formal response, won't you?"

"This *is* our formal response," replied Rowny. Later he elaborated colloquially, telling Karpov that a freeze was "a bummer, an absolute no-no." The U.S., he said, had an obligation to pursue simultaneously the reduction of Soviet nuclear forces and the modernization of its own. Both were necessary for the sake of stability. Karpov found this view "revealing of the essence of the American position," and as such, totally unacceptable.

As was their practice, the Soviets did not withdraw the freeze proposal, despite the American rejection. They left it on the table, but Karpov soon laid another initiative alongside it. This became known, earnestly on the Soviets' part and sarcastically on the Americans', as the Kremlin's "reductions proposal." It would have lowered the SALT II ceiling on the total number of strategic delivery vehicles (intercontinental bombers, SLBMs, and ICBMs) from 2,250 to 1,800 in exchange for American agreement that there would be no addition to forward-based systems. In other words, no new American missiles in Europe. As Gromyko had already broadly hinted, the Soviet willingness to accept any strategic arms-control agreement beyond SALT II was linked explicitly to American acceptance of the Soviet position in INF, which demanded cancellation of the new NATO deployments. The Kremlin seemed to have decided to make stopping the American Euromissiles the prime objective of START as well as INF.

The Tomahawk ground-launched cruise-missile program in particular would already have been halted by the Soviets' INF freeze; now it would be further blocked not once but twice in START. In addition to the proposed ban on new forward-based systems, there was a prohibition on the deployment of all forms of long-range cruise missiles, whether launched from land, sea, or air. Significantly, however, development, testing, and production of those weapons would be permitted, allowing the Soviets to catch up with the U.S.

Long-range ground- and sea-launched cruise missiles had been banned in the protocol to the SALT II treaty, but that protocol had already expired (or would have expired had the treaty itself ever come formally into force). Air-launched cruise missiles, ALCMs, had been permitted under the SALT II treaty proper, which was still being observed by both sides even though it had never been ratified. Each side was allowed a limited number of bombers armed with ALCMs, and the U.S. was already taking advantage of that provision by converting B-52s into cruise-missile carriers. Under the Soviets' START proposal, that program would have to be scrapped. If the U.S. was going to try to take away the Soviet advantage in heavy ICBMs granted in SALT I, the Kremlin was going to try to take away the American advantage in ALCMs granted in SALT II.

Even as they pulled back a pawn, however, their offer to lower the overall number of strategic bombers and missiles indicated that they might give up some other pieces later on. They might propose a new, still-undefined subceiling on MIRVed ICBMs. SALT II included a similar subceiling of 820. The U.S.S.R. already had nearly 800 MIRVed ICBMs, so if the new subceiling in their START proposal was significantly below the SALT II level, it would mean the Kremlin might be willing to retire some of its SS-17s. At the same time, there was nothing to suggest that they would give up any of their more formidable SS-18s and -19s—and there were numerous, emphatic assertions to the contrary. Krasnoslav Osadchiyev, the Council of Ministers' representative, stressed that the MIRVed ICBMs were "the absolute mainstays of our defense" and that the U.S.S.R. was not willing to accept anything like the drastic reductions Reagan had proposed.

The Soviets were holding back on the details of their proposal, such as the level they would accept for a MIRVed ICBM subceiling, until they learned more about the American position. They were particularly curious about exactly how the two phases of START were supposed to work. Their curiosity was justified: that same question was still a matter of bitter contention back in Washington. The U.S. delegation in Geneva was authorized to agree in principle to numerical limits in Phase I on bombers at approximately current levels, but only after the Soviets raised the issue. The Soviets, quite naturally, did raise it, since bombers figured in both their freeze and reduction proposals. They did not like what they heard, since the Americans declared that any ceiling on bombers in Phase I would have to cover the Backfire.

The exchanges that then took place had a familiar and melancholy ring to those on both sides who had been through SALT. The U.S. insisted that the Backfire was a heavy bomber, or strategic weapon. The Soviets denied this, saying it was a "medium bomber," intended for use against targets at less than intercontinental range. The American rejoinder was that what mattered were "capabilities, not intentions," and the Backfire had intercontinental capability. General Viktor Starodubov, the military officer who doubled as head of the Soviet delegation at the Standing Consultative Commission (SCC), ridiculed this claim by asking for volunteers from the American delegation who would be prepared to ride aboard the Backfire on an intercontinental flight. The implication was that it would be a one-way, suicide mission. Donald Tice said he was willing to go. "I've never been to Havana, so I'd enjoy the free ride," he said, thus suggesting that the Backfire could attack the continental U.S. and land safely in Cuba. The whole issue of the Backfire promised to be particularly contentious. The Soviets regarded the question as having been closed once and for all in SALT II with Brezhnev's letter to Carter. Their leader had given his word; for the new American administration to be reopening the question was, they suggested, not just an "unworthy trick" but a personal insult to the prestige and honor of Brezhnev. The Americans were just as adamant that the exemption of Backfire from SALT II was a flaw that must be corrected.

Cruise missiles, supposed to be a Phase II issue for the Americans, were an immediate concern for the Soviets. The U.S. negotiators could discuss limitations on numbers of bombers, but there was to be no distinction between those armed with ALCMs and those with gravity bombs, and no discussion whatsoever of sea-launched cruise missiles. The Soviets were alternately incredulous and indignant that the U.S. would refuse to discuss limits on cruise missiles until Phase II. Any American proposal that neglected cruise missiles was "not comprehensive or equal."

Of all the claims made by the Reagan Administration in defense of its proposal, the proposition that slow-flying weapons were less threatening than fast-flying ones triggered the angriest Soviet reaction. "So what if a missile takes hours rather than minutes to reach us?" challenged Karpov. "What makes it a first-strike or surprise-attack weapon is how much warning we have that it's coming, and in the case of cruise missiles, that warning might be a matter of minutes. The whole purpose of the things, after all, is to avoid detection." Aleksei Obukhov, the Foreign Ministry representative and Karpov's deputy, argued that "a cruise missile can get to its target with minimal warning time through stealthy means just as a ballistic missile can get to its target with minimal warning time through fast flight speed."

Rowny would listen to Soviet objections with the expression of a stern but persevering schoolmaster dealing with a pupil who is both obstreperous and a bit dim-witted. "If that's what you think," he would reply, "then you obviously don't understand what we're telling you and we'll explain it again." He would then repeat everything he had said earlier.

"We still want to know about cruise missiles," said Karpov at one point. "Don't tell us what phase they are in; tell us what you're willing to do about them."

"That's what we mean by phases," replied Rowny. "Phase I is Phase I, and Phase II is Phase II. We'll discuss cruise missiles when we make progress in Phase I."

"How can you expect us to buy a pig in a poke [or, in the literal Russian idiom he used, 'a cat in a sack']?" Karpov asked. "You say we should reduce our [ballistic] missiles in this first phase, yet you won't tell us what you'll give up in exchange in the second."

Every time the Soviets raised the Phase II issues they wanted to talk about, bombers and cruise missiles, the Americans brought up that other Phase II issue, the one that represented a further demand on the Soviets— ballistic-missile throw-weight. Rowny himself was utterly dedicated to meeting the secret target figure of 2.5 million kilograms, and referred to it constantly in conversations with his staff. The Soviets must have it "hammered into their skulls," he said, that "an obvious result of the collateral restraints we are seeking in Phase I would be significant reductions in throw-weight."

The Soviets' stock reply was that throw-weight was not a fair or appropriate unit of account and they did not want to discuss the subject. They would go back to their own favorite subjects, particularly cruise missiles.

Just as they had suggested lowering the subceiling on MIRVed ICBMs from the SALT II level, the Soviets floated the possibility of limiting "nuclear charges"—a term that seemed to include cruise missiles and other bomber armaments as well as ballistic warheads—but they dodged all American attempts to find out what sort of limit they had in mind. First, they wanted the U.S. to admit that the warheads on cruise missiles were also nuclear charges and must be limited in the agreement. A futile dialogue ensued: "When are you going to give us some numbers on nuclear charges?" the Americans would ask. "When are you going to tell us about cruise missiles?" the Soviets would reply.

Rowny did not seem to mind. After his years as the odd-man-out in SALT, and with his conviction that the U.S. had caved in to Soviet negotiating tactics too often in the past, he was rather enjoying the opportunity to be unyielding and, as he put it once, to "watch the other guys squirm and go up the wall a bit. It's no more Mr. Nice Guy with me." He told his staff that he was perfectly prepared to "hold off the Russians on this cruise-missile thing until hell freezes over if necessary."

As long as he was in Geneva, however, Rowny was open to arguments about negotiability. He eventually became persuaded that something more needed to be said about cruise missiles. In early August, Rowny suggested to Washington that the status of cruise missiles be at the top of the list of issues on which the Administration should review its position.

One Walkout and Many Lectures

At their first meeting, Rowny had delivered a short lecture to Karpov, using some of the Russian phrases he had picked up over the years: they knew both the issues and each other well enough to avoid wasting time or eroding good will by engaging in nastiness. There was, however, a protracted if rather petty bit of nastiness over a matter of procedure that Rowny decided to use as a test of will and a demonstration of the new, tougher quality of the American approach to relations with the U.S.S.R., at all levels and on all issues. It concerned the protocol for dividing up into post-plenary sessions, the smaller, less formal groupings that took place following the full-dress plenary sessions. Members of one delegation would pair off with their assigned counterparts from the other, then be joined by lower-ranking experts. Rowny objected to the Soviets' long-established practice of stacking their delegation with extra experts and sometimes doubling up on members assigned to the smaller groups, with the result that the Americans were often outnumbered. He told Karpov that the sessions would be "more efficient and businesslike" if the members split up one on one with their interlocutors: "No more MIRVing your post-plenary teams."

The Soviets balked. Karpov explained that the Soviet delegation was a mixture of old hands and new blood. He was particularly concerned that Osadchiyev, as a newcomer, should have a military man at his side during post-plenaries. As Karpov put it to Rowny, "We have seasoned birds and fledglings in our group." Rowny retorted, "All my delegates are equal; we have no fledglings." He insisted that smaller, more evenly matched groups should form. But at the next meeting the Soviets practically fell over each other to stick together before the Americans could split them up. Two American members—the Pentagon civilian representative, Michael Mobbs, and another delegate, William Spahr—found their opposite numbers already seated together, rather than separately, as Rowny wanted. As arranged, Mobbs and Spahr turned on their heels and left the room rather than join the larger groups. It was the first walkout of START.

The issue finally brought the two chief negotiators to a heated confrontation during a cocktail party. "To us Soviets, form is often as important as substance," Karpov protested. "You Americans don't understand form! You don't realize that form and substance can be the same thing sometimes!" Rowny said yes, he did understand the importance of form, which is precisely why he was making an issue out of the question of small groups. Once he let the Soviets dictate question of "venue and procedure," he would be letting them dictate the agenda, and that would lead to their being able to dictate the terms of an agreement itself. "You're trying to use this point to take over the running of other arrangements," he said.

"Well," replied Karpov, "if you do understand the importance of form, why is the American side trying to change the form now, after all this time?"

"Because," said Rowny, "you're dealing with a new set of Americans. And you're dealing with me."

It all ended in a compromise. Post-plenaries would follow Rowny's rules of order at the U.S. headquarters, while the Soviets could do it the old way on their own turf. Whatever it may have accomplished, the episode did not raise Rowny in the estimation of the Soviets—or in that of some of his own countrymen, especially when he sent back a cable to Washington playing up the incident and boasted to colleagues about how he had "hung tough, and the other guy blinked."

Rowny and Karpov browbeat each other about the favorite slogans and code words of their governments. Rowny emphasized the goals of equality and stability, both of which meant in practice depriving the Soviets of ICBMs while letting bombers and cruise missiles "run free." When Karpov countered with his side's insistence on "equal security," Rowny retorted that the phrase could have no meaning as long as the U.S. alone refrained from aggression. "Get yourselves better attitudes and international behavior," he said, "and you won't have the same defense needs." When Karpov tried to elaborate on a recent proposal by Gromyko that the superpowers join in a pledge to renounce the first use of nuclear weapons, Rowny cut him off abruptly. The matter was one of "utilization policy," he said; it had "no place in our talks."

As the round drew to a close, Rowny drafted an eight-page report on how the talks had gone and circulated it to all the agency heads who had been involved in arms control. It struck many of its readers as a mixture of self-delusion and self-congratulation. Rowny professed to be encouraged that "we got a lot further than I expected we would in identifying the points of difference." He was given to flattering himself for having impressed the Soviets with his experience, toughness, and ability to "cut through the nonsense." Unlike SALT II, he said, START was "remarkably free of polemics."

In fact, a good day in START contained far more polemics, and far less progress, than a bad day in SALT. Rowny was spending much of his time staging walkouts and delivering lectures in part because there was relatively little real business to transact, given the uncertainties and unresolved conflicts within the American position and the chasm separating the two sides. Rowny sent a condensed version of his report to William Clark with the request that it be forwarded to the President. In this paper, Rowny congratulated the President for the Administration's successful, though razor-thin, victory in Congress over the advocates of a nuclear-weapons freeze.* Among other things, said Rowny, the defeat of the freeze resolution had strengthened his hand as a negotiator. He meant that if the new programs like MX, Trident II, Stealth, and cruise missiles had been discarded by the Congress, he would not have been able to use them for bargaining in Geneva.

---

*On August 6, the House of Representatives backed Administration arms policies against proponents of an immediate freeze by a margin of two votes (204–202); a freeze resolution in the Senate had died in the Foreign Relations Committee in June.

A Busy, Bitter Recess

But the fact was that those weapons, and above all cruise missiles, had yet to be dealt into Rowny's hand by the Administration. It was questionable that they ever would be. Dividing START into two phases and consigning cruise missiles and throw-weight to Phase II had seemed a clever compromise back in May when the Administration cobbled together its opening proposal. But, once they had made the move from Washington to Geneva, and from dealing with each other to dealing with the Soviets, U.S. officials discovered that the phasing gimmick was a handicap. The two-phase structure of START deprived the negotiators of leverage against the Soviets, while it increased the leverage of Perle and the Pentagon against the State Department.

As the two principal elements in Phase II, cruise missiles and throw-weight were like quarrelsome Siamese twins: they were mismatched in almost every way, but they were impossible to separate. Once the interagency review of START got underway during the first recess, it quickly degenerated into a dialogue that was oddly similar to the one that had taken place with the Soviets in Geneva, and every bit as futile. The State Department would ask, "What about cruise missiles?" and the Pentagon would respond, "What about throw-weight?"

During a meeting with Secretary Shultz, James Goodby suggested that the U.S. had what he called a "window of opportunity" to get a deal in START. The window might stay open for about a year. The INF talks were under the deployment deadline of late 1983; the Soviets were clearly most anxious to negotiate severe limits on the upgrading of NATO missiles, and it was possible that they would be more forthcoming in START as long as there was a chance of progress in INF. Also, Reagan had about a year before the onset of the next presidential election season would complicate decision-making. For their part, the Soviet leaders might be eager to consolidate their gains in arms control before the passing of Brezhnev and the other members of the gerontocracy brought on a transition period, during which their successors would have difficulty signing a lasting agreement, or perhaps would be disinclined to do so.

As on other occasions when he was being lobbied on arms control, Shultz was Buddha-like. He listened attentively but impassively, and he took no stand. He had just emerged from the struggle over whether the Administration should abandon its zero proposal in INF and endorse Nitze's walk-in-the-woods fallback. He had seen the President side with Weinberger against a key aspect of that plan, the sacrifice of the Pershing II. Shultz was not ready to enter a similar fray over START, so the issue remained deadlocked.

.   .   .

There was another piece of unfinished business that had been, and would remain, largely hidden from view, but it was related to a matter of intense public debate: could a nuclear war be fought and won? For the experts, the question eni.ailed the three r's: reload, refire, and reconstitution. Could the Soviets store large numbers of back-up (or reload) missiles, reconstitute their forces after absorbing an American nuclear strike, fire the missiles from launchers that had already been used—and thus have an advantage in a war? If that danger was real, and could play a decisive part in determining the winner, what could the U.S. do to forestall it? The more feasible one considered a controlled, protracted nuclear conflict, the more compelling was the argument that the U.S. should insist in INF on the prohibition of refire SS-20s, and that it should insist in START on monitoring and limiting the inventory of all Soviets ICBMs, deployed and undeployed.

The Reagan White House and Pentagon were giving more thought than previous administrations to the development of a nuclear war-fighting and war-winning capability. This was evident in the Defense Guidance and the targeting master plan that had so preoccupied the Joint Chiefs of Staff during the optioneering over START early in the year. If there was one individual in the Administration who personified the seriousness with which it took the task of nuclear-war fighting, he was Thomas K. Jones, Deputy Under Secretary of Defense for Research and Engineering, Strategic and Theater Nuclear Forces. T. K. Jones, as he was called, had worked for Paul Nitze on SALT and for private industry as a weapons expert. He was a friend and protégé of Richard Perle's.

A tall, slim, mild-mannered, scholarly-looking man with modishly styled, prematurely gray hair and an oddly distracted, almost mechanical way of speaking, Jones struck a number of people who met him as the human prototype for C-3PO, the interpreter-droid in the *Star Wars* saga. He found himself the center of a roiling controversy when in a newspaper interview he ventured the opinion that the U.S. could not only survive an all-out nuclear war but could regain its prewar gross national product in a few years, if only everyone built backyard bomb shelters: "If there are enough shovels to go around, everybody's going to make it. It's the dirt that does it."

Jones and others in the Pentagon were working with "post-exchange recovery scenarios," some of which covered periods as long as five years and assumed as many as a hundred million dead on each side. It was part of Jones's critique of SALT II that the treaty

would limit firepower in a short-spasm war, but would leave completely uncapped the firepower that the Soviets could bring to bear in a protracted war. That's another incentive for them to plan for a protracted war. It's well known that the Soviets have the capacity to reload their launchers, while we don't have any reloadable arms. Our silos aren't designed for it. Theirs are. Our silos are built by engineers with a one-shot mentality; theirs are built by artillery guys. An artillery piece is meant to fire lots of shells.

The analogy was somewhat misleading. A spare artillery shell can be loaded in an instant. What Jones was calling reload ICBMs would have to be taken out of storage facilities, put on railroad cars, transported hundreds of miles to transshipment points, loaded onto trucks and hauled, along with a great deal of cumbersome equipment, to silos for launching. Moreover, the Soviets would have to carry out this time-consuming and complicated procedure while a nuclear war was in progress. It was true that they did rehearse the procedure in peacetime, but that was largely because SALT II had banned the storage of extra missiles near launchers.

Jones believed that, despite the logistical problems, the Soviets might put their refire capability to use in a militarily threatening way. He argued that negotiations should involve the toughest possible prohibition against having such a capability and the toughest verification measures to make sure the prohibition was obeyed. In INF, Jones was one of those who fought hard to get the Soviets to accept concessions to provide no-refire verification and thus prevent the Soviets from storing reload SS-20s in a nearby vehicle. In START, too, Jones and Perle were determined to make sure that the U.S. ended up with the right, in Jones's words, to "monitor all production and storage facilities, with on-site monitoring during the initial round of inspections, then inventory and production counts to come afterwards. This will mean intrusive on-site inspection, but the Soviets will accept it if they want real arms control."

As it happened, the Soviets were beginning to suggest that, in certain circumstances, they might accept "cooperative measures," including possibly on-site inspection. One reason may be that they were worried about cruise missiles, which were notoriously difficult to verify because they were so small and mobile, and which represented an American advantage. It was almost certainly with cruise missiles in mind that they were shifting from their standard declaration about the adequacy of "national technical means" (spy satellites and remote ground stations) to a new, cryptic formulation: "verification must be adequate for the system being verified." But, even if they gave up their traditional objection that on-site inspection constituted an infringement on their sovereignty, nothing in these hints suggested that they would permit the kind of intrusion that Jones envisioned. Making that point, however, was difficult in the atmosphere of the Reagan Administration because it entailed consideration of what was negotiable.

The question of what to do about refire and reconstitution had originally been intended for presidential attention, and resolution, at the NSC meeting that was devoted largely to collateral restraints (the sublimits of 210/110 on heavy and medium ICBMs) on June 25, the day that Rowny and his team took off for Geneva. As quickly became apparent at that meeting, so much disagreement remained at the interagency level that there was no way it could be resolved by the NSC. So, like decisions on phasing and the fate of cruise missiles, a decision on the nature of a refire ban was postponed.

T. K. Jones had been under tight wraps for some months, ever since the uproar over his "enough shovels" line. But the growing intramural dispute over refire brought him out. He decided to attend interagency meetings to argue the Pentagon's side of the case. "The trouble with you guys," he said in one meeting with representatives of the other government agencies, "is that you only think about the first salvo. We've got to think about the second, and the third, and maybe the fifth or sixth."

Yet, even conceding for the sake of argument that reconstitution was a legitimate military problem, quite a few experts throughout the government felt strongly that it was not an appropriate problem for arms control to deal with. U.S. military intelligence knew the location of Soviet storage sites and rail lines that could be used to transport extra missiles to launching areas, and these could be targeted in the Single Integrated Operational Plan, or SIOP. The U.S. could be far more certain of hitting those targets with its warheads than it could be of forcing the Soviets to give the U.S. in START a search warrant to conduct on-site inspection at factories and storage areas from one end of the U.S.S.R. to the other.

The debate over whether the U.S. could or should limit the inventory of all Soviet missiles was neither the finest nor the happiest hour for the intelligence community. Earlier in the year, Weinberger and Perle had enlisted the support of William Casey and one of his top aides, Henry Rowen. Rowen had spoken favorably about a "refire ban" in the Senior Interagency Group well before the START proposal had even taken shape, and Casey seconded Weinberger's call for the same thing at the first NSC meeting on START April 21.

The only senior intelligence official to question the wisdom of trying to ban excess undeployed missiles and then verify such a ban had been Admiral Bobby Inman. At the NSC meeting on May 21, Inman had argued strenuously against what he saw as the pernicious absolutism of his colleagues. He warned against "an inflated view of what on-site inspection can accomplish." Even *with* on-site inspection, the U.S. would still be a long way from certainty that the Soviets were not cheating. Inspectors, he pointed out, could be fooled as easily as satellites—sometimes much more easily. Fred Iklé passed Weinberger a note, prompting Weinberger to ask of Inman, "But you would concede that on-site inspection would improve verification?"

"It might," replied Inman, "but to what benefit and at what cost? We shouldn't expect to achieve Soviet agreement to on-site inspection unless we're prepared to give up something that they want very much."

By August, however, when the issue came to a head again, Inman had left the government, and Casey and Rowen still favored a refire ban in principle. Knowing their bosses' view, the career experts began producing papers and making oral presentations that were couched in equivocations, jargon, abstruse technical disclaimers, and platitudes. As Casey himself put it at a number of meetings, "We can verify anything if we have enough information." That suggested the U.S. should do everything it could to get enough information, but it begged the question of how much information the U.S. could realistically expect to get.

Perle and the Office of the Secretary of Defense were seeking "inventory limits" on all missiles, deployed and undeployed. Each side would be allowed 850 deployed missiles, plus an additional allotment for purposes of test firings, spares, etc. The figure of 10 to 15 percent was often cited as a reasonable allowance above the ceiling on deployed missiles. Anything beyond that limit would be a violation of the treaty. Verification of compliance required that the Soviets declare where their inventories were and that the U.S. have the right to inspect any suspicious-looking factory, warehouse, railway car, or rail-to-road transshipment point, as well as launch sites. The more secret the Soviet facility, the more open it should be to American inspection. The State Department favored a less ambitious proposal that would represent a strengthening of the rapid-reload restrictions in SALT II.

Rowny's position on verification was, as on almost everything else, Hamlet-like. Having heard Weinberger make his pitch for on-site inspection, Rowny told a member of his staff, "He's making my negotiating job harder." But then he quickly added, "Of course, that may be *his* job. No one ever told me that this was supposed to be easy, nor is it Weinberger's responsibility to make it so." For the record, Rowny took the position of "not excluding" a provision for on-site inspection, but to look for other, less intrusive, more negotiable ways of assuring Soviet compliance.

As time went on, and Perle had a chance to work on him in quiet chats and phone calls at the end of the day, Rowny's stance hardened. He did not want to appear to be deterred from seeking tough provisions by questions of "mere" negotiability. "I'm not going to let negotiability drive my instructions," he said on a number of occasions. Nor did he want to end up on the State Department's side in the increasingly polarized interagency process.

When the question of what to do about refire came before the NSC on August 9, George Shultz started a discussion of the problem that ended up undercutting his own department's position and reinforcing the Pentagon's. At first, he followed his talking points closely, concentrating on the argument that, almost no matter how intrusive the accompanying verification measures, any set of measures designed to prohibit the Soviets from hiding excess missiles other than at launch sites was basically unverifiable. More-over, for the U.S. to rely on such measures would be self-deluding: "We might think we've solved the problem when actually we haven't at all." There could never be a certainty that somewhere hidden away in that vast and secretive country there was not a secret stockpile of missiles the U.S. knew nothing about. "Someday," said Shultz, "we might see some suspicious behavior, and when we challenge them, they would say, 'Yeah, we've got 20,000 extra missiles. What are you going to do about it?' "

Now the Secretary of State was departing from the script his aides had prepared for him. By voicing this concern, he was lending support to the Pentagon. It was the danger of just this kind of Soviet breakout that led Weinberger, Perle, and T. K. Jones to want an inventory limit. Shultz had no intention of changing sides or bolstering the Pentagon's position. He was simply trying to keep an open mind. He had been spared having to listen to the hours, weeks, and months of debate that had gone on at the lower levels of the government, where the battle lines were already firmly drawn. He was using an NSC meeting to think and worry out loud, and to seek useful answers to genuine questions.

Reagan was in a similar situation. He said he could imagine the possibility that Shultz had described, but he still thought that the inhibition against cheating posed by the high probability that at least some of the illegally stored missiles might be discovered would serve as "some deterrent" against the Soviets' taking a chance. Nevertheless, he still had his doubts. "Why," he inquired, "is it really all that important [whether the Soviets cheat or not]? Will there be anyone or anything left after we've hit them?"

The answer came from the new chairman of the Joint Chiefs, General John Vessey. He agreed with the skepticism implicit in Reagan's question. For some time, the Chiefs had tended to downplay the danger of what the Soviets could do with excess missiles once a war was underway. The danger that Vessey and his military colleagues worried about was one of breakout and blackmail, not fighting a war. If the Soviets had a hidden, illegal inventory of missiles that they could suddenly make use of in a crisis, they would be in a far stronger position to dictate terms to the U.S. In other words, it was precisely the possibility that Shultz had raised of the Soviets' suddenly being able to confront the U.S. with a hitherto undetected back-up arsenal that made Vessey feel that "reconstitution is a real issue, and one we've got to try to get a handle on by somehow limiting refire."

Shultz interjected that he could see how the worries about whether the Soviets had a large stockpile of excess missiles and could reconstitute their forces might contribute to "the perception of overwhelming [Soviet] advantage" and that perception, in turn, "could have political consequences." He conceded that "Cap's got a point on this." This line was getting to be a refrain in the Administration's deliberations.

Reagan himself went further. He said he could see how there was enormous uncertainty about how much confidence could be achieved with on-site inspection and he agreed with Shultz that the U.S. must not kid itself on that score. But it would be indefensible for the Administration in effect to throw up its hands and walk away from the issue. The Administration would be held accountable—by the Senate, he implied—if it failed even to try to improve verification in a way that narrowed the Soviets' latitude to cheat. Then and there he decided that the proposed measures—i.e., an inventory limit and whatever verification arrangements were necessary to enforce it—were "far from perfect, but they are better than nothing."

That left the question of how many excess missiles should be allowed. During much of the preliminary work on the refire issue, the figure of 10 to 15 percent had been bandied about as a reasonable "overage" for missiles that could be used in tests and training exercises. But McFarlane reported that the figure had risen dramatically—to 30 to 50 percent. The Joint Chiefs of Staff wanted a high number of excess missiles because they were planning on producing and stockpiling many more MXs than they would actually deploy.

Reagan exclaimed, "Gee! That seems awfully high. What good does that do if we're trying to make sure that the Soviets don't have a lot of leftover missiles?" The Pentagon representatives shifted uneasily in their chairs. Vessey, somewhat defensively, explained that because the MX was a new weapons system the U.S. needed to manufacture a lot more than it would actually deploy (the plan of the Air Force at that time was to produce as many as 250 missiles and deploy 100 of them). This feature of the Pentagon's position was greeted back at the State Department with disgust and derision. Once again, as with the 850 launcher ceiling, the Chiefs had complicated the design of the U.S. proposal by bending it to fit American military requirements.

Rowny wanted as much flexibility as possible in the timing and manner in which to confront Karpov with what could only be an unpleasant surprise. He said that it would be "the feat of the century" if he could get the Soviets to accept on-site inspection. He clung to the hope that he might pull off that feat if he could ease Karpov into a discussion of the issue in the right way, gradually and gently, as part of the "broader dialogue on stability" in which Rowny so wanted to engage the Soviets. The delegation was instructed to tell the Soviets the U.S. was concerned about nondeployed missiles and the problem would have to be addressed in a treaty. The Soviets listened closely, their eyebrows arched skeptically. After a delay to check with Moscow, Karpov said that the American proposal sounded "contrived and artificial"; surely whatever problem was posed by the existence of extra missiles could be handled with a SALT II–like measure proscribing refire and rapid-reload.

Cross Purposes

The Administration had worked itself into a frenzy over the inventory limit, which was essentially a side issue. Verification does not become a central issue in arms control until there is some possibility of an agreement to be verified. The far more relevant question of what to do about cruise missiles —and thus advance the negotiations—had been left to languish.

Perle was still holding out for exempting ALCMs from START unless and until the Soviets accepted significant constraints on their anti-aircraft defenses. Even more troublesome were long-range SLCMs. Goodby still felt that the only solution was to ban them altogether. Burt was for trading them off against the Soviet Backfire bomber. He now believed that of all the weapons on the agenda in START the sea-launched cruise missile was unique, in that it had very real value as a conventionally armed weapon, as a long-range anti-ship weapon, and as a tactical, or regional (as opposed to strategic), weapon, especially in what he called "Third World contingencies, when we're looking for a way to project power ashore." Many of the same things were true of the Backfire. Backfire and sea-launched cruise missiles were, he said, "classic gray-area systems." That made the SLCM a good piece of negotiating coinage for extracting Soviet concessions on Backfire.

Perle's position was similar to the one he was then taking in INF with regard to ground-launched cruise missiles. He agreed that SLCMs could be useful to the Navy as conventional weapons. For that reason it was essential, he felt, to make sure that START did not interfere with them. Verifying the distinction between conventionally armed and nuclear-armed SLCMs was extremely difficult. Moreover, since SLCMs were easier to hide on ships than ALCMs were on planes, verifying SLCMs in general was, he said, "an insurmountable problem." Therefore his solution was simple: no limits whatsoever on sea-launched cruise missiles.

On the issue of refire ICBMs and the reconstitution of strategic forces during a nuclear conflict, Perle had invoked verification as a reason for the most stringent possible constraints, and the most intrusive "cooperative measures" for monitoring those constraints. The difficulty of verifying an inventory limit on undeployed missiles was, to him, all the more reason to seek tight limits and to acquire whatever inspection rights might be necessary to overcome the difficulties of verification. Yet, on the issue of SLCMs, Perle invoked verification as a reason not to seek any limits at all. He was blunt about the difference between the two cases: ICBMs were a Soviet advantage, so the U.S. had to worry about cheating; cruise missiles were an American advantage, so the worry did not arise.

Perle was now alternately boycotting the process and obstructing it when he participated. Jonathan Howe, in his capacity as chairman of the START

Interagency Group, kept phoning Perle, the principal Pentagon member, and saying, "Richard, we really need your office's input on this cruise-missile question. . . . Richard, where's your paper on cruise missiles?"

"We're working on it, Jon. . . . Patience, Jon, this is a complicated business. We don't want to rush. We're not going to be stampeded."

So the American negotiators in Geneva were still unable to talk about cruise missiles. When they tabled a proposed schedule of reductions for deployed ballistic missiles and warheads, the Soviet reply was: "You should call this a buildup schedule. Where is the schedule for reductions in cruise missiles?" Rowny in turn became convinced that the Soviets were stonewalling because they were waiting to see how the INF talks were going. "That's not right," replied Aleksei Obukhov of the Foreign Ministry. "We're waiting to see how these negotiations are going, and when you're going to get serious in them." When asked why the Soviets were so clearly holding back on revealing the details of their bargaining position, Karpov commented tartly, "You're not ready for it."

In mid-October, Goodby enlisted the help of John McNeill, a lawyer who was a veteran of SALT, to produce a paper that would lay out the "basic elements" of an agreement. It preserved the concept of a treaty that would be implemented in phases, but it allowed the U.S. to specify to the Soviets early in the negotiations what limits on cruise missiles would come into effect in a subsequent phase of the treaty. Rowny submitted this draft to the U.S. delegation. Perle's representative Michael Mobbs argued that it violated the President's orders by trying to make cruise missiles negotiable while transparently seeking to undermine the goal of throw-weight limits. Rowny sent the paper back to Washington for consideration by the START Interagency Group in early November. There it sat, too hot to handle.

At meeting after meeting, the State Department representatives and the negotiators would ask that cruise missiles be put on the table in the next round. In reply, Perle, or his deputy Ronald Lehman, would deliver the same speech: "If you take anything from Phase II, you take everything from Phase II." Then Perle gave the screw another turn: "It no longer makes any sense to preserve two phases," he said. "We can't put on the table those Phase II items in which we have an advantage—cruise missiles—without at the same time dealing with something in which the Soviets have a very significant advantage, throw-weight. One way or another, we'll have to make the resolution of issues in Phase I contingent on how other issues are resolved in Phase II. In which case, we won't have two phases any more."

He had, for some time, been building the case for collapsing the phases into a single negotiation toward a single agreement, and he stepped up that effort as the bureaucracy prepared for an NSC meeting on START in late January 1983. This was more than just a replay of the old debate over the extent to which the outcome of Phase I would depend on certain commitments in Phase II, or whether implementation of a Phase I agreement could begin without concrete progress in Phase II negotiations. It was a matter of doing away with phases altogether, abandoning the compromise that Burt and the Chiefs had engineered in the spring. With the changing of the guard in the military high command, the Chiefs were no longer key players.

That meant Rowny was more important as a swing vote. He became the object of intensive lobbying by both sides. Rowny was notorious for changing his mind—and for letting Perle change it. He would tend to side with the State Department while he was in Geneva, but once he returned to Washington, he fell again under Perle's influence. An Interagency Group meeting was coming up on Monday, January 17, as part of the preparation for an NSC meeting the following week. The Friday before, Rowny reassured his delegation and a number of State Department officials that he still opposed collapsing the two phases and making a throw-weight ceiling an immediate goal of START. But over the weekend Perle called Rowny and made a deal.

Rowny told Perle he felt vulnerable to the Soviet charge that the U.S. was holding back in the negotiations, and the best way to rebut the charge was to come forward with a Basic Elements paper along the lines of what Goodby and McNeill had drafted in Geneva. Perle replied that he and the Office of the Secretary of Defense would let Rowny do so if he would support them on the collapse of the two phases. Rowny agreed, and at the Interagency Group meeting on Monday, he shocked his colleagues from State by changing his position 180 degrees. They immediately concluded that Perle had been at work.

At the National Security Council meeting on January 25, Shultz was once again isolated against Weinberger, Rowny, and the Arms Control Agency, with the Joint Chiefs of Staff sitting out the debate. Once again, just as he had been during the final stages of preparing the President's Eureka proposal, McFarlane had to thread his way between conflicting objectives. There was growing sentiment in favor of keeping cruise missiles and throw-weight closely linked and moving them in tandem forward into Phase I. At the same time the State Department felt—and McFarlane agreed—that collapsing the phases would jeopardize the credibility, not to mention the negotiability, of the U.S. position.

The result, in the form of McFarlane's National Security Decision Directive, was another tortured compromise. Rowny would be granted his request to table a Basic Elements paper, which would "not alter the basic U.S. approach to phased negotiations." He would be instructed to make clear to the Soviets that the new American willingness to discuss limits on cruise missiles—and that meant ALCMs only—would be dependent on Soviet willingness to discuss throw-weight.

Edwin Meese treated the NSDD as an ingenious piece of statecraft. "A concept of two phases still exists," he explained, "but the discussion has been broadened. It shows our flexibility." Burt, Eagleburger, and others at the State Department were relieved but less impressed. They saw the NSDD as a noble effort at damage-limitation by McFarlane, but one that hardly solved the problem, or made Rowny's job any easier. To the tune being played over and over in Geneva Rowny could now add another stanza: "What about limits on throw-weight?"

Rehearsals in the Bubble

The START negotiating round in early 1983 reached new lows, both between the U.S. and the Soviet delegations and among the Americans themselves. Rowny, now that he was back in Geneva and therefore thinking about negotiability again, wanted to table a Basic Elements paper that would catch the Soviets' attention with a precise proposal on cruise missiles while keeping the throw-weight aspect vague. That plan won the approval of the delegation as a whole, except for Perle's representative, Michael Mobbs. He announced that he would not accept the group's decision. After a complicated and heated dispute, he gathered up his papers and declared, "I am under instructions to go home." There was a flurry of phone calls across the Atlantic, and the NSC staff split the difference. In the Basic Elements paper ALCMs would be handled the delegation's way, and throw-weight would be handled the Pentagon's way. Both proposed limits would be defined, and Mobbs could stay in Geneva.

Once the Basic Elements paper was on the table, the Americans tried to play it up as "a constructive and responsive step, conducive to progress: now bomber limitations and cruise missile loadings are discussible." The Soviets' comeback was swift and dismissive: "It's no concession at all. As far as we're concerned, those matters have always been discussible. You'll recall we've raised them for discussion more than once." Then they would ask over and over again, in plenary and post-plenary exchanges: "Why are only ALCMs limited in your draft?"

Because, came the American reply, GLCMs are covered in INF: "The President has proposed banning them from the face of the earth." The Soviets had heard that one before. They knew those words meant also banning SS-20s from one end of the U.S.S.R. to the other. "And what about SLCMs?"

"Well, SLCMs pose serious verification problems. Have you got any ideas?"

"Yes," said the Soviets. "Ban them from the face of the earth."

Osadchiyev went further with a sardonic crack: "You've already made cruise missiles into Stealth weapons: they're invisible in these negotiations and invulnerable to limitation."

The Soviets had used their own recess to do some fairly detailed though tendentious analysis of the proposed treatment of ballistic missiles. They were now ready to complain a bit more elaborately than before that in the hypothetical and "totally excluded" event that they were to accept the American proposal, the result would be a "90 percent cut in our most valued systems." The real purpose of START, said Karpov, was to "emasculate" Soviet defenses.

Rowny responded, "We'll give you the benefit of the doubt and assume that you really don't understand." He and his team then devoted an entire plenary session, on February 22, to an "analytical and illustrative examination of how our proposal would impact on your forces and options." It was a tiresome exercise for both sides. It did nothing to sway the Soviets, and for the American negotiators, the preparation for plenaries was becoming a rare form of torture. Rowny would assemble his troops in the "bubble" (or "padded cell" as some of its inmates came to refer to it), the specially designed, bug-proof chamber in the Botanic Building where secrets could be openly discussed. Then he would subject his colleagues to a not-so-dramatic reading of the entire script of his plenary statement for the upcoming session.

Two days later, Rowny devoted another long plenary statement to analyzing the impact of the Soviet proposal on U.S. forces. Once again, the principal topic was cruise missiles. The Soviets had been, from the beginning of START, insisting on a prohibition of all cruise missiles—ALCMs, SLCMs, and GLCMs—with ranges more than 600 kilometers. This was "totally unacceptable," said Rowny. Moreover, it represented an attempt to renege on SALT II. In that treaty, the Soviets had accepted an allowance for ALCMs on specially designated heavy bombers.

"You accepted ALCMs before," said Rowny. "Why can't you accept them now?"

Karpov's reply was abrupt and something less than a full answer: "We didn't just accept ALCMs before. We accepted SALT II. You did not. Now you want something different from SALT II, and we want a ban on ALCMs."

Another provision in the Soviet proposal would have effectively blocked the Trident II program, to which the Soviets had also resigned themselves in SALT II. The U.S. would not be able to deploy Trident II SLBMs on the Trident submarines that were already coming into service; the Navy would have to go back to the drawing board and develop an entirely new, smaller submarine just for the new missile. "That would take ten years," protested Mobbs.

Osadchiyev replied sourly, "Well, at this rate, we're going to be talking for at least ten years, so that's no problem. Besides, your proposal involves certain inconveniences for us. If you insist on letting this process drag out, it is not necessarily our side that will suffer. Before we had to negotiate from a position of being five years behind. Now we're not behind you. Nor do we intend to be, ever again."

A number of Americans sensed that on both the ALCM and SLBM issues, the Soviets were making purely tactical demands. Their purpose was to show that two could play the game of repudiating SALT and using arms-control proposals to "emasculate" the other side's weapons programs. They were also probably setting up tactical concessions to make when the time was ripe. But that point had not arrived. On March 10, Karpov pronounced judgment on the whole round: "You're still not interested in doing business."

Nor was his own side. The Soviets were going through the motions of a negotiation while waiting to see what happened to the American proposal, what happened in INF, what happened with the Administration's defense budget and MX plan, and what happened more generally in the American political arena.

The Hit List

In mid-March, morale among the Americans in Geneva fell even further. Here the contrast with INF was largely a matter of the personalities of the two chief negotiators. In INF, there was little sign of progress and dwindling hope, but Nitze still commanded immense respect from his delegation. Rowny's standing could not have been more of a contrast. His susceptibility to Perle's influence when he was in Washington was a source of confusion and discouragement. His ponderous style made staff meetings an ordeal. His efforts at bonhomie often came across as buffoonery, and he had a knack for making everyone else feel foolish when he made a fool out of himself, especially when he made fun of the enterprise in which they were all engaged. At a birthday party for one of the secretaries in the Botanic Building, Rowny pulled out his harmonica and asked his colleagues to sing along while he played "the arms control theme song." Dutifully, but none too joyously, they joined in. The song was "I'm Forever Blowing Bubbles."

There had been rumors for weeks that before leaving Washington in January, Rowny had prepared a "secret hit list" with derogatory comments about members of his own delegation and officials of the Arms Control Agency. Rowny's stonefaced response to the rumor was simply, "There is no hit list."

In early March the story leaked in Washington that Rowny had indeed given Kenneth Adelman, the controversial director-designate of the Arms Control Agency, a memorandum commenting on various officials. Goodby, for example, was declared suspect on grounds of being too eager for an agreement.

Rowny's initial response was to release a statement regretting the revelation of "talking points prepared for me" and denying that they reflected his thinking either at the time they were written or at present. The phrasing—prepared for, not by, Rowny—was widely noted. In a speech to his staff about the whole affair, Rowny tried to change his image from Captain Queeg to General MacArthur. He struck the pose of a seasoned, battle-scarred old soldier who for decades had always been willing to lead the charge, to deflect the fire from his troops, and to take the heat. "It's a first principle with me," he said, "that the buck stops with the guy in command." Just when it looked as if he was going to accept responsibility for the memo, Rowny added, "However, this case is exceptional," and he owed it to the delegation to pass the buck. The memo, he declared, was the doing of his long-time aide, Samuel Watson. The disgust among Rowny's troops was now complete. They all knew that, while the memo may have come out of Watson's typewriter, the contents came straight from Rowny.

Almost every day more of the Rowny memo leaked out. A copy was now in the hands of the Senate Foreign Relations Committee, which was still considering, more skeptically than ever, Adelman's nomination. Members of that committee told Senator Gary Hart that he too was mentioned on the hit list. Rowny's message to Adelman included a request that Hart, an arms-control advocate and occasional official visitor to Geneva, be kept away from the talks. Furious over what he called "a total lack of understanding over how our system works and the balance of powers between the two branches of the government," Hart called for Rowny's dismissal.

What had begun as a new, embarrassing, and potentially disastrous wrinkle in the Adelman affair had now raised questions about whether Rowny himself could survive. The director of the Arms Control and Disarmament Agency and the chief U.S. arms-control negotiator had come to symbolize the ineptitude and deviousness that many critics, particularly on Capitol Hill, associated with the Administration's arms-control policies as a whole. One of those critics, Congressman Les Aspin, told Robert McFarlane, "If you guys want to buy yourselves some political running room for START, there are two ways you can do it. You can change the players—fire Rowny and Adelman; otherwise you've got to change the negotiating position."

Rowny and Adelman stayed in place. But, with the Congress's attention now thoroughly engaged, the Administration's negotiating position did begin to change.

16 The Outsiders Step In

At the end of 1982, President Reagan met over breakfast with William Clark to review the old year and look ahead to the new. As the meeting was later described by Robert McFarlane at a press briefing, Reagan told Clark that he believed there would be an opportunity in 1983 to make real progress with the Soviets in arms control, and it was time for a major new political offensive. But, to capitalize on that opportunity, there would have to be allied cohesion in INF and congressional backing for his defense program. The first goal seemed to be well in hand. The allies were holding firm on deployment. But the President was concerned about Congress. He directed Clark, George Shultz, and Caspar Weinberger to begin work on Capitol Hill. The key inside man for this campaign, the one who coordinated the approaches of cabinet members and undertook many of his own, was McFarlane himself.

The White House wanted it to seem that Reagan was taking the initiative. In fact, the Administration was reacting to the imminent danger of a congressional mutiny over the MX. In addition to being expensive and controversial, the missile was also homeless. Some thirty-three schemes had been proposed, and Congress had not liked any of them, including "the shell game" (moving the missile around within a cluster of holes), "the race track" (moving it around a loop with protective shelters along the way), "Big Bird" (keeping it constantly airborne on a cargo plane), and "DUMB" (deep underground missile basing, with a corkscrew-like device fitted on the missile launcher that would burrow up to the surface for firing).

The thirty-fourth suggestion, "Closely Spaced Basing," or "Dense Pack," had aroused more opposition and ridicule than any of its predecessors. Under this scheme, the survivability of the American missiles would depend upon a phenomenon called fratricide, whereby incoming Soviet warheads were supposed to destroy each other, or at least throw each other sufficiently off course to miss many of the American silos. The plan thus attempted to make a virtue out of vulnerability; it would "work" by seeming to invite a massive blitz by Soviet nuclear weapons.

Les Aspin remarked that the MX was in trouble partly because it had acquired such a high "snicker factor." Edward Rowny hardly helped when he linked the prospects for progress in START to congressional approval of Dense Pack. "A decision not to deploy the MX/CSB [Closely Spaced Basing] would not only undercut my negotiating leverage, but would require a reassessment of our START proposal," he told the Senate. Such a reassessment could only be taken to mean that, unless Congress supported the Administration on the MX, the U.S. would adopt an even tougher negotiating posture toward the Soviets in Geneva. Rowny's threat made no new friends for the Administration on Capitol Hill when it desperately needed them.

Congress was beginning to consider seriously the alternative of abandoning the multiple-warhead MX altogether and developing instead a small, single-warhead, mobile missile that would neither threaten nor tempt a preemptive strike. A formidable array of officials within the Administration had tried and failed in early 1982 to make START an incentive for de-MIRVing on both sides and, on the American side, to replace the MX with what Paul Nitze called "little guys." This effort had failed because the Joint Chiefs of Staff, with the support of the State Department, had succeeded in using START instead to reinforce the rationale for MX by pushing for a low launcher ceiling. Such a ceiling made sense only if both sides put as many warheads as possible on as few rockets as possible.

By 1983, de-MIRVing was no longer esoteric; it had become fashionable. Little guys, under the nickname Midgetman, now had promoters ranging from liberal Democratic congressmen to moderate Republicans to Henry Kissinger. Suddenly it seemed that everyone had a plan for how to break the stalemate in START. Every plan seemed, one way or another, to feature de-MIRVing. And de-MIRVing meant, at the very least, deemphasizing the MX. If the missile was to go forward at all, it should be primarily as an inducement for the Soviets eventually to join the U.S. in a move toward small, single-warhead ICBMs.

A new theme cropped up in White House briefings on START. McFarlane started saying that the President saw the MX as roughly analogous to the anti-ballistic missile (ABM) system over which the Nixon Administration and Congress had locked horns in the late 1960s. Had Congress not approved Nixon's program to deploy the ABM in 1969, there would probably never have been a SALT I ABM Treaty in 1972 since the Soviets would have had little incentive to restrict their own ABM system. "We've got to replicate that now," McFarlane quoted the President as saying.

For that analogy to be plausible, two unlikely things had to happen. First, the MX had to be accepted as a genuine bargaining chip—something the U.S. would actually give up, or at least severely curtail, in exchange for the right concessions on the Soviet side. Second, START had to seem as promising as SALT had been at the time of the ABM debate. Yet long-standing Administration policy held that the MX was needed in any event, no matter what START accomplished, and anyone could see that the deadlock in Geneva left little hope of progress in START.

The White House tried to generate optimism about the negotiations by changing its rhetoric. The new watchwords were to be bipartisanship, compromise, flexibility, and continuity. "It is terribly important to rebuild a bipartisan consensus on defense and national security that will stick from administration to administration," declared Thomas Reed, a senior member of the NSC staff working to save the MX. Reed, McFarlane, and others did their best to make the public and the Congress forget that they were speaking for a President who had made much of his determination to repudiate the arms-control policies of his predecessors.

The White House was now taking the line that Reagan needed the MX as an inducement for the Soviets to negotiate seriously in START. The fact was that the President wanted the MX so badly that Congress could now use the threat of canceling it as an inducement for him to negotiate seriously. As it happened, the principal negotiations throughout 1983 were not between the U.S. and the Soviet Union, but between the White House and the Congress.

The New START Gang

The Administration needed not just a new tone for its policies; it needed new substance. McFarlane and a few other presidential aides realized that the Administration could probably not come up with a new START position by itself. Its policymaking apparatus was too cumbersome and too divided. As McFarlane set out to define it in practice, "rebuilding a bipartisan consensus" was going to have to be a code word for active, though disguised, collaboration between a small circle of presidential aides and a small circle of moderate legislators and experts from previous administrations. The White House would publicly ask advice from a council of wise men, whisper in their ear what sort of advice would be helpful, then use their response to ram new policies through an impacted, fractious bureaucracy.

Presidents have often used blue-ribbon commissions when they needed new ideas or new support for old ones that have run into trouble. Reagan had set up a commission on the MX before, early in his Administration. But that panel, chaired by Charles Townes, a Nobel Prize–winning physicist from Berkeley, had focused narrowly on the MX-basing problem itself, not on the broader political and arms-control context. In 1982, the commission had given Dense Pack a lukewarm blessing, which did neither the panel nor the basing plan much good in the eyes of Congress.

This time, the White House decided to put together a commission that could, given the nature of its membership and the scale of its mandate, not only save the MX from congressional opposition but rescue the Administration's START policy from itself.

The chairman of the commission was Brent Scowcroft, and his right-hand man was James Woolsey, a young, highly regarded lawyer with experience in government and defense matters. Here were the most respected representatives of the center-right of what Richard Perle had disparaged as "the old SALT gang." Scowcroft had been Kissinger's deputy on the National Security Council staff, Gerald Ford's special assistant for national security affairs, and a member of Jimmy Carter's General Advisory Committee on Arms Control. He was also a retired Air Force lieutenant general who had fought long and hard for the MX.

Woolsey had been an adviser to the U.S. SALT delegation, a member of the NSC staff under Nixon, and Under Secretary of the Navy during the Carter Administration. But lately he had been making a new, more conservative reputation for himself by writing and speaking about the inadequacy of past arms-control agreements and the need for stronger ("more robust") U.S. defenses. He was on close terms with Richard Perle, and occasionally served as an adviser to Senator John Glenn, the most conservative of the Democrats then positioning themselves to run for President in 1984. Scowcroft and Woolsey had served together on the Townes panel, so they had lived through the futility of thinking about the MX as a purely military problem and did not intend to make that mistake again.

McFarlane knew both Scowcroft and Woolsey well. They drew up a list for the rest of the commission. The members and senior counselors were the sort of people the Administration had spurned for the previous two years. Scowcroft's former boss, Henry Kissinger, was on it, along with Kissinger's old debating partner on the throw-weight issue, James Schlesinger. So were Harold Brown and one of his principal deputies, William Perry, and Lloyd Cutler, a Washington lawyer who had worked for Jimmy Carter in the forlorn effort to get SALT II ratified. The one White House insider was Thomas Reed. It was a textbook example of ticket balancing, with something for almost every constituency—except for the anti-MX forces.* This was a commission

---

*Reed resigned from the White House staff, but not from the commission, after questions arose about his having engaged in possible stock-trading improprieties. Vice-President George Bush had some influence on the selection of the commissioners, particularly Nicholas Brady, an investment banker who had helped Bush in his presidential campaign in 1980 and served briefly as an interim, appointed senator from New Jersey. Other members were the most prominent discard from the Reagan Administration, Alexander Haig; two former Republican defense secretaries, Melvin Laird and Donald Rumsfeld; two former CIA directors, Richard Helms and John McCone; William Clements, a Deputy Secretary of Defense under Nixon and Ford who had been one of the godfathers of the cruise-missile program; John Deutch, an MIT scientist who was both an arms-control liberal and a former aide to Schlesinger; John Lyons, an A.F.L.-C.I.O. vice-president and the chairman

that McFarlane intended to have praise the MX, albeit faintly, not bury it.

Although not on the roster of the commission, another key figure in the background was Les Aspin, the Democratic congressman, who had been warning the White House for some time that it was going to have to change its START team or its game plan or both if it wanted to avoid the loss of the MX. Aspin had been pro-SALT and, for a while at least, pro-freeze. Now he was pro-MX, staking out what he called "the middle position that ICBM vulnerability matters, but it's not cause for panic; we need the MX to threaten Soviet ICBMs just enough so that they'll have an incentive to cut back on their biggest ones." That view made Aspin suspect among some of his fellow liberals, but it also made him indispensable to the Administration in its new effort to build a bipartisan consensus. He was the linchpin of that effort on the Hill. Aspin stayed in close touch with other influential legislators, such as Congressman Albert Gore, Jr., one of the most vigorous proponents of de-MIRVing and Midgetman. Aspin was also a close friend of Woolsey's.

Reagan established the President's Commission on Strategic Forces at the beginning of January, and the panel plunged into an intensive series of meetings, numerous small conferences, and interviews with more than two hundred experts. Much of the testimony and advice the commission received was in favor of developing a small, single-warhead ICBM to be based on vehicles that would roam around military reservations; the launchers would be specially hardened against nuclear blasts. The combination of mobility and hardening was supposed to make the new missiles highly survivable. Meanwhile, Woolsey, Scowcroft, and Aspin were meeting over the weekends at their homes, talking about how to guide the commission's deliberations and shape its recommendations. McFarlane stayed in close touch with this inner circle. As the commission moved into its final stage, its members held breakfast meetings with key congressmen like Gore.

The commission's report, drafted largely by Woolsey, appeared on April 6. It was a wide-ranging, artfully crafted compromise. It questioned whether the U.S. faced a "window of vulnerability." So much for a phrase and a concept close to the Administration's heart. This disavowal, though it did reflect the judgment of the members, was also necessary to reinforce the logic of their recommendation to base the MX in fixed silos as a stop-gap until the Midgetman could be developed. If the silos were in fact vulnerable to Soviet attack, it would make little sense to put MX missiles in them. The report also criticized the notion that reductions for their own sake were necessarily good for strategic stability. Specifically, it called on the Adminis-

---

of its committee on defense issues; and Levering Smith, a retired vice-admiral who had been heavily involved in developing new weapons systems.

tration to raise the 850-launcher ceiling in START, since that feature of the proposal—while dramatizing the Administration's desire for deep reductions—would increase the ratio of warheads to targets on both sides and therefore increase the plausibility of a first strike, just as Perle, Nitze, Rostow, and liberal outside critics like Herbert Scoville had pointed out at the time of the Eureka proposal. The report also contained an oblique but unmistakable recommendation that the Administration seek more realistic, negotiable objectives than those embodied in its proposal.

Aspin thought it was important that no one seem too pleased about the report. He had his own political motives. As a liberal Democrat, he wanted to downplay the impression that he was helping a conservative Republican President save the most controversial single item in his defense program. Aspin cautioned Weinberger, "Cap, don't crow when this comes out; we need you to grouse." When Reagan endorsed the commission enthusiastically, Aspin complained to McFarlane. "Couldn't the White House be a little less gracious about this?" he asked facetiously. "Couldn't it look as though you're being dragged kicking and screaming into a new START position? Otherwise, Congress isn't going to believe that you're really moving."

Aspin was also concerned that liberals not wax too enthusiastic either, since that would make the Pentagon and the right wing think that the Administration was being set up for massive compromises. The essence of the whole maneuver was for everyone involved to think he was coopting everyone else, but for no one to think he was being coopted. Richard Burt encountered Aspin at a party and told him the coalition that was forming between the Hill and the commission "may yet get this goddamned Administration off the dime in arms control; just keep the pressure up."

The Build-Downers

On May 24 Aspin's fellow legislators in the House approved resolutions to release funding for further development of the MX. The next day the Senate passed the same resolution. There, too, the Administration found itself having to deal with an impatient, influential arms-control lobby that had its own idea for saving MX and START. The plan was a so-called guaranteed mutual build-down, whereby the addition of each new weapon must be accompanied by the retirement of several old weapons.

The principal advocates of this scheme were two Republicans, William Cohen of Maine and Charles Percy of Illinois, the chairman of the Foreign Relations Committee, and a Democrat, Sam Nunn. All three were advocates of arms control. They were critical of what they saw as the intransigence and impracticality of the Administration's position in START, but they were also against both the freeze and the groundswell of sentiment to kill the MX. They saw the build-down as a moderate alternative to the freeze; it would allow the U.S. simultaneously to reduce and to modernize its arsenal, the professed commitment of the Administration. In fact, its advocates contended that the build-down was more true to the goal of reductions than was the START proposal. The build-down sought "comprehensiveness": the deployment of cruise missiles, like new ballistic warheads, would require the removal of older weapons on more than a one-for-one basis. The Administration's approach virtually exempted cruise missiles from arms control, permitting a vast proliferation of those weapons and thus quite likely paving the way for a net increase in strategic weapons by the 1990s.

The build-down acquired considerable support in the Senate not just because of its conceptual merits, but because, like the de-MIRVing and Midgetman scheme, it filled a vacuum. The Administration had not been able to come up with an arms-control policy that had broad support, and partly for that reason its rearmament program was foundering. The Congress was offering ideas that seemed to make sense for both halves of the national security, diplomacy and defense.

Cohen published an article about the build-down early in January. Ronald Reagan liked the simplicity of the idea; he liked the way it reconciled modernization with reductions. The President telephoned the senator right away and said he was struck by its "compatibility" with START. He overlooked its incompatibility with his own cherished distinction between fast-flyers and slow-flyers.

However, the experts who were making policy in Reagan's name saw almost immediately that the build-down would entail trade-offs between bomber armaments and ballistic missiles, and largely because of this they did not like it at all. They much preferred to accommodate the de-MIRVers and would-be godfathers of Midgetman, who, like the Administration itself, were concentrating on ballistic missiles. But the build-down continued to gather so much support in the Senate that the White House felt obliged to continue making receptive, appreciative noises about how it might be incorporated into START. In May, shortly before the vote on the MX scheduled for the end of that month, Reagan wrote Nunn, Cohen, and Percy, giving the idea of a build-down the most general and noncommittal blessing, saying that it had merit "if formulated and implemented flexibly, and negotiated within the context of our modified START proposal."

Privately, however, Reagan's aides were eager for build-down to go away. "Let's hope," said McFarlane to his staff after a frosty meeting with Cohen, "we can kill the build-down with kindness." The White House tried to study the plan to death. McFarlane told Nunn and Cohen that the build-down scheme was being "thoroughly scrubbed" in the START Interagency Group but that there were a number of troubling questions about whether it was "practical or not." Would the process of taking out old weapons for every new one added begin before there was a more comprehensive agreement? If so, that would be unfair to the U.S., since the Soviets had nearly completed their modernization program, while the U.S. was just beginning its own. What was a new warhead and what wasn't? Was a cruise missile, or a gravity bomb, to be given equal weight with an SS-18 ballistic warhead?

"You're nitpicking," Cohen replied. "Your attitude is one of looking for problems as an excuse not to accept the thing." Cohen warned the Administration to keep in mind that support for the MX in Congress was still "eggshell thin."

The Throw-Weight Restoration Movement

The wise men of the Scowcroft Commission had spoken; carefully selected outsiders had provided the impulse that McFarlane and others had hoped would get things moving inside the Administration. The result was a movement, all right, but it turned out to be another scramble, with State and the Pentagon tugging harder than ever in opposite directions.

Part of the problem was that precisely because the criticisms contained in the Scowcroft Commission's report were so oblique, they were easy to ignore. Perle, for example, was able to deny that the commission was "calling for fundamental change in our arms-control policy—I can't find it anywhere." Moreover, the only specific feature of START that the report recommended altering was the 850 launcher ceiling, which Perle had opposed all along for the same reason the commission did. Now he wanted to reshape the START proposal on the table in Geneva to conform with the option he had tried and failed to get the President to accept a full year before, replacing the low launcher ceiling with a low ballistic-missile throw-weight ceiling.

Like theologians arguing some particularly controversial theory of the nature of good or evil on the basis of a single verse in some holy text, Perle and the other throw-weight enthusiasts based their case on a few scattered sentences in the report, particularly the statement that "attention to throw-weight limitations" in the Administration's START proposal was "consistent with the Commission's recommended program." In another passage, the report urged using arms control to induce the Soviets to "join [the] evolution [toward small mobile missiles] and forgo the current advantages they have in the ability to attack hard targets and to barrage large areas with their preponderance in throw-weight." The commission had given a very general endorsement to "relatively simple agreements . . . that exert pressure to reduce the overall number and destructive power of nuclear weapons," and it called for equal numbers of warheads of roughly equivalent yield—a passage that Harold Brown later described as "a sop to the throw-weight freaks."

It turned out to be much more than a sop; it was an opportunity. Perle's office prepared a draft letter to be sent over the President's signature to the Senate assuring the legislators that the Administration had every intention of complying with the recommendations of the Scowcroft Commission, and it then cited those passages that Perle had seized upon as an endorsement of throw-weight as a unit of account of START. The NSC staff blocked the letter, but in congressional testimony and in articles for newspaper op-ed pages, Weinberger's office continued to work in as many references as it could to throw-weight as "the key measure of strategic capability."

In late May, Aspin arranged for Perle to meet for lunch with a group of congressmen who held the swing votes on the MX. Gore, one of the principal champions of de-MIRVing and Midgetman, listened to Perle preach the merits of throw-weight limits. He became convinced that Perle was trying to sabotage the negotiations, to assure that a bargain was never reached. Afterward Gore told Scowcroft, McFarlane, and Kenneth Adelman in no uncertain terms that his very qualified support for the MX would depend not just on the presence in the new START position of a higher launcher ceiling, but also on the absence of any direct limits on throw-weight.

Adelman had become Perle's principal ally outside the Pentagon. He assured Gore that he was "open-minded" on the issue of throw-weight, then went back to the Arms Control Agency and told a group of colleagues, "We're just going to have to bear this cross of all these little congressmen with their bright ideas and their political-psychological hangups about how it's somehow immoral to try to reduce the Soviet threat by the measure in which it's most threatening."

In conversations with Jonathan Howe and Robert McFarlane, Scowcroft objected to Perle's tactics and warned sternly that the commission would not allow its report to be misused by the Pentagon. Restoring throw-weight as a unit of account would backfire on Capitol Hill, he predicted: "We [the Commission] think that a punitive attempt through arms control to force the Soviets into unilateral throw-weight reductions is not the way to go. Any revision of START in that direction would be counterproductive; it would be disastrous." Howe and McFarlane agreed and were therefore glad to have Scowcroft's message. Howe called it "a silver bullet" to use against Perle. Among the veterans of the great throw-weight debate of 1982, there were wry jokes about "the Throw-Weight Restoration Movement," and it was at this time that handmade signs appeared on walls in the offices of the State Department: "Real Men Don't Need Throw-Weight!"

George Shultz was not a veteran of this old debate, and he had been on the receiving end of considerable lobbying by Weinberger. Much to the dismay of his staff, he remarked in early June, "Cap has a point about throw-weight"—almost an exact echo of what the President had said the year before, leading McFarlane to insert the secret limit of 2.5 million kilograms into Phase I of START.

Burt undertook to persuade Shultz that "Cap's point" about throw-weight was all wrong. He placed in front of Shultz a set of plastic scale models of Soviet and American ICBMs. Pointing to the Minuteman III, Burt said, "This little missile here is twice as destructive with its new warheads [the Mark-12A] as it was with its old ones, yet its throw-weight has remained unchanged." Technology had rendered throw-weight far less important than it used to be. If warheads could be given virtually pinpoint accuracy, and if their explosive power could be increased by more efficient packing of their thermonuclear charge, it was a waste of time, and of negotiating capital, to focus excessively on throw-weight. This was an old and familiar point, and Shultz came back with the equally old and familiar counterpoint: excessive throw-weight of the sort that the Soviets had accumulated on their ICBMs still translated into an unacceptable opportunity for loading extra MIRVs onto the rockets. This much Shultz had learned from his many talks with Weinberger, and he knew it was an issue about which Weinberger was passionate.

So Burt lost another one to the Pentagon. Weinberger, for his part, in addition to enlisting, or at least neutralizing, Shultz, also hoped to make common cause with the new Joint Chiefs of Staff. At the time of the original Eureka proposal, the old Chiefs still had high hopes for the MX; de-MIRV-ing and Midgetman were prematurely dismissed as the pipedreams of the theoreticians. Now, a year later, in response to the Scowcroft Commission and pressure from Capitol Hill, the Administration had virtually adopted de-MIRVing and a commitment to Midgetman. As a result, the new Chiefs had to think much more seriously than their predecessors about protecting Midgetman from Soviet attack. That meant looking afresh at the problem of throw-weight.

The Soviets' undisputed advantage in ICBM throw-weight had always posed a problem of breakout, as the Chiefs had acknowledged. An excess of throw-weight had always entailed the possibility that someday the Soviets might suddenly increase the number of MIRVs on their ICBMs. The question was whether that breakout would be militarily useful to the Soviet Union and therefore militarily threatening to the U.S.

As long as the principal American concern was with the survivability of the U.S.'s hardened ICBM silos, such as those housing Minuteman and now envisioned for the MX as well, the problem was manageable. Soviet hard-target-kill capability was largely a function of accuracy, and honing accuracy meant extensive testing. SALT II prevented the Soviets from testing large ICBMs with more warheads than would actually be deployed; that prohibition deprived them of the option of increasing their arsenal of highly accurate, hard-target-killing MIRVs in a relatively short time.

Midgetman, it was assumed, would be deployed not in hardened underground silos, but on mobile launchers that would roam around military reservations. That meant worrying less about the accuracy of individual Soviet warheads and more about the possibility of a barrage. If the Soviets could blanket U.S. military reservations with blasts that would obliterate mobile launchers on the surface, then Midgetman would be vulnerable. The warheads to carry out such an attack did not need to be particularly accurate; they needed only to have a high yield, or destructive force, which would not require extensive flight testing. Damage to so-called area targets was primarily a function of yield, and yield in turn was a function of throw-weight. So throw-weight was a valid measure of the threat of barraging.

It was this line of thinking that led Vessey and his fellow officers to accept Weinberger's and Perle's argument that, in the event that the Office of the Secretary of Defense did not succeed in getting a direct, explicit limit on missile throw-weight in START, then there must at least be a "codification" of the amount of throw-weight resulting from indirect limits—i.e., on launchers and warheads. How codification would actually work was never clearly defined; different individuals and offices had different plans. But the general idea was that the U.S. would calculate the maximum throw-weight the Soviets could accumulate under whatever launcher and warhead ceilings were included in the agreement; that number would then be plugged into the agreement as a cap to preclude an increase in throw-weight later. That way, the Soviets would be prevented from developing some new, larger ICBM that circumvented the State Department's much-vaunted indirect limits on throw-weight, thereby achieving "throw-weight breakout" with which to barrage Midgetman reservations.

Complicated and hypothetical as all this was, it had a simple and immediate consequence: the Chiefs would not actively oppose Weinberger and Perle the way their predecessors had done. Also, whatever it was supposed to mean at the Pentagon, codification of throw-weight was destined to have the eventual effect in Geneva of reinforcing Rowny's stubbornness on the issue. It exacerbated tensions between him and his delegation, and sharpened Soviet antagonism. Rowny had long been concerned that the Soviets might develop a new medium ICBM that would have greater throw-weight than the SS-19. He often said he could see the pressure building, particularly from the State Department, to relax the collateral restraints on missile launchers "to the point of meaninglessness," as he put it: "I'm not going to the Senate and stand behind a treaty that doesn't deal with throw-weight."

When the time came to present a draft treaty for START, Rowny announced to his delegation that he wanted to make sure that "the Soviets can't exceed a theoretical maximum of throw-weight" of around 3 million kilograms, based on a "snapshot" of the forces that each side would be allowed under an agreement. That way, "we'd have an insurance policy against throw-weight creeping upwards" as the Soviets brought on new missiles. Rowny had the support of Michael Mobbs. What they were pushing for meant that the Soviets would have to accept a direct limit on throw-weight even if the main provisions of the treaty were the indirect limits of the warhead and launcher ceiling. "I want both direct and indirect limits on throw-weight," said Rowny, "so that the direct ones will take up the slack if the indirect ones are relaxed."

Around the State Department there was muttering about how Rowny had thrown a new monkey wrench into the works: how to deal with "throw-weight creep." (Within the delegation in Geneva, Mobbs became known as "our very own throw-weight creep.") Recognizing that the government as a whole would immediately become deadlocked if asked to settle the matter, Robert Einhorn, the Arms Control Agency's representative, cabled his agency recommending that the issue be finessed. James Timbie, still the chief "backstopper" for the delegation, devised what he hoped would be a suitably cryptic reference in the draft treaty to "appropriate measures to deal with destructive capability and potential." That phrase was the working euphemism for throw-weight, and everyone knew what it meant, including the Soviets. "Throw-weight," they kept saying over and over again, "is not an acceptable unit of account."

This whole wrangle had come about because the Midgetman was seen to be more vulnerable to the Soviet big missiles than Minuteman. Thus, the movement inside the Administration to restore throw-weight as the unit of account had received an ironic and certainly unintended boost from the de-MIRVing proponents on Capitol Hill.

Half a Loaf

The question of how to revise the START proposal to take account of the Scowcroft Commission's recommendations went before the National Security Council on June 7, 1983. The State Department favored raising the 850 launcher ceiling to a level around 1,200 (the level State had originally wanted the President to propose at Eureka), doing away with the 2,500 ceiling on land-based warheads (which Karpov had told Rowny was the single most unacceptable and "discriminatory" figure in the entire U.S. package), limiting new types of ICBMs to single warheads (thus promoting de-MIRVing), and offering new, somewhat more lenient collateral restraints on heavy missiles. Instead of the 210/110 aggregate for heavy and medium ICBMs, which would require the Soviets to cut their combined SS-18 and SS-19 force by more than two-thirds and eliminate their SS-17s altogether, State recommended limiting heavy missiles by a half to 150, with no separate limit for medium missiles.

Jimmy Carter had proposed a similar 50 percent cut in the SS-18s as part of his Comprehensive Proposal of March 1977, and he had included a sweetener that the Reagan Administration was not prepared to offer now: cancellation of the MX program. Then, the Soviets had turned him down flat. Once again, the State Department option had the appearance of negotiability only by comparison with the existing START proposal, and by comparison with what Perle wanted to do, which was reintroduce direct limits on throw-weight.

Anticipating stiff opposition from the Pentagon, the State Department advised Shultz to present a compromise plan. The U.S. would give the Soviets a choice of ways to accommodate the American concern with large ICBMs: either they could accept a direct limit on ballistic-missile throw-weight, without separate limits on specific categories of land-based ICBMs, or they could accept the 210/110 collateral restraints on heavy and medium ICBMs as already proposed. The idea originated with Burt and Goodby. They discussed it with Adelman and Howe, so that it might be the unified position of State and ACDA. It was sure to appeal to McFarlane, who had made a specialty of brokering half-a-loaf compromises of just this sort. In this near-anarchy of decisionmaking, the State Department's compromise ended up, almost willy-nilly, as the basis of a new National Security Decision Directive.

Reagan set the tone for that document when he told Clark after the NSC meeting, "I don't want to enshrine one specific approach, or one set of numbers. If there's another solution to the problem, I don't want to be precluded from trying that, too. I would like to get a good agreement, but I'm not going to grovel for just any piece of paper. On the other hand, let's not go for all or nothing if it means we end up getting nothing."

Did that mean changing the basic structure of START? "I don't want to alter our proposal at this time," Reagan said, implying that he wanted to be in a position that would allow him to alter it later. Clark met with the NSC staff after talking to Reagan and paraphrased his boss's thinking this way: "He wants to be seen as moving and he wants to get ready to move, but he doesn't want to move all that much yet."

As usual, it fell to McFarlane to translate these Delphic utterances and conflicting desires into instructions to the government and the negotiators —and into a presidential statement for Reagan to read to the press in the Rose Garden of the White House. The most tortuous passage of the document he prepared was:

> We believe, as does the Scowcroft Commission, that stability can be increased by limitations on the destructive capability and potential of ballistic missiles. As a consequence, we will continue to propose such constraints which indirectly get to the throw-weight problem while

making clear to the Soviets our readiness to deal directly with the corresponding destructive capability if they prefer.

The next day, TASS complained that the President's announcement "does not in any way affect the essence of Washington's position [which is] directed, as before, at gaining military superiority and pressing the Soviet Union into unilateral disarmament." In Geneva, Osadchiyev commented tartly that "Your idea of 'flexibility' is to give a condemned man the choice between the rope and the ax."

Nor was Perle's response to the presidential decision much more favorable than the Soviets'. He complained in the Interagency Group that the presidential directive circulated after the June 7 NSC meeting was filled with "ambiguities that are going to come back to haunt us." While throw-weight was still a factor, it had become less specific. The absence of a stated permissible level was a troublesome departure from the position of the previous year. "A vague decision simply means that issues remain contentious. In the absence of a presidential decision on the appropriate level, the whole U.S. government will continue to argue about what the level should be. The President is being badly served. People acting on his behalf are prolonging and intensifying the discord. They're refusing to face up to the issue."

He did not like the collateral restraints now being couched in language about flexibility: "There's a whole trend in the process now away from concepts and levels that mean something in the real world. All this 'flexibility' stuff is just the foreplay for massive concessions down the road."

Perle's reputation as the Administration's No. 1 anti-arms-control bogeyman and his vocal irritation came in handy at the White House. He was made the in-house straw man. Administration officials encouraged liberal and moderate legislators to infer that the most troublesome features of the U.S. position (the 2,500 and 210/110 subceilings) would soon be relaxed, over Perle's objections. Perle was said to be at last bureaucratically isolated, his ability to veto progress circumscribed; McFarlane was now fully in control, and the President was listening closely to Scowcroft.

Some congressmen may have been fooled, but Scowcroft certainly was not. He knew his name was being used by the White House as a *Good Housekeeping* seal of approval, just as his commission's report had been used earlier by Perle to reinstate throw-weight. As pressure from Capitol Hill continued to build, Reagan had extended the commission's term and expanded its mandate to advise him on arms control. In fact, however, the President was noticeably unreceptive to Scowcroft's advice.

The first week in July, Scowcroft met with Reagan and warned him that there was still a great deal of skepticism on the Hill about the Administration's commitment to arms control, not to mention the chances of an agreement. The President reacted angrily, complaining about what he called the "ill will" of anyone in Congress who would doubt his sincerity. He and every responsible official working for him had said over and over that there was a new flexibility to the American position in START. But Scowcroft did not let up: "Even though you can convey that to some of those who are wavering on the Hill, Mr. President, it is not likely to mean much, given the general perception of the character of Ed Rowny, for whom flexibility tends to be a dirty word." Rowny, he continued, is "perceived as a road block."

Once again, Reagan stiffened. That perception was unfair, he retorted. He strongly reaffirmed his support for Rowny. Reagan had two reasons for sticking by Rowny. One was that Rowny had firm backing from the right wing on the Hill, and Reagan was already under some suspicion in conservative quarters for having allowed veterans of SALT and détente to advise him on defense and arms control.

The President also had a more personal reason to like Rowny. One of his deepest objections to arms control was the way American negotiators had, he believed, tended to reach for an agreement for its own sake. Here, finally, was a negotiator who knew how to say "no" as firmly and as frequently as the Soviets knew how to say "nyet." Rowny could out-stonewall the master stonewallers. Reagan, in short, appreciated Rowny and wanted to keep him for all the reasons that the pro-arms-control lobby on the Hill wanted him out.

17 New Swords, New Shields

One purpose of START was to get the Soviet Union to adopt roughly the same sort of strategic arsenal as the U.S., to rely less on the SS-18 and more on smaller missiles. The emerging consensus in Washington was that the U.S. would develop the MX as a counter to the large, MIRVed Soviet ICBMs but that Midgetman was the real weapon of the future. As it happened, the Soviets were already well along on a program to do part of what the U.S. professed to want them to do: they were developing what Robert McFarlane nicknamed "the Midgetmanski," a light, mobile, single-warhead ICBM. The trouble was that they were also developing an "MXski," a new, MIRVed ICBM, presumably as an eventual replacement for the SS-19 and, no doubt, as a counter to the MX. That was not what the U.S. had in mind at all.

The two-pronged Soviet program was arguably a violation of SALT II. Two men who had joined the Administration at the beginning only to be quickly expelled for their extreme views, Michael Pillsbury and David Sullivan, were now working for a group of right-wing senators, and they seized upon this latest instance of what they considered outright Soviet cheating. The SALT II treaty had limited each side to one new type of ICBM. The U.S.'s new type would be the MX. Midgetman was still just an idea, a gleam in its proponents' eyes. It would not be ready for testing, much less deployment, until long after SALT II had been replaced by a START agreement, or strategic arms control had broken down entirely. The Soviets, by contrast, seemed to have two new types of ICBM already well underway. In October 1982, they had flight-tested a weapon in the medium (SS-19/MX) class from the test site at Plesetsk, near the White Sea. American intelligence dubbed it the SS-X-24, or alternatively, the PL-4, and the Soviets officially notified the U.S. that this was to be their one new type permitted under SALT II.

The PL-4 was propelled by solid fuel. That made it potentially more efficient, reliable, and easier to move than the liquid-fueled SS-17, -18, and -19. (Liquid fuel is bulky; it corrodes; and if it leaks, it can catch fire or explode. The Soviets had mastered solid-fuel technology only slowly and with difficulty. The U.S. had made the transition when it shifted from Titan to Minuteman in the early 1960s.)

Meanwhile, the Soviets had been dropping hints at START that, in addition to technological breakthroughs, they were also making a conceptual one: they were facing up to the problem of ICBM vulnerability. In the past, they had always dismissed that concern as a myth invented by the Americans to justify new programs like the MX, to discredit SALT, and to impute warlike intentions to the Soviet Union. Yet, even as they admitted that the problem of ICBM vulnerability existed, they were certainly not going to accept it as any more of a problem for the U.S. than for themselves. On the contrary, they claimed that the instability was the U.S.'s fault—the Minuteman III with its improved Mark-12A warhead, the Pershing II, the Trident II, the MX, and the cruise missile all threatened to make Soviet land-based forces vulnerable to an American surprise attack. The Soviets suggested that one solution to the problem of vulnerability was to make land-based missiles mobile. Once again, the discussion hit a dead end. Rowny and his colleagues were not authorized to say anything about land mobiles, since, at that point in 1982, the Reagan Administration had yet to make up its mind on the subject.

Then, in February 1983, there was a very different sort of test from Plesetsk. Whatever it was, the missile was not the medium, MIRVed PL-4. The new one was smaller, seemed designed to carry one warhead, and was suspiciously similar to an old, abandoned ICBM called the SS-16. The SS-16, which had been first detected by U.S. intelligence ten years earlier, would have been the Soviet version of Midgetman if it had worked properly, which it didn't, and if it had been permitted under SALT, which it wasn't. The SS-16 was a three-stage, intercontinental version of the two-stage, intermediate-range SS-20 that had so upset the nuclear balance in Europe. Like the SS-20, the SS-16 was mobile. If the Soviets had perfected the SS-16, they would have been able to stockpile its third stage and, in an international crisis, rapidly convert mobile IRBM launchers (SS-20s) into ICBM launchers—a classic and ominous form of breakout. In SALT, the Carter Administration got the Soviets to abandon the SS-16 program and accept a ban on any new missile of that type.

That accomplishment, while significant, was made easier by the fact that the SS-16 was a lemon. For a missile to be truly mobile it must be designed to use solid fuel. The Soviets had deployed one solid-fuel ICBM already, the SS-13, but it was apparently not reliable. Only about 60 were in service, and they were deployed on fixed launchers at Plesetsk. Two subsequent attempts to develop mobile solid-fuel missiles, the SS-14 and -15, failed miserably, and the third, the SS-16, had already experienced a series of blowups and fizzles when SALT II nipped the program in the bud. Only with the SS-20 did the U.S.S.R. really have a solid-fuel land-based rocket that worked properly.

Now, in February 1983, along came the test of a solid-fuel, three-stage, probably single-warhead missile that looked to be about the same size as the

SS-16. It was dubbed PL-5, later the SS-X-25. If PL-5 was in fact a resurrection of the SS-16, it would violate the SALT II prohibition against that program; if it was not the SS-16, it could be a violation of the SALT II prohibition against more than one new type of ICBM. The Reagan Administration decided to challenge the Soviets on PL-5. Richard Burt demanded an explanation from Dobrynin's deputy, Oleg Sokolov, while Kenneth Dam did the same with Dobrynin himself. The U.S. delegation to the Standing Consultative Commission eventually made a representation of its own in Geneva. The Soviet reply was predictable: PL-5 was neither the SS-16 come back from the grave nor a new type of ICBM; it was a new model, or "modification," of the old SS-13, which was permitted under SALT.

Other Soviets, speaking privately, offered a less legalistic and more plausible explanation. The PL-4 and PL-5 should be seen in the spirit of equality between the superpowers. Anything the U.S. could do, the U.S.S.R. could do, too, and the two new missiles were the Soviet answer to the MX and Midgetman. Furthermore, they said, the PL-5 was part of their response to the prospective deployment of new American missiles in Europe and the American "betrayal" of SALT II.

By June 1983, the Administration had come to accept PL-4 and PL-5, "MXski and Midgetmanski," as part of the new strategic equation that START must address. Scowcroft and the State Department both urged that, in adjusting its proposal during the summer, the Administration formally propose a "modernization restraint" allowing each side one new type of MIRVed ICBM, but permitting additional new types with single warheads. In preparing Reagan for the June 7 NSC meeting, McFarlane used the PL-5 as an argument for raising the launcher ceiling but not eliminating it altogether. The absence of any launcher limits at all would pose the threat of a new version of breakout, he explained. While the U.S. was just beginning to think seriously about Midgetman, its Soviet counterpart was already undergoing its first flight tests. A START agreement that set no launcher limits at all would leave the Soviets in the position of "suddenly flooding the market with Midgetmanskis." Reagan dutifully echoed this point at the NSC meeting.

ABMs in the Background

In March 1983, Reagan had astounded the world, including some members of his own Administration, by proposing an all-out, Manhattan Project–like campaign to develop comprehensive, space-based anti-ballistic-missile defenses for the U.S. He believed his "Star Wars" speech offered a way out of the paradox of deterrence. Instead of keeping the peace through reliance on offensive weapons that threatened catastrophic destruction and possible global suicide, the U.S. would deter Soviet attack with an impenetrable defense. To many, however, the President's proposal promised to lead only to the militarization of space and a surge in the arms race. Even the Administration's top defense scientist, Richard DeLauer, the Under Secretary of Defense for Research and Engineering, pointed out about six weeks after the Star Wars speech that the proposed defensive system could be overcome by Soviet offensive weapons unless it was to be coupled with an offensive-arms-control agreement. "With unconstrained proliferation" of Soviet warheads, said DeLauer, "no defensive system will work."

Yet, at the very time that the Administration decided to press ahead with the Star Wars concept, the constraints placed on Soviet weapons by SALT were eroding, as the nearly simultaneous appearance of the PL-4 and PL-5 made clear, and the START negotiations were going nowhere. Moreover, despite Administration disclaimers to the contrary, an all-out R & D program on military space technology would surely violate SALT I, which prohibited the development and testing as well as deployment of ABMs in space.

The Reagan Administration had been looking for a way out of the ABM treaty from the moment it entered office. Edward Rowny, in his public appeal for the MX as part of his "bargaining kit" in START, had broadly hinted that the MX required some sort of ballistic-missile defense (BMD); BMD would mean drastically amending if not scrapping altogether the ABM treaty. The White House and State Department had done their best to suppress such talk in public, since the Administration had enough trouble on Capitol Hill without giving the impression that it was planning to scrap the ABM treaty.

But the emergence of PL-5 brought the issue to the surface. If the Soviets were about to "go mobile" with their ICBMs, as the PL-5 suggested, then they would be on the advantageous side of a "mobility gap." The Kremlin could ensure the survivability of its ICBMs by moving them around. The U.S. was a long way from getting its own mobile ICBM, the Midgetman. Despite its current fashionability, the idea of a land-mobile ICBM had repeatedly run into serious trouble with the American public. Rowny, for one, doubted that Midgetman would fare any better, and a number of professional military experts, especially those who had been fighting for the MX, agreed. They saw Midgetman as a passing fad—"the strategic equivalent of the Hula-Hoop," as one senior aide to the Joint Chiefs put it. The U.S. might, in the end, simply not have the option of going mobile. Therefore, it had to protect its ICBMs by other means. That meant ballistic-missile defense.

Rowny said privately on numerous occasions that he regarded the ABM treaty as "an historical mistake" because it "tied our hands forever." In public, he took a position more consistent with long-established American policy. In the final days of SALT I, on May 9, 1972, the chief U.S. negotiator, Gerard Smith, had, under instructions from Washington, read the Soviets a unilateral statement. The key passage was: "If an agreement providing for more complete strategic offensive arms limitations were not achieved within five years, U.S. supreme interests could be jeopardized. Should that occur, it would constitute a basis for withdrawal from the ABM Treaty." The linkage between offensive and defensive arms control had also been written into law as an amendment to the articles of ratification of the ABM treaty.

According to its provisions, the treaty was to be reviewed by the two countries every five years. There had been a review in 1977, during the Carter Administration, and another was scheduled for 1982. For the Reagan Administration, the review process provided an opportunity for Rowny, Perle, and others to hold the ABM treaty hostage to START.

Almost since the day he had arrived on the job the year before, Rowny had been pushing the idea of folding the formal review of the ABM treaty, at least initially, into START. He felt time was running out on the 1972 treaty. Defensive arms control could exist only in tandem with offensive arms control. Rowny was fond of comparing ABMs and ICBMs to shields and spears. Two adversaries arm themselves with shields and spears, then agree to throw away the shields. But if one side starts making more and longer spears, then sooner or later the other side has to think seriously about retrieving its shields. The trouble with this analogy, in the view of many, was that shields can never deflect nuclear spears, and as DeLauer and others recognized, the absence of limits on spears makes the development of shields all the more fruitless.

Before the autumn 1982 round of START began, Rowny was authorized to make a plenary statement reminding the Soviets that the 1972 ABM Treaty had always been closely linked to, and dependent on, a complementary agreement limiting offensive weapons. He pointedly referred to the 1972 Jackson amendment to the articles of ratification of the treaty, which the Soviets knew were largely the work of Richard Perle.

The Soviets listened impassively during the plenary session, but immediately afterward they fanned out in force to ask their American opposite numbers what Rowny was really saying. Was this a threat that the U.S. might abrogate the 1972 treaty if there was no progress in START? If so, the Soviets said indignantly, they must remind the Americans that, as a matter of principle, the U.S.S.R. would never negotiate under the pressure of ultimatums. When the Standing Consultative Commission—the joint U.S.-Soviet body that considered questions of compliance—took up a detailed review of the ABM Treaty, Richard Perle did his best to emphasize that the threat was real enough. He tried to prevent General Richard Ellis, the former commander of the Strategic Air Command and now head of the U.S. SCC delegation, from making a concluding statement. The Soviets should understand that the U.S. considered the status of the ABM Treaty an open question, and the absence of a concluding statement would suggest that the U.S. considered the review open-ended.

So yet another shadow hung over the negotiations, yet another reason for Soviet uncertainty and suspicion. To Soviet ears, the U.S. seemed to be saying that it had a right to develop a new MIRVed ICBM and a new single-warhead mobile one, but the Soviet Union did not. It seemed to be saying that the Soviet Union must abide by SALT, but the U.S. might not. And, at the same time, the Administration sounded as though it was getting ready to declare a new round in the defensive arms race simultaneously with a new round in the offensive arms race.

Later in 1983, the Administration turned up evidence that the Soviets might already have a head start in developing and deploying defensive systems. The discovery concerned radar, a perennially troublesome issue in the Standing Consultative Commission. The ABM treaty contained a prohibition against using or testing radars designed for anti-aircraft defenses "in an ABM mode." Neither side was allowed to test, at the same time and at the same site, ABM interceptors and radars designed for anti-aircraft defenses. These provisions were intended to make it harder for either side to upgrade its conventional air defenses into a network of ABM defenses.

The U.S. had, for some time, been voicing two particular concerns in the SCC. One had to do with certain large radars that the Soviets insisted were for legitimate military purposes recognized in SALT I, such as early warning of an enemy attack, but which the U.S. suspected might be used as the basis for a nationwide ABM system. The other concerned activity near Sary-Shagan, on the banks of Lake Balkhash in Kazakhstan, where the Soviets tested a number of weapon systems, including ABMs. From time to time, they would launch a dummy ballistic warhead into the area and fire an ABM interceptor at it. They would concurrently turn on their air-defense radar in the area. The Soviets could claim they were doing so simply for purposes of checking their instrumentation and for "range safety," to make sure all that hardware flying about stayed on course. They even argued that air defense itself was legitimate for range safety, since the U.S. might attack the facility. (Range instrumentation and safety radars were exempted from SALT I limits at the insistence of the U.S. military.)

The American suspicion, however, was that the Soviets were "teaching" their air-defense radar how to track incoming warheads and thus illegally developing a new ABM system in violation of SALT I. Before the Reagan Administration came into office, the U.S. had engaged in several years of intricate and quite fruitful discussion about what air-defense radar was permitted during ABM tests. The issue seemed, even by the new Administration's lights, to be under control.

But then, in 1983, American reconnaissance satellites spotted a giant radar facility near Abalakovo in the Krasnoyarsk region of central Siberia, deep inside the U.S.S.R. It was as tall as a fifty-story building and nearly as large as two football fields. Each side was allowed early-warning radars to track incoming enemy warheads, but only "at locations along the periphery of its national territory and oriented outward." This one seemed much too far inland to qualify as permissible. Moreover, it was suspiciously close to a cluster of SS-18 and single-warhead SS-11 ICBM fields to the south, near the Mongolian border. It had the earmarks of being part of a new ABM facility, illegal under SALT I.

For critics of SALT and proponents of a hard line in START, the Abalakovo radar became the most compelling and damning piece of evidence that the Soviets were cheating. There was intensive bickering over whether merely to raise questions (the State Department's preference) or flatly accuse the Soviets of cheating (the Pentagon's). The U.S. made representations at the Standing Consultative Commission, Perle accused the State Department of "playing the role of apologist for the Soviets," and the right wing on Capitol Hill put pressure on the Administration. As a result, the White House ordered a comprehensive report on alleged Soviet violations of arms-control treaties.

While the incident was generally recognized as the most serious case to date of a possible Soviet violation, there were still ambiguities in the language of the treaty that might be used to excuse it. The Soviets claimed that the radar was for tracking their satellites in space, a function permitted by SALT I. Once again, the Soviets seized the opportunity to declare their innocence while protesting the effrontery of nitpicking about compliance with a treaty for which the U.S. seemed to have so little respect.

Building and Unbuilding Confidence

With SALT in danger of coming unraveled, with START so unpromising, and with the demand for arms control rising on the homefront, the Administration began looking for ways of extracting a consolation prize from the shambles in Geneva. The White House was also looking ahead to the 1984 presidential election and thinking about how useful it would be for the President to hold a summit meeting with Yuri Andropov. Both sides knew that there would have to be an agreement of some kind to justify a summit.

One possibility was an accord on confidence-building measures, or CBMs. These were arrangements by which the superpowers communicated with each other about their military activity. They were meant to make arms-control agreements easier to verify and to reduce the danger of war occurring through miscalculation or misunderstanding. SALT was full of CBMs. The establishment of the Standing Consultative Commission was one. Another was the provision in SALT II for each side to supply the other with a "data base," or inventory, of its weapons covered by the agreement. There were also rules established by SALT II to reduce the risk that one side might mistake test launches by the other for the beginning of a nuclear attack.

There were two problems with CBMs. One was that proposed measures often served to build the confidence of one side at the expense of the other. For example, the Soviets had floated the idea of "ASW-free patrol zones" for their submarines. ASW meant anti-submarine warfare. The U.S. had a dual advantage, both defensive and offensive, in this arena: its own anti-submarine warfare was superior to the Soviets', and its submarines were far less vulnerable to Soviet ASW. So the creation of ASW-free zones might reduce a crucial American advantage.

The other problem with CBMs was that they had little utility or credibility in a vacuum, apart from arms agreements. They only made sense, in Brent Scowcroft's phrase, as "frosting on the cake." The Reagan Administration, he added, "doesn't even have a cake in the oven." Rowny seemed to think he could use CBMs as a substitute for the cake, as the basis for an agreement and a summit.

During Reagan's tour of Europe in June 1982, he had given a series of speeches in which he had called for a worldwide crusade against Soviet Communism; at the same time, he asked the Soviets to join in a series of confidence-building measures. These were warmed-over, slightly expanded versions of measures already provided for in SALT II. In an effort to create the illusion of constructive advances in the U.S. position, Rowny devoted two plenary speeches during the fall 1982 round of START to elaborating on Reagan's proposals, and later, with the help of Goodby and others on the delegation, he refined some of the proposed measures.

The Soviets greeted this American enthusiasm for confidence-building measures with a barrage of rhetorical questions. If the U.S. was so interested in building up confidence, why did Ambassador Rowny continue to refuse to discuss Andrei Gromyko's proposal for a bilateral pledge on no-first-use of nuclear weapons? And how could the U.S. representatives talk about improving confidence in an atmosphere poisoned by President Reagan's proclamation of an anti-Soviet crusade and his description of the U.S.S.R. as "the focus of evil in the modern world"?

Far from giving up, the Administration was now pursuing a CBM agreement in direct contacts between Shultz and Dobrynin. Shultz had been reluctant to use the Dobrynin back channel that had been so critical during SALT to Henry Kissinger and, to a lesser extent, Cyrus Vance. But Shultz decided to open it partly because of the growing eagerness at the White House for progress in time to be of help to the President in the election.

The U.S. proposal for CBMs now featured secure military communications links between the superpowers; an upgrading of the Moscow-Washington Hot Line to include high-speed facsimile transmissions; upgrading the communications of each side's embassy with its capital; and multilateral negotiations on nuclear terrorism. Within the government, these were regarded as something of a joke—"arms-control junk food" was a common phrase around the State Department. The measures were either cosmetic to the point of being frivolous or sure to be utterly unacceptable to the Soviets (a link between the military communications of the two sides, for example, would be seen in Moscow as a trick to compromise Soviet secrets and security). There was muffled derision of the notion that being able to transmit pictures over the Hot Line would help avoid nuclear war.

Rowny found it no laughing matter. "What if we ever had to send a map or a chart?" he asked. "Good point, Ed," retorted a skeptical colleague. "Why don't you add touch-tone dialing while you're at it?" At one point, consideration was given to making the Hot Line a voice link—i.e., a real telephone—in addition to the existing teleprinter. One reason that idea went nowhere was that many officials, having seen movies about fictional crises in which American presidents "get on the Hot Line to the Kremlin," thought that it already was a telephone.

While dismissing most of the other proposals the U.S. was making, Dobrynin said that his government might be willing to upgrade the Hot Line. Shultz commented to an aide after the meeting: "Big deal. We can't get a summit out of that."

In early August, a middle-level delegation from the Pentagon and NSC staff went to Moscow for more negotiations on CBMs. They came home with nothing except a reiteration of Soviet interest in upgrading the Hot Line. In Geneva, Rowny pressed Karpov to join him in setting up, under the aegis of START, a separate working group on CBMs. Karpov agreed, but only on the condition that anything accomplished in that working group would have to be part of a final agreement on strategic arms reduction; a separate agreement on CBMs was not acceptable. The Soviets then dragged their feet until the last possible minute, as though to underscore their refusal to let the quest for CBMs proceed in the absence of progress on START itself.*

Fudging and Budging

Having himself been persuaded that CBMs were no substitute for START, Shultz tried to use the Dobrynin channel to stimulate progress on the central issues. His hope was that, if the U.S. relaxed its constraints on warheads and

---

*The working group was finally established in early December 1983, with Michael Mobbs as the American chairman. The Soviets were still in their old habit of double-teaming that had so annoyed Rowny earlier: their side was co-chaired by Osadchiyev and a Foreign Ministry official.

launchers and indicated a willingness to negotiate meaningful limits on cruise missiles, the Soviets would reciprocate. During the spring of 1983, at the urging of his staff, he decided to signal flexibility on the U.S.'s part, see if there was any on the Soviets', and do so in a way that bypassed the Pentagon.

Shultz was uneasy and proceeded in the most gingerly way so as to minimize any trouble he might have with Weinberger. During a meeting with Dobrynin about CBMs, with Weinberger sitting in, Shultz suggested that the ambassador come back on another occasion "so that we can talk a bit about START." Shultz felt his trail was covered; he had issued the invitation in front of Weinberger, so he could not be accused of arranging the meeting behind Weinberger's back.

The gathering took place in the State Department and included Shultz's own advisers and Rowny, but no one from the Pentagon. The secretary put a number of questions to Dobrynin that had been suggested by Goodby and others. The Soviet proposal on the table in Geneva included a ceiling of 1,800 on strategic launchers (bombers and missiles). Was there some lower level that the U.S.S.R. might be willing to consider? The Soviet proposal also called for a total ban on all types of long-range cruise missiles. Surely Moscow realized that such a ban was unacceptable to the U.S. At the very least, would it be willing to accept partial limits on air-launched cruise missiles, along the lines of what had already been agreed in SALT II? The Soviets must also recognize that the Reagan Administration was adamant about including the Backfire as a strategic weapon. Was there any flexibility there? And what about Soviet heavy missiles? As part of the right agreement, could there be some reductions? And with forward-based systems already on the table in INF, the Soviets must see the unreasonableness in subjecting them to double jeopardy by trying to ban the Pershing IIs and Tomahawks in START.

It was a fishing expedition without bait, since Shultz was in a position to offer no specific American concessions. Dobrynin said he would get back to Shultz with the answers. When he did so, the answers were: No, no, and no, with one maybe thrown in. The only hint of give was on the question of air-launched cruise missiles. Dobrynin said there might be a way of limiting ALCMs, but it would have to be in the context of a total ban on sea- and ground-launched cruise missiles. That would hardly be a great step forward, since the Soviets had already agreed to permit ALCMs in SALT II, and it would still mean banning the GLCMs destined for Western Europe. As in discussions Shultz was holding with Dobrynin on INF at the same time, the State Department had succeeded only in getting the Soviets to reiterate their hard line at a higher level; the approach had also let the Soviets know that the American line might be softening.

When the Pentagon civilians found out what had happened, Perle reacted not so much with fury as with disgust and condescension. The State Department's overture to Dobrynin had been, he felt, amateurish and utterly botched. While he took some satisfaction from what he considered its ineptitude, Perle was more on guard than ever against State's "shenanigans." Rowny was worried that once he returned to Geneva he would be left out of the real action. He drafted a confidential memorandum insisting not only that he be kept apprised of whatever went on between Shultz and Dobrynin, but that he be summoned home to sit in.

Undaunted, Goodby prepared a list of follow-up questions, but Burt decided to abort the exercise, on the ground that it risked turning into "a sterile conversation, like the one in Geneva."

Dobrynin was not sure what to make of the whole episode. He had rather expected more sessions, since Shultz had initiated the exchange. In earlier, better days, when dealing with Kissinger and Vance, Dobrynin had found that numerous meetings were necessary in order to make progress. Each side had to feel the other out, with one hinting at tentative concessions to see if the other would respond. There also had to be mutual confidence that each participant could float ideas without being held to them later as though his government had made a formal concession. Kissinger used to receive Dobrynin in the Map Room at the White House for one-on-one sessions, during which Richard Nixon would occasionally telephone Kissinger, in part to remind Dobrynin that Kissinger was acting on behalf of the President.

Shultz, by contrast, insisted on being backed up by a large cast of characters. His tone may have hinted that changes were possible on the U.S. side, but he had offered nothing specific. So why should the Administration have expected much in return, at least initially? As it was, Dobrynin had tipped his hand ever so slightly on the treatment of ALCMs. Hardly a major concession, to be sure, but still something to follow up on. The absence of any follow-up left Dobrynin more inclined than ever to write this Administration off as simply "not serious."

When the Reagan Administration did finally get around to offering a formal change in its position in early June, it hardly met the Soviet definition of serious. The U.S. was still committed to a definition of stability that the Soviets were unlikely to accept either in theory or in practice, since that definition was based on missile throw-weight and warheads. As McFarlane put it, "We're ready to show flexibility as long as the other side does, and as long as the other side joins us in meeting our basic objectives. There's more than one way to skin a cat." But, however the cat was skinned, the result would have to be massive reduction in Soviet ICBMs.

Still, the Soviets were not willing to let the U.S. take the lead even in what they regarded as phony concessions. When the Administration indicated it would raise the 850 ceiling on SLBM and ICBM launchers right away and perhaps later relax the 210/110 subceiling on heavy and medium ICBM launchers, the Soviets eased the strictures they were proposing on ALCMs and SLBMs, and tabled an elaboration of their own reductions plan, with a variety of sublimits under the 1,800 ceiling on total strategic launchers (intercontinental bombers, SLBMs, and ICBMs). All these sublimits existed in SALT II, although at higher levels. What the Soviets were doing now was lowering the levels somewhat in keeping with the reduction they had already proposed for an overall ceiling in START.

It was almost certainly the proposal that the Soviets had intended to make in SALT III. It would indeed have been an improvement on SALT II, insofar as there would have been fewer Soviet MIRVed ICBMs. SALT II had set the subceiling at 820; the new Soviet proposal included a subceiling of 680. But the U.S.S.R. would still have been permitted more than 7,000 ICBM warheads (compared to the 2,500 the U.S. had proposed) and over 11,000 ballistic-missile warheads on land and sea (compared to the 5,000 ceiling to which the Reagan Administration was committed).* Also the whole package of reductions had a string attached: Soviet willingness to make these reductions was still conditioned on American cancellation of the Pershing II and Tomahawk deployments in Western Europe.

A year or even six months earlier, the Administration probably would have seized upon the Soviet proposal as proof that the Kremlin refused to accept American objectives and was using START to stall and score propaganda points. But now the Administration was looking desperately for evidence of progress, the more so if it could claim that its own much-advertised flexibility had stimulated the Soviets to show some of their own. Therefore, leaks out of Washington interpreted the Soviet move as a hopeful sign, and a vindication of American policy to date.

In fact, the Administration was still fighting over its policy, especially on cruise missiles and throw-weight. The State Department had wanted from the beginning to include limits in START on sea-launched cruise missiles. At one point it had looked as though the Joint Chiefs of Staff might go along, thus risking the wrath of John Lehman, Richard Perle, and others. The staff of the Joint Chiefs had even come up with a way to limit SLCMs and to verify that limit. It was an idea based on SALT II's treatment of air-launched cruise missiles. Just as the Air Force was permitted under the treaty to put its ALCMs on specially designated, visually distinctive bombers, the Navy would put its SLCMs on specially designated, visually distinctive ships.

---

*If the new Soviet missile, the PL-4, or SS-X-24, turned out to have 10 warheads, and if the Soviets replaced all their SS-17s and -19s with SS-24s, then the entire MIRVed ICBM force—all 680 launchers under their proposal—could have 10 warheads each (the SS-18 already had 10). Hence there could be a total of 6,800 warheads on their MIRVed ICBMs, plus however many they deployed on single-warhead ICBMs.

But the Chiefs themselves did not go along with their staff. By the summer of 1983, they were firmly aligned with the Office of the Secretary of Defense on the principle that SLCMs "do not belong in START." The Pentagon took the view that SLCMs were too valuable as weapons to use against Soviet ships and to "project power ashore." The nuclear-armed land-attack SLCM variant was less valued by the Navy than either the conventionally armed anti-ship or land-attack version. The START delegation recommended that the U.S., therefore, at least be willing to ban nuclear-armed SLCMs, but since it was almost impossible to make the type of armament on an individual SLCM itself visually distinctive, the Administration decided not to accept any restriction on SLCMs.

As it now stood, the Administration's proposal came down to a three-part choice that the U.S. was giving the Soviet Union. In their oral accompaniment to a new draft treaty that was formally presented in July, the U.S. negotiators were to say: (1) the Administration's collateral restraints of 2,500 land-based warheads, 210 heavy and medium missiles, and 110 heavy missiles would "remain on the table," if only as a reminder of how unreasonable the original START proposal had been and therefore how reasonable the U.S. was being now; (2) "However, we will be prepared to discuss with you some direct limit on throw-weight at a number to be negotiated"; and (3) "If neither of these proposals appeals to you, then we're prepared to listen to any constructive proposal you have to deal with destructive capability and potential [i.e., throw-weight]."

"These are not accommodating changes," said Aleksei Obukhov. "They're totally within the framework of what you've been trying to do all along, which is force one-sided and unreasonable reductions on us." The U.S., he said, was still determined to make "dead souls" out of the Soviet Union's most valued weapons.

The Goodby Plan

There was one last attempt on the part of Administration officials to break the impasse. It came, predictably enough, from within the State Department, and its principal designer was James Goodby. This was to be his last contribution to START. Working in a hopelessly stagnated negotiation as the State Department's representative and at the same time as Rowny's deputy was barely tolerable. Being named prominently on Rowny's hit list in January had been the last straw. He was determined that he would not return to START for the fall round.*

---

*Goodby was eventually named ambassador to the Conference on Disarmament in Europe (CDE) that opened in Stockholm in January 1984.

Goodby had played a key role in designing earlier interagency compromises: the two-phase "consensus approach" of May 1982, the inclusion of cruise missiles and bombers that fall, and the presidential alteration of the proposal in June 1983. But in all of those instances, because of bureaucratic politics, Goodby had included throw-weight as a prominent part of the package. The Pentagon was able to keep pushing throw-weight from the periphery back to the center. His idea this time was to graft the hierarchy of launcher sublimits that the Soviets were then proposing as a successor to SALT II onto a hierarchy of warhead ceilings, thus preserving some of the main goals the U.S. was seeking, particularly reductions in MIRVed ICBMs.

The Soviet launcher sublimits were unacceptable all by themselves not just because they were too high, but because they allowed too many warheads and too much freedom to mix between ballistic-missile warheads and bomber weapons. That freedom gave the Soviets a right to devote most of their strategic weapons to missile warheads and thus to maintain a substantial lead over the U.S. in that important category. However, if sublimits could be applied to the aggregate of warheads and bomber armaments, not just to the launchers as the Soviets had proposed, the freedom to mix would be constrained, and a mutually acceptable compromise might result. Throw-weight could be handled as part of a separate, undefined subceiling, or it could be left out of the package altogether. Also, there might be a provision for phasing out SS-18s by prohibiting a successor heavy missile to replace the SS-18 when it became obsolete in fifteen years or so.

Goodby's scheme involved American concessions in both concept and concrete military consequence, and it had a number of key points in common with the alternative approaches to strategic arms control favored in Congress, particularly by the build-downers. Goodby was willing to move significantly toward the Soviets and toward SALT II in allowing some "aggregation" of bombers with missiles. The U.S. would be giving up what had been an ironclad premise of the Reagan Administration: that ballistic missiles must be treated as separate from, and unequal to, slow-flying bombers and cruise missiles. The hardest number for the Reagan Administration to swallow in Goodby's scheme was a ceiling of 7,400 on an aggregate of MIRVed ballistic-missile warheads and ALCMs.

But the Soviets were being asked to swallow hard, too. Goodby's proposed ceiling of 5,000 on MIRVed ballistic-missile warheads—that is, an aggregate of land- and sea-based MIRVs—was about half of what U.S. intelligence calculated that the Soviets were planning to acquire. Another ceiling of 3,000 on MIRVed ICBM warheads, or land-based MIRVs alone, was also much less than the Soviet program called for.

Under his scheme, each side could, in theory, have 8,000 single-warhead missiles, as long as it had no strategic bombers and, of course, no MIRVs.

It was aimed at encouraging the development of single-warhead ballistic missiles, in keeping with new dogma about the stabilizing virtues of such weapons. This feature would appeal to the Scowcroft Commission and de-MIRVing enthusiasts on Capitol Hill.

Goodby designed the scheme with an added feature in mind—one that might improve its negotiability with the Soviets. A pair of launcher and warhead subceilings could be added to cover intermediate-range weapons, perhaps with sub-subceilings to distinguish between bombers (FB-111s and Backfires), ballistic missiles (SS-20s and Pershing IIs), and cruise missiles (Tomahawks). Thus, the plan would lend itself easily to the eventual merger of START and INF.

Burt had been thinking along much the same lines. Nearly a year before, in a memo to Shultz, Burt had argued that Administration objectives to date in START were hopelessly unrealistic. Then, in a much more detailed follow-up memo, Burt laid out his ideas about how the two negotiations could be merged. The first order of business was to adjust the START package so as to build in an aggregate ceiling for bombers and missiles, to come up with "more reasonable" collateral restraints, and to hold open the possibility of allowing the Soviets to keep SS-20s and the U.S. to deploy its own Pershing IIs and Tomahawks under a "comprehensive" set of ceilings.

Goodby's plan as refined during the summer was well suited to just that possibility. He hoped it would permit the summit that the White House was now so interested in having. He first checked the idea with Burt and Howe, then laid it out in a memo to Rowny in late July. While everyone was initially wary of it, and tinkered with its details, the plan became the basis of a memorandum co-signed by Burt and Howe to Shultz on August 11, headed "A New Framework for START." The choice of words was meant to appeal to conflicting desires at the White House. The President and his political advisers were looking for something "new," since the old approach clearly was not working. But they did not want to appear to be abandoning their basic proposal, so the old initials START were preserved in the Burt-Howe memo. Most important was the word "framework." It suggested that perhaps there was a way to build something rather quickly on which an agreement could rest—something skeletal and makeshift that could provide a platform on which Reagan might meet with the Soviet leadership before the 1984 election.

18 Too Many Cooks

Of all the contenders for a new approach to START, the Goodby plan would have been by far the most negotiable with the Soviets. It was hardly negotiable at all within the U.S. government. In Washington, the plan suffered from precisely those features that would have made it promising in Geneva: its structural similarity to SALT II and to the Soviet proposal; the presence of a limited freedom to mix slow-flying bombers with fast-flying ballistic missiles and air-launched cruise missiles with ballistic warheads; and the downplaying of direct limits on throw-weight. Its detractors would later dismiss it as "SALT II½."

The plan also suffered from an accident of timing. At the moment when the State Department ought to have been waging a full-scale campaign in its behalf, the most logical campaigner, Richard Burt, was almost completely preoccupied with INF. Burt's principal friend in court at the White House and his partner at so many key moments in the past, Robert McFarlane, was also unavailable. With the Middle East heating up, Reagan had appointed McFarlane as his special envoy to the region. McFarlane retained the title of deputy head of the NSC staff, but not even his prodigious energies allowed him to deal with INF and START while trying to handle Israel and Lebanon. McFarlane had brought Perle's deputy, Ronald Lehman, over to the NSC staff, so now Lehman was the ranking expert on arms control at the White House. Lehman prided himself on "being able to work for one boss at a time"—he no longer felt obligated to advance Perle's views—but he did not have McFarlane's standing in the government, nor did he have McFarlane's rapport with Burt.

Also, just about the time that George Shultz was seriously studying the Goodby plan as something that he might propose to Andrei Gromyko at their scheduled meeting in Madrid in early September, the Soviets shot down the Korean airliner. At a meeting of a special committee that had been set up to study alternative approaches to START, Jonathan Howe's deputy, Robert Dean, observed, "I'm afraid that a good idea has been shot down in flames over the Sea of Japan."

On Capitol Hill, however, the airliner crisis brought only a momentary easing in the pressure on the Administration to find a new and more promising START proposal. By early October, when Rowny's delegation was preparing to return to Geneva, it was plain that Congress would insist on getting into the act.

The Kitchen Gets Crowded

There were two arms-control lobbies in Congress, one in each chamber: the de-MIRVers, or Midgetmanners, in the House and the build-downers in the Senate. Over time, considerable coordination had developed between them. For example, Albert Gore, the Democratic representative from Tennessee, and a member of his staff, Leon Fuerth, kept in close touch with Senator William Cohen and his adviser, Alton Frye, the Washington director of the Council on Foreign Relations. The legislators had figured early in the spring of 1983 that they could exert more leverage on the Executive Branch by maintaining parallel, rather than unified, initiatives; their hope was to whipsaw the Administration.

But by the summer, as START sank deeper into stagnation and the Administration continued to try to keep the congressmen at bay, the two lobbies decided to join forces. That meant merging their plans. They needed an intermediary, someone who would serve as an honest broker between the two house of Congress—and, simultaneously, between Congress and the Administration. That role fell to Brent Scowcroft. The congressmen saw him as a friendly and credible channel for conveying their views to the White House, where he was entitled to a respectful hearing as the chairman of the President's commission on strategic arms.

Scowcroft and his colleague on the commission, James Woolsey, held a series of meetings with the key members of Congress, their aides, a small number of other outsiders, and selected members of the Administration. The result, after many months of brainstorming and wheeling-and-dealing, was a new approach to START. It was ingenious in its ramifications for nuclear deterrence and arms control, eclectic in its political and ideological sponsorship, but daunting in its complexity.

The new scheme managed to incorporate the 5,000-warhead ceiling from the Eureka proposal, the inducement to de-MIRVing favored by the Midgetmanners, and a schedule for reductions that met the demands of the build-downers. The hardest feature for the Administration to accept was its comprehensiveness—it called for lumping bombers and their armaments, including cruise missiles, together with ballistic missiles and their warheads.

A related feature in the plan was more ambiguous. This was an overall ceiling on "potential destructive capacity." A similar phrase ("destructive capability and potential") was by now well established in the lexicon of the Reagan Administration, and in the negotiating record of START, as synonymous with ballistic-missile throw-weight. However, as used by the congressional arms-control lobby and the Scowcroft Commission, the index would cover bombers as well. In that respect, it was a further attempt to commit the Administration to recognizing the asymmetrical but essentially equivalent nature of the superpowers' arsenals and to seeking trade-offs between American and Soviet areas of advantage.

Thus, the scheme had much in common with the Goodby plan. There was the basis for a four-way alliance: among the Midgetmanners in the House, the build-downers in the Senate, the Scowcroft Commission, and the State Department. But Scowcroft and his confederates were more interested in finding a common denominator between their own preferences and those of the Pentagon. That seemed both more important and more difficult than satisfying the State Department. Quite simply, they took State for granted. Shultz, Burt, and Howe had been pushing for movement for months; they could be counted on to climb aboard any bandwagon once it got going. There was a vague awareness among the outsiders that State had developed its own alternative approach to START, although the details of the Goodby plan were closely held even within the government.

As word got out that such a plan existed, there was some thought in the commission and on Capitol Hill of making the State Department proposal the basis of a short-term accord—a bird in the hand—so that a formal arms-control agreement could be in place while the two sides engaged in what were likely to be protracted negotiations over a more ambitious solution to the problem of strategic stability. But that idea never went anywhere. In Les Aspin's phrase, the State alternative was "too much like SALT II and therefore anathema to the conservatives." It was the conservatives and the Pentagon, not the liberals and State, that Scowcroft, Aspin, and Woolsey wanted to enlist in the process of breaking the stalemate in START.

The key man at the Pentagon was, of course, still Richard Perle. For some time Perle had been worried that the President would come under irresistible political pressure to make a START deal in 1984. The temptation would be to make a few cosmetic changes in SALT II and accept something similar to what the Soviets were offering. That, Perle felt, would certainly be the State Department's recommendation. He needed a strong counterposition. Returning to his original preference for a low ceiling on ballistic-missile throw-weight was out of the question; it would be seen as a step backward, away from the possibility of an agreement and a summit. He needed a plan that appeared to offer some concession on the issue of bomber limits.

Perle had lunch at the end of March with Walter Slocombe, Perle's predecessor in the Carter Administration. Slocombe was not associated with the Scowcroft Commission, but his former boss, Harold Brown, was, and Slocombe was a friend of Woolsey's. Slocombe and Perle themselves were friendly adversaries. When he had been on the inside and Perle had been on the outside, Slocombe had regarded Perle as intellectually the most formidable of the SALT critics. Now that their roles were in some ways reversed, Slocombe was just as critical of START as Perle had been of SALT. He was particularly critical of Perle's dogged pursuit of a low limit on ballistic-missile throw-weight. If that was a realistic goal, Slocombe used to say, then the Administration was asking too little: "Any Administration that thinks it can get the Soviets to take down two-thirds or more of their most modern and powerful missiles should also be asking for the restoration of the Romanov monarchy and the establishment of Judaism as the state religion."

During their lunch, Perle said he was thinking hard about "new ways to solve the problem" of START, but there still had to be some sort of overall limit on throw-weight. Slocombe replied that an overall limit would never be acceptable to the Soviets or to the Congress unless it somehow included bombers and cruise missiles. To Slocombe's surprise, Perle said he did not object to the "principle" of including bombers and their armaments as long as it could be done in a way that "recognized the higher level of threat posed by ballistic weapons." Perle said he had been thinking about the possibility of a combined measure for bomber payload and missile throw-weight.

Slocombe was intrigued. Almost immediately after the lunch, he got in touch with his friend Woolsey and said, "My God, something must be wrong, because Richard Perle and I agree on something. If you can believe in miracles, I don't think you guys"—the commission and the congressmen —"are all that far apart from him." Unlike some of his colleagues, Woolsey was prepared to accept Perle's sincerity; he defended him against charges that his demand for "higher standards" was just a cover for a determination to sabotage arms control altogether.

Woolsey had also staked out a position somewhat right of center in the great throw-weight debate; he believed that real arms control did need throw-weight. As the principal drafter of the original Scowcroft Commission report, he had made sure that there was passing, but approving, mention of the Administration's attempt to limit throw-weight—the lines that Perle had seized upon in support of the throw-weight restoration movement. It was Woolsey's hope that a new approach to START would find some way of dealing with throw-weight more negotiably than the Administration's did, but that would still establish the precedent that throw-weight mattered and should somehow be accounted for in arms control. That way, a new Administration, be it Democratic or moderate Republican, would be less likely to ignore throw-weight in its own arms-control proposals.

Woolsey told Scowcroft that Perle was "ripe for a little discreet massaging, and won't necessarily go on the warpath against us." During the summer, Woolsey and Perle, who both lived in the Maryland suburbs, ran into each other at a neighborhood swimming pool. Woolsey congratulated Perle for having come up with "the very interesting idea" of aggregating bomber payload and missile throw-weight. He also had Perle over to his house for coffee with Scowcroft to talk the matter over. Scowcroft meanwhile had been in touch with Aspin, Nunn, and a number of other key people in Congress. The trick was to come up with an index of destructive capability that included bombers and cruise missiles but was heavily weighted against ballistic missiles. While none of those involved would ever admit it in so many words, the fact was that Richard Perle had, ever so casually, brought the Scowcroft Commission and the congressional arms-control lobby round to his criterion for a new approach to START. The State Department was left in the lurch.

The task of figuring out a new way to measure and limit destructive capability fell to Glenn Kent, a retired Air Force general and nuclear-weapons expert. Kent had worked with Scowcroft on the Townes panel, which had tried and failed to come up with a basing scheme for the MX that was invulnerable to congressional preemptive strikes. He was now helping Sam Nunn refine the build-down scheme. Kent was one of the fathers, if not grandfathers, of the American concern with ballistic-missile throw-weight. In 1961, when Perle was still in school, Kent had been a colonel on sabbatical at Harvard arguing in vain with civilian arms-control experts that they had better pay more attention to the sheer size and lifting power of Soviet rockets. And that was nearly a decade before the era of MIRVs began.

Kent was the ultimate numbers-cruncher. He had something like a genius for taking abstract concepts of nuclear peace and strategies for nuclear war and converting them into mathematical equations. Until now, he had been working on different ways of calculating destructive potential in ballistic missiles. Now along came Scowcroft, in the midsummer of 1983, and said, "Glenn, let's look at another way to get at throw-weight. START is a non-starter, and one reason is that it doesn't take sufficient account of bombers. Is there any way to factor in bombers?"

In effect, Kent saluted and went back to his note pad and his blackboard and his calculator. Assisting him now was another military man turned professional defense intellectual, Ted Warner. Both were attached to the Washington office of the Rand Corporation. Warner, a retired Air Force officer like Kent, had helped the Joint Chiefs of Staff do battle with Perle over the throw-weight issue in 1981–82. Kent and Warner put their heads together and came up with what became known as the compulsory double build-down approach to START.

At the heart of the plan was the amalgamation of two units of account for strategic arms control—warheads and destructive potential. To the State Department and the Soviet government, both of which believed that the primary unit of account should be launchers, Kent and Warner had nothing to offer. Kent particularly felt that launchers "are just plain the wrong currency, the wrong way to go."

The double build-down introduced new numbers, new regulations, new forms of measurement, and even new terminology. The unit of account that would subsume warheads and destructive potential was to be a "standard weapon station," the lowest common denominator of a superpower's aggregate "strategic attack capability." This unit might represent a gravity bomb, a cruise missile, a short-range attack missile, or a ballistic missile warhead of a certain permissible size. Oversized warheads counted extra; warheads on MIRVed missiles might also count extra. The elusive concept of "bomber throw-weight" varied depending on how the bomber was armed: a bomber equipped with cruise missiles counted more than a bomber carrying gravity bombs.

The overall name "double build-down" came from the stipulation that each side would have to reduce by certain set percentages over time both the number of ballistic-missile warheads and the number of standard weapon stations.

Kent and Warner put together a ten-page briefing paper, complete with charts. It read like a Chinese menu, if not a menu in Chinese. There was something for almost everyone, and various combinations of interested parties could pick and choose various combinations of features that suited their tastes. For those who, like the President and the build-downers, wanted to see reductions, there were two categories in which dramatic reductions would be achieved (warheads and standard weapon stations). For those who wanted to protect the B-1, Trident, MX, and other new weapons, the plan "allows for modernization of strategic systems."

For those on Capitol Hill and on the Commission who wanted to see Midgetman thrive instead of the MX, there were bonuses for the development of single-warhead ICBMs. In fact, the new rules and limits were so heavily prejudiced against large MIRVed ICBMs that the plan would appeal to those who wanted the MX to die but did not want to have to kill it themselves. (Aspin commented to his colleagues, "Why don't we let arms control get rid of the MX and thus spare ourselves [the Congress] having to do it?") At the same time, those who wanted the MX to survive could see that the MX was still allowed, and that it was less sharply restricted than the largest Soviet missiles.

To appeal to the Joint Chiefs of Staff, who were not enamored of Midgetman but were preparing to live with it and worry about its vulnerability, Kent and Warner pointed out on the first page of their paper that "reduced barrage potential encourages fielding of a small ICBM on a hardened mobile transporter over an extensive deployment area." For those who cared about reducing ballistic-missile throw-weight—there it was, tucked away in the concept of standard weapons stations. For those who wanted to see comprehensiveness and the aggregation of bombers and missiles, that was there, too. Thus the plan managed to appeal to both the hard-liners and the soft-liners simultaneously, or at least to those who could understand it.

However, double build-down also had several shortcomings. Its ingenuity was matched by its complexity. It was complicated partly because it was the brainchild of technicians but also because it was intended to be a grand synthesis, with something for everyone.

Even assuming Reagan could explain it to the American people, how could he expect Edward Rowny, or anyone else, to negotiate it? In their attempt to break out of the rut of SALT and START, Kent and Warner had succeeded too well. Their approach was so innovative that the Soviets were likely to react to it by throwing up their hands in despair at this latest example of the American penchant for trying to start over in strategic arms control.

However, since they were including something for everyone, the designers had tried to tempt the Soviets as well. Unlike START, the new plan seemed at first to be asking roughly equal cutbacks on both sides. Both started with about 8,500 ballistic warheads; by 1992, they would have to come down to 5,000—the only figure Kent and Warner were retaining from the Administration's START proposal. By their calculations, the U.S. would be starting with a few more than 16,000 standard weapon stations, the Soviet Union with a few less. Both would have to cut back to 8,500 by 1996. Only when one looked at the consequences for each side's existing and prospective programs did the problem of negotiability become apparent. The U.S. could follow the straight lines of double build-down and still proceed with most if not all of the new programs to which it was committed; quite a few of the weapons to be given up were slated for retirement and replacement anyway. This was far less true on the Soviet side. The Soviets would have to retire many more weapons that they considered valuable if not indispensable.

Partly because the Kent-Warner scheme was so complex, Senator Cohen's adviser, Alton Frye, devised a somewhat simpler plan, offering it as a "compatible alternative." He believed it to be more negotiable as well as more comprehensible, but his bottom line still entailed a very large subtraction in Soviet ICBMs over time.*

While Soviet objections were easy enough to anticipate, they were not uppermost in the minds of the Administration and its many would-be partners in a new initiative. Given the yearning for consensus, double build-down seemed to be the order of the day. In mid-August, Les Aspin publicly released a letter to Scowcroft calling on the commission to produce a new START proposal that met a series of criteria spelled out in an accompanying "essay." Aspin had consulted closely with Scowcroft on the drafting of the

---

*For an excellent history of the evolution of the double build-down, as well as an explication of his own version, see Frye's article "Strategic Build-Down," *Foreign Affairs,* Winter 1983/84.

letter; Woolsey had helped him write the essay; the criteria were designed to invite a proposal along the lines of double build-down. Scowcroft's half of the script called for him to appear before the press and say he thought "build-down fits well with what it is that the Commission has recommended." Flying across the country to attend the funeral of Henry Jackson, who had died the week of the Korean airliner affair, Nunn and Cohen conceived a similar letter to Scowcroft, which they released jointly in mid-September. Nunn publicly credited Glenn Kent with devising "the ingredients for a bipartisan consensus."

The Treaty of Pennsylvania Avenue

The Administration knew a steamroller when it saw one. Ronald Lehman appealed for Reagan to be allowed into the driver's seat, if only for a brief photo opportunity: "The President has got to have a piece of this," said Lehman plaintively. "There's got to be something here for him to call his own. You can't leave him in the position of having a major area of his responsibility overhauled outside the Executive Branch."

Aspin was willing to let the Administration tinker with the presentation and even the substance of the plan "so as to avoid the appearance that they're farming out an important element of their foreign policy." To that end, he was fully prepared to enter into a "kabuki dance," as long as the choreography included adoption of the new plan. Scowcroft agreed. Rather than have the commission formally recommend the new approach to the Administration, he tried hard, in a series of meetings at the White House, to persuade William Clark and Lehman that the Administration should come forward on its own with some version of double build-down.

However, the Administration was too divided and disorganized to seize even the appearance of initiative. The only strong inhouse advocates for changing START were the White House political operatives—James Baker, Richard Darman, and Kenneth Duberstein, the White House's chief of congressional liaison. Duberstein in particular kept warning, "Don't overestimate how much time the Korean airliner business has bought us on the Hill; we've got to give those guys something, or we'll lose the MX."

"Those guys" were Nunn, Cohen, Percy, Aspin, Gore, and Congressman Norman Dicks, sometimes called "the Gang of Six." Along with Scowcroft, they met with Clark on September 21 to press their package of criteria for a new proposal. The criteria were deliberately and obviously drawn up with the double build-down in mind. Clark sought to assure them that the Administration shared their goals. The President was about to give a speech at the United Nations General Assembly presenting a number of concessions in INF, and he wanted to be able to say in the same speech that he had bipartisan support for his approach to START. The congressmen let it be known that this claim would be premature until they saw the final version of the proposal. Clark promised them an answer in a week. On September 29, the National Security Council met.

It was decided to placate the double build-downers by proposing a schedule for annual reductions in ballistic-missile warheads. Instead of simply being informed that they had to reduce to 5,000 by a given year, the Soviets would be told to reduce by a certain percentage each year until the end point. It was hardly an addition that would make the U.S. position more attractive to the Soviets, but the Administration hoped it would make it superficially more similar to the first half of the double build-down, the requirement that old weapons be retired in greater numbers than new weapons were added.

The other, far more important and controversial half of the double build-down, the aggregation of slow-flyers and fast-flyers, was set aside to be the subject of further study. The formal replacement of ballistic-missile throw-weight with some kind of broader, aggregated measurement of destructive potential as the unit of account for START would not yet be incorporated into the proposal, but it might be later on. At the end of September and beginning of October, the congressmen and Scowcroft negotiated intensively and sometimes acrimoniously with the White House over the language in which this promise would be couched. On September 30, Clark and Lehman presented a draft of a memorandum to the congressmen. It was deliberately vague and qualified with what Cohen called "waffle words." He warned, "It's going to have to be a lot firmer before I'm going to support it."

Clark said it was the best the Administration could do.

"That's just not acceptable," replied Cohen.

Clark grew angry. Turning to the others in the room, he said, "We can't satisfy this guy."

"Not with something like this, you can't," said Cohen.

Lehman launched into a long, anguished protest that "we've gone the last mile."

"You better not have," said Cohen, "or you're not going to have me with you."

Clark and Lehman were trying to preserve the President's cherished principle of separate and unequal treatment for destabilizing fast-flyers and stabilizing slow-flyers. The congressmen were pressing for the Administration to accept, once and for all, the concept of offsetting asymmetries—the idea that the Soviet reliance on large, land-based ballistic missiles did not necessarily mean that Soviet forces were superior to, and more dangerous than, the American strategic triad. The corollary of that notion for arms-control negotiations was that the Administration must endorse unequivocally the validity of trading off bombers and their armaments (especially cruise missiles) against ballistic missiles and their warheads. Scowcroft made this case vigorously to Shultz, who in turn made it to Reagan himself. After listening to Shultz, the President agreed to accept the principle of offsetting asymmetries and to incorporate the pursuit of trade-offs between fast- and slow-flyers in START. Shultz and Scowcroft felt this was potentially a major turning point in the education of Ronald Reagan.

The negotiations continued well into Monday, October 3. At a final meeting in the Situation Room, the congressmen and the NSC officials were still haggling over the wording of the memorandum when Reagan and Vice-President Bush put in a brief appearance to give their blessing to the deal. The dispute was down to a single word, whether the Administration would, as Lehman wanted, commit itself to "exploring" trade-offs between bombers and missiles or, as the congressmen wanted to say, "seek" such a trade-off. "We're so close," said Nunn to the President, "that we should not let one word get in our way. Let's find a substitute." Lehman then suggested a new verb: the U.S. would "negotiate" the trade-off. "That sounds good to me," said Reagan, and the deal was sealed.

In the final document, which Aspin jokingly called "the Magna Carta," it was agreed to leave START, with some slight further amendments, formally on the table as a sop to the Administration. The U.S. would propose setting up a new joint Soviet-American working group to explore the double build-down. The initial U.S. proposal in those parallel talks would be for an annual 5 percent cut in missile warheads or a reduction based on modernization, whichever produced the greater reduction. For example, two land-based MIRVs might be retired for every new one added; SLBM warheads might be converted on a three-to-two basis; smaller, single-warhead ICBMs could be traded in on a one-for-one basis. Thus, sea-based MIRVs would be treated more leniently than land-based ones, and Midgetman-like weapons would be treated most leniently of all.

To give all these carefully laid plans credibility, James Woolsey would join the delegation and would serve as a member of a special joint Soviet-American working group on double build-down that Rowny would propose to Karpov. That way, the Scowcroft Commission and the build-downers would have their man in Geneva. Aspin could not have been blunter: "If Ed Rowny came back and said double build-down won't fly, I wouldn't believe him; but I trust Jim Woolsey to give it a real try and to report back to us honestly." The outsiders' hope was that eventually, and perhaps even rather quickly, Woolsey's enterprise would leave Rowny's in the dust, and the real negotiations would take place in the double-build-down working group.

The congressmen emerged from the Situation Room October 3 immensely pleased with themselves. One after another, they stepped before microphones and proclaimed that the long-sought "bipartisan consensus" had finally been achieved, and that now the President had the basis for an arms-control agreement that could definitely be ratified by the U.S. Senate.

The next day Ronald Reagan met with congressional leaders and delivered one of his most affecting, emotional speeches to date on arms control. Humanity had always lived with the threat of war, he said, but "now people talk about wiping out civilian populations. Doesn't that alone argue for eliminating nuclear weapons?" For the first time, meeting with that group and on that subject, he received a standing ovation. Then the President went into the sunlit Rose Garden to give his START negotiators an upbeat send-off to Geneva. The congressmen were deliberately not included in the public ceremony in order to play down the fact that the Administration had given in to the Hill.

Reagan publicly welcomed Woolsey as a member-at-large of the delegation. Then, looking at Rowny, Reagan said, "You and your team go with the certain knowledge that you're negotiating with the full support of the American people. Our bipartisan support is stronger than ever before, and you carry with you fair, equitable proposals that are in the interest of both nations and all humankind. . . . The door to an agreement is open [the same line Reagan had used the week before at the UN when presenting his new initiatives for INF]. All the world is waiting for the Soviet Union to walk through."

The delegation was returning to Geneva with two proposals, an old one that the Soviets had already rejected in its essence and the outlines of a new one that would require the Soviets to abandon both the precedent of SALT and their own position in START. Rowny had barely arrived for the opening session of the new round when the Soviet news agency TASS complained that the latest changes in the American position were "vague, obscure and unclear." The redundancy may have reflected the Soviets' bafflement over garbled and incomplete American press reports about the build-down, which were the Kremlin's only source of information.

However, while it would take them a while to digest the fine points of the build-down, if and when those details were ever offered officially, the Soviets were not for a minute taken in by Reagan's claim that the entire U.S. government was now united behind a single, sustainable position. Dobrynin told Aspin and Cohen that his superiors in Moscow regarded the double build-down as "pure propaganda." Besides, how could the Soviet government take it seriously when the Pentagon, the State Department, and Rowny were all reported by the press to be against it?

The confusion on the American side was now all but hopeless, and the divisions, rather than being healed, ran as deep as ever through what passed for a U.S. negotiating position. The Legislative Branch had, in effect, fired the Executive Branch for gross incompetence in arms control; then the legislators had dictated the substitution of their own proposal for the Administration's; then they had conspired with the Administration to cover up the fractiousness that remained. Rowny returned to Geneva suggesting, at least to Soviet ears, that the old START proposal was the real one and that build-down was an ornament to placate the Congress. He stressed to Karpov that the "basic position of this Administration has not changed." Karpov and Dobrynin both cited this as further evidence that "Ambassador Rowny is not a serious man."

The congressmen thought the build-down was now the real proposal, and that Woolsey was in Geneva to make sure it was given a chance. But the Soviets could be forgiven some puzzlement over Woolsey's role. Karpov's staff prepared biographical material that highlighted Woolsey's background as a Democrat, an official of the Carter Pentagon, and an occasional adviser to Senator John Glenn, who was running for President. A number of Soviet negotiators asked, only half in jest, whether Woolsey was in Geneva to represent the current Administration or the next one.

Quite possibly, the Soviets' almost instantaneous rejection of the double build-down was a reflex reaction to other issues and to the general atmosphere. INF, not START, was the preoccupation of the hour (the new American missiles were due in Europe in a matter of weeks). Soviet-American relations were still at the nadir to which they had sunk as a result of the Korean airliner affair; moreover, with Andropov infirm and invisible, the Kremlin leadership seemed to be suffering from a kind of paralysis of its own; it was even less capable than usual of adjusting to sudden shifts in American policy.

At the same time, however, Karpov and his colleagues had some reason for skepticism about how new the American proposal really was with the addition of double build-down. In presenting the plan to the Soviets, Rowny focused on the missile-warhead half of the build-down, which seemed to them to discriminate against MIRVed ICBMs just as much as the old proposal had. Partly because the interagency process back in Washington had not produced detailed instructions for him, Rowny gave only sketchy presentations of the variable ratios that would guide the build-down and of the concept of an aggregated index of potential destructive capacity. Once again, the Soviets understood enough to see that this was weighted against MIRVed ICBMs. The scheme, said Osadchiyev, was "based on artificial distinctions [between bombers and missiles] and is clearly designed to emasculate our strategic forces."

The Americans were making much of their congressionally mandated willingness to limit bombers and cruise missiles in a spirit of "comprehensiveness." But in fact, even under the START proposal as it had been amended earlier in the year, bombers and air-launched cruise missiles were already on the table. So this feature looked to the Soviets to be neither new nor adequate, especially since they were given to understand that the offer extended only to ALCMs. Sea-launched cruise missiles still seemed to be exempt.

"Old poison in new bottles," said Karpov. He dismissed the idea of a working group to study the build-down as a "worthless exercise."*

Meanwhile, the State Department harbored hopes that neither half of the hybrid position on the American side of the table would turn out to be the ultimate proposal, and that some version of the Goodby plan—Burt and Howe's "new framework for START"—still had a chance.

The United States quite simply no longer knew what it wanted in strategic arms control, much less how to get it. START, as such, was dead. Whether strategic arms control would be revived with a coherent, negotiable new proposal from the American side was, at the end of the year, uncertain at best. On December 8, two weeks after their comrades had walked out of the INF talks, Karpov and his delegation ended the fifth round of START with an announcement that, "in view of the deployment of new U.S. missiles in Europe, which has already begun, changes in the global strategic situation make it necessary for the Soviet side to review all problems under discussion." The U.S.S.R. refused to agree to a date for resumption of the talks. If the talks did resume, the agenda would be more complicated, and the Americans' expectations would have to be far more modest.

---

*Early the next year, there were indications that the Soviets might have been less dismissive of the double build-down had the timing been different, the atmosphere better, and the American official presenting it someone other than Rowny. In February 1984, Senator Cohen traveled to Moscow with a Democratic colleague, Joseph Biden of Delaware, and Alton Frye. Their purpose was to urge Soviet reconsideration of the double build-down, and they seemed to make some progress. The officials with whom they met—Andrei Gromyko's deputy, Georgi Kornienko, Deputy Premier Vladimir Kuznetsov, and Alexander Bessmertnykh of the Foreign Ministry—were far more responsive than Karpov, Dobrynin, and other Soviets had been when the double build-down had been presented by Rowny in Geneva the previous fall.

It was likely that the Kremlin's positive reception of these guests was motivated, at least in part, by a desire to exploit the obvious tensions within the U.S. government and to encourage any and all critics of the Administration's own START policy; Cohen and Biden were, after all, members of the loyal opposition. It was worth recalling that a little more than a year before, as the West German elections approached, Yuri Andropov had received the leader of the West German opposition, Hans-Jochen Vogel, and exuded far more flexibility about INF than his negotiators were showing in Geneva. Nevertheless, Cohen, Biden, and Frye came home to Washington convinced that the double build-down might still stand a chance as the basis for an eventual agreement.

Epilogue

So sweeping was the change that the Reagan Administration sought in arms control that it deserved to be called a revolution. In fact, members of the Administration used that word to describe what they were trying to accomplish, as did many of their supporters in Congress and outside the government. Others claimed that their movement was more of a reformation, a return to the verities of American national-security policy in the pre-SALT, pre-détente era.

Revolution and reformation have in common a compulsion to reject the existing order, with all its perceived abuses and follies. The President and his men had been determined as much as possible to wipe out vestiges of the old regime. That meant altering if not scrapping the diplomacy that had held sway since the 1950s, discrediting if not discarding the agreements that earlier administrations had signed, and mistrusting if not purging many public servants who were identified with the old order.

But the new policies, quite simply, had not succeeded in their own avowed terms. In 1980 Ronald Reagan had promised that as President he would promptly and purposefully begin negotiations leading to arms reductions. His proposals emerged anything but promptly, and their nature contributed both to a breakdown in negotiations and to a buildup in armaments, Soviet as well as American. He had also promised to pursue policies that would reinforce the solidarity of the Western alliance and generate a bipartisan consensus of support in Congress. As it happened, however, the Reagan policies had, by the end of 1983, touched off a backlash against the Administration both at home and abroad. The consequence was the beginnings of a basic shift by the Administration, away from the positions so firmly held for three years, back toward an approach similar to the one the President had inherited but had wished to repudiate when he came into office.

Yet even this reorientation seemed to follow a long-since-established pattern, the one that has been chronicled in this book: policy made and remade in response to politics.

. . .

Political pressure, from the allies and from Congress, had forced the Administration in 1981–82 to enter negotiations in the first place; further pressure had forced the Administration in 1983 to modify its opening proposals with the adoption of the interim solution in INF and the incorporation of the double build-down in START. But those were accommodations with Reagan's constituencies in the West, not with the Soviets, and both negotiations collapsed anyway. As a result, the Administration came under greater pressure than ever in 1984 to resume the talks, not just with additional modifications but with genuinely new proposals.

Having seen the necessity of a fresh initiative, the President stepped into the process long enough to set a new tone, just as he had done in the past. In a speech on January 16, he proclaimed 1984 to be "a year of opportunities for peace." Those opportunities arose, he claimed, because his policies of the previous three years had succeeded: the buildup in American defenses permitted the U.S. now to be more forthcoming if talks were resumed:

> We're stronger . . . than we were three years ago. Our strength is necessary to deter war and to facilitate negotiated solutions. Soviet leaders know it makes sense to compromise only if they can get something in return. But America can now offer something in return. Strength and dialogue go hand in hand. We're determined to deal with our differences peacefully through negotiations. We're prepared to discuss the problems that divide us and to work for practical, fair solutions on the basis of mutual compromise. We will never retreat from negotiations.

"Compromise"—a word that Reagan's advisers had learned to leave out of papers that went to the NSC, not to mention drafts of presidential speeches—appeared here twice in a single passage, and was implied in virtually every sentence, particularly the last. The speech was dramatically different from the battle cries in the early days of the Administration, when negotiations themselves were regarded as a form of retreat if not capitulation.

As usual, however, Reagan's intervention was vague on details and inconclusive in its effect. He had long been disposed to think that presidential statements established policies, when in fact they often touched off new rounds of internal fighting over policy. So it had been with his zero-option speech on INF in November 1981, and his Eureka speech on START in May 1982; and so it was with his January 16, 1984, speech.

While it was filled with suggestions of his willingness to modify the U.S. negotiating position, neither in the preparations for the speech nor in its follow-through was there a determination of the next move to make at the table in Geneva, or even whether to make one at all. Once again, Reagan showed himself unable to engage decisively in the policymaking process. The struggle continued within the ranks of his Administration over what he had meant, what he wanted, and how it should be translated into proposals for the negotiations and into general strategy for the conduct of Soviet-American relations.

That struggle remained ideological as well as bureaucratic; at issue were differing philosophies over how to deal with the Soviets. The combatants, their interests, and their tactics were the same: the State Department, particularly Richard Burt, fought for compromise against the Pentagon, particularly Richard Perle, while the National Security Council staff, particularly Robert McFarlane, tried to arbitrate, reconcile, synthesize. Now, as before, the result was not so much synthesis as further paralysis.

The Kremlin, too, followed much the same tactics as it had the previous three years: it sought to maximize, and if possible capitalize on, Reagan's political discomfiture; to see how far he might move in his own positions before making any commitment to meet him halfway; and meanwhile to match the Administration blow for blow, feint for feint, gesture for gesture, in the propaganda competition. If the Americans published a list of alleged Soviet violations of SALT and other arms-control agreements, then the Soviets would go public in *Pravda* with their own accusations.* If Ronald Reagan could give a conciliatory but noncommittal speech, then *Pravda* could publish a purported interview with Yuri Andropov in which the terminally ill and invisible leader would send a few ambiguous signals of flexibility so as to encourage nervous doves in the West to put more pressure on their hawkish leaders.

At the same time, the Soviets could not have been less ambiguous in conveying their skepticism about whether Administration policy, as opposed to Administration rhetoric, had changed. Andrei Gromyko quickly denounced Reagan's speech as a "hackneyed ploy," motivated by American election-year politics: "It is deeds that are needed, not verbal exercises." The principal deed the Soviets were interested in was the reversal of the West's major achievement in "the Year of the Missile"—the initial deployment of Pershing IIs and Tomahawks in Europe. Even Andropov's somewhat

---

*The Administration's fifty-page classified report, alleging "an expanding pattern of Soviet violations or possible violations," went to Congress on January 23. It was preceded by a published outline of its contents. The testing of the PL-5, or SS-X-25, was said to be a "probable violation" of SALT II, and the giant radar under construction at Abalakovo in Siberia was said "almost certainly" to constitute a violation. Those charges are reviewed in Chapter 17.

The Soviet counterstrike came a few days later, when Moscow presented a detailed list of supposed American violations. The Soviet note contained old accusations, and—presumably to match the American complaint about Abalakovo—a newer accusation that the U.S. had upgraded major military radar stations on its Atlantic and Pacific coasts "and also in the southern direction [toward the Gulf of Mexico]" in such a way as to make them capable of serving a comprehensive antimissile system.

milder interview in *Pravda* repeated the standard charge that the U.S. had "torpedoed" the Geneva negotiations with the introduction of these new missiles.

There were cryptic Soviet hints—dropped by diplomats and amplified by semi-official spokesmen such as members of foreign-policy institutes in Moscow—that the atmosphere for resuming INF talks might be improved if the U.S. left in place the few missiles it had already deployed as bargaining chips, but suspended further deployments "to give negotiations a chance." The Reagan Administration, however, continued to display its conviction that the way to deal with the Russians was to keep the new weapons coming until the Soviets agreed to a deal; freezes were part of the Soviet bag of tricks. Reagan himself said that a moratorium on further INF deployments "would be a retreat, and it would not do anything to speed up negotiations if we now fell back and delayed deploying."

Thus, the Soviets had locked themselves into a position in which they could not start talking again in INF unless, at a minimum, the U.S. stopped deploying, while the U.S. had locked itself into a position where it could not stop deploying unless, at a minimum, the Soviets started talking. That meant that if the issues on the agenda of INF were to be dealt with at all, they would probably have to be transferred to START.

A merger of INF and START was exactly what many West European and American experts outside the Administration were recommending. Proponents pointed out that the distinction between intermediate-range and strategic systems had always been artificial; combining the two talks might break the logjam, facilitating trade-offs between the two categories of weaponry.

The Administration, however, resisted this proposal as well, determined to avoid making it appear that the Soviet walkout from INF had succeeded and that the U.S. was now acquiescing to pressure from the U.S.S.R. There was also concern about "multilateralizing" START. If the issues of INF— American weapons on West European soil—were placed on the table in START, the U.S. would be permitting in START the same sort of West European kibitzing and Soviet political mischief-making within the alliance that had so acutely complicated the American conduct of INF. A combined INF and START negotiation might degenerate into a wrangle over which intermediate-range weapons belonged on the agenda, and that would make it all the more difficult to address the various problems of intercontinental weapons, daunting enough in their own right.

Moreover, the very possibility of combining the talks raised the question of who would do the talking for the American side—Paul Nitze or Edward Rowny. Rowny was, by statute, the President's chief negotiator for nuclear arms control, and therefore senior to Nitze; Nitze, moreover, had blotted his copybook within the Administration by embarking on his various walks in the woods and walks in the park, and by being so pessimistic about the political consequences of INF deployment for NATO. And yet, almost everyone realized that Nitze was by far the more capable and credible negotiator.

Some members of the Administration and outside advisers were casting about for a new channel and a new negotiator, perhaps a super-envoy like Henry Kissinger or Brent Scowcroft, of the sort the President was using in Central America and the Middle East. Richard Burt was hoping that the time had finally come to activate the existing channel between the State Department and the Soviet embassy: Secretary of State George Shultz would step up the frequency of his contacts with Ambassador Anatoly Dobrynin, and Burt would go to work in a parallel channel with Dobrynin's deputy, Oleg Sokolov.

What was jokingly referred to around the corridors of government as "the urge to merge" or "the surge to merge" was in fact just another manifestation of everyone's frustration with the breakdown of policymaking and diplomacy alike. Merger was essentially a matter of form; the substance of policy remained largely undefined—and to the extent that it was defined, it was heatedly contested.

Aside from the question of whether to fold INF into START, uncertainty and division over the next move afflicted START in its own right. The State Department, with Shultz now solidly behind his assistants Burt and Jonathan Howe, was committed to the proposition that the old START proposal had outlived its usefulness, and that pretending otherwise was diplomatically fruitless and politically dangerous. State wanted to sound out the Soviets on the Goodby plan, now called the "framework approach." This might allow the two sides to reach an interim agreement on some general limits, with the details to be negotiated later. That cluster of general limits, or framework, would establish one set of ceilings and subceilings for launchers and another for missile warheads and bomber armaments, including cruise missiles. The key features were its rough similarity to SALT II and to the Soviet START proposal, and the "freedom to mix" that it permitted between ballistic weapons and bomber weapons.

The precedent that some advocates of the framework approach had in mind was the Vladivostok Accord that Gerald Ford and Leonid Brezhnev had signed in 1974. It established one aggregate for strategic ballistic missiles and intercontinental bombers (2,400) and another for MIRVed ballistic missiles (1,320), as well as some general principles (the Soviets could keep their 308 heavy missiles, and American forward-based systems would not count); the accord tided SALT II over the delay in the negotiations that had been caused by Watergate and Richard Nixon's resignation.

But the Vladivostok Accord, of course, had come about in circumstances very different from those that now prevailed. The American Administration in 1974, then dominated by Henry Kissinger, knew generally what it wanted in SALT and how to get it; and the two sides in the negotiation had been moving toward an agreement when Watergate intervened. By contrast, the Reagan Administration in 1984 still shared no common understanding of what it wanted in START, much less about how to get it, and its earlier negotiations with the Soviets had not been interrupted by external events but had simply reached a dead end. Burt and Howe had finally persuaded Shultz that the framework approach was a way out, but the Pentagon remained as hostile to the plan as ever.

The sterile arguments of the past three years had by now become not just institutionalized but ritualized. In early January, a small group of key Administration policymakers met for a day and a half at the Wye Plantation, a retreat run by the Aspen Institute in Maryland, to discuss alternative approaches to START. The principal participants were Burt, Howe, Perle, Rowny, Kenneth Adelman, and, on behalf of the National Security Council staff, Ronald Lehman.

The meeting was shrouded in secrecy. Participation was, in bureaucratic parlance, confined to "principals plus one." Perle brought Michael Mobbs, his office's representative on the START delegation. Rowny brought his aide-de-camp, Samuel Watson (the same trusty sidekick whom Rowny had, a year earlier, tried to blame for the famous hit list). Rowny's choice of Watson meant that his principal deputy, Ambassador Sol Polansky—James Goodby's successor as chief State Department representative on the START delegation —was excluded. That fact alone said much about the extent of Rowny's estrangement from his own delegation and from the State Department.

During the meeting, Rowny warned, "Now is not the time to be shifting our position. The Soviets are in disarray within their own leadership; they've behaved unacceptably in the negotiations; they've refused to negotiate seriously; they've walked out. If we change our position now, we'd seem to be giving in to their tactics. We'd be rewarding them. We'd encourage them to do more of that kind of thing. This is a time for steadiness."

Perle resorted to a tactic he had used in the high-level arms-control group chaired by Kenneth Dam the year before, asking broad, basic questions— "Let's go back to fundamentals; let's ask ourselves where exactly have we come these past fifteen years," and the like. His purpose seemed to be to lead the discussion away from the questions of practical policy at hand. Perle offered his own very blunt answer to one of the most basic questions about arms control. "This stuff is a soporific," he said with some passion. "It puts our society to sleep. It does violence to our ability to maintain adequate defenses."

The State Department representatives, Burt and Howe, were willing to talk philosophy, too, but with a very different thrust from Perle's. Howe, a Navy man, spoke a number of times about the need to "rechart our course" and "trim our sails"—meaning, let's go for a far less ambitious agreement than the one the Administration had been seeking in START.

The meeting ended in the creation of yet another interagency committee that spent the next few months refining alternatives of the framework approach for eventual consideration by the National Security Council. The State Department, the Arms Control and Disarmament Agency, and the Joint Chiefs of Staff all had their preferred variations of the original Goodby plan, with minor adjustments and differences; ACDA and the Chiefs wanted a separate subceiling for heavy ICBMs at half the current Soviet level, while State was still trying to restrict heavies indirectly.* But what mattered was that Perle and the Office of the Secretary of Defense refused to join in the process, and did their best to block it.

Shultz wanted to suggest the framework approach to Andrei Gromyko during a meeting in Stockholm in mid-January, but he did not dare raise that possibility in the normal interagency process, where Perle would be waiting in ambush. So Shultz did something that hardly came naturally to him and that underscored the failure of Reagan's cherished goal (originally shared by Shultz) of governing by Cabinet consensus: Shultz bypassed the rest of the government and went directly to the President.

Burt and Howe had prepared a set of talking points for the meeting with Gromyko. The talking points included one page—No. 3 in the sheaf of papers that Shultz would take to Stockholm—outlining the framework approach. The other agencies submitted their own proposed talking points. By and large, they stressed American concern over Soviet compliance with SALT, asserted American flexibility in the vaguest terms, and invited the Soviets to show more flexibility of their own in START. Shultz took the whole batch to the President and McFarlane and displayed them as an example of how divided the government still was. Reagan asked in some exasperation, "Can't you just mix them together, George?" That, of course, had been the way out of previous interagency impasses.

Shultz replied that he would, of course, stress to Gromyko those points on which all the agencies agreed, but that he needed "some kind of a hook

---

*Yet another variation of the framework approach was being promoted by Zbigniew Brzezinski. In a newspaper article at the end of January, he urged the Administration to shift "from a comprehensive agreement to a limited interim agreement, confined to a few aggregate categories" —strategic launchers and warheads. Reagan heard Brzezinski expound on this plan on a Sunday television talk show and telephoned him to say it sounded interesting. With this expression of presidential interest, the Brzezinski variant of the framework approach was added to those being considered in the interagency process.

in case Gromyko nibbles." Reagan was looking for diplomatic gestures that would be compatible with the tone he was setting in his January 16 speech, so he authorized Shultz to use Page 3 of the State Department talking points if Gromyko did nibble.

The five hours that Shultz spent with Gromyko in Stockholm were not a successful fishing expedition, at least on the issue of nuclear arms control. The negotiations on conventional arms reductions in Europe—the Mutual Balanced Force Reduction talks, which the Soviets had also suspended— might be resumed in Vienna in March, and the Administration prepared to see if progress could be made there. But on START and INF, Gromyko was so unforthcoming that Shultz felt unable to say more than that a comprehensive, "technical" agreement was proving elusive and so perhaps there should be a "conceptual" agreement first. This was as close as he felt he could appropriately come to making use of his presidential authorization to raise the possibility of the framework plan.

After the Stockholm meeting, Shultz told McFarlane and Caspar Weinberger over breakfast how "tough and difficult" Gromyko had been on nuclear arms control. McFarlane expressed regret and frustration that Gromyko's attitude had made it impossible for Shultz to sound him out on "our new approach." McFarlane was careful not to call it a new proposal. Nonetheless, Weinberger pricked up his ears: the discussion confirmed his already aroused suspicion that the State Department had embarked on some new departure of its own.

"This is outrageous!" Perle complained when he learned what had happened. "The Office of the Secretary of Defense is entitled to a full read-out of that meeting! We're being steamrollered!" He began talking once again about resigning from the government.

Yet Burt and Howe were feeling anything but smug. They could hardly be complacent in the knowledge that the State Department was able to present its plans to the President only by hiding them from the Pentagon. As it was, Shultz had gotten only the vaguest of blessings from Reagan to explore new paths; there was no interagency consensus; without a consensus, there could be no concrete proposal; and without a proposal, the U.S. had little with which to lure the Soviets into a genuine negotiation.

The President and his principal advisers, James Baker and Michael Deaver, were only dimly aware of the framework approach. Baker in particular, who was following the national-security debate more closely than others in the presidential inner circle, knew that Burt had plans to promote a new START position, but he did not regard the matter as pressing; if the debate required presidential adjudication, Baker was counting on McFarlane and the NSC staff to come up, as they had so often before, with a half-a-loaf compromise between the State Department and Pentagon positions. McFarlane's own view was that the U.S. must not seem too eager to make new concessions, especially in the face of Gromyko's intransigence in Stockholm; it was the Soviets' turn to move.

Andropov's death and replacement by Konstantin Chernenko was itself an occasion for fresh bickering in Washington. The State Department argued that the changing of the guard in the Kremlin presented a golden opportunity for a new American initiative; the Pentagon was inclined to the view that now, more than ever, the U.S. must hold to the line it had laid down so as to impress the new Soviet leadership with American consistency and resolve.

The White House itself saw the Soviet succession as an opportunity not so much for a change in policy as for an escalation in the rhetorical peace offensive. Vice-President George Bush traveled to Moscow to attend Andropov's funeral and to meet Chernenko. He proclaimed there that "the mood was good, the spirit was excellent. It signals that we can go from here." Reagan reiterated his heightened hopes for a summit.* He also stressed that the time had come for "quiet diplomacy" with the Soviets; proposals should be advanced and discussed behind closed doors, not proclaimed publicly.

These were welcome words to Shultz and Burt. But what those proposals might be, Reagan did not say. Indeed, Reagan did not know. He did know, however, that he did not want to be seen to be budging while the Soviets were still stonewalling. At an NSC meeting in late March, the President repeated a number of times that whatever new approaches he would allow his emissaries to explore, the U.S. would make "no preemptive concessions." Perle picked up the phrase and emphasized it in public as a presidential endorsement of his own dogged holding action against "progress for its own sake." The Soviets, meanwhile, were just as adamant that they would not budge unless and until the U.S. led the way with concrete concessions. Nor did they share the Administration's eagerness for movement before the American presidential election: they knew that progress of any kind, for any reason, could only help Reagan get reelected. When, therefore, Scowcroft traveled to Moscow in early March with a personal letter from Reagan to Chernenko proposing what amounted to a back channel at the highest level, the Soviet leader refused to see him, and Scowcroft declined to meet with one of Andrei Gromyko's aides instead.

---

*He did so, however, in terms not likely to entice the Soviets. Meeting with American reporters over breakfast shortly after Chernenko's rise to supreme power, Reagan commented, "I've never been in Marine One [the White House helicopter] flying at a low altitude over our cities and looking down at the homes that our working people live in without fantasizing what it would be like to have Soviet leaders with me and be able to point down and say, 'That's where the workers of America live; they live like that; how long are you going to cling to that system of yours that can't provide anything like that for your people?' "

Thus, even as the U.S. adopted new gambits, the stalemate with the U.S.S.R. continued.

The men who had come into office vowing such ambitious changes in arms control approached the end of their first term facing a highly disagreeable choice: they could settle for nothing, no agreement of any kind, which might mean the utter collapse of the enterprise the superpowers had begun a generation before to regulate their rivalry in its most dangerous aspect; or they could scramble desperately for what would perforce be a modest stop-gap, a face-saver, an election-eve "quick fix" of the sort that Perle, Rostow, Rowny, and others had so often vowed to prevent. Such an agreement might sustain the battered arms-control process for a while, permitting a fuller salvage operation later and, eventually perhaps, significant progress. Or they could lay the groundwork for the resumption of talks early in a second term, hoping that it might then be possible to negotiate a durable replacement for the steadily eroding structure of SALT. But in adopting that expedient, too, the Administration would be leaving behind many of the assumptions and aspirations with which it had come into office.

The Reagan revolution in arms control was over.

Index

A Note About the Author

Strobe Talbott is diplomatic correspondent for *Time* magazine, based in Washington, D.C. Eduated at Hotchkiss, Yale, and Oxford, where he was a Rhodes Scholar, he has been on the *Time* staff for thirteen years. He won the Edward Weintal Award in 1981 for distinguished writing on foreign affairs and is the author of several other books, among them *Endgame: The Inside Story of SALT II* and, most recently, *The Russians and Reagan.* In 1970 and 1974 Talbott translated and edited two volumes of memoirs by Soviet Premier Nikita Khrushchev.

A Note About the Type

The text of this book was set by CRT in a film version of a typeface called Times Roman, designed by Stanley Morison (1889–1967) for *The Times* (London) and first introduced by that newspaper in 1932.

Among typographers and designers of the twentieth century, Stanley Morison was a strong forming influence as a typographical advisor to The Monotype Corporation, as a director of two distinguished English publishing houses, and as a writer of sensibility, erudition, and keen practical sense.

Composed by The Haddon Craftsmen, Inc., Scranton, Pennsylvania.
Printed and bound by Fairfield Graphics, Fairfield, Pennsylvania.
Designed by Iris Weinstein.